STERLING
Test Prep

MCAT®

Practice Tests

Biological & Biochemical
and
Chemical & Physical Foundations
of Living Systems

9th edition

We strive to provide the highest quality preparation materials.
Be the first to report any error, typo or inaccuracy in the content of this publication
to info@onlinemcatprep.com and receive a $10 reward per correction.

9 8 7 6 5 4 3 2 1

ISBN 13: 978-0-9892925-1-1

Sterling Test Prep products are available at special quantity discounts for sales, promotions, premed counseling offices and other educational purposes.

For more information contact our Sales Department at

Sterling Test Prep
276 Washington Street #305
Boston, MA 02108

info@onlinemcatprep.com

Dear Future Doctor!

Congratulations on making the right decision by choosing this book as part of your MCAT® preparation!

Scoring well on the MCAT® is important for admission into medical school. To achieve a high MCAT® score you need to develop skills to properly apply the knowledge you have and quickly choose the correct answer. You must solve numerous practice questions that represent the style and content of the MCAT®. Understanding key science concepts and how to apply them is more valuable on the MCAT® than memorizing formulas and terms which is unlikely to significantly increase your score.

This book is different from the majority of other MCAT® science prep books. While other books either only superficially review science topics or provide practice questions with brief explanations, this book presents the science material in an MCAT-style test format and provides detailed explanations. These explanations discuss why the answer is correct and – more importantly – why another answer that may have seemed correct is the wrong choice. The explanations include the foundations and details of important science topics needed to answer related questions on the MCAT®. By reading these explanations carefully and understanding how they apply to solving the question, you will learn important concepts and the relationships between them. This will prepare you for the MCAT® and will significantly improve your score.

This book is designed to reflect the content of the new MCAT® 2015. It contains 4 Biological & Biochemical Foundations of Living Systems and 4 Chemical & Physical Foundations of Biological Systems MCAT® practice tests. Each test contains 59 passage-based and independent questions with the appropriate combination of biology, biochemistry, organic chemistry, general chemistry and physics topics tested on the MCAT®.

All the questions are prepared by our science editors that possess extensive credentials, are educated in top colleges and universities and have been admitted to medical school with stellar MCAT® scores. Our editors are experts on teaching sciences, preparing students for the MCAT® and have coached thousands of premeds on admission strategies.

We wish you great success in your future medical profession and look forward to being an important part of your successful preparation for the MCAT®!

Sterling Test Prep Team

140821gdx

Other products by Sterling Test Prep:

- **MCAT 1,200 Physics Practice Questions**
- **MCAT 1,200 Biology & Biochemistry Practice Questions**
- **MCAT 1,800 General Chemistry Practice Questions**
- **MCAT 1,800 Organic Chemistry & Biochemistry Practice Questions**
- **MCAT Organic Chemistry Review Notes**
- **MCAT General Chemistry Review Notes**
- **MCAT Physics Review Notes**
- **MCAT Biology Review Notes**

Online CBT Testing

The practice tests included in this book are also available in an online format. Our advanced testing platform allows you to take the tests in the same CBT (computer based test) format as the AAMC's official MCAT®.

We strongly advise you to use this feature for several reasons. Taking test on the computer (which you will do on test day) is a very different experience from working with a book. Our proprietary testing platform is designed to fully simulate the actual MCAT®. Practicing the tests online, under timed conditions, helps you get accustomed to computer testing and have a smoother experience during the real MCAT®.

By using our online CBT testing, you will get a Scaled Score and will also receive your personalized Diagnostics Report. This report includes detailed statistics on your individual performance on each test and categorizes questions by topics and difficulty level. This will allow you to assess your knowledge of each subject and topic, identify the areas where you need to spend more time preparing and compare your performance to the performance of other test takers.

To take online tests visit:
www.MasterMCAT.com/bookowner.htm

If you are satisfied with the content of this book, share your opinion with other readers by publishing your review on Amazon.com and receive free access to our online practice resources in appreciation of your time and effort.

After you publish your review, create a user account at www.MasterMCAT.com and send us an email to receive the instructions for your free access.

If you have any concerns about the material, email us and we will do our best to resolve any issues.

Table of Contents

MCAT® Strategies

It is a common mistake to think that the MCAT® assesses only general knowledge, critical thinking skills and the ability to select the correct answer from the information provided. While MCAT® is targeting all of these abilities, it is still mostly a science test. To succeed on the MCAT®, a student must possess the foundational knowledge and analytical ability to apply this knowledge to science questions.

Many students believe they are prepared to sit for MCAT® if they took college-level biology, physics, biochemistry, organic and general chemistry. In fact, all the applicants competing for medical school admission took these courses. The MCAT® questions come from a wide range of topics for each of these disciplines. However, most college courses, due to time constrains and class sizes, can't cover these subjects in the breadth and depth needed to ace the MCAT®. Students need to invest additional time and effort in studying to prepare specifically for the MCAT® and most students who achieve high scores report that they spent significant amounts of time in preparation for this test. Practicing MCAT-style questions and test is the most important component of preparation for achieving a high MCAT® score.

In addition to studying, there are strategies, approaches and perspectives that you should learn to apply on the MCAT®. On the test, you need to think and analyze information quickly. This skill cannot be gained from a college course, a review prep course or a text book. But you can develop it through repetitive practice and focus.

Intimidation by information. Test developers usually select material for the test that will be completely unknown to most test takers. Don't be overwhelmed, intimidated or discouraged by unfamiliar concepts. While going through a question, try to understand all the relevant material available, while disregarding the distracter information. Being exposed to strange sounding topics and terms that you are not familiar with is normal for this test.

Do not feel disappointed that you're not very familiar with the topic. Most other test takers are not familiar with it either. So, stay calm and work through the questions. Don't turn this into a learning exercise either by trying to memorize the information (in a passage or question) that was not known to you before because your objective on the test is to answer questions by selecting the correct answers.

Find your pace. Everybody reads and processes information at a different rate. You should practice to find your optimal rate, so you can read fast and still comprehend the information. If you have a good pace and don't invest too much time in any one question, you should have enough time to complete each section at a comfortable rate. Avoid two extremes where you either work too slowly, reading each and every word carefully, or act panicky and rush through the material without understanding.

When you find your own pace that allows you to stay focused and calm, you will have enough time for all questions. It is important to remember, that you are trying to achieve optimal, not maximum, comprehension. If you spend the time necessary to achieve a maximum comprehension of a passage or question, you will most likely not have enough time for the whole section.

You should practice MCAT® tests under timed conditions to eventually find your optimal pace. This is why we recommend that you practice the tests from this book on our website (www.MasterMCAT.com/bookowner.htm) where you will get a scaled score and your personalized Diagnostics Report.

Don't be a perfectionist. The test is timed, and you cannot spend too much time on any one question. Get away from thinking that if you spent just one more minute on the question you'll get it right. You can get sucked into a question that you lose track of time and end up rushing through the rest of the test (which may cause you to miss even more questions). If you spend your allocated per-question time and still not sure of the answer, take the best pick, take a note of the question number and move on. The test allows you to return to any question and change your answer choice. If you have extra time left after you answered all other questions on that section, return to that question and take a fresh look. Unless you have a sound reason to change your original answer, don't change your answer choice.

You shouldn't go into the MCAT® thinking that you must get every question right. Accept the fact that you will have to guess on some questions (and maybe get them wrong) and still have time for every question. You goal should be to answer as many questions correctly as you possibly can.

Factually correct, but actually wrong. Often MCAT® questions are written in a way that the incorrect answer choice may be factually correct on its own, but doesn't answer the question. When you are reading the answer choices and one choice jumps out at you because it is factually correct, be careful. Make sure to go back to the question and verify that the answer choice actually answers the question being asked. Some incorrect answer choices will seem to answer the question asked and are even factually correct, but are based on extraneous information within the question stem.

Narrow down your choices. When you find two answer choices that are direct opposites, it is very likely that the correct answer choice is one of the two. You can typically rule out the other two answer choices (unless they are also direct opposites of each other) and narrow down your search for the correct choice that answers the question.

Experiments. If you encounter a passage that describes an experiment, ask some basic questions including: "What is the experiment designed to find out?", "What is the experimental method?", "What are the variables?", "What are the controls?" Understanding this information will help you use the presented information to answer the question associated with the passage.

Multiple experiments. The best way to remember three variations of the same experiment is to focus on the differences between the experiments. What changed between the first and the second experiment? What was done differently between the second and the third experiment? This will help you organize the information in your mind.

Passage notes. Pay attention to the notes after a passage. The information provided in those notes is usually necessary to answer some questions associated with that passage. Notes are there given for a reason and often contain information necessary to answer at least one of the questions.

Look for units. When solving a problem that you don't know the formula for, try to solve for the units in the answer choices. The units in the answer choices are your clues for understanding the relationship between the question and the correct answer. Review what value is being sought in the question. Sometimes you can eliminate some wrong answers because they contain improper units.

Don't fall for the familiar. When in doubt, it is easy to choose what you are familiar with. If you recognize a term in one of the four answer choices, you may be tempted to pick that choice. But don't go with familiar answers just because they are familiar. Think through the other answer choices and how they relate to the question before making your selection.

Don't get hung up on the passage. Read through the passage once briefly to understand what items it deals with and take mental notes of some key points. Then look at the questions. You might find that you are able to answer some questions without using the information in the passage. With other questions, once you know what exactly is being asked, you can read through the passage more effectively looking for a particular answer. This technique will help you save some time that you otherwise would have overinvested in processing the information that has no benefit to you.

Roman numerals. Some questions will present three or four statements and ask which of them are correct. For example:

   A. I only
   B. III only
   C. I and II only
   D. I and III only

Notice that statement II doesn't have an answer choice dedicated to it. It is likely that statement II is wrong and you can eliminate answer choice C. This narrows your search to three choices. However, if you are confident that statement II is part of the answer, you can disregard this strategy.

Extra Tips

• With fact questions that require selecting among numbers, don't go with the smallest or largest number unless you have a reason to believe it is the answer.

• Use the process of elimination for questions that you're not clear about. Try to eliminate the answer choices you know to be wrong before making your selection.

• Don't fall for answers that sound "clever" and don't go with "bizarre" choices. Only choose them if you are confident that the choice is correct.

• None of these strategies will replace the importance of preparation. But knowing and using them will help you utilize your test time more productively and increase you probability for successful guessing when you simply don't know the answer.

CHEMICAL & PHYSICAL FOUNDATIONS OF BIOLOGICAL SYSTEMS

PART I.I

MCAT® Practice Tests

MCAT Chemical & Physical Foundations of Biological Systems

Practice Test #1

59 questions   95 minutes

For explanatory answers see pgs. 119-154

For CBT online format of this test that provides Diagnostics Report with performance statistics, difficulty rating of each question and other features visit:

www.MasterMCAT.com

Most questions in the Physical Sciences test are organized into groups, each containing a descriptive passage. After studying the passage select the one best answer to each question in the group. Some questions are not based on a descriptive passage and are also independent of each other. If you are not certain of an answer, eliminate the alternatives you know to be incorrect and then select an answer from the remaining alternatives. Indicate your selected answer by marking the corresponding answer on your answer sheet. A periodic table is provided for your use. You may consult it whenever you wish.

Periodic Table of the Elements

1 H 1.0																	2 He 4.0
3 Li 6.9	4 Be 9.0											5 B 10.8	6 C 12.0	7 N 14.0	8 O 16.0	9 F 19.0	10 Ne 20.2
11 Na 23.0	12 Mg 24.3											13 Al 27.0	14 Si 28.1	15 P 31.0	16 S 32.1	17 Cl 35.5	18 Ar 39.9
19 K 39.1	20 Ca 40.1	21 Sc 45.0	22 Ti 47.9	23 V 50.9	24 Cr 52.0	25 Mn 54.9	26 Fe 55.8	27 Co 58.9	28 Ni 58.7	29 Cu 63.5	30 Zn 65.4	31 Ga 69.7	32 Ge 72.6	33 As 74.9	34 Se 79.0	35 Br 79.9	36 Kr 83.8
37 Rb 85.5	38 Sr 87.6	39 Y 88.9	40 Zr 91.2	41 Nb 92.9	42 Mo 95.9	43 Tc (98)	44 Ru 101.1	45 Rh 102.9	46 Pd 106.4	47 Ag 107.9	48 Cd 112.4	49 In 114.8	50 Sn 118.7	51 Sb 121.8	52 Te 127.6	53 I 126.9	54 Xe 131.3
55 Cs 132.9	56 Ba 137.3	57 La* 138.9	72 Hf 178.5	73 Ta 180.9	74 W 183.9	75 Re 186.2	76 Os 190.2	77 Ir 192.2	78 Pt 195.1	79 Au 197.0	80 Hg 200.6	81 Tl 204.4	82 Pb 207.2	83 Bi 209.0	84 Po (209)	85 At (210)	86 Rn (222)
87 Fr (223)	88 Ra (226)	89 Ac† (227)	104 Rf (261)	105 Db (262)	106 Sg (266)	107 Bh (264)	108 Hs (277)	109 Mt (268)	110 Ds (281)	111 Uuu (272)	112 Uub (285)		114 Uuq (289)		116 Uuh (289)		

	58 Ce 140.1	59 Pr 140.9	60 Nd 144.2	61 Pm (145)	62 Sm 150.4	63 Eu 152.0	64 Gd 157.3	65 Tb 158.9	66 Dy 162.5	67 Ho 164.9	68 Er 167.3	69 Tm 168.9	70 Yb 173.0	71 Lu 175.0
†	90 Th 232.0	91 Pa (231)	92 U 238.0	93 Np (237)	94 Pu (244)	95 Am (243)	96 Cm (247)	97 Bk (247)	98 Cf (251)	99 Es (252)	100 Fm (257)	101 Md (258)	102 No (259)	103 Lr (260)

CHEMICAL & PHYSICAL FOUNDATIONS
MCAT® PRACTICE TEST #1: ANSWER SHEET

Passage 1

1 : A   B   C   D
2 : A   B   C   D
3 : A   B   C   D
4 : A   B   C   D
5 : A   B   C   D

Passage 2

6 : A   B   C   D
7 : A   B   C   D
8 : A   B   C   D
9 : A   B   C   D
10 : A   B   C   D
11 : A   B   C   D

Independent questions

12 : A   B   C   D
13 : A   B   C   D
14 : A   B   C   D
15 : A   B   C   D

Passage 3

16 : A   B   C   D
17 : A   B   C   D
18 : A   B   C   D
19 : A   B   C   D
20 : A   B   C   D

Passage 4

21 : A   B   C   D
22 : A   B   C   D
23 : A   B   C   D
24 : A   B   C   D
25 : A   B   C   D
26 : A   B   C   D

Independent questions

27 : A   B   C   D
28 : A   B   C   D
29 : A   B   C   D
30 : A   B   C   D
31 : A   B   C   D

Passage 5

32 : A   B   C   D
33 : A   B   C   D
34 : A   B   C   D
35 : A   B   C   D
36 : A   B   C   D

Passage 6

37 : A   B   C   D
38 : A   B   C   D
39 : A   B   C   D
40 : A   B   C   D
41 : A   B   C   D
42 : A   B   C   D

Independent questions

43 : A   B   C   D
44 : A   B   C   D
45 : A   B   C   D
46 : A   B   C   D

Passage 7

47 : A   B   C   D
48 : A   B   C   D
49 : A   B   C   D
50 : A   B   C   D
51 : A   B   C   D
52 : A   B   C   D

Independent questions

53 : A   B   C   D
54 : A   B   C   D
55 : A   B   C   D
56 : A   B   C   D
57 : A   B   C   D
58 : A   B   C   D
59 : A   B   C   D

This page is intentionally left blank

Passage 1
(Questions 1–5)

A capacitor (condenser) is a passive electronic component consisting of a pair of conductors separated by a dielectric (nonconducting substance). When a voltage potential difference exists between the conductors, an electric field is present in the dielectric. This field stores energy and produces a mechanical force between the plates. The effect is greatest between wide, flat, parallel, narrowly separated conductors. An ideal capacitor is characterized by a single constant value, capacitance measured in farads.

A parallel-plate capacitor is the simplest capacitor and consists of two parallel conductive plates separated by a dielectric with permittivity (ε). Permittivity describes how an electric field affects a dielectric medium and is determined by the ability of a material to polarize in response to the field.

Two parallel metal plates of a parallel-plate capacitor are connected to a voltage source which maintains a potential (V) across the plates. An electric field (E) is created between the plates because positive charges collect on one side of the capacitor and negative charges on the other side. The magnitude of the electric field is related to the potential and the separation between the plates according to:

$$V = Ed$$

where V is measured in volts, E in joules/mole, and d in meters.

When placed between the plates, a charged particle experiences a force in magnitude by:

$$F = qE$$

where q is charge of particle in Coulombs, and F is force in Newtons.

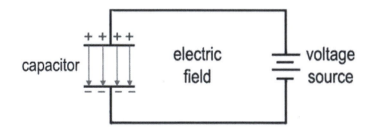

Figure 1. Parallel-plate capacitor

1. How is the electric field affected when the distance between the plates is increased by a factor of 3 but the voltage remains constant?

    A. stays the same
    B. decreases by factor of 3
    C. increases by factor of 3
    D. decreases by factor of 9

2. How does the force on the helium nucleus compare to the force on the proton when both, a proton and a bare helium nucleus, are placed between the plates of a parallel-plate capacitor?

    A. the same
    B. there is no force on the helium nucleus
    C. force on the helium nucleus is two times greater
    D. force on the helium nucleus is four times greater

3. How is an electric field affected if the voltage between the plates is increased by a factor of 9?

    A. it increases by a factor of 9
    B. it increases by a factor of 3
    C. it decreases by a factor of 9
    D. it increases by a factor of 81

4. Which graph best illustrates the relationship between the potential (V) and electric field (E)?

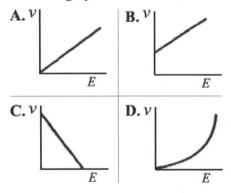

5. What happens to the force on a proton between the plates if the separation of the plates is decreased by a factor of 2?

    A. it decreases by a factor of 2
    B. it decreases by a factor of 4
    C. it increases by a factor of 2
    D. it stays the same

Passage 2
(Questions 6–11)

There are two types of interactions within molecules (intramolecular) and three types of interactions between molecules (intermolecular). Intramolecular forces include covalent and ionic bonds. Intermolecular interactions include van der Waals forces, dipole-dipole, and hydrogen bonds.

Interaction type	Bond	Energy (kJ/mol)
Intramolecular forces	Covalent bond	155 – 650
	Ionic bond	350 – 550
Intermolecular forces	van der Waals	0.1 – 4
	Dipole-dipole	3 – 5
	Hydrogen bond	3 – 7

Table 1. Bond energies

The boiling point of a substance is the temperature at which the vapor pressure of the liquid equals the environmental pressure that surrounds the liquid. A liquid in a vacuum has a lower boiling point than a liquid at atmospheric pressure. A liquid in a high pressure environment has a higher boiling point than when the liquid is at atmospheric pressure. The boiling point of liquids depends upon the environmental pressure.

The boiling point of a solution increases in proportion to the strength of intermolecular forces.

6. The atomic radius of I compared to Br is:

A. smaller
B. greater
C. the same
D. cannot be determined

7. Why do boiling points of HF and H_2O deviate from the expected trend?

A. Cl and O are elements of the second and third period
B. H_2O and HF are relatively small molecules
C. H_2O and HF molecules are less polarizable
D. H_2O and HF molecules form hydrogen bonds

8. Why are van der Waals interactions weaker than dipole-dipole interactions?

   A. dipole-dipole interactions occur only with ionic bonded compounds
   B. dipole-dipole is an electrostatic interaction between the molecules
   C. van der Waals interactions rely on temporary momentary flux of electron density
   D. van der Waals interactions require a large surface area of molecules

9. Which type of intramolecular forces binds the atoms within the molecule of $CaCl_2$?

   A. van der Waals
   B. hydrogen
   C. ionic
   D. covalent

10. Which of the following best describes why boiling points are better indicators of the strength of intermolecular bonding than melting points?

   A. vaporization is easier to measure
   B. vaporization requires less energy than melting
   C. vaporization requires more energy than melting
   D. melting point involves factors such as crystalline lattice structures

11. As the period increases, the boiling points of noble gases increase because the bonds are:

   A. weaker due to larger atoms being more polarizable
   B. stronger due to larger atoms being more polarizable
   C. weaker due to larger atoms being less polarizable
   D. stronger due to larger atoms being less polarizable

Questions 12 through 15 are not based on any
descriptive passage and are independent of each other

12. Which statement is true for bases?

A. Strong bases are always corrosive
B. Strong bases readily accept protons from weak acids
C. Weak bases do not react with strong acids
D. Weak bases completely dissociate into ions in H_2O

13. Which of the following is the correct statement about the relationship between the temperature of hot water at 80°C and its heat content?

A. Temperature measures the average potential energy of the molecules and heat
  measures the stability
B. Temperature and heat and have no relationship
C. Heat is the energy transferred due to the difference in their temperatures
D. Temperature and heat mean the same measure but use different numerical scales

14. Body 1 moves toward Body 2 which is at rest. The mass of Body 2 is twice the mass of Body 1.

After collision, the bodies stick together. What fraction of initial speed of Body 1 do the two bodies move at after the collision?

A. 2/3
B. 1/2
C. 1/3
D. 1/4

15. Mike sits on a stationary sled (total mass of Mike + sled = 100 kg) on a skating rink with smooth ice and holds a 2 kg ball. If he throws the ball at a speed of 10 m/s, what is the speed at which Mike and the sled move?

A. 0.1 m/s
B. 0.2 m/s
C. 0.4 m/s
D. 0 m/s

This page is intentionally left blank

Passage 3
(Questions 16–20)

When light in the ultraviolet region of the electromagnetic spectrum shines on a phosphor, the phosphor fluoresces and emits light in the visible region of the spectrum. Fluorescent lamps utilize this principle and are very efficient light sources. The lamp is a glass tube with inside walls coated with a phosphor. The tube has a large length-to-diameter ratio (to reduce the power loss at each end of the tube) and is filled with argon gas mixed with mercury vapor. Inside both ends of the tube are tungsten electrodes covered with an emission material.

The two main parts in a fluorescent lamp are a gas-filled tube (bulb) and the magnetic (or electronic) ballast. An electrical current from the ballast flows through the gas (mercury vapor), causing emission of ultraviolet light. The ultraviolet light then excites a phosphor coating on the inside of the tube which emits visible light. Electrons are liberated at the cathode and accelerated by an applied electric field. These free electrons encounter the mercury gas, ionizing some mercury atoms and exciting others. Since it requires more energy to ionize atoms than excite electrons, more excitation than ionization occurs.

When the excited electrons revert to their ground state, they radiate ultraviolet photons which strike the phosphor coating electrons and excite them to higher energy states. The excited electrons in the phosphor return to their ground state in several steps, producing radiation in the visible region of the spectrum. Not every fluorescent lamp emits the same color of radiation and color depends on heavy metal compounds within the phosphor. New phosphor compositions have improved the color of the light emitted by fluorescent lamps and some light from new lamps is similar in color to standard incandescent lamps.

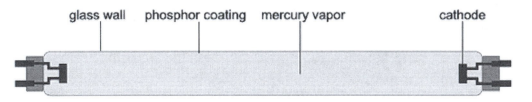

glass wall   phosphor coating   mercury vapor   cathode

Figure 1. Fluorescent lamp

The fluorescent lamp shown operates at 100 volts and draws 400 milliamps of current during normal operation. Only 25% of the lamp's power is converted to light, while the remaining 75% dissipates as heat which keeps the lamp at its optimal working temperature of 40°C.

16. Which of the following best describes light emitted when excited electrons in the phosphor coating revert to the ground state in more than one step?

   A. greater energy than light absorbed
   B. same wavelength as light absorbed
   C. longer wavelength than light absorbed
   D. higher frequency than light absorbed

17. In addition to light emitted in the visible spectrum, the lamp also emits a small proportion of ultraviolet light. This ultraviolet light is incident on a metal that has a minimum energy necessary to free an electron (work function) of 3.0 eV. If the frequency of the incident light is 1.2×10^{15} Hz, what is the kinetic energy of an electron ejected from the metal? ($h = 4.14 \times 10^{-15}$ eV·s)

   A. 1.83 eV
   B. 4.13 eV
   C. 7.96 eV
   D. 9.66 eV

18. What is the explanation of why some fluorescent light bulbs glow for a short period after the power supply has been turned off?

   A. incandescence of hot ionic gas within the bulb surface
   B. emission of light stored as vibrational kinetic energy in the phosphor coating
   C. dissipation of electric charge built up on the bulb's surface
   D. electrons returning to the ground state from excited states

19. How much light energy is emitted by the fluorescent lamp after 5 hours?

   A. 72 kJ
   B. 180 kJ
   C. 1,800 kJ
   D. 720 kJ

20. What is the wavelength of the light emitted by the fluorescent lamp when an electron of phosphor coating falls from an excited state to a lower energy state emitting a photon with energy of 3.04 eV? (Planck's constant $h = 4.14 \times 10^{-15}$ eV·s, and $c = 3 \times 10^{8}$ m/s)

   A. 30 nm
   B. 400 nm
   C. 1200 nm
   D. 3600 nm

Passage 4
(Questions 21–26)

Electron configuration is the arrangement of electrons of an atom or molecule and describes the way electrons are distributed in orbitals of the atomic or molecular system. The periodic table of elements uses the electron configuration of atoms as a main principle, and electron configuration describes the sharing of electrons within chemical bonds.

The ground state of an atom refers to the state when all the electrons of an atom occupy orbitals of the lowest energy levels. For example, the ground state for fluorine is $1s^2 2s^2 2p^5$, for phosphorus is $1s^2 2s^2 2p^6 3s^2 3p^3$ and for chlorine is $1s^2 2s^2 2p^6 3s^2 3p^5$.

When an atom in the ground state absorbs energy, its electron is promoted to a higher energy level, and a dark band appears on its absorption spectrum. Absorption spectrum shows the fraction of incident electromagnetic radiation absorbed by the material over a range of frequencies. Every chemical element has absorption lines at several particular wavelengths corresponding to the differences between the energy levels of its atomic orbitals.

When the excited electron returns to the ground state, a photon is emitted and produces a bright band on the emission spectrum. Absorption and emission spectra provide important information about the energy levels of the electrons within atoms and ions.

Hydrofluoric acid (HF) is created by reacting hydrogen (H_2) and fluorine (F_2) gasses:

$$H_2(g) + F_2(g) \rightleftarrows 2\ HF(g) \quad \Delta H = -269\ \text{kJ/mol}$$

Reaction 1

In aqueous solutions of hydrofluoric acid (HF), the electron configuration of the conjugate base F^- may be determined by absorption spectroscopy. In the ground state, the fluoride ion's additional electron occupies the outer position in the 3s subshell as: $1s^2 2s^2 2p^4 3s^1$.

21. Gaseous hydrogen fluoride is formed by reacting hydrogen and fluorine in a closed container (Reaction 1). What is the result of increasing the reaction temperature when the reaction reaches equilibrium?

A. [HF] increases due to increased rate of reaction
B. [HF] increases due to a decrease in enthalpy of forward reaction
C. [HF] decreases due to an exothermic forward reaction
D. [HF] decreases due to an increase in molar quantity of gas of the forward reaction

22. Which of the following is the conjugate base of the unknown hydrogen halide?

A. Xe   C. I
B. Xe⁻   D. Ⅰ

23. Which of the following statements is true for the ground state electron configurations of conjugate bases of two hydrogen halides?

A. electrons are absent   C. they are configurations of two metals
B. electrons are excited   D. they are configurations of two inert gases

24. Which of the following represents the electron configuration of a chlorine atom in excited state?

A. $1s^2 2s^2 2p^4 3d^1$ C. $1s^2 2s^2 2p^6 3s^2 3p^4 4s^1$
B. $1s^2 2s^2 2p^6 3p^1$ D. $1s^2 2s^2 2p^1 3s^2 3d^2$

25. What does the absorption spectrum of an excited conjugate base (X^-) of the hydrogen halide (HX) show?

A. red shift   C. no absorption
B. dark bands   D. bright bands

26. What is pH of 0.1 M solution of hydrogen bromide?

A. 0.1
B. 1.0
C. 2.0
D. 7.0

Questions 27 through 31 are not based on any descriptive passage and are independent of each other

27. Which of the following elements is the most electronegative?

   A. H
   B. K
   C. Cl
   D. Mg

28. In a KCl molecule, how many electrons are shared in the potassium-chlorine bond?

   A. 1
   B. 2
   C. 3
   D. 0

29. What is the molarity of a 2N concentration of H_2SO_4 completely dissociated in water?

   A. 1 M
   B. 2 M
   C. 3 M
   D. 4 M

30. The car, with its engine off, slows down as it coasts. Which of the following statements is true about the forces acting on the car?

   A. no forces are acting on the car
   B. net force is zero while there are forces acting on the car
   C. net force acting on car does not equal zero
   D. none of the above statements can be concluded

31. Which of the following conclusions best describes each of the hydrogen halides and bonding between hydrogen and halide atoms?

   A. smaller halide atoms have stronger bonds
   B. smaller halide atoms have weaker bonds
   C. hybrids of smaller halide atoms have greater lengths
   D. hybrids of greater lengths are associated with stronger bonds

This page is intentionally left blank

Passage 5
(Questions 32–36)

In fluid dynamics, drag refers to forces that oppose the relative motion (resistance) of an object through a fluid (liquid or gas). Drag forces act in the direction opposite the oncoming flow velocity. Unlike other resistive forces (e.g. dry friction), drag forces depend on velocity. When an object moves through a fluid, the drag force retards its motion with a magnitude expressed by:

$$F_{drag} \approx -\frac{1}{2}\, CA\rho v^2,$$

Equation 1

where C, drag coefficient, is a dimensionless constant, A is cross-sectional area of object normal to flow direction, ρ is density of the fluid, and v is velocity of object relative to fluid.

Equation 1 applies to fluids with an onset of turbulence that develops whirls and eddies. For an undisturbed fluid, the drag force is actually greater than the value in Equation 1. Reynolds number, also a dimensionless constant, determines the extent to which a fluid is disturbed.

$$R_e = \rho v l / \eta,$$

Equation 2

where l is linear size of object and η is viscosity (stickiness) of fluid.

Substance	ρ (kg/m^3)	η (kg/m s)
Air	1.3	1.8×10^{-5}
Water	1.0×10^3	1.0×10^{-3}
Mercury	1.36×10^4	1.5×10^{-3}
Methanol	0.9×10^3	5.7×10^{-4}
Benzene	0.8×10^3	6.0×10^{-4}

Table 1.

For R_e values greater than 100, Equation 1 for F_{drag} is relatively accurate. Reynolds number also determines the onset of turbulence in the fluid. When R_e is greater than 2×10^5, the fluid develops whirls and eddies that break off from the flow in an unpredictable manner and turbulence is observed.

Viscosity is a measure of the resistance of a fluid which is being deformed by stress (shear or extensional). Viscosity characterizes a fluid's internal resistance to flow and may be thought of as a measure of fluid friction and describes "thickness" of a fluid. Thus, water is "thin" with a lower viscosity, while molasses is "thick" with a higher viscosity. The less viscous a fluid is, the greater its ease of movement and flow.

32. What should be the minimum velocity of the car with the linear size of 3 m (*l*) for turbulence to develop behind it ($\rho = 1.3$ kg/m³, $\eta = 1.8 \times 10^{-5}$ kg/m·s)?

A. 0.24 m/s

B. 0.5 m/s

C. 0.84 m/s

D. 0.92 m/s

33. What minimum velocity makes Equation 1 true for a cube with dimensions 2 x 2 x 2 m moving through the air ($\rho = 1.3$ kg/m³, $\eta = 1.8 \times 10^{-5}$ kg/m·s)?

A. 1.1×10^{2} m/s

B. 3.3×10^{-2} m/s

C. 4.8×10^{-3} m/s

D. 6.9×10^{-4} m/s

34. What thrust would be exerted by a fish swimming in the ocean at constant 3 m/s velocity with dimensions of 0.1 x 0.1 x 0.1 m ($C = 0.2$, $\rho = 1.0 \times 10^{3}$ kg/m³)?

A. 0.09 N   **B.** 9 N   **C.** 90 N   **D.** 3×10^{5} N

35. What is the drag force on the 1000 kg car with dimensions 1.5 m high, 2 m wide, and 3 m long if it is moving at 20 m/s ($\rho = 1.3$ kg/m³, $C = 0.25$)?

A. 10 N   **B.** 100 N   **C.** 200 N   **D.** 1,950 N

36. For solving Equation 1, what is the effective cross-sectional area (*A*) for a car with dimensions 1.5 m high, 2 m wide, and 3 m long?

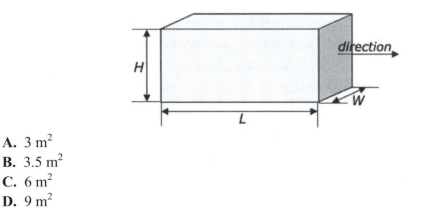

A. 3 m²

B. 3.5 m²

C. 6 m²

D. 9 m²

Passage 6
(Question 37–42)

In an average household some very toxic substances may be found. For example, oven cleaners and drain cleansers dissolve organic substances such as grease, fat, hair, and skin because these substances contain concentrated solutions of sodium hydroxide (NaOH). Like all strong aqueous bases, NaOH hydrolyzes protein peptide and ester linkages.

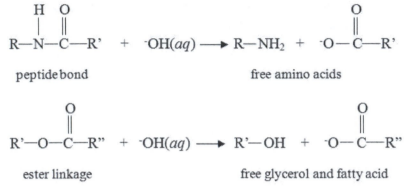

Household bleach is a 5% (by mass) solution of sodium hypochlorite (NaClO) and H_2O. The hypochlorite ion ($^-$ClO) is a mild oxidizing agent and toxic when ingested internally. Low concentrations of chlorine gas are also present within bleach solutions.

Another common household toxic substance is ammonia (NH_3). NH_3 is a strong ligand and gas at room temperature. If NH_3 is inhaled in high concentration, death can ensue due to irreversible exclusion of O_2 from the hemoglobin within the red blood cell. The same mechanism is observed for death caused by carbon monoxide (CO) poisoning.

$$4\ NH_3(g) + Hb \cdot 4\ O_2(aq) \rightarrow Hb \cdot 4\ NH_3(aq) + 4\ O_2(g)$$

NH_3 Poisoning

Most US deaths in the household caused by chemicals are due to toxic gases formed when ammonia and bleach come in contact with each other. Harmful insidious vapors containing hydrazine (H_2NNH_2), chloroamine ($ClNH_2$) and hydrogen chloride (HCl) are released from the reaction of bleach and ammonia solutions.

$$n\text{NaOCl}(aq) + n\text{NH}_3(aq)$$
$$\text{Bleach} \qquad \text{Ammonia}$$
$$\downarrow$$
$$H_2NNH_2(aq) + ClNH_2(aq) + HCl(aq)$$

For consumer safety, warning notices are required on the labels of these chemicals. A safety precaution is to never mix two substances with different active ingredients because a cloud of toxic fumes could result.

37. Which one of the following statements is true?

    A. N_2H_4 cannot act as a ligand
    B. N_2H_4 experiences dipole interactions, not hydrogen bonds
    C. O_2 is a better Lewis base than either NH_3 or CO
    D. vapor pressure of NH_3 at room temperature is greater than 760 torr

38. Which of the following statements is true for ammonia?

    A. NH_3 is a weak base and weak acid
    C. NH_3 is a strong acid and weak base
    B. NH_3 is a strong acid and strong base
    D. NH_3 is neither an acid nor a base

39. The formal charges of atoms in the hypochlorite ion (ClO^-) are:

    A. 0 for Cl and –1 for O
    C. –1 for Cl and 0 for O
    B. +1 for Cl and –2 for O
    D. –1/2 for both the Cl and O atoms

40. Ammonium chloride (NH_4Cl) is formed when bleach and ammonia are mixed together. What is the phase of ammonium chloride at room temperature?

    A. plasma   **B.** gas   **C.** solid   **D.** liquid

41. The shapes of NH_3 and NH_2Cl are identical. Which one of the following molecules also has a trigonal pyramidal shape?

    A. iodine trifluoride (IF_3)
    C. hypochlorous acid (HOCl)
    B. hydronium ion (H_3O^+)
    D. hydrochloric acid (HCl)

42. Electrolytes dissociate into anions and cations in water. Which of the following compounds is/are NOT electrolytes?

    I.   Chloramine
    II. Hydrazine
    III. Hydrogen chloride

    A. I only
    B. II only
    C. I & II only
    D. I, II & III

> Questions 43 through 46 are not based on any
> descriptive passage and are independent of each other

43. A 1 kg block slides back and forth on a frictionless table while attached to the free end of an anchored spring. If the spring constant (k) is 9 N/m, what is the frequency of motion with a period ($T = 2\pi\sqrt{m/k}$)?

    A. 0.25 Hz

    B. 0.5 Hz

    C. 2 Hz

    D. 4 Hz

44. The displacement of an object in simple harmonic motion is expressed as: $x = 3\cos(\omega t + \pi/3)$ (t in sec and x in cm). At which of the following positions (x) will the block have the greatest speed?

    A. 0 cm

    B. 3/2 cm

    C. 3 cm

    D. $3\sqrt{3}/2$ cm

45. When the following equation is balanced, what is the sum of the coefficients?

$Hg + HCl \rightarrow HgCl_2 + H_2$

    A. 1

    B. 4

    C. 5

    D. 7

46. When the following equation is balanced, what is the coefficient of $Mg(OH)_2$?

$(NH_4)_2SO_4 + Mg(OH)_2 \rightarrow NH_3 + H_2O + MgSO_4$

    A. 1

    B. 2

    C. 3

    D. 4

This page is intentionally left blank

Passage 7
(Questions 47–52)

Radio waves carry information by varying a combination of the amplitude, frequency and phase of the wave within a frequency band. The radio waves which carry information in a standard broadcast are an example of electromagnetic radiation. These waves are disturbance, not of a material medium, but of electric and magnetic fields. In linearly polarized wave, the electric field points perpendicular to propagation of the wave although its magnitude varies in space and time. The magnetic field points in a direction perpendicular to the wave propagation and to electric field, and two fields propagate in phase.

The electromagnetic radiation is generated by an antenna, which is a metal rod that points perpendicular to the wave propagation. An alternating current is generated in the antenna, whose frequency is the same as the radiation produced. The electric field of the resulting electromagnetic radiation points along the same axis as the current.

The electric field of the electromagnetic radiation encounters electrons on the receiving antenna, which is also a metal rod. The electric field creates a current along the receiving antenna. Transmission and reception can be enhanced by having the length of the antenna one quarter of the wavelength of the electromagnetic wave.

The following questions refer to a transmitting antenna which points vertically and a receiving antenna which points directly to the north. The speed of light (c) is 3×10^8 m/s.

47. According to the passage, what is the best orientation of the receiving antenna?

    A. any orientation   **C.** vertical

    B. east/west   **D.** north/south to point towards the transmitting antenna

48. According to the passage, what is the reasonable length for an efficient antenna when the frequency of the alternating current in the transmitting antenna is 10^7 Hz?

    A. 150 m   **C.** 30 m

    B. 75 m   **D.** 7.5 m

49. Which of the following statements is the best description of energy flow between two antennas?

    A. kinetic to electromagnetic to kinetic

    B. electrical to electromagnetic to electrical

    C. electromagnetic to electrical to electromagnetic

    D. mechanical to electromagnetic to mechanical

50. What is the direction of the electric field vector of the radiation for a point between the two antennas referenced in the passage?

    A. east / west   **C.** north / south

    B. up / down   **D.** north / south and east / west

51. According to the passage, how is a current on the receiving antenna created by the electric field?

    A. electrons are promoted to higher energy orbitals by the electric field

    B. resistance of antenna is changed by the electric field

    C. electrons are polarized by the electric field

    D. force on electrons is exerted by the electric field

52. What is the direction of the magnetic field vector of the radiation for a point between the two antennas referenced in the passage?

    A. east / west   **C.** north / south

    B. up / down   **D.** north / south or east / west

Questions 53 through 59 are not based on any
descriptive passage and are independent of each other

53. Which compound consists of only carbon and hydrogen?

    A. carbohydrate   **B.** hydrocarbon   **C.** homolog   **D.** isomer

54. Which of the following statements is correct about naturally occurring monosaccharides?

    A. The ratio of L and D-isomers varies widely depending on the source
    B. The L and D-isomers occur in equal ratios
    C. The D-isomers predominate
    D. The L-isomers predominate

55. The following structure's IUPAC name is:

    A. 2-chloro-1-ethylcyclohexane
    B. Chloro-ethylcyclohexane
    C. 1-chloro-2-ethylcyclohexane
    D. 2-ethyl-l-chlorohexane

56. Which of the following is true for a reducing sugar?

    A. It can reduce Cu^{2+} but not Ag^+ **C.** It contains a b(1→1) link
    B. It has an acetal group   **D.** It has a hemiacetal group

57. Which amino acid, unlike all others, does NOT contain a chiral carbon?

    A. Histidine   **B.** Glycine   **C.** Cysteine   **D.** Phenylalanine

58. Which of the following terms is used to describe the structure of the cell membrane?

    A. mosaic model   **C.** fluid model
    B. diffusion model   **D.** fluid mosaic phospholipid bilayer model

59. Which of the following molecules is a ketone?

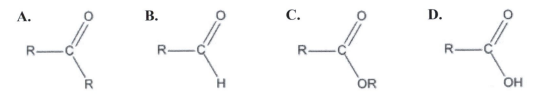

MCAT Chemical & Physical Foundations of Biological Systems

Practice Test #2

59 questions

For explanatory answers see pgs. 155-192

For CBT online format of this test that provides Diagnostics Report with performance statistics, difficulty rating of each question and other features visit:

www.MasterMCAT.com

Most questions in the Physical Sciences test are organized into groups, each containing a descriptive passage. After studying the passage select the one best answer to each question in the group. Some questions are not based on a descriptive passage and are also independent of each other. If you are not certain of an answer, eliminate the alternatives you know to be incorrect and then select an answer from the remaining alternatives. Indicate your selected answer by marking the corresponding answer on your answer sheet. A periodic table is provided for your use. You may consult it whenever you wish.

Periodic Table of the Elements

1 H 1.0																	2 He 4.0
3 Li 6.9	4 Be 9.0											5 B 10.8	6 C 12.0	7 N 14.0	8 O 16.0	9 F 19.0	10 Ne 20.2
11 Na 23.0	12 Mg 24.3											13 Al 27.0	14 Si 28.1	15 P 31.0	16 S 32.1	17 Cl 35.5	18 Ar 39.9
19 K 39.1	20 Ca 40.1	21 Sc 45.0	22 Ti 47.9	23 V 50.9	24 Cr 52.0	25 Mn 54.9	26 Fe 55.8	27 Co 58.9	28 Ni 58.7	29 Cu 63.5	30 Zn 65.4	31 Ga 69.7	32 Ge 72.6	33 As 74.9	34 Se 79.0	35 Br 79.9	36 Kr 83.8
37 Rb 85.5	38 Sr 87.6	39 Y 88.9	40 Zr 91.2	41 Nb 92.9	42 Mo 95.9	43 Tc (98)	44 Ru 101.1	45 Rh 102.9	46 Pd 106.4	47 Ag 107.9	48 Cd 112.4	49 In 114.8	50 Sn 118.7	51 Sb 121.8	52 Te 127.6	53 I 126.9	54 Xe 131.3
55 Cs 132.9	56 Ba 137.3	57 La* 138.9	72 Hf 178.5	73 Ta 180.9	74 W 183.9	75 Re 186.2	76 Os 190.2	77 Ir 192.2	78 Pt 195.1	79 Au 197.0	80 Hg 200.6	81 Tl 204.4	82 Pb 207.2	83 Bi 209.0	84 Po (209)	85 At (210)	86 Rn (222)
87 Fr (223)	88 Ra (226)	89 Ac† (227)	104 Rf (261)	105 Db (262)	106 Sg (266)	107 Bh (264)	108 Hs (277)	109 Mt (268)	110 Ds (281)	111 Uuu (272)	112 Uub (285)		114 Uuq (289)		116 Uuh (289)		

	58 Ce 140.1	59 Pr 140.9	60 Nd 144.2	61 Pm (145)	62 Sm 150.4	63 Eu 152.0	64 Gd 157.3	65 Tb 158.9	66 Dy 162.5	67 Ho 164.9	68 Er 167.3	69 Tm 168.9	70 Yb 173.0	71 Lu 175.0
†	90 Th 232.0	91 Pa (231)	92 U 238.0	93 Np (237)	94 Pu (244)	95 Am (243)	96 Cm (247)	97 Bk (247)	98 Cf (251)	99 Es (252)	100 Fm (257)	101 Md (258)	102 No (259)	103 Lr (260)

CHEMICAL & PHYSICAL FOUNDATIONS OF BIOLOGICAL SYSTEMS
MCAT® PRACTICE TEST #2: ANSWER SHEET

Passage 1

1 : A   B   C   D
2 : A   B   C   D
3 : A   B   C   D
4 : A   B   C   D
5 : A   B   C   D
6 : A   B   C   D

Passage 2

7 : A   B   C   D
8 : A   B   C   D
9 : A   B   C   D
10 : A   B   C   D
11 : A   B   C   D

Independent questions

12 : A   B   C   D
13 : A   B   C   D
14 : A   B   C   D
15 : A   B   C   D

Passage 3

16 : A   B   C   D
17 : A   B   C   D
18 : A   B   C   D
19 : A   B   C   D
20 : A   B   C   D
21 : A   B   C   D
22 : A   B   C   D

Passage 4

23 : A   B   C   D
24 : A   B   C   D
25 : A   B   C   D
26 : A   B   C   D
27 : A   B   C   D

Independent questions

28 : A   B   C   D
29 : A   B   C   D
30 : A   B   C   D
31 : A   B   C   D
32 : A   B   C   D

Passage 5

33 : A   B   C   D
34 : A   B   C   D
35 : A   B   C   D
36 : A   B   C   D
37 : A   B   C   D
38 : A   B   C   D

Passage 6

39 : A   B   C   D
40 : A   B   C   D
41 : A   B   C   D
42 : A   B   C   D
43 : A   B   C   D

Independent questions

44 : A   B   C   D
45 : A   B   C   D
46 : A   B   C   D
47 : A   B   C   D

Passage 7

48 : A   B   C   D
49 : A   B   C   D
50 : A   B   C   D
51 : A   B   C   D
52 : A   B   C   D

Independent questions

53 : A   B   C   D
54 : A   B   C   D
55 : A   B   C   D
56 : A   B   C   D
57 : A   B   C   D
58 : A   B   C   D
59 : A   B   C   D

This page is intentionally left blank

Passage 1
(Questions 1–6)

The combustion of fuel occurs with an oxidizer (usually air) in a combustion chamber of an internal combustion engine. The expansion of high temperature and pressure gases, produced by combustion, directly applies force to a movable component of the engine generating useful mechanical energy. Internal combustion engines form carbon monoxide (CO) and oxides of nitrogen including nitrogen monoxide (NO) and nitrogen dioxide (NO_2). These gases enter the atmosphere and undergo several reactions.

NO is a colorless gas which spontaneously reacts with oxygen forming NO_2. NO_2 is a reddish-brown gas and can react with H_2O to form nitric acid (HNO_3) which causes increased rain acidity. At low temperatures NO_2 molecules dimerize forming dinitrogen tetroxide (N_2O_4) molecules.

NO_2 and CO also react in the atmosphere in the following reaction:

$$NO_2(g) + CO(g) \rightarrow NO(g) + CO_2(g)$$

Reaction 1

The reaction mechanism involves two steps:

(1a) $NO_2(g) + NO_2(g) \rightarrow NO_3(g) + NO(g)$ *slow step*

(1b) $NO_3(g) + CO(g) \rightarrow NO_2(g) + CO_2(g)$ *fast step*

The Earth's atmosphere (stratosphere) contains an ozone (O_3) layer at relatively high concentrations which absorbs 93-99% of the sun's high frequency ultraviolet light. Ozone is created by ultraviolet light striking oxygen molecules (O_2), and splitting them into atomic oxygen (O) which combines with O_2 to create ozone, O_3.

NO and CO gases are ozone-depleting compounds. Before NO and CO gases entered the atmosphere and reacted with ozone, the ozone level was in equilibrium maintained by a photochemical process. Self-propagating chain reactions disrupt the dynamics of the ozone layer by the mechanism below:

(2a) $NO(g) + O_3(g) \rightarrow NO_2(g) + O_2(g)$

(2b) $NO_2(g) + O(g) \rightarrow NO(g) + O_2(g)$

Net reaction:

$$O_3(g) + O(g) \rightarrow 2\ O_2(g)$$

Reaction 2

1. For ozone to be maintained in dynamic equilibrium, what must be true about the rate of the ozone-depleting process?

A. equal to zero
B. less than rate of ozone formation

C. equal to rate of ozone formation
D. greater than rate of ozone formation

2. The ozone-depleting reactions described in the passage are noxious because the destructive chemical:

A. is more reactive than ozone
B. is repeatedly regenerated

C. is produced in large quantities
D. diffuses into stratosphere with ozone layer

3. Which of the following is a true statement about the mechanism of Reaction 1?

A. step 1a determines the overall rate of reaction
B. step 1b is the rate-limiting step of reaction
C. adding catalyst increases activation energy of reaction
D. NO is an intermediate and not final reaction product

4. After adding more NO_2(g) to Reaction 1:

A. equilibrium constant decreases
B. equilibrium constant increases

C. reaction proceeds in the reverse direction
D. reaction proceeds in the forward direction

5. A 1 L vessel at 400°C contains the following equilibrium concentrations: [NO] = 0.2 M, [CO_2] = 0.04 M, [NO_2] = 0.01 M and [CO] = 0.2 M. What is the equilibrium constant of Reaction 1?

A. 0.5
B. 1.0
C. 2.0
D. 4.0

6. Which of the following is necessary for maintaining the ozone layer in absence of ozone depleting chemicals?

A. electromagnetic radiation
B. atmospheric pressure

C. nitrogen oxides
D. water vapor

Passage 2
(Questions 7–11)

The speed of longitudinal waves (e.g. sound waves) through a fluid medium is expressed as:

$$v = \sqrt{\frac{\beta}{\rho}}$$

Equation 1

where B is bulk modulus and ρ is density of medium.

The formula for the speed of longitudinal waves moving through a solid is the same as for waves moving through fluid medium, except B is replaced by Young's modulus (Y). At constant temperature, an increased pressure of fluid medium results in a decreased volume. The bulk modulus is the ratio that describes this effect:

$$B = \frac{F/A}{\Delta V/V_0}$$

Equation 2

where F/A is external pressure, ΔV is the change in volume of the medium and V_0 is initial volume.

Because increased pressure always results in decreased volume, a minus sign is required for B to be positive. Fluids with a higher bulk modulus are less affected by changes in external pressure than fluids with a lower bulk modulus.

The Young's modulus of a solid expressed by the same ratio as for bulk modulus of fluids, except the denominator is replaced by $\Delta L/L_0$, where L is length of solid.

Material	Modulus (N/m^2)	Density (kg/m^3)
Air	$B = 1.4 \times 10^5$	1.2
Water	$B = 2.2 \times 10^9$	1,000
Aluminum	$Y = 7.0 \times 10^{10}$	2,700
Copper	$Y = 1.4 \times 10^{11}$	8,900
Lead	$Y = 1.6 \times 10^{10}$	11,340
Gold	$Y = 7.8 \times 10^{10}$	19,300

at 23°C and 1 atm

Table 1. Moduli and densities for various materials

7. From Equation 1 and Table 1, the speed of sound through water is approximately 1,500 m/s. What is the wavelength of a 50-kHz sound wave emitted by a humpback whale underwater?

    A. 0.3 cm   **B.** 1.5 cm   **C.** 3.0 cm   **D.** 15.0 cm

8. What is the ratio of the speed of sound moving through gold to thw speed of sound moving through water?

    A. 0.0135   **B.** 0.135   **C.** 1.35   **D.** 13.3

9. At 0°C and 1 atm, the speed of sound in hydrogen gas is four times greater than the speed of sound in air. What is the reason for this difference between the speeds of sound in these two mediums?

    A. H_2 gas is significantly more compressible than air
    B. H_2 molecules have a lower mass and therefore move faster when subjected to sound wave
    C. H_2 molecules experience smaller London dispersion forces than N_2 and O_2
    D. H_2 gas is denser than air at STP (standard temperature and pressure)

10. If a block of aluminum with volume (V_0) is taken to an underwater depth (d) of greater than 1,000 m, ρ is density of the water and B is the bulk modulus of aluminum, which of the following expressions describes the change in volume of the block?

    A. $\dfrac{V_0\rho g d}{B}$ **B.** $\dfrac{V_0}{B\rho g d}$ **C.** $\dfrac{B\rho g d}{V_0}$ **D.** $\dfrac{B}{V_0\rho g d}$

11. In vulcanized rubber, the speed of sound is 45 m/s. How long does it take for a 650 Hz sound wave to pass through a 0.50 m cube of vulcanized rubber?

    A. 0.45 ms
    B. 4.5 ms
    C. 9.3 ms
    D. 11.1 ms

Questions 12 through 15 are not based on any
descriptive passage and are independent of each other

12. In a physics experiment, carts run along a level frictionless one-dimensional track. Cart A is 2 kg and cart B is 3 kg. Initially cart A moves to the right at 0.4 m/s, and cart B moves to the left at 0.5 m/s. After cart A & B collide, they stick together.

Note: movement to the right is positive while movement to the left is denoted as negative.

Before collision, what is the total momentum of the system?

A. 0.7 kg m/s   **C.** 2.3 kg m/s
B. –0.7 kg m/s   **D.** –2.3 kg m/s

13. From question 12, what is the magnitude of the final velocity of the two carts?

A. 3.5 m/s   **C.** –0.14 m/s
B. 7.14 m/s   **D.** –1.6 m/s

14. A hoisting mechanism pulls a 1,000 kg block on wheels at a slow speed up the hill with an incline $\emptyset = 40°$. The block starts at ground level, and the hoisting mechanism exerts a power 3,000 Watts, for 100 seconds, where $g = 10$ m/s^2.

With no friction and 100% efficiency, what is the height above horizontal that the mechanism pulls the block to?

A. 10 meters   **C.** 30 meters
B. 20 meters   **D.** 40 meters

15. Which type of energy flow is the most efficient?

A. electric energy to potential energy
B. electric energy to kinetic energy
C. potential energy to kinetic energy
D. potential energy to electric energy

This page is intentionally left blank

Passage 3
(Questions 16–22)

The rate of reaction for reactants (starting material) or products in a particular reaction is defined as how fast the reaction takes place. Several laboratory techniques are used to determine the order of a reaction. The rate-determining step, not the overall equation, is necessary to predict the rate of the reaction.

For example, the following reaction occurs in three steps:

$$A + D \rightarrow F + G$$

Step 1 (*slow*)	$A \rightarrow B + C$
Step 2 (*fast*)	$B + D \rightarrow E + F$
Step 3 (*fast*)	$C + E \rightarrow G$

Reaction 1

In the reaction pathway above, the rate-determining step is the first step. Therefore, the overall reaction rate equals the rate of the first step, k_1 [A], where k is rate constant. Rate constants are denoted as k_x, where x is step number.

Sometimes it is preferable to measure the rate of a reaction relative to one reactant or product. For second-order reaction, excess of one reactant is included in the reaction mixture. A pseudo first-order reaction is when only a small portion of excess reactant is consumed and its relative concentration remains constant. To analyze enzyme activity, a new rate constant k′ equals the product of the original rate constant k, and concentration of reactant in excess.

The reaction rate may depend on the concentration of the intermediates and is common if the rate-determining step is not the first step. In this case, the concentration of intermediates must be derived from the equilibrium constant of the preceding step.

In electrochemistry, the Nernst equation can be used (in conjunction with other information) to determine the equilibrium reduction potential of a half-cell in an electrochemical cell. For redox reactions at equilibrium, the reaction rate is proportional to voltage produced by two half-cells as expressed by equation:

$$E = E^\circ_{tot} - (RT/zF) \ln([C]^c[D]^d / [A]^a[B]^b)$$

Equation 1

where, T = absolute temperature, R = 8.314 J/K·mol, z = # electrons transferred and F = 9.6485 x 10^4 C/mol.

16. Which of the following expressions is true for the reaction at equilibrium?

I. $E = E°$ II. $k_1/k_{-1} = 1$ III. $\ln([C]^c[D]^d/[A]^a[B]^b) = zFE°/RT$

A. I only   **B.** II only   **C.** I and III only   **D.** III only

17. What would be the electromotive force of the galvanic cell of the following system at 298K?

$$Zn(s)|Zn^{2+}(0.2M)\|Cu^{2+}(0.02M)|Cu(s)$$
$$E°_{cell} = +1.10V$$

A. 1.07V   **B.** 1.13V   **C.** 1.10V   **D.** 0.05V

18. To test the rate of Step 3 in Reaction 1, a solution containing concentration of 0.1 M of E and 50 M of C was prepared. After the reaction was 50% complete, the rate was calculated. If the reaction was pseudo first-order, the calculated rate will differ from the true rate by:

A. 0.2%   **B.** 0.1%   **C.** 0.05%   **D.** 0.02%

19. Catalysts are effective in increasing the rate of a reaction because they:

A. increase the value of equilibrium constant
B. increase the energy of activated complex
C. lower activation energy
D. decrease the number of collisions between reactant molecules

20. The reaction of A and B is catalyzed by enzyme P. With P in large excess, concentrations of A and B produced the following initial results.

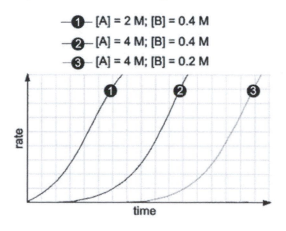

Which of the following rate expression best describes the reaction?

A. rate = $k'[A]^x$
B. rate = $k'[B]^y$
C. rate = $k'[A]^x[B]^y$
D. rate = $k'[A]^x[B]^y[P]^z$

21. In galvanic cells, what is the result of increasing the concentrations of reactants?

A. both voltage and spontaneity increase
B. voltage increases, while reaction spontaneity remains constant
C. reaction rate increases, while voltage and reaction spontaneity remain constant
D. reaction spontaneity increases, while the voltage remains constant

22. If Step 2 was the rate-determining step of Reaction 1, which of the following equations would be the correct expression for the rate?

A. rate = $k_1 k_2 [D] / k_{-1}[C]$
B. rate = $k_1 k_2 [D] / k_{-1} k_{-2}[C]$
C. rate = $k_1 k_2 [A][D] / k_{-1} k_{-2}[C]$
D. rate = $k_1 k_2 [A][D] / k_{-1}[C]$

This page is intentionally left blank

Passage 4
(Questions 23–27)

A section of copper tubing has three cross sectional areas, A_1, A_2, A_3, which are decreasing in size. Fluid is moving through the tube at a constant rate. To measure hydrostatic pressure, narrow columns of identical diameter extend vertically from each of three sections of the tube.

Bernoulli's equation describes fluids in motion at the same elevation by the following equation:

$$P + \tfrac{1}{2}\rho v^2 = \text{constant}$$

where P is pressure, ρ is density and v is speed of the flow.

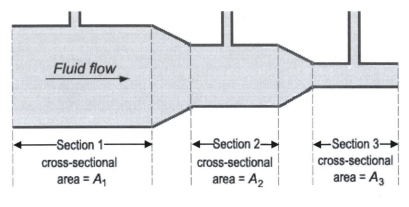

Figure 1.

Note: Assume the fluid flows in non-turbulent manner and the fluid is incomprehensible

23. If the ratio of A_1 to A_2 is tripled, then the v_1 to v_2 ratio of flow speeds will:

A. increase by a factor of 3
B. increase by a factor of 9
C. decrease by a factor of 3
D. decrease by a factor of 9

24. If the cross-sectional area of Section 2 is 12 cm² and the fluid is flowing through that section at a velocity of 10 cm/s, the velocity of the fluid flow in Section 1 with a cross-sectional area of 30 cm² will be:

    A. 2 cm/s
    B. 4 cm/s
    C. 8 cm/s
    D. 10 cm/s

25. Fluids A and B pass through Tubes 1 and 2 at equal rates of flow. The cross-sectional area of Tube 1 is greater than Tube 2. Which of the following would best explain the equal rate of flow?

    A. Fluid A has a greater viscosity than Fluid B
    B. Fluid A is less dense than Fluid B
    C. Fluid A has less velocity than Fluid B
    D. Fluid A has a greater vapor pressure than Fluid B

26. Which of the following correctly describes the relationship of pressure readings from each cross-sectional area?

    A. $P_1 > P_2 > P_3$
    B. $P_1 < P_2 < P_3$
    C. $P_1 < P_2 = P_3$
    D. $P_1 = P_2 < P_3$

27. What is the pressure difference between Sections 1 and 3 if the fluid velocity in Section 1 is 0.4 m/s and in Section 3 it is 0.6 m/sec and the density is 1000 kg/m³?

    A. 10 Pa
    B. 100 Pa
    C. 200 Pa
    D. 1000 Pa

> Questions 28 through 32 are not based on any
> descriptive passage and are independent of each other

28. A woman jumps from an airplane with a parachute. After an initial accelerating thrust, she falls at a constant speed (terminal velocity) in a straight vertical vector. Are the forces on the woman balanced during the latter portion of her fall?

    A. yes because she is falling at a constant velocity
    B. no because gravity is greater than drag force
    C. no because gravity is not balanced by other forces
    D. no because forces are balanced only for stationary objects

29. When there is one force acting on an object, what can be concluded?

    A. object is moving in a straight line at a constant speed
    B. object is accelerating or decelerating
    C. object is moving at a constant speed but not necessarily in a straight line
    D. none of the above may be concluded

30. Which one of these aqueous solutions has a pH greater than 7.0?

    A. 0.1 M KCN
    B. 0.25 M HCN
    C. 0.5 M NH_4Cl
    D. 1.0 M HClO

31. A radio is producing 30 W of sound and the listener is 5 m away. What would be the intensity of sound energy at the listener's ear if the sound travels equally in all directions?

    A. 0.5 W/m^2
    B. 0.095 W/m^2
    C. 90 W/m^2
    D. 9,000 W/m^2

32. A massless meter stick is placed on a fulcrum at its 0.3 m mark. A 5 kg object is placed on the meter stick at its 0.2 m mark. An object of what mass must be placed at the 0.8 m mark to establish torque balance?

    A. 1 kg
    B. 2 kg
    C. 5 kg
    D. 10 kg

Passage 5
(Questions 33–38)

The ideal gas law uses the following equation to describe the state of an ideal gas:

$$PV = nRT$$

where P is pressure, V is volume, n is number of moles of gas, R is the ideal gas constant, and T is the temperature of the gas.

The gas particles in a container are constantly moving at various speeds characterized by the Maxwell distribution shown in the figure below.

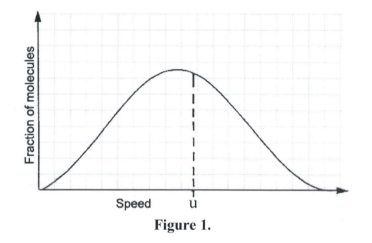

Figure 1.

When two particles collide, their velocities change. However, for a gas in thermal equilibrium, the velocity distribution of the gas as a whole remains unchanged.

The average kinetic energy (E) of the gas is:

$$E = (\tfrac{1}{2})mu^2$$

Equation 1

where m is mass of one particle and u is root mean square (rms) speed of gas particles.

$$u = [1/n(v_1^2 + v_2^2 + \ldots + v_n^2)]^{1/2}$$

Equation 2

where n is number of gas particles; rms is different than average speed.

For an ideal gas: $E = (3/2)\, nRT$

Equation 3

where n is number moles of gas.

Combining Equations 1 and 3:

$$u = (3RT/M)^{1/2}$$

Equation 4

where M is the molar mass of gas particles.

l is the mean free path (mfp) which is the average distance a particle travels between collisions. The mfp is expected to be larger for gases at a low pressure because of the greater space between gas particles and for gases where gas particles are small.

The following expression for the mfp supports these assumptions:

$$l = kT/(2^{(1/2)}\pi s^2 P)$$

Equation 5

where s is the atomic diameter (typically 10^{-8}), k is the Boltzmann constant and P is pressure.

In addition to colliding with each other, gas particles also collide with the container walls. If the container wall has a pinhole that is small compared to the mfp of the gas, and a pressure differential exists across the wall, gas particles escape (effusion) through the pinhole without affecting Maxwell's distribution.

The effusion rate is described by the equation:

$$dN_{eff}/dt = A(P-P_1) / (2\pi MRT)^{1/2}$$

Equation 6

where N_{eff} is the number of moles of effusing particles, A is the area of the pinhole, P and P_1 – pressure on the inside and outside of the container walls respectively, and $P > P_1$.

33. For a mixture of two noble gases, G_X and G_Y, which escape through the same pinhole, what is the relative rate of effusion?

A. 1

B. $P_Y (M_Y)^{1/2} / P_X (M_X)^{1/2}$

C. $A_Y (M_Y)^{1/2} / A_X (M_X)^{1/2}$

D. $(M_Y / M_X)^{1/2}$

34. Which of the following conditions imply a shorter mean free path (mfp) of a gas?

A. pressure of the gas is increased

B. pressure of the gas is decreased

C. number of gas particles per unit volume is decreased

D. distance between collisions is increased

35. For an ideal gas, the average kinetic energy can be directly related to:

A. Boltzmann constant

B. universal gas constant

C. temperature

D. rms speed

36. If a vessel contained the following gas mixture in equal amounts of NH_3, H_2, O_2 and Cl_2 and had a pinhole, which gas would have the highest rate of effusion?

A. NH_3

B. H_2

C. O_2

D. Cl_2

37. At 298K, which of the following gases will have the smallest rms speed?

A. N_2

B. O_2

C. Cl_2

D. CO_2

38. Which of the following provides for a standard pressure and temperature?

A. 1 atm and 273 K   C. 760 mm Hg and 273 K

B. 760 Torr and 0°C   D. all of the above

Passage 6
(Questions: 39–43)

A man stands on a scale at the surface of the Earth. The scale reading is the magnitude of the normal force which the scale exerts on the man. To a first approximation, there is a balance of forces and the magnitude of the gravitational force is the magnitude of the scale's force:

$$F_{grav} = \frac{GM_{Earth}\,m}{R_{Earth}^2}$$

Equation 1

where G is Newton's constant, M_E is the mass of Earth and R_E is the radius of Earth.

The force of gravity (F_{grav}) and the reading of the scale (g) is proportional and the mass (m) of object:

$$F_{grav} = mg$$

Equation 2

where g has the value $GM_E/R_E^2 = 9.8 \text{ m/s}^2$.

There are several approximations made and to calculate the scale reading, idealizations need to be accounted for.

For example, consider the rotation of Earth. If a person is standing on a scale at the equator, there is a centripetal acceleration because he is moving in a circle. The scale will not give a reading equal to the force of gravity (Equation 1).

Because the Earth is not a perfect sphere, the distance from the center of the Earth to the equator is greater than the distance from the center of the Earth to a pole by about 0.1%.

Additionally, the contours of the Earth vary at different location so g would have to be measured at an exact location to determine an exact value of the effective acceleration due to gravity.

39. At the equator, if a man stood on a scale, how would the scale read compared to the reading for the same man standing on a non-rotating Earth?

 A. the same as on a non-rotating Earth
 B. depends on where the man is
 C. greater than on a non-rotating Earth
 D. less than on a non-rotating Earth

40. Which of the following gives the best expression for the velocity of a man standing at the equator of a rotating Earth when T_{day} is the time of one rotation and equals 1 day?

 A. $2\pi R_E / T_{day}$ B. $2\pi g T_{day}$ C. R_E / T_{day} D. $g T_{day}$

41. How would the reading of the scale of a man standing at the South pole compare to the scale reading of the same man standing at the equator of an identical but not rotating Earth?

 A. readings would be the same
 B. reading at the South pole would be greater
 C. reading at the South pole would be less
 D. there is not enough information to answer this question

42. If the period of the man's motion is known, what variables are needed to calculate the centripetal force on him?

 A. radius of Earth   C. mass of man and radius of Earth
 B. velocity of man and radius of Earth   D. mass and velocity of man and radius of Earth

43. Which of the following force diagrams best describes a man standing on a scale at the equator of rotating Earth?

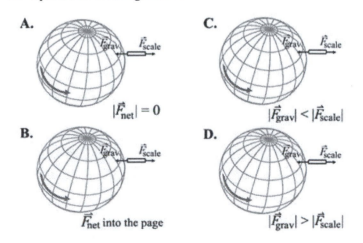

Questions 24 through 47 are not based on any
descriptive passage and are independent of each other

44. What will be the approximate pH after adding 0.7 moles NaOH to a buffer solution
that contains 0.15 moles $NaNO_2$ and 1.5 moles HNO_2 with the initial pH of 2.4?

    A. 0.7

    B. 3.4

    C. 4.4

    D. 5.4

45. A calorimeter consisting of two nested Styrofoam cups with a lid is used to measure
energy. What is the primary purpose of using two Styrofoam cups?

    A. increase the heat capacity of the calorimeter by increasing its mass

    B. reduce the likelihood of the cups tipping over by increasing their mass

    C. reduce conduction through Styrofoam due to a thicker barrier

    D. reduce convection through Styrofoam due to a thicker barrier

46. Two balls of 500 grams each move in opposite directions after an isolated collision.
Ball 1 moves at 0.3 m/s in the negative x direction and Ball 2 moves at 0.6 m/s in the
positive x direction. What was the total momentum of this system before the collision?

    A. -0.15 kg·m/s

    B. -0.45 kg·m/s

    C. 0.15 kg·m/s

    D. 0.45 kg·m/s

47. A white billiard ball with a mass of 250 g moves at 0.9 m/s, strikes a purple billiard
ball, at rest, with a mass 200 g. After the collision, the white ball moves with a velocity of
0.5 m/s. What is the velocity of the purple ball after collision?

    A. 1.0 m/s

    B. 0.5 m/s

    C. 1.25 m/s

    D. 0.75 m/s

This page is intentionally left blank

Passage 7
(Questions 48–52)

Ionic compounds are solids composed of ions with opposing charges held together by strong electrostatic attraction (ionic bonds). Typically, the positively charged portion consists of metal cations and the negatively charged portion is an anion or polyatomic ion. Ionic compounds are usually hard, brittle and have relatively high melting and boiling points.

In the solid phase, ionic compounds are poor conductors because there are no mobile ions or electrons present. However, in aqueous solutions or molten state, the mobile ions are free to conduct electric current. When dissolved in water, ionic compounds establish equilibrium between the solid phase and free ions. Low solubility ionic compounds are known as *slightly soluble salts*.

Ionic compounds dissolve in polar solvents, especially one that ionize (e.g. water, ionic liquids). They are typically more soluble in other polar solvents (e.g. alcohols, acetone, dimethyl sulfoxide). Ionic compounds usually do not dissolve in nonpolar solvents (e.g. diethyl ether or petrol). The conjugate acid of the strong base has no tendency to combine with a H_2O to produce an OH^- ion.

When the oppositely charged ions in the solid ionic compound are surrounded by the opposite pole of a polar molecule, the solid ions are pulled out of the lattice into the liquid. When this force is greater than the electrostatic attraction of the lattice, the ions dissolve in the liquid.

Reaction 1 illustrates the example when solid silver chloride enters the following equilibrium:

$$AgCl(s) \rightleftarrows Ag^+(aq) + Cl^-(aq)$$

Reaction 1

This dissolution of a salt is a thermodynamic process which depends on temperature. At 25° C, the solubility constant of AgCl is 1.8×10^{-10}.

Solvation, dissolution and *solubility* are related concepts though distinct from one another. Solvation is an interaction of a solute with the solvent and leads to stabilization of the solute species in the solution. Dissolution is a kinetic process quantified by its rate. Solubility quantifies the dynamic equilibrium state achieved when the rate of dissolution equals the rate of precipitation.

To identify an unknown slightly soluble salt an experiment is conducted. It is known that the salt forms a cation when it is dissolved in water. The cation is a weak acid which can therefore be titrated with a strong base. By adding aliquots of NaOH to an aqueous solution of the unknown salt, the following titration curve is obtained:

According to the IUPAC (International Union of Pure and Applied Chemistry), an ionic compound's common name is written using two words. The name of the cation is first, the oxidation number in parentheses, followed by the name of the anion.

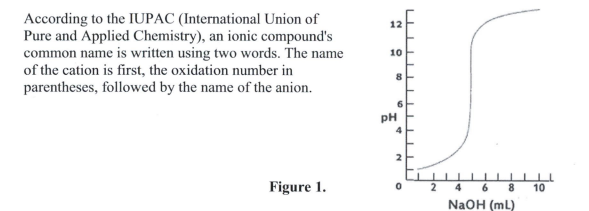

Figure 1.

48. Which of the following statements is true, given that the K_{sp} of AgBr is 5.4×10^{-13}, and the K_{sp} of AgI is 8.5×10^{-17}?

    A. AgBr is less soluble than AgI
    B. AgBr is more soluble than AgI
    C. More energy is required for solvation of AgBr than of AgI
    D. The dissolution process of AgBr is more exothermic than that of AgI

49. From the titration curve for the unknown salt (Figure 1), the unknown salt is most likely:

    A. monoprotic   **B.** diprotic   **C.** amphiprotic   **D.** amphoteric

50. What is the hydrogen ion concentration, when 4 mL of NaOH is added to the aqueous solution of the unknown salt?

    A. 1.0×10^{-2} M   **B.** 1.0×10^{-3} M   **C.** 1.0×10^{-4} M   **D.** 1.0×10^{-5} M

51. Which of the following buffers would best maintain a solution at pH 7.35 at 23°C?

    A. SSC ($pK_a = 7.0$)   **C.** Tricene ($pK_a = 8.05$)
    B. K_2HPO_4 (aq) ($pK_a = 7.2$)   **D.** Citric acid ($pK_a = 4.76$)

52. Which of the following occurs when KBr is added to a solution of AgBr(s) that is at equilibrium at 23°C?

    A. Increase of the solubility constant   **C.** Formation of more AgBr(s)
    B. Decrease of the solubility constant   **D.** More AgBr(s) goes into solution

Questions 53 through 59 are not based on any descriptive passage and are independent of each other

53. Which statement correctly explains why enzymes are very effective catalysts?

   A. Enzyme can convert a normally endergonic reaction into an exergonic reaction
   B. Enzymes release products very rapidly
   C. Enzymes bind very tightly to substrates
   D. Enzyme stabilizes the transition state

54. How many carbon atoms are in a molecule of heptane?

   A. 4   B. 5   C. 7   D. 9

55. In the presence of a competitive inhibitor, what changes are expected in kinetics?

   A. K_M appears to increase while V_{max} remains the same
   B. K_M appears to increase while V_{max} decreases
   C. K_M appears to decrease while V_{max} remains the same
   D. K_M appears to decrease, while V_{max} decreases

56. Two compounds that consist of the equal number of the same atoms but have a different molecular structure are:

   A. hydrocarbons   B. isomers   C. homologs   D. isotopes

57. What agent causes the formation of a cyclobutane thymine dimer?

   A. Propylmethanesulfonate   C. N-ethyl-N'nitro-N-nitrosoguanidine
   B. Ultraviolet radiation   D. DNP

58. In relation to each other, α-D-fructofuranose and β-D-fructofuranose are:

   A. conformational isomers   C. epimers
   B. anomers   D. enantiomers

59. Which of the following structures represents an amide (protein) bond?

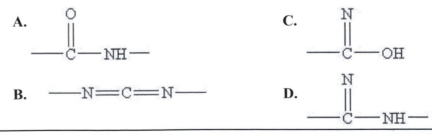

MCAT Chemical & Physical Foundations of Biological Systems

Practice Test #3

59 questions

For explanatory answers see pgs. 193-232

For CBT online format of this test that provides Diagnostics Report with performance statistics, difficulty rating of each question and other features visit:

www.MasterMCAT.com

Most questions in the Physical Sciences test are organized into groups, each containing a descriptive passage. After studying the passage select the one best answer to each question in the group. Some questions are not based on a descriptive passage and are also independent of each other. If you are not certain of an answer, eliminate the alternatives you know to be incorrect and then select an answer from the remaining alternatives. Indicate your selected answer by marking the corresponding answer on your answer sheet. A periodic table is provided for your use. You may consult it whenever you wish.

Periodic Table of the Elements

1 H 1.0																	2 He 4.0
3 Li 6.9	4 Be 9.0											5 B 10.8	6 C 12.0	7 N 14.0	8 O 16.0	9 F 19.0	10 Ne 20.2
11 Na 23.0	12 Mg 24.3											13 Al 27.0	14 Si 28.1	15 P 31.0	16 S 32.1	17 Cl 35.5	18 Ar 39.9
19 K 39.1	20 Ca 40.1	21 Sc 45.0	22 Ti 47.9	23 V 50.9	24 Cr 52.0	25 Mn 54.9	26 Fe 55.8	27 Co 58.9	28 Ni 58.7	29 Cu 63.5	30 Zn 65.4	31 Ga 69.7	32 Ge 72.6	33 As 74.9	34 Se 79.0	35 Br 79.9	36 Kr 83.8
37 Rb 85.5	38 Sr 87.6	39 Y 88.9	40 Zr 91.2	41 Nb 92.9	42 Mo 95.9	43 Tc (98)	44 Ru 101.1	45 Rh 102.9	46 Pd 106.4	47 Ag 107.9	48 Cd 112.4	49 In 114.8	50 Sn 118.7	51 Sb 121.8	52 Te 127.6	53 I 126.9	54 Xe 131.3
55 Cs 132.9	56 Ba 137.3	57 La* 138.9	72 Hf 178.5	73 Ta 180.9	74 W 183.9	75 Re 186.2	76 Os 190.2	77 Ir 192.2	78 Pt 195.1	79 Au 197.0	80 Hg 200.6	81 Tl 204.4	82 Pb 207.2	83 Bi 209.0	84 Po (209)	85 At (210)	86 Rn (222)
87 Fr (223)	88 Ra (226)	89 Ac† (227)	104 Rf (261)	105 Db (262)	106 Sg (266)	107 Bh (264)	108 Hs (277)	109 Mt (268)	110 Ds (281)	111 Uuu (272)	112 Uub (285)		114 Uuq (289)		116 Uuh (289)		

	58 Ce 140.1	59 Pr 140.9	60 Nd 144.2	61 Pm (145)	62 Sm 150.4	63 Eu 152.0	64 Gd 157.3	65 Tb 158.9	66 Dy 162.5	67 Ho 164.9	68 Er 167.3	69 Tm 168.9	70 Yb 173.0	71 Lu 175.0
*														
†	90 Th 232.0	91 Pa (231)	92 U 238.0	93 Np (237)	94 Pu (244)	95 Am (243)	96 Cm (247)	97 Bk (247)	98 Cf (251)	99 Es (252)	100 Fm (257)	101 Md (258)	102 No (259)	103 Lr (260)

CHEMICAL & PHYSICAL FOUNDATIONS OF LIVING SYSTEMS
MCAT® PRACTICE TEST #3: ANSWER SHEET

Passage 1

1 : A B C D
2 : A B C D
3 : A B C D
4 : A B C D
5 : A B C D

Passage 2

6 : A B C D
7 : A B C D
8 : A B C D
9 : A B C D
10 : A B C D
11 : A B C D

Independent questions

12 : A B C D
13 : A B C D
14 : A B C D
15 : A B C D

Passage 3

16 : A B C D
17 : A B C D
18 : A B C D
19 : A B C D

Passage 4

20 : A B C D
21 : A B C D
22 : A B C D
23 : A B C D
24 : A B C D

Independent questions

25 : A B C D
26 : A B C D
27 : A B C D
28 : A B C D
29 : A B C D

Passage 5

30 : A B C D
31 : A B C D
32 : A B C D
33 : A B C D
34 : A B C D
35 : A B C D
36 : A B C D

Passage 6

37 : A B C D
38 : A B C D
39 : A B C D
40 : A B C D
41 : A B C D

Independent questions

42 : A B C D
43 : A B C D
44 : A B C D
45 : A B C D

Passage 7

46 : A B C D
47 : A B C D
48 : A B C D
49 : A B C D
50 : A B C D
51 : A B C D
52 : A B C D

Independent questions

53 : A B C D
54 : A B C D
55 : A B C D
56 : A B C D
57 : A B C D
58 : A B C D
59 : A B C D

This page is intentionally left blank

Passage 1
(Questions 1–5)

Geological time scale is a system for measuring change occurring on wide-ranging time scales. This system helps scientists describe the timing and connections between events that took place throughout Earth's history. Isotopic dating shows that the Earth is about 4.5 billion years old.

Eon is a time period of over one-half billion years. Some ecological changes (like the slow building of mountain ranges) take eons or can occur during extremely brief periods when dramatic geologic changes (e.g. earthquakes) make a significant impact. Physical effects account for much of the geologic changes, but many geological processes are based on chemical reactions. For example, the formation of limestone caves involves aqueous carbonic acid interacting with limestone rock strata (layers with consistent composition).

This process is illustrated by the following reactions:

$$CO_2(g) + \text{pressure} \overset{H_2O}{\longleftrightarrow} CO_2(aq)$$

Reaction 1

$$CO_2(aq) + H_2O(l) \leftrightarrow H_2CO_3(aq)$$

Reaction 2

$$H_2CO_3(aq) \leftrightarrow H^+(aq) + HCO_3^-(aq)$$

Reaction 3

$$CaCO_3(s) + H^+(aq) \leftrightarrow Ca^{2+}(aq) + HCO_3^-(aq)$$

Reaction 4

Atmospheric carbon dioxide dissolves in water (Reaction 1). The concentration of dissolved carbon dioxide (at atmospheric pressure and 25°C temperature) is low. However, the concentration would be much higher in the fissures and cracks of the limestone because they may have higher pressure. Then, the dissolved carbon dioxide reacts with water and forms carbonic acid (Reaction 2) which then dissociates (Reaction 3) and the acidic hydrogens enter into reaction with limestone (Reaction 4) and dissolve it.

Eventually, water drains from the caves leaving a web of cracks filled with dissolved limestone which then exits the cracks and gets exposed to the lower pressure within the cave interior. Reactions 1 through 4 reverse resulting in the calcium carbonate precipitation. Stalactites (mineral formations that hang from the cave ceiling) form when this precipitation occurs before a drop of dissolved limestone leaks out of the cave ceiling; stalagmites (formations that rise from the floor) form if the precipitate builds-up on the cave floor.

1. Which of the following statements is true for this reaction?

$$HCO_3^- + HCl \leftrightarrow H_2CO_3 + Cl^-$$

   A. HCO_3^- is a base and Cl^- is its conjugate acid
   B. HCO_3^- is a base and H_2CO_3 is its conjugate acid
   C. Cl^- is an acid and HCl is its conjugate base
   D. HCl is an acid and HCO_3^- is its conjugate base

2. Which of these compounds is a strong acid?

   A. H_2CO_3
   B. CF_3CO_2H
   C. HNO_3
   D. H_3PO_4

3. The main component of stalagmites is:

   A. H_2CO
   B. $Ca(HCO_3)$
   C. Ca_2CO_3
   D. $CaCO_3$

4. Given that many acids contain an H^+ ion and many bases contain OH^- ions, how is BCl_3 (containing neither H^+ nor OH^-) classified?

   A. Lewis acid
   B. Lewis base
   C. Brønsted-Lowry acid
   D. Brønsted-Lowry base

5. What would be an approximate pH of a 1.0 M solution of $CaCO_3$ if it was water soluble?

   A. 1
   B. 4
   C. 6
   D. 8

Passage 2
(Questions 6-11)

During the winter Olympics, a ski jumper travels down an inclined track. He comes to the end of the track, leaves the take off ramp, passes through the air and lands on the slope.

The skier's trajectory through the air is shown in Figure 1. The take off ramp from which he left the track is at a 30° angle to the horizontal. The track is at an angle of θ to the horizontal and the slope is inclined at a 45° angle.

A ski jumper starts off stationary at the top of the track, but once he pushes off, he accelerates down the track, and then takes off from the ramp. The vertical height between the top of the track and its lowest point is 65 m, and the vertical height between the top of the ramp and its lowest point is 15 m.

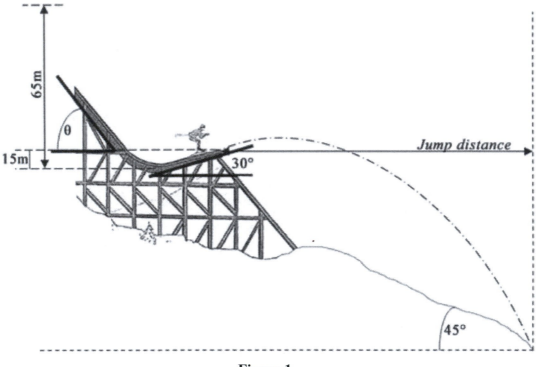

Figure 1

The jump distance is the distance traveled by the skier in the air from leaving the ramp to landing on the slope. Sometimes, a skier may slightly jump when leaving the jump ramp to increase the jump distance by increasing the vertical velocity.

Assume that the friction between the skis and the slope is negligible and ignore air resistance. Acceleration (due to gravity) = 9.8 m/s²

Note: $\cos 30° = \frac{\sqrt{3}}{2}$, $\sin 30° = 0.5$, $\cos 45° = \frac{\sqrt{2}}{2}$

---

6. If θ is 45°, what is the acceleration of a 90 kg skier going down the track?

A. 3.4 m/s^2 **C.** 9.8 m/s^2
B. 6.9 m/s^2 **D.** 14.7 m/s^2

7. Which of these factors would increase a ski jumper's jump distance?

   I.   increased angle of incline θ of the track
   II. increased vertical height h of the track
   III. increased total mass of the ski jumper

A. I only   **C.** III only
B. II only   **D.** I and II only

8. If the vertical height of the jump ramp was increased from the original 15 meters while the skier's starting point on the track is unaffected, how would the speed of a skier leaving the ramp change?

A. remains the same   **C.** decreases
B. increases   **D.** depends on the ramp's incline angle

9. What would occur if a skier used skis of a greater surface area?

A. pressure exerted on the slope by the skis increases
B. pressure exerted on the slope by the skis decreases
C. normal force of the slope on the skier increases
D. normal force of the slope on the skier decreases

10. When the skier skis down the track or if he fell the same vertical height, how would the work done by gravity on the skier in each case compare?

A. ˙Equal amounts of work would be done
B. More work would be done on the skier when he falls
C. Less work would be done on the skier when he falls
D. Depends on the track incline angle

11. Another skier takes off from a point farther down the ramp and leaves it at a speed of 12 m/s traveling in the air for 5 s. What is the total horizontal distance traveled by the ski jumper between take off and landing on the slope?

A. 12 m   **B.** 6√3 m   **C.** 30√3 m   **D.** 60 m

> Questions 12 through 15 are not based on any
> descriptive passage and are independent of each other

12. There are two poles (X and Y) of cylindrical shape where pole X has a greater cross sectional area than pole Y. Both poles at their bases experience a force of their weight. If the poles themselves are of equal weight, the pressure at the base of which pole will be greater?

    A. pressure will be equal for pole X and Y
    B. pressure will be greater for pole X than for pole Y
    C. pressure will be greater for pole Y than for pole X
    D. pressure will depend on the relative height of the two poles

13. Which of these aqueous solutions has the lowest pH?

    A. 0.5 M HF
    B. 1.5 M NaClO
    C. 0.4 M HBr
    D. 1.0 M KCl

14. Given that the penetration depth difference for *gamma* rays and *beta* particles is about two $\log_{10}$ units, how many times deeper does a *gamma* ray penetrate lead compared to a *beta* particle?

    A. 2
    B. 4
    C. 20
    D. 100

15. Given that the cornea has a larger refractive index for violet light than for yellow light, where would the focus for a beam of violet light land considering that the yellow light is focused on the retina?

    A. at the same place.
    B. behind the retina and the yellow light focus
    C. in front of the retina and yellow light focus
    D. both in front of and behind the retina

This page is intentionally left blank

Passage 3
(Questions 16-19)

The transition metals are defined by valence electrons that have d subshells. These elements in the fourth through seventh period of the periodic table undergo sequential filling of the d subshell. For example, in the third period, elements like Cr, Mn, Fe and Co, undergo sequential filling of orbitals in the $3d$ subshell. They have a general electron configuration $[Ar]\ 4s^x\ 3d^y$ where $[Ar]$ is the electron configuration for the noble gas argon, x is the number of electrons in the $4s$ subshell and y is the number of electrons in the $3d$ subshell.

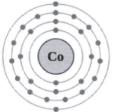

For cobalt in the $+2$ oxidation state (Co^{2+}) the electron configuration is $[Ar]\ 3d^7$. In transforming from a neutral ($+0$) to an oxidized ($+2$) state, the cobalt atom must first lose two electrons from the $4s$ subshell.

Generally, transition metals may assume multiple oxidation states. Even though metals usually form basic oxides (e.g., Na_2O) and nonmetals usually form acidic oxides (e.g., SO_3), transition metal oxides, depending on the oxidation state of the metal, may be either acidic or basic. For example, Mn_2O_7 is highly acidic while MnO is basic.

This behavior of the oxides (i.e. anhydrides) may be better explained in terms of the elemental hydroxides.

Reactions of the manganese oxides, Mn_2O_7 and MnO, with H_2O are as follows:

$$
\begin{array}{cl}
& \overset{\displaystyle O}{\underset{\displaystyle O}{\overset{\displaystyle \|}{\underset{\displaystyle \|}{Mn}}}} \\
1) & Mn_2O_7 + H_2O \rightarrow 2\,H-O-Mn-O
\end{array}
$$

$$2)\qquad MnO + H_2O \rightarrow Mn(OH)_2$$

The difference in behavior between the two oxides and their hydroxides is the result of the relative sizes of the metal-oxygen (M-O) electronegativity difference ($\Delta\chi_{M-O}$). Electronegativity (χ) is the propensity by atoms within a molecule to attract electrons towards their nuclei. An atom's χ is affected by both its atomic number and the distance of its valence electrons from the positively charged nucleus.

When $\Delta\chi_{M-O}$ is less than $\Delta\chi_{O-H}$, the oxygen-hydrogen (O-H) bond has ionic character and the proton may dissociate. Therefore, the metal hydroxide is an acid. This behavior is observed in metal anhydrides where the metal has a high oxidation state (greater than $+5$).

Conversely, when $\Delta\chi_{M-O}$ is greater than $\Delta\chi_{O-H}$, the metal-hydroxide (M-OH) bond has ionic properties, and the hydroxide is basic. Generally, metal anhydrides are basic when the oxidation state of the metal is less than or equal to $+4$.

16. After two oxides of the same transition metal, Compound A and Compound B, are placed separately into two vessels of aqueous media, Compound A produced an acidic solution while Compound B produced a basic solution. From this observation, what can be concluded about the metal-oxide bonding in these compounds?

    A. The bonding in Compound A is more covalent and the bonding in Compound B is more ionic

    B. The bonding in Compound A is more ionic and the bonding in Compound B is more covalent

    C. The bonding in Compound A is more polar than the bonding in Compound B

    D. The bonding in both compounds is nonpolar

17. Knowing that manganese is a transition metal that is able to assume the oxidation states 0, +1, +2, +3, +4, +5, +6 or +7, a chemist attempted to identify the oxidation state of manganese in an oxide of an unknown formula of Mn_xO_y. He dissolved the compound in water completely and measured the pH of the solution to be 6.0. Which of the following empirical formulas is the most likely one for the Mn_xO_y?

    A. MnO

    B. MnO_2

    C. Mn_2O_3

    D. Mn_2O_7

18. Which of the following would NOT be paramagnetic based on the provided electronic configurations?

    A. Co^{2+} — $[Ar]\ 3d^7$

    B. Cd — $[Kr]\ 5s^2\ 4d^{10}$

    C. V — $[Ar]\ 4s^2\ 3d^3$

    D. Mn — $[Ar]\ 4s^2\ 3d^5$

19. Which of these metals is the LEAST reactive considering the closed-shell and half-closed shell characteristics?

    A. Sc(s)

    B. Na(s)

    C. Ag(s)

    D. Rb(s)

Passage 4
(Questions 20–24)

When a light wave passes slantingly from one medium to another, the angle at which it emerges from the boundary between the media is different from the angle at which it strikes it. The change is called refraction and is caused by change in the medium composition.

The relationship between the angle of refraction (θ_2) and the angle of incidence (θ_1) is described by Snell's law.

$$n_1 \sin \theta_1 = n_2 \sin \theta_2$$

Snell's law

n_1 = the refractive index of medium 1, n_2 = the refractive index of medium 2.

Refractive index = c/v, where c = speed of light (vacuum) and v = speed of light (medium). For air, $n \approx 1$.

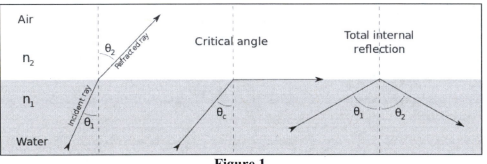

Figure 1

When a light wave encounters a medium with a refractive index smaller than that of the medium it was traveling through, it may exhibit the phenomenon of total internal reflection. This happens when the angle the wave strikes at is greater than or equal to the critical angle θ_c for the two media.

For any two media where $n_1 > n_2$, $\sin \theta_c = n_2/n_1$.

Figure 2 shows a classic experiment where white light passes through a prism with a 1.67 refractive index and the emerging light strikes a screen opposite the light source as a color spectrum.

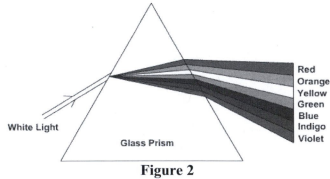

Figure 2

For each material medium, n slightly varies depending on the frequency of light wave going through it and the n value increases with increasing frequency. For instance, with any change in medium, violet light has greater refraction than yellow light.

Variability in n causes a prism to disperse white light into its component wavelengths of different colors. The various wavelengths that come out of the prism at different angles appear as a spectrum.

20. To determine the relative magnitude of the wavelengths emitted from yellow and violet light sources, the likely conclusion is that the shorter of the two wavelengths is emitted from the:

    A. yellow light source because yellow light's refraction is lower than the violet light's
    B. violet light source because violet light's refraction is lower than the yellow light's
    C. yellow light source because yellow light's refraction is greater than the violet light's
    D. violet light source because violet light's refraction is greater than the yellow light's

21. What is the approximate velocity of light as it passes through the prism shown in Figure 2?

    A. 0.6×10^8 m/s   **C.** 5.0×10^8 m/s
    B. 1.8×10^8 m/s   **D.** 9.0×10^8 m/s

22. When indigo light passes through a nesosilicate medium and strikes the silicate-air border, the smallest angle that results in a total internal reflection is approximately $25°$. Based on this information, what is the refractive index of nesosilicate? *Note:* $\sin 25° = 0.4$

    A. 4.0   **B.** 2.5   **C.** 0.4   **D.** 0.25

23. A ray of light travelling through the air hits the surface of a transport medium at a $65°$ angle to the normal and continues though the medium at an angle of $30°$ to the normal. What is the approximate refractive index of this medium? *Note*: $\sin 30° = 0.5$, $\sin 65° = 0.9$

    A. 0.55   **B.** 1.4   **C.** 1.8   **D.** 4.5

24. If green light has a wavelength of 5.1×10^{-7} m in air, what is its frequency?

    A. 1.6×10^{14} Hz   **C.** 5.9×10^{14} Hz
    B. 5.1×10^{14} Hz   **D.** 1.6×10^{15} Hz

Questions 25 through 29 are not based on any
descriptive passage and are independent of each other

25. The air streams that provide frictionless sliding along the track for two carts are shut off while the carts are moving. What is the ratio of the frictional force exerted on the heavier cart to the frictional force exerted on the lighter cart, given that the heavier cart is twice the mass of the lighter one?

    A. 1 : 2   **B.** 1 : 4   **C.** 2 : 1   **D.** 4 : 1

26. Susan and Mike are playing on a 4 meter seesaw with a fulcrum in the middle. Susan is 30 kg and sits on the end, while Mike, 40 kg, sits so that they balance. The seesaw itself is uniform and balanced. How far from the end should Mike sit in order to achieve balance?

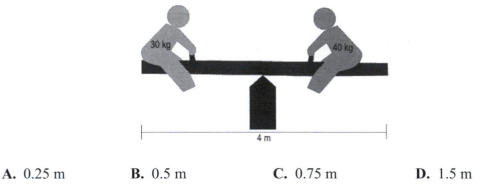

    A. 0.25 m   **B.** 0.5 m   **C.** 0.75 m   **D.** 1.5 m

27. What is the pH of a 0.05 *M* solution of acetic acid? *Note:* The K_a for acetic acid is 2×10^{-5}.

    A. 0.05   **B.** 0.1   **C.** 1.0   **D.** 3.0

28. Charge Q is at a distance of 15 cm from a charge q_1 and 60 cm from charge q_2. What is the ratio of q_1 to q_2 if Q experiences an attractive force of 0.4 mN (milliNewtons) to q_1 and a repulsive force of 0.8 mN to q_2?

    A . –1/32   **B .** –1/8   **C .** –1   **D .** –2

29. Given that a wave with a period of 0.006 seconds is traveling at 36 m/s, what is the wavelength?

    A. 0.166 m   **B.** 0.216 m   **C.** 0.432 m   **D.** 2.16 m

This page is intentionally left blank

Passage 5
(Questions 30–36)

Thermochemistry is the study of energy and heat related to chemical reactions and/or physical transformations. A reaction may release (i.e. exothermic) or absorb (i.e. endothermic) heat or release (i.e. exergonic) or absorb (i.e. endergonic) energy to predict (along with considerations to entropy) if the reaction is spontaneous (i.e. energetically favorable) or non-spontaneous (i.e. energetically unfavorable). A phase change may also release heat (e.g. melting and boiling).

Thermochemistry focuses on these energy changes with particular focus on the system's energy exchange with its surrounding. Thermochemistry is useful in predicting relative reactant and product quantities throughout the course of a reaction. In combination with entropy (i.e. a measure of disorder), it is also used to predict whether a reaction is spontaneous (i.e. products are more stable than reactants) or non-spontaneous (i.e. reactants are more stable than products), favorable or unfavorable. Thermochemistry integrates the concept of thermodynamics with concepts of energy in the formation of chemical bonds. It can be used to calculate heat capacity, heat of formation, entropy, enthalpy, free energy and calories.

During the heating of 504 g of water to boiling, 4 g of it was lost to vaporization. Most of this water was lost near the boiling point.

In a 23°C room, a 250 g pewter pot was filed with 500 g of the boiling water. The pot and water were allowed to cool to 75°C and 100 g of water was transferred from the pot into an insulated thermos.

The specific heat of the pewter pot is 0.17 J/g·K and that of water is 4.2 J/g·K. The entire procedure was done under a pressure of 1.0 atm.

Note: heat of fusion of water = 80cal/g, heat of vaporization of water = 540cal/g, heat capacity of water = 4.184 J/K and 4.184 J = 1 calorie.

30. The heat transferred from the boiling water to the pewter pot is called:

A. enthalpy
B. entropy
C. heat capacity
D. specific heat

31. During boiling, how much energy is necessary to evaporate 4 g of water?

A. 0.74 kJ   B. 9.0 kJ   C. 13.5 kJ   D. 135 kJ

32. Given that after the water is transferred to the thermos, its temperature falls quickly from 75°C to 71.8°C as it achieves thermal equilibrium with the thermos flask, what is the heat capacity of the thermos?

A. 10.8 J/K   B. 27.3 J/K   C. 38.3 J/K   D. 54.6 J/K

33. Which of these graphs best represents the cooling curve for the pewter pot contents when placed in a cooler set at –25°C?

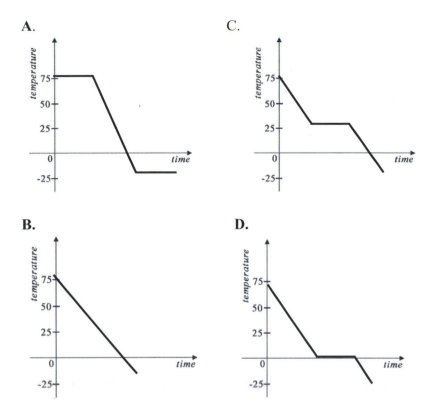

34. Which of the following systems has the lowest entropy?

A. Water at 100°C   **C.** Ceramic plate at 70°C

B. Steam at 100°C   **D.** Water at 50°C

35. After 100 g of the water has been transferred to the thermos, the pewter pot with its contents at a temperature of 75°C was placed on the insulated warmer that transfers 500 cal/min to the water. What is the water's temperature after being placed on the warmer for 10 minutes? *Note:* assume no significant heat transfer with the surroundings.

A. 79.2°C   **B.** 83.1°C   **C.** 87.2°C   **D.** 91.5°C

36. As an alternative for keeping the water hot, the pewter pot can be placed on a block heated in an oven to 250°C. A block of which of the following substances is best able to keep the water hot?

A. silver (specific heat = 0.23 J/g·K)   **C.** glass (specific heat = 0.84 J/g·K)

B. titanium (specific heat = 0.52 J/g·K)   **D.** aluminum (specific heat = 0.90 J/g·K)

Passage 6
(Questions 37–41)

The circulatory system in the body functions to distribute blood, lymph, nutrients and hormones to and from the cells within the organism. Several factors control the flow of blood through the human vascular system. The rate of flow (Q) is directly proportional to the pressure difference (ΔP) between different points along the system and inversely proportional to the resistance (R) of the system:

$$Q = \Delta P / R$$

Equation 1

The resistance (R) is determined by the length (L) of the blood vessel, the viscosity (η) of blood and the radius (r) of the blood vessel:

$$R = \frac{8\eta L}{\pi r^4}$$

Equation 2

Under normal conditions, the length of the blood vessel and the viscosity of the blood are negligible and therefore, the resistance is insignificant. However, certain conditions cause changes in the blood composition which alters the viscosity. Veins are more compliant (expand and contract in response to pressure changes) since there is less smooth muscle surrounding them in contrast to arteries which are surrounded by thick muscularity. The flow of blood through the major arteries can be approximated by the equations of ideal flow.

The dynamics of blood and fluid movement from capillaries to body tissue (i.e. interstitial space) and back to capillaries are driven by the differences in pressure. The net movement depends on the difference between the hydrostatic pressure of the blood in the capillaries (P_c) and that of interstitial fluid outside the capillaries (P_i). The difference between the osmotic pressure of the capillaries (π_c) of approximately 25 mmHg and the osmotic pressure of the interstitial tissue fluids (π_l) (which is negligible) is called *oncotic* pressure. The difference in hydrostatic and oncotic pressure determines the direction of fluid movement (whether the fluid moves into or out of the capillary) and is calculated as:

$$\Delta P = (P_c + \pi_l) - (P_i + \pi_c)$$

Equation 3

The sum of $P_c + \pi_l$ is the force acting to move fluid into the interstitial space from the capillaries, while the sum of $P_i + \pi_c$ is the force acting to move fluid into the capillaries from the interstitial space.

Note: 1 atm = 760 Torr = 760 mmHg.

37. The body increases red blood cell count as the art of adaptation to living at high altitudes. Ignoring other physiological compensating factors, what effect will this change have on the flow of blood?

A. increased due to increased viscosity

B. decreased due to increased viscosity

C. increased due to decreased viscosity

D. decreased due to decreased viscosity

38. According to the diagram of systemic circulation below, which of the following is true?

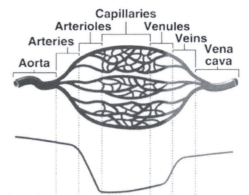

Vascular architecture of organs is in:

A. parallel, total peripheral resistance is greater than the resistance of individual organs

B. parallel, total peripheral resistance is less than the resistance of individual organs

C. series, total peripheral resistance is greater than the resistance of individual organs

D. series, total peripheral resistance is less than the resistance of individual organs

39. The dilation and constriction of the blood vessels regulates the blood flow to the various systems in the body. For example, after ingesting a large meal, the blood vessels supplying the digestive system will dilate to increase their radii by 25% and the flow of blood to the digestive system will be about:

A. 25% of the original flow

B. 75% of the original flow

C. 125% of the original flow

D. 250% of the original flow

40. Given that the cross sectional area of the aorta is approximately 5 cm^2 and the speed of the blood in the aorta is 20 cm/sec, what is the average blood speed in the major arteries if their cross sectional area is 4 cm^2?

A. 2 cm/sec   **B.** 8 cm/sec   **C.** 25 cm/sec   **D.** 100 cm/sec

41. The hydrostatic pressure of the capillary at the venular end of skeletal muscle capillaries is 15 mmHg, hydrostatic pressure of the interstitial fluid is 0 mmHg and oncotic pressure in the interstitial fluid is 3 mmHg. Under these conditions, blood moves from the:

A. interstitial to the capillary, with a pressure of 7 mmHg

B. interstitial to the capillary, with a pressure of 13 mmHg

C. capillary to the interstitial, with a pressure of 7 mmHg

D. capillary to the interstitial, with a pressure of 13 mmHg

Questions 42 through 45 are not based on any
descriptive passage and are independent of each other

42. What is the K_b value of $^-$OH, given that the K_a of H_3O^+ is 1.75×10^{-5} ?

A. 3.3×10^{-7} **B.** 5.3×10^{-8} **C.** 5.7×10^{-10} **D.** 10

43. The two lowest notes on the piano are A_0 (28.6 Hz) and $A\#_0$ (30.1 Hz). If the notes are played simultaneously, the resulting sound seems to repeatedly turn off and on. How much time exists between the successive "on" sounds?

A. 0.66 s   **B.** 1.5 s   **C.** 28.6 s   **D.** 30.1 s

44. In the Hubble Space Telescope (HST) the incoming light is focused by the primary mirror of a 2.4 m diameter onto the detection apparatus. Considering that the HST is used to observe galaxies in visible light, which of the following is the closest estimation for the resolution?

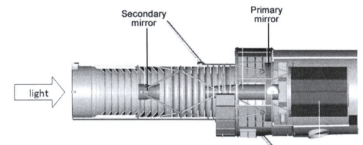

Cross section of the Hubble Space Telescope. Length: 13 m; diameter: 4.3 m

A. 2.4×10^{-7} radians   **C.** 13.56×10^{-7} radians
B. 24.0×10^{-7} radians   **D.** 1356.0×10^{-7} radians

45. The Hubble Space Telescope is also equipped with ultraviolet light detectors. Assuming diffraction limitation, how would the resolution for the ultraviolet compare to the one for visible light?

     A. About the same as for visible light
     B. Higher than for visible light
     C. Lower than for visible light
     D. Sometimes lower and sometimes higher than for visible light

This page is intentionally left blank

Passage 7
(Questions 46–52)

Explosive is a reactive substance containing a large amount of potential energy which may be chemical energy (e.g. nitroglycerin), pressurized gas (e.g. gas cylinder) or nuclear energy (e.g. uranium-235 or plutonium-239). An explosion occurs when this potential energy is released suddenly. Explosions often produce light, sound, heat and pressure. Explosive materials are categorized by the speed at which they expand where materials that detonate at speeds faster than the speed of sound are *high explosives* and the others are *low explosives*.

Oxidation-reduction reactions are the most common type of chemical reactions. Redox reactions that result from strong oxidizing and strong reducing agents are highly exothermic. The amount of heat produced from these reactions is directly proportional to the strengths of the oxidant and the reductant.

Compounds that contain an electropositive atom (e.g., C, H, alkali earth metals) in a nonpositive (i.e. charged) oxidation state are reducing agents. Alternatively, a reducing agent has two or more electropositive atoms that are covalently bonded together. A reductant's strength is proportional to the eletropositivity and the oxidation state of the atom. Some mild reducing agents are $H_2(g)$, $C(s)$, $S(s)$, metal powders and butane. Strong reducing agents like alkali metals are rarely used to make explosives because it is difficult to prevent the spontaneous detonation that takes place when they are exposed to atmospheric oxygen.

Compounds which contain a highly electronegative atom (such as F, O, N, Cl) in a nonnegative (i.e. charged) oxidation state are oxidizing agents. Alternatively, an oxidizing agent has two or more highly electronegative elements that are covalently bonded together. An oxidant's strength is proportional to the electronegativity and oxidation state of the atoms. Some *strong* oxidizing agents are Cl_2, H_2O_2, $NaNO_3$, $KMnO_4$ and $NaClO_4$.

46. Which of these compounds is one of the components of gun powder, in addition to charcoal (pure carbon) and elemental sulfur?

A. LiCl
B. $NaNO_3$

C. Manganese
D. CaF_2

47. With the reaction mechanism below, Zn metal is attacked by hydrochloric acid. Why would Cu metal NOT be affected by HCl?

$$Zn(s) + 2HCl\,(aq) \rightarrow ZnCl_2\,(aq) + H_2\,(g)$$

A. Cu^+ is a stronger oxidant than H^+
B. Zn is a stronger oxidant than H^+
C. Zn is a stronger oxidant than Cu
D. Cl^- is a stronger oxidant than Zn, but is a weaker oxidant than Cu

48. All of these compounds, when mixed with lithium metal, will make it explode EXCEPT:

A. argon gas
B. nitric oxide

C. chlorine liquid
D. sulfuric acid

49. In which of these compounds oxygen atom is most highly oxidized?

A. O_2^- **B.** H_2O_2 **C.** F_2O **D.** N_2O

50. The chemical rockets of a space shuttle use a liquid fuel that is a mixture of liquid hydrogen and oxygen which produce highly exothermic reactions. Which of these fuel mixtures is most likely to release more energy than H_2 and O_2?

A. H_2 and Cl_2 **B.** H_2 and I_2 **C.** H_2 and F_2 **D.** H_2 and Br_2

51. Which of the following compounds is used in household bleach which consists of 94-97% water and 3-6% of a mild oxidizing agent that contains electronegative atoms with a +1 or +2 oxidation state?

A. KCl   **B.** $NaClO_3$ **C.** NaClO   **D.** $NaIO_4$

52. Which one of these mixtures would produce an explosion when heated?

A. RbF and Cu powder
B. CH_4 and NH_3

C. H_2O_2 and Cl_2
D. $KMnO_4$ and Mn powder

Questions 53 through 59 are not based on any
descriptive passage and are independent of each other

53. Given that enzyme is a catalyst, which of the following statements is correct?

A. The enzyme is not changed over the course of an enzyme-catalyzed reaction
B. Reaction that is normally catalyzed by the enzyme will not take place without an enzyme
C. Enzyme-catalyzed reaction is always exergonic
D. Enzymes increase the rate of a reaction though a mechanism different than in uncatalyzed reaction

54. Which statement best explains how the inhibitor binds to the enzyme in noncompetitive inhibition?

A. The inhibitor binds to a site other than the active site only after the substrate binds
B. Either before or after the substrate binds, the inhibitor binds to a site other than the active site
C. The inhibitor binds to the active site only after the substrate binds
D. The inhibitor binds to a site other than the active site only before the substrate binds

55. Which enzyme activity is associated with the termination factor ρ?

A. Helicase   B. Exonuclease   C. Endonuclease   D. Topoisomerase

56. Monomers of a polysaccharide are linked together by:

A. Glycosidic bond   C. Phosphate ester bond
B. Peptide bond   D. Glucotide bond

57. In animal cell membranes, cholesterol:

A. acts as a receptor site for hormones on the surface of membranes
B. broadens the temperature range of optimum membrane fluidity
C. blocks the association of the fatty acyl chains of phospholipids at high temperature
D. aids in the transport of small hydrophobic molecules across the membrane

58. Why are triacylglycerols NOT found in cell membranes?

A. Because they are not abundant in cells
B. Because they are charged at biological pH
C. Because they are amphipathic
D. Because they are not amphipathic

59. Which of these molecules is aromatic?

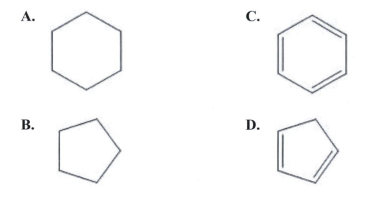

A.

B.

C.

D.

MCAT Chemical & Physical Foundations of Biological Systems

Practice Test #4

59 questions

For explanatory answers see pgs. 233-270

For CBT online format of this test that provides Diagnostics Report with performance statistics, difficulty rating of each question and other features visit:

www.MasterMCAT.com

Most questions in the Physical Sciences test are organized into groups, each containing a descriptive passage. After studying the passage select the one best answer to each question in the group. Some questions are not based on a descriptive passage and are also independent of each other. If you are not certain of an answer, eliminate the alternatives you know to be incorrect and then select an answer from the remaining alternatives. Indicate your selected answer by marking the corresponding answer on your answer sheet. A periodic table is provided for your use. You may consult it whenever you wish.

Periodic Table of the Elements

1 H 1.0																	2 He 4.0
3 Li 6.9	4 Be 9.0											5 B 10.8	6 C 12.0	7 N 14.0	8 O 16.0	9 F 19.0	10 Ne 20.2
11 Na 23.0	12 Mg 24.3											13 Al 27.0	14 Si 28.1	15 P 31.0	16 S 32.1	17 Cl 35.5	18 Ar 39.9
19 K 39.1	20 Ca 40.1	21 Sc 45.0	22 Ti 47.9	23 V 50.9	24 Cr 52.0	25 Mn 54.9	26 Fe 55.8	27 Co 58.9	28 Ni 58.7	29 Cu 63.5	30 Zn 65.4	31 Ga 69.7	32 Ge 72.6	33 As 74.9	34 Se 79.0	35 Br 79.9	36 Kr 83.8
37 Rb 85.5	38 Sr 87.6	39 Y 88.9	40 Zr 91.2	41 Nb 92.9	42 Mo 95.9	43 Tc (98)	44 Ru 101.1	45 Rh 102.9	46 Pd 106.4	47 Ag 107.9	48 Cd 112.4	49 In 114.8	50 Sn 118.7	51 Sb 121.8	52 Te 127.6	53 I 126.9	54 Xe 131.3
55 Cs 132.9	56 Ba 137.3	57 La* 138.9	72 Hf 178.5	73 Ta 180.9	74 W 183.9	75 Re 186.2	76 Os 190.2	77 Ir 192.2	78 Pt 195.1	79 Au 197.0	80 Hg 200.6	81 Tl 204.4	82 Pb 207.2	83 Bi 209.0	84 Po (209)	85 At (210)	86 Rn (222)
87 Fr (223)	88 Ra (226)	89 Ac† (227)	104 Rf (261)	105 Db (262)	106 Sg (266)	107 Bh (264)	108 Hs (277)	109 Mt (268)	110 Ds (281)	111 Uuu (272)	112 Uub (285)		114 Uuq (289)		116 Uuh (289)		

	58 Ce 140.1	59 Pr 140.9	60 Nd 144.2	61 Pm (145)	62 Sm 150.4	63 Eu 152.0	64 Gd 157.3	65 Tb 158.9	66 Dy 162.5	67 Ho 164.9	68 Er 167.3	69 Tm 168.9	70 Yb 173.0	71 Lu 175.0
†	90 Th 232.0	91 Pa (231)	92 U 238.0	93 Np (237)	94 Pu (244)	95 Am (243)	96 Cm (247)	97 Bk (247)	98 Cf (251)	99 Es (252)	100 Fm (257)	101 Md (258)	102 No (259)	103 Lr (260)

CHEMICAL & PHYSICAL FOUNDATIONS OF BIOLOGICAL SYSTEMS
MCAT® PRACTICE TEST #4 ANSWER SHEET

Passage 1

1 : A   B   C   D
2 : A   B   C   D
3 : A   B   C   D
4 : A   B   C   D

Passage 2

5 : A   B   C   D
6 : A   B   C   D
7 : A   B   C   D
8 : A   B   C   D
9 : A   B   C   D

Independent questions

10 : A   B   C   D
11 : A   B   C   D
12 : A   B   C   D
13 : A   B   C   D

Passage 3

14 : A   B   C   D
15 : A   B   C   D
16 : A   B   C   D
17 : A   B   C   D
18 : A   B   C   D

Passage 4

19 : A   B   C   D
20 : A   B   C   D
21 : A   B   C   D
22 : A   B   C   D
23 : A   B   C   D

Independent questions

53 : A   B   C   D
54 : A   B   C   D
55 : A   B   C   D
56 : A   B   C   D
57 : A   B   C   D
58 : A   B   C   D
59 : A   B   C   D

Independent questions

24 : A   B   C   D
25 : A   B   C   D
26 : A   B   C   D
27 : A   B   C   D
28 : A   B   C   D

Passage 5

29 : A   B   C   D
30 : A   B   C   D
31 : A   B   C   D
32 : A   B   C   D
33 : A   B   C   D
34 : A   B   C   D
35 : A   B   C   D

Passage 6

36 : A   B   C   D
37 : A   B   C   D
38 : A   B   C   D
39 : A   B   C   D
40 : A   B   C   D
41 : A   B   C   D

Independent questions

42 : A   B   C   D
43 : A   B   C   D
44 : A   B   C   D
45 : A   B   C   D

Passage 7

46 : A   B   C   D
47 : A   B   C   D
48 : A   B   C   D
49 : A   B   C   D
50 : A   B   C   D
51 : A   B   C   D
52 : A   B   C   D

This page is intentionally left blank

Passage 1
(Questions 1–4)

A cylindrical pole stands vertically with one end attached securely to the ground. The pole is made of a homogeneous material with a density of 6000 kg/m³, its length is 12 m and cross sectional area is 0.03 m². Figure 1 shows the pole and three hypothetical cross sections at 4-meter intervals.

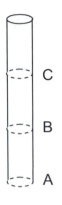

Figure 1.

The pole can be considered a very rigid spring that follows *Hooke's Law* which states that stress is directly proportional to strain:

$$F = -kx$$

Equation 1

where F is the restoring force exerted by the spring on that end (N or kg·m/s²), *k* is a constant referred to as the *rate* or *spring constant* (N/m or kg/s²) and *x* is displacement of the spring's end from its equilibrium position (a distance in meters).

If some object is placed at the top of the pole, the pole gets compressed by an amount proportional to that object's weight. But if the object's mass is significant enough to bend the pole, Hooke's law no longer applies. Assume that the pole above acts as a Hooke's Law spring until it collapses.

Young's modulus of elasticity (*E*) is the ratio of stress (units of pressure) to strain (dimensionless). Therefore, Young's modulus has units of pressure (*p*). Pressure is the ratio of the force over the area to which that force is applied.

Young's modulus is similar to the spring constant in Hooke's Law and Equation 1 shows that *E* depends on the stress (σ) exerted on an object.

$$E = \frac{\text{tensile stress}}{\text{tensile strain}} = \frac{\sigma}{\varepsilon} = \frac{F/A_o}{\Delta L/L_o}$$

Equation 2

where E = Young's modulus (modulus of elasticity);

F = force exerted on an object under tension;

A_0 = original cross-sectional area through which the force is applied;

ΔL = amount by which the length of the object changes;

L_0 = original length of the object.

Strain (ε), the fractional change in length the body undergoes is defined as:

$$\varepsilon = \frac{\Delta L}{L_0}$$

Equation 3

One also must consider that in reality, a pole needs to be able to support its weight. If the diameter of a pole is fixed, there is a limit to the pole's height. The stress (σ) on the pole exerted by its own weight is $\sigma = \rho g h$ at any point, where ρ is the density of the pole, h is the height of the pole above that point and g is acceleration due to gravity.

Note: for the pole above, $E = 945$ N/m^2; the acceleration due to gravity, $g = 9.8$ m/s^2.

1. What is the relative value of the Young's modulus for a metal pole if it undergoes minimal fractional change in length while subject to significant stress?

A. large and positive

C. small and positive

B. large and negative

D. small and negative

2. Which of the following expressions best represents the pressures at each of the pole's cross sections A, B, and C?

A. $\sigma_A = \sigma_B = \sigma_C$　　**B.** $\sigma_A < \sigma_B > \sigma_C$　　**C.** $\sigma_A > \sigma_B > \sigma_C$　　**D.** $\sigma_A < \sigma_B < \sigma_C$

3. Which expression corresponds with how tall the pole could get before buckling under its own weight if it collapses when compressed by more than a factor of ε_c?

A. $\dfrac{\varepsilon_c}{E}$　　　　**B.** $\dfrac{\varepsilon_{cg}}{E}$　　　　**C.** $\dfrac{Eg}{\rho\varepsilon_c}$　　　　**D.** $\dfrac{E\varepsilon_c}{\rho g}$

4. What is the pressure of the pole's weight (Figure 1) at cross section B?

A. 8.0×10^2 Pa　　**B.** 1.3×10^3 Pa　　**C.** 4.8×10^4 Pa　　**D.** 4.8×10^5 Pa

Passage 2
(Questions 5–9)

Energy is an indirectly observed quantity of matter that comes in many forms such as potential energy, kinetic energy, radiant energy and so on. In physics and chemistry, heat is energy transferred from one body to another by thermal interactions. The transfer of energy can occur in a variety of ways, among them conduction (i.e. collision of particles), radiation, (i.e. propagation of energy without matter) and convection (i.e. transfer of heat with any fluid or gas movement). Heat is not a property of a system or body, but is associated with a process of some kind, and is synonymous with heat flow and heat transfer.

Heat flows from hotter to colder systems, occurs spontaneously and is always accompanied by an increase in entropy. The second law of thermodynamics states that the entropy of an isolated system never decreases because isolated systems spontaneously evolve towards thermodynamic equilibrium – the state of maximum entropy where there is no net flow of matter or energy. The second law of thermodynamics prohibits heat flow directly from cold to hot systems.

Several thermodynamic definitions are very useful in thermochemistry. A system is the specific portion of the universe that is being studied. Everything outside the system is considered the surrounding or environment. A system may be an *isolated system* – when it cannot exchange energy or matter with the surroundings (e.g. an insulated bomb calorimeter), a *closed system* – when it can exchange energy but not matter with the surroundings (e.g. a steam radiator), or an *open system* – when it can exchange both matter and energy with the surroundings (e.g. a pot of boiling water).

A system undergoes a process when one or more of its properties changes. A process relates to the change of state. An *isothermal* (i.e. same temperature) process occurs when the temperature of the system remains constant. An *isobaric* (i.e. same pressure) process occurs when the pressure of the system remains constant. An *adiabatic* (i.e. no heat exchange) process occurs when no heat exchange occurs.

To produce acetic acid (i.e. table vinegar) in a lab from inexpensive starting materials, a researcher can use carbon dioxide and water. Reaction 1 shows how these two compounds react to produce carbonic acid:

$$H_2O(l) + CO_2(g) \rightarrow H_2CO_3(aq) \quad \Delta G° = 8.5 \text{ kJ/mol}$$

Reaction 1

If the researcher can find the correct catalyst, the following reaction produces acetic acid:

$$2CO_2(g) + 2H_2O(l) \rightarrow CH_3COOH(l) + 2O_2(g)$$

$$\Delta H° = 873 \text{ kJ/mol}$$

$$\Delta S° = 3 \text{ J/mol•K}$$

Reaction 2

Substance	ΔH°f (kJ/mol)	ΔG°f (kJ/mol)
$H_2CO_3(aq)$	−700	−623
$H_2O(g)$	−241.8	−237.1
$CO_2(g)$	−393.5	−394.4
$CH_3COOH(l)$	−484	−389
$C_6H_{12}O_6(aq)$	−1271	−917

Table 1. Enthalpies and free energies of formation for several compounds

5. What is the $\Delta G°f$ value for $H_2O(l)$?

    A. 0 kJ   **B.** −229.0 kJ   **C.** −237.5 kJ   **D.** −246.0 kJ

6. For Reaction 2 to occur spontaneously, what condition must be satisfied (assuming that ΔH and ΔS are independent of temperature)?

    A. The temperature is sufficiently high

    B. It never occurs spontaneously because $\Delta G°$ is positive

    C. The correct catalyst is found

    D. The temperature is sufficiently low

7. For Reaction 1, what is the value of the thermodynamic equilibrium constant at 298 K? *Note:* $\ln x = 2.3 \log_{10} x$; the universal gas constant (R) is 8.3145 J/mol·K.

    A. 2×10^{-17} **B.** 4×10^{-2} **C.** 1   **D.** 25

8. What is the entropy change (ΔS) for the formation of acetic acid from its elements under standard conditions?

    A. −3.19 kJ/mol·K   **C.** 0.319 kJ/mol·K

    B. −0.319 kJ/mol·K   **D.** 3.19 kJ/mol·K

9. Under standard conditions, would $H_2O(g)$ decompose into its elements spontaneously?

    A. Yes, H_2O cannot exist in the gaseous phase at 25°C

    B. Yes, entropy increases

    C. No, $\Delta G°$ for the reaction is positive

    D. No, the reaction is endothermic

Questions 10 through 13 are not based on any descriptive passage and are independent of each other

10. Which element has the electronic configuration $[Ar]\ 4s^2\ 3d^3$?

   A. titanium   **B.** vanadium   **C.** chromium   **D.** molybdenium

11. The energy of photons emitted by the mercury vapor is:

   A. equal to the energy of electric current
   B. equal to the voltage across the fluorescent tube
   C. less than the energy difference between electron orbitals of mercury atoms
   D. equal to the energy difference between electron orbitals of mercury atoms

12. Isocyanic acid is not an oxidizing agent. Therefore the structure of HCNO is:

   A. H — N ══ O — N   **C.** N — O ══ C — H
   B. C ══ N — O — H   **D.** O ══ C ══ N — H

13. How many molecules are present in Y grams of a compound with a molecular mass of X, assuming the Avogadro's constant is A?

   A. $\dfrac{XY}{A}$ **B.** $\dfrac{YA}{X}$ **C.** $\dfrac{Y}{XA}$ **D.** XYA

This page is intentionally left blank

Passage 3
(Questions 14–18)

Elastic collision is a collision between two bodies where the sum of their linear momenta ($P_1 + P_2$) has the same value before and after the collision. The total kinetic energy (KE) of the system remains unchanged because none of the system's kinetic energy is converted into other forms (e.g. heat, light, sound) of energy.

The conservation of the total momentum demands that the total momentum before and after the collision is the same, and is expressed by the equation:

$$m_1\vec{u}_1 + m_2\vec{u}_2 = m_1\vec{v}_1 + m_2\vec{v}_2.$$

Likewise, the conservation of the total kinetic energy is expressed by the equation:

$$\frac{m_1 u_1^2}{2} + \frac{m_2 u_2^2}{2} = \frac{m_1 v_1^2}{2} + \frac{m_2 v_2^2}{2}.$$

where m_1 and m_2 are the masses, u_1 and u_2 the velocities before the collision, and v_1 and v_2 are the velocities after collision.

The main condition that makes a collision perfectly elastic is the absence of friction. This condition usually exists at atomic and subatomic levels whereby atoms and nuclear particles often undergo ideal elastic collisions. This condition is not achievable for macroscopic bodies on the earth and all such bodies produce collisions that are not perfectly elastic because some of the kinetic energy of each body gets converted into other energy forms.

To simulate motion and contact free of friction, researchers run experiments that involve miniature carts sliding along a track. Carts are supported by air streams projecting from the track's surface and this allows them to slide almost free of friction.

Physicists set up an experiment involving the collision of two such carts whereby light springs are attached to the front and back of each cart. These springs undergo compression and extension and obey Hooke's law. The masses of the carts are 2 kg and 4 kg. When the air streams are turned off, the coefficient of kinetic friction is less than 0.01, therefore frictional effects can be disregarded. When the carts slide toward each other, immediately prior to the collision, the speed of the lighter cart is 4 m/s and that of the heavier one is 2 m/s.

14. Which of the following sequences represents corresponding energy transfers when the two carts approach each other, collide and separate?

   A. elastic potential → kinetic → elastic potential
   B. kinetic → elastic potential → kinetic
   C. kinetic → heat → gravitational potential → heat → kinetic
   D. heat → kinetic → heat → gravitational potential

15. What is the total kinetic energy of the system immediately before the collision?

   A. 8 J
   B. 12 J
   C. 16 J
   D. 24 J

16. If the experiment is conducted on an elevated platform inclined at an angle of 50° to the horizontal, what is the magnitude of the component of the sliding cart's weight (i.e. *mg*) normal to the plane?

   A. *mg* sin 50°
   B. *mg* cos 40°
   C. *mg* sin 40°
   D. None of the above

17. If the experiment was designed in a way that the collision between carts was perfectly inelastic, what would be the energy dissipation for the collision?

   A. 0 J
   B. 2 J
   C. 8 J
   D. 12 J

18. In a system where two objects undergo an ideal elastic collision, which of the following statements is valid?

   I.   Momentum (ρ) is conserved
   II. Kinetic energy (KE) is conserved
   III. Velocity of each object remains unchanged

   A. I only
   B. II only
   C. I and II only
   D. II and III only

Passage 4
(Questions 19–23)

Alpha (α), beta (β) and gamma (γ) particles are destructive to biological molecules because they are able to ionize atoms they collide with. In living organisms, ionization of compounds ultimately results in some type of biochemical dysfunction because ionized molecules typically lose all their useful activity. Limited exposure to these particles on the cellular level is typically not fatal because the majority of the damaged molecules can be replaced. However, if cellular DNA is struck by several decay particles, the damage to the DNA molecule is usually fatal for the cell.

Occasionally, a nonessential (e.g. non-coding) region of the DNA may be damaged causing the genome of the cell to be altered (mutated) but not resulting in phenotypic changes or in cell death. If the damaged gene affects cell replication (i.e. tumor suppressor gene or oncogene), that cell may become cancerous and replicate uncontrollably.

The destructiveness of ingested radioisotopes may be graded as alpha > beta > gamma rays. External exposure hazards vary significantly, with the potential biohazard depending on the penetrability of the particle. Figure 1 illustrates the average penetration depth of alpha, beta and gamma rays through various media. Alpha radiation consists of a helium nucleus and would not penetrate through a sheet of paper. Beta radiation consists of electrons and is not able to penetrate an aluminum plate. Gama radiation consists of atomic nuclei decay and requires over 1cm of dense shielding such as lead.

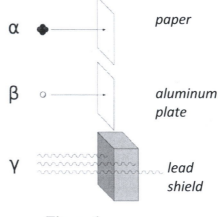

Figure 1.

In 1986, the catastrophe at the Chernobyl nuclear power plant released into the atmosphere vast amounts of highly toxic radioisotopes such as cesium-137, strontium-90, and iodine-131. All of them are short-lived radioisotopes, with half-lives of 30 years, 28 years and 8 days, respectively, and all are beta (β^-) emitters. As these radionuclides settled from the atmosphere, they contaminated the soil and water over hundreds of thousands of square kilometers within Ukraine and Scandinavia. Today, nearly one million people in the countries of the former Soviet Union may be suffering from some physiological effects associated with chronic exposure to radiation from the Chernobyl nuclear power plant accident.

19. Why was strontium-90 (^{90}Sr) responsible for the high occurrence of bone marrow cancer following the Chernobyl disaster?

   A. ^{90}Sr is chemically similar to Be, a major component of bone matrix
   B. ^{90}Sr is chemically similar to Ca and is incorporated into the bone matrix
   C. ^{90}Sr is an essential component of hemoglobin synthesized in the bone marrow
   D. ^{90}Sr decays into ^{90}Y, a stable isotope and is a heavy metal that gets incorporated into the bone matrix

20. The daughter nucleus of ^{137}Cs is:

   A. ^{136}Xe   **B.** ^{137}Xe   **C.** ^{136}Ba   **D.** ^{137}Ba

21. In constructing a barrier to penetration by *gamma* radiation, which material would be the best substitute for lead?

   A. Neon   **B.** Platinum   **C.** Radon   **D.** Silicon

22. Which of the following statements is true about the depth of penetration of radioactive decay in products?

   A. It increases with the increase in magnitude of the particle's charge
   B. It decreases with the increase in magnitude of the particle's charge
   C. It increases with the increase of the particle's mass
   D. It decreases with the increase of the particle's mass

23. Considerable radiation burns on the skin, throat and lungs of a patient indicate that this person had been recently exposed to high concentrations of:

   A. ^{210}Po, an *alpha* emitter   **C.** ^{59}Ni, decay by electron capture
   B. ^{137}Cs, a *gamma* emitter   **D.** ^{15}O , a positron emitter

Questions 24 through 28 are not based on any
descriptive passage and are independent of each other

24. If three moles of Cu_2S are consumed in the following reaction, how many moles of solid copper are produced?

$$Cu_2S \rightarrow 2Cu + S$$

    A. 2
    B. 3
    C. 6
    D. 9

25. What is the best expression for K_{eq} in the following reaction: $H_2(g) + Cl_2(g) \rightleftarrows 2HCl(g)$?

    A. $[H_2][Cl_2] / [HCl]$
    B. $[HCl]^2 / ([H_2][Cl_2])$
    C. $[HCl] / ([H_2][Cl_2])$
    D. $[H_2][Cl_2] / [HCl]^2$

26. All of the following statements about chemical formulas are true EXCEPT:

    A. Molecular formula can be derived from the empirical formula and molecular weight
    B. Molecular formula can be identical to the empirical formula
    C. Molecular formula cannot be identical to the empirical formula
    D. Empirical formula can be derived from the molecular formula

27. What type of intermolecular bonding occurs between C_5H_{12} molecules?

    A. van der Waals
    B. hydrogen
    C. ionic
    D. covalent

28. All of the following conditions are correct for ionic bond formation EXCEPT:
    A. transfer of electrons between two atoms.
    B. valence orbitals need to be filled.
    C. sharing of pairs of electrons between atoms
    D. electronegativity difference between the two atoms is greater than 1.7

This page is intentionally left blank

Passage 5
(Questions 29–35)

In all types of collisions (assuming no external forces acting), the total momentum vector p_{total} is conserved and expressed by the equation $p'_{total} = p_{total}$, where prime denotes *after* the collision and no prime – *before*. Each component of momentum (p_x and p_y) is conserved separately. For an object of nonzero mass m, including an atom, $p = mv$. Under conditions where an external force F exists and acts for a time interval Δt, the resulting change in momentum is expressed as $\Delta p = F\Delta t$.

A photon is the quantum of light and other electromagnetic waves. Photons do not have a mass. For a photon, the magnitude of the momentum is expressed by $p = E/c$, where E is the photon's energy and c is the speed of light. The photon's energy is:

$$E = hf$$

Equation 1.

where h is Planck's constant and f is the frequency of the light.

The photon's frequency f and wavelength λ are related by the equation:

$$\lambda f = c.$$

Equation 2.

The constant $h = 4.1 \times 10^{-15}$ eV·sec $= 6.6 \times 10^{-34}$ J·sec, and the speed of light c = 3 $\times 10^8$ m/sec $= 3 \times 10^{17}$ nm/sec.

When an atom absorbs a photon, an electron can be excited to a higher energy level. The difference in energy between the original and the higher levels is equal to the energy of the photon (E). If no higher level exists so that the difference in energy equals E, the photon will not be absorbed, which means the atom will be transparent to photons of energy E. Likewise, when an electron falls from a higher to a lower energy level, a photon is emitted.

When an atom absorbs or emits a photon, momentum (p) is conserved:

$$p'_{atom} = p_{atom} + p_{photon}$$

Equation 3. Conservation of momentum

29. If a stationary atom with a mass of 3 x 10^{-27} kg absorbs a photon of energy 3.0 x 10^{-19} J, what is the magnitude of the atom's velocity after the absorption?

A. 0.1 m/s   **B.** 0.3 m/s   **C.** 3.0 m/s   **D.** 27 m/s

30. If a 7.2 eV photon is in the vicinity of an atom that is in its ground state and the next energy level is 8.7 eV above the ground state, then the:

A. atom's momentum changes in proportion to the energy of the photon
B. atom absorbs the photon, but no electron will move to a different energy level
C. photon passes the atom and has no effect
D. photon causes one of the electrons to be ejected from the atom

31. Given that the photon's wavelength is 600 nm, what is its frequency?

A. 1.8 x 10^{19} sec^{-1} **B.** 5.0 x 10^{14} sec^{-1} **C.** 1.8 x 10^{14} sec^{-1} **D.** 5.0 x 10^{20} sec^{-1}

32. An atom experiences a head-on collision with a photon that travels in the opposite direction and which has twice the magnitude of the momentum. The atom absorbs the photon and, as a result:

A. moves along the initial path with increased speed   **C.** reverses direction
B. moves along the initial path with decreased speed   **D.** ceases motion

33. An atom has the magnitude of momentum p and the velocity vector perpendicular to a heavy barrier. What is the magnitude of the change in the atom's momentum after it strikes the barrier in elastic collision?

A. p **B.** $2p$ **C.** $4p$ **D.** $8p$

34. Which of the following is/are measure of momentum?

I. N·sec   II. kg·m/sec   III. J·sec/m

A. I only   **B.** I & II only   **C.** II & III only   **D.** I, II, & III

35. If an initially stationary atom with a mass of 4.5 x 10^{-26} kg emits a photon of energy 4.0 x 10^{-19} J, what is the magnitude of the atom's momentum after the emission?

A. 1.2 x 10^{-11} kg·m/s   **C.** 1.3 x 10^{-27} kg·m/s
B. 1.2 x 10^{-27} kg·m/s   **D.** 7.5 x 10^{-11} kg·m/s

Passage 6
(Questions 36–41)

The first modern definition of acids and bases was proposed by Svante Arrhenius and resulted in Arrhenius receiving the Nobel Prize in Chemistry in 1903. According to Arrhenius, an acid is a substance that dissociates in water to form hydrogen (H^+) ions. Thereby, an acid increases the concentration of H^+ ions in an aqueous solution. This protonation of water yields hydronium (H_3O^+). The use of H^+ is regarded as shorthand for H_3O^+, because a bare proton (H^+) does not exist as a free species in an aqueous solution. An *Arrhenius base* is a substance that dissociates in water to form hydroxide (OH^-) ions. Thereby, a base increases the concentration of OH^- ions in an aqueous solution.

The Arrhenius definitions of acidity and alkalinity apply only to aqueous solutions and refer to the concentration of the solvent ions. By this definition, pure H_2SO_4 and HCl dissolved in toluene are not acidic, and molten KOH and solutions of sodium amide in liquid ammonia are not alkaline.

The *universal aqueous acid–base definition* of the Arrhenius concept is described as the formation of a water molecule from a proton and hydroxide ion. This leads to the definition that in Arrhenius acid–base reactions, a salt and water are formed from the reaction between an acid and a base. This is a neutralization reaction where:

$$acid + base \rightarrow salt + water$$

Arrhenius definition defines acids as compounds that dissociate a proton when mixed with water or when reacting with another substance. The proton is always closely associated with at least one water molecule, therefore sometimes it's identified as H_3O^+. In the past it was believed that all acids contained oxygen (in Greek "oxygen" means "acid-forming"), but the elemental analysis of hydrochloric acid refuted this proposition.

Acids with the low ionization percentage are weak acids and acids that are almost 100% dissociated are considered strong acids. There are thousands of compounds that are technically acids, majority of which are weak organic acids.

The acid's relative strength is identified by its K_a value (a dissociation constant). The following table provides dissociation constants for some common acids.

Name	Formula	Acidity constant (K_a)		
Acetic acid	$HC_2H_3O_2$	1.8×10^{-5}		
Carbonic acid	H_2CO_3	$K_{a1} = 4.5 \times 10^{-7}$	$K_{a2} = 4.7 \times 10^{-11}$	
Citric acid	$C_6H_8O_7$	$K_{a1} = 7.1 \times 10^{-4}$	$K_{a2} = 1.7 \times 10^{-5}$	$K_{a3} = 6.4 \times 10^{-6}$
Hydrochloric acid	HCl	1.3×10^{6}		
Hydrocyanic acid	HCN	6.2×10^{-10}		
Lactic acid	$H_6C_3O_3$	1.4×10^{-4}		
Nitric acid	HNO_3	2.4×10^{1}		
Nitrous acid	HNO_2	7.1×10^{-4}		
Oxalic acid	$H_2C_2O_4$	$K_{a1} = 5.4 \times 10^{-2}$	$K_{a2} = 6 \times 10^{-5}$	
Phosphoric acid	H_3PO_4	$K_{a1} = 7.25 \times 10^{-3}$	$K_{a2} = 6.31 \times 10^{-8}$	$K_{a3} = 3.98 \times 10^{-13}$
Sulfuric acid	H_2SO_4	$K_{a1} = 2.4 \times 10^{6}$	$K_{a2} = 1.2 \times 10^{-2}$	

Table 1.

36. To neutralize 20 mL of 1.0 M HNO$_2$, what is the necessary volume of 0.5 M NaOH?

A. 4 mL   **B.** 10 mL   **C.** 20 mL   **D.** 40 mL

37. Which of these mixtures can be used as a buffer solution?

A. HBr and NaBr
B. KHCO$_3$ and Na$_2$CO$_3$

C. HNO$_3$ and NaNO$_2$
D. H$_4$C$_2$O$_2$ and KCN

38. Which ion is the conjugate base of oxalic acid (H$_2$C$_2$O$_4$)?

A. C$_2$O$_4^{2-}$ **B.** HC$_2$O$_4^{-}$ **C.** H$_2$C$_2$O$_4^{+}$ **D.** H$_3$C$_2$O$_4^{+}$

39. Which curve correctly reflects the titration curve for oxalic acid when it is completely titrated with NaOH?

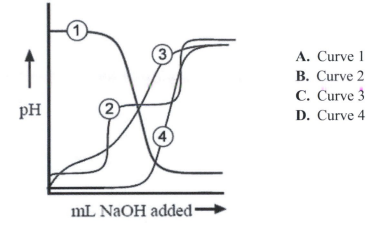

A. Curve 1
B. Curve 2
C. Curve 3
D. Curve 4

40. Which of the following acids is the strongest?

A. Acetic acid
B. Carbonic acid

C. Citric acid
D. Lactic acid

41. When 0.2 moles of NaOH is added to 0.4 moles HCN (hydrocyanic acid), what is the approximate pH?

A. 4.3   **B.** 5.7   **C.** 9.2   **D.** 12.1

Questions 42 through 45 are not based on any descriptive passage and are independent of each other

42. On a distant planet, rain consists of sulfuric acid droplets in a carbon dioxide atmosphere. Compare a raindrop on Earth to the same size and mass drop of sulfuric acid on the distant planet. The acceleration due to gravity is the same on both planets. Which of these factors affects the terminal velocity of the rain drop?

     I.   Chemical composition of the drop
     II. Temperature of the atmosphere
     III. Pressure of the atmosphere

  A. I only   **B.** I & II   **C.** II & III   **D.** I, II & III

43. Why are intermolecular forces in dry ice (CO_2) weaker than intermolecular forces in frozen water?

  A. carbon dioxide is nonpolar while water is polar
  B. carbon dioxide molecules have more kinetic energy than water molecules
  C. carbon dioxide cannot exist in the liquid phase at one atmosphere while water can
  D. carbon dioxide has a much higher molecular weight than water

44. Which of the following family of elements do lithium, sodium and potassium belong to?

  A. alkali metals   **C.** transition elements
  B. alkaline earth metals   **D.** lanthanides

45. In a chemical reaction, a compound accepts a pair of electrons from:

  A. oxidant   **C.** proton acceptor
  B. reductant   **D.** oxidant and reductant

Passage 7
(Questions 46–52)

The eye of a mammal collects light and focuses it onto the retina which consists of a multitude of cells that are able to detect that light. The interface between air and the cornea is where most of the refraction and focusing of incoming light rays occurs. The eye lens changes the focal length so the image projects precisely on the retina for the eye to be able to focus light from objects that are very close and very far.

The eye's ability to distinguish waves coming from different directions is known as *spatial resolution*. If a distant object emits two separate light beams, the human eye can distinguish the two separate lights because the light from the two sources approaches the eye from two directions, but if the light source is too far away from the eye, it lacks the resolution (i.e. ability to distinguish two separate lights) and they appear as one.

Resolution is measured in degrees or radians. For example, if a human eye can distinguish two lights emitted by two sources 1.5 m apart from each other and 1 km away from the observer, the angular separation of the lights is approximately 1.5 m/1000 m = 1.5×10^{-3} radians. The resolution of the eye is 1.5×10^{-3} rad or 0.09 degrees (since 1 rad = 57°) or 5 seconds of an arc. To a good approximation, the angular separation of two light sources (or any objects) is the ratio of spatial separation (Δx) to distance from the point of reference (L). Therefore, the smaller the resolution angle the better the resolution.

The spatial resolution of the eye (and any other detector) is limited by *diffraction,* which is essentially the spreading of waves. When waves pass through an aperture, they spread on the other side forming an angle given by:

$$\theta_{\text{diff}} = \frac{\lambda}{d}$$

Equation 1.

where θ_{diff} is measured in radians, λ = wavelength, and d = the diameter of the hole through which the waves pass. Diffraction is the physical limit of the resolution. The actual resolution of a detector may be much lower than given by Equation 1 if it is designed poorly.

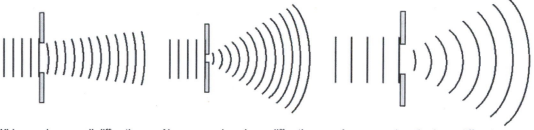

Wide opening - small diffraction   Narrow opening - large diffraction   Large wavelength - large diffraction

Figure 1.

The properly functioning human eye is limited by diffraction.

Color	Wavelength (nm)
Red	625 - 740
Orange	590 - 625
Yellow	565 - 590
Green	520 - 565
Blue	500 - 520
Indigo	435 - 500
Violet	380 - 435

* 1 nm = 10^{-9} m

Table 1. The visible light spectrum

46. What should be the approximate power of the appropriate corrective lens for an eye that does not focus correctly if the front to back length of the eye is 0.025 m, but the focusing power of the resting eye is 30 diopters?

A. 5 diopters
B. 10 diopters
C. –5 diopters
D. –10 diopters

47. Being adapted to seeing at night, a cheetah's eye has a much larger lens than a human eye and a larger pupil. However, a cheetah's eye resolution is not superior to that of almost diffraction limited human eye. Which of these statements is the most likely explanation for a cheetah's eye lack of resolution?

A. The larger pupil limits the amount of directional information entering the eye
B. The larger pupil allows more light to enter the eye
C. The large lens causes spherical aberration
D. The large lens causes chromatic aberration

48. What is the frequency of yellow light?

A. 5.3 x 10^{14} Hz
B. 1.9 x 10^{13} Hz
C. 1.7 x 10^{15} Hz
D. 1695 Hz

49. A painting of Camille Pissarro consists of a multitude of pure color dots of 0.002 m diameter. When a viewer looks at the painting from a far enough distance, the dots blend together and a coherent image is visible. Given that the resolution of an observer's eye limited by diffraction is 2 x 10^{-4} radians, how far away must he or she stand to be able to make out the image?

   A. 2 m away   **B.** 4 m away   **C.** 10 m away   **D.** 20 m away

50. When the human eye with the front to back length of 0.024 m focuses on a 0.02 m bead located 0.25 m away, what is the size of the image on the retina?

   A. 10^{-4} m   **B.** 10^{-3} m   **C.** 0.0002 m   **D.** 0.002 m

51. To photograph distant landscapes, an engineer designed a camera with a lens that focuses the light on a detector. While the camera is diffraction limited, the resolution is not good enough. Which solution would improve the camera's resolution?

   A. Make the lens bigger
   B. Design the lens from a more transparent material
   C. Change the lens shape
   D. Decrease the distance from the lens to the detector

52. When the human eye with the front to back length of 0.025 m focuses on a 0.02 m bead located 0.25 m away, what angle is subtended by the bead in the view of the eye?

   A. 2.3°   **B.** 4.6°   **C.** 10.3°   **D.** 20.6°

> Questions 53 through 59 are not based on any
> descriptive passage and are independent of each other

53. If glucose provides the anomeric carbon atom in a glycosidic link, the resulting compound is a:

   A. glucosamine   **B.** glucoside   **C.** glycan   **D.** glycoside

54. The impaired synthesis of sphingomyelins or cerebrosides most likely affects the proper formation of:

   A. blood groups   **C.** cell to cell communication
   B. nerve cells   **D.** cell surfaces

55. Which of these molecules is a tertiary amine?

    A. R_2NH^+ **B.** R_3N **C.** R_2NH **D.** RNH_2

56. The disaccharide below is formed by joining two monomers of D-glucose. Its name is:

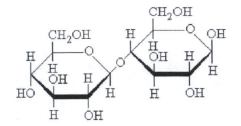

    A. α-D-glucopyranosyl-(1→3)-β-D-glucopyranose
    B. β-D-glucofuranosyl-(1→4)-β-D-glucofuranose
    C. α-D-glucopyranosyl-(1→4)-α-D-glucopyranose
    D. β-D-glucopyranosyl-(1→4)-β-D-glucopyranose

57. Which amino acid is the C-terminal group in the peptide Gly–Ala–Val–Phe–Tyr ?

    A. Tyr   **B.** Val   **C.** Ala   **D.** Gly

58. Sterols are steroids with:

    A. 5 fused rings compared to the 4 fused rings of cholesterol
    B. hydroxyl groups at both position C-3 and C-17
    C. hydroxyl group at position C-3
    D. hydroxyl group at position C-17

59. Which of the following molecules is cis-2,3-dichloro-2-butene?

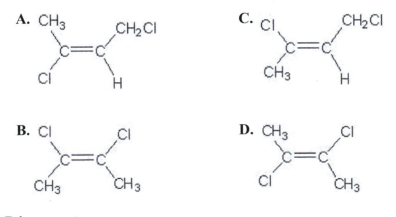

B is correct.

PART I.II

Explanatory Answers

CHEMICAL & PHYSICAL FOUNDATIONS OF BIOLOGICAL SYSTEMS
MCAT® PRACTICE TEST #1: ANSWER KEY

Passage 1
1 : B
2 : C
3 : A
4 : A
5 : C

Passage 2
6 : B
7 : D
8 : C
9 : C
10 : D
11 : B

Independent questions
12 : B
13 : C
14 : C
15 : B

Passage 3
16 : C
17 : A
18 : D
19 : B
20 : B

Passage 4
21 : C
22 : D
23 : D
24 : C
25 : B
26 : B

Independent questions
27 : C
28 : D
29 : A
30 : C
31 : A

Passage 5
32 : D
33 : D
34 : B
35 : C
36 : A

Passage 6
37 : D
38 : A
39 : A
40 : C
41 : B
42 : C

Independent questions
43 : B
44 : A
45 : C
46 : A

Passage 7
47 : C
48 : D
49 : B
50 : B
51 : D
52 : A

Independent questions
53 : B
54 : C
55 : C
56 : D
57 : B
58 : D
59 : A

Passage 1
(Questions 1-5)

A capacitor (condenser) is a passive electronic component consisting of a pair of conductors separated by a dielectric (nonconducting substance). When a voltage potential difference exists between the conductors, an electric field is present in the dielectric. This field stores energy and produces a mechanical force between the plates. The effect is greatest between wide, flat, parallel, narrowly separated conductors. An ideal capacitor is characterized by a single constant value, capacitance measured in farads.

A parallel-plate capacitor is the simplest capacitor and consists of two parallel conductive plates separated by a dielectric with permittivity (ε). Permittivity describes how an electric field affects a dielectric medium and is determined by the ability of a material to polarize in response to the field.

Two parallel metal plates of a parallel-plate capacitor are connected to a voltage source which maintains a potential (V) across the plates. An electric field (E) is created between the plates because positive charges collect on one side of the capacitor and negative charges on the other side. The magnitude of the electric field is related to the potential and the separation between the plates according to:

$$V = Ed$$

where V is measured in volts, E in joules/mole, and d in meters.

When placed between the plates, a charged particle experiences a force in magnitude by:

$$F = qE$$

where q is charge of particle in Coulombs, and F is force in Newtons.

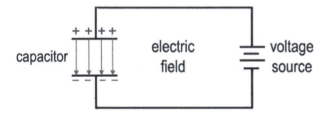

Figure 1. Parallel-plate capacitor

1. How is the electric field affected when the distance between the plates is increased by a factor of 3 but the voltage remains constant?

   A. stays the same   **C.** increases by factor of 3

   B. decreases by factor of 3   **D.** decreases by factor of

B is correct.

According to the equation ($V = Ed$), the electric field and the plate separation are inversely related. An increase in d by a factor of 3 results in a decrease in E by a factor of 3.

A capacitor (i.e. condenser) stores energy in an electric field and contains at least two electrical conductors separated by a dielectric (i.e. insulator) often made of glass, air, paper and vacuum. For example, a capacitor may consist of metal foils separated by a thin layer of insulating film and is used as part of electrical circuits in many common electrical devices. The conductors hold equal and opposite charges on their facing surfaces, and the dielectric develops an electric field.

When there is a potential difference (i.e. voltage) across the conductors, a static electric field develops across the dielectric, causing positive charge to collect on one plate and negative charge on the other plate.

The capacitance is greatest when there is a narrow separation between large areas of conductor plates. The dielectric between the plates passes a small amount of leakage current. Capacitors are widely used in electronic circuits for blocking direct current while allowing alternating current to pass, to smooth the output of power supplies, to stabilize electric power transmission systems for voltage and power flow.

An ideal capacitor is characterized by a single constant value, capacitance (measured in farads). A farad (F) is the charge in coulombs that a capacitor will accept to change the potential across it by 1 volt.

One *volt* is the difference in electric potential across a wire when an electric current of one ampere dissipates one watt of power. A *coulomb* is 1 ampere × second, the ratio of the electric charge on each conductor to the potential difference between them.

The capacitor is a reasonable general model for electric fields within electric circuits. An ideal capacitor is wholly characterized by a constant capacitance C, defined as the ratio of charge $\pm Q$ on each conductor to the voltage V between them:

$$C = \frac{Q}{V}$$

Sometimes charge build-up affects the capacitor itself and causes its capacitance to vary. In this case, capacitance is defined in terms of incremental changes:

$$C = \frac{dq}{dv}$$

2. How does the force on the helium nucleus compare to the force on the proton when both, a proton and a bare helium nucleus, are placed between the plates of a parallel-plate capacitor?

  A. the same
  B. there is no force on the helium nucleus
  C. **force on the helium nucleus is two times greater**
  D. force on the helium nucleus is four times greater

C is correct.

A helium nucleus has two protons (refer to its atomic number on the Periodic table), so the bare helium nucleus has two times greater charge than a proton.

3. How is the electric field affected if the voltage between the plates is increased by a factor of 9?

    A. it increases by a factor of 9   **C.** it decreases by a factor of 9
    B. it increases by a factor of 3   **D.** it increases by a factor of 81

A is correct.

From $V = Ed$, if separation distance between the plates is unchanged, the electric field also increases by a factor of 9.

4. Which graph best illustrates the relationship between the potential (V) and electric field (E)?

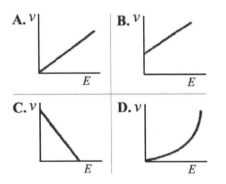

A is correct.

The voltage (V) and electric field (E) are proportional and the values of each increase accordingly as shown in graph A.

For B, the equation would be $V = Ed + V_0$.

5. What happens to the force on a proton between the plates if the separation of the plates is decreased by a factor of 2?

    A. it decreases by a factor of 2   **C. it increases by a factor of 2**
    B. it decreases by a factor of 4   **D.** it stays the same

C is correct.

If the separation of the plates decreases by a factor of 2, then the electric field increases by a factor of 2.
Therefore, the force on the proton increases by a factor of 2.

Passage 2
(Questions 6–11)

There are two types of interactions within molecules (intramolecular) and three types of interactions between molecules (intermolecular). Intramolecular forces include covalent and ionic bonds. Intermolecular interactions include van der Waals forces, dipole-dipole, and hydrogen bonds.

Interaction type	Bond	Energy (kJ/mol)
Intramolecular forces	Covalent bond	$155 - 650$
	Ionic bond	$350 - 550$
Intermolecular forces	van der Waals	$0.1 - 4$
	Dipole-dipole	$3 - 5$
	Hydrogen bond	$3 - 7$

Table 1. Bond energies

The boiling point of a substance is the temperature at which the vapor pressure of the liquid equals the environmental pressure that surrounds the liquid. A liquid in a vacuum has a lower boiling point than a liquid at atmospheric pressure. A liquid in a high pressure environment has a higher boiling point than when the liquid is at atmospheric pressure. The boiling point of liquids depends upon the environmental pressure.

The boiling point of a solution increases in proportion to the strength of intermolecular forces.

6. The atomic radius of I compared to Br is:

A. smaller
B. **greater**
C. the same
D. cannot be determined

B is correct.

This is a general Periodic table trend where radius increases moving down and to the left on the Periodic table. Elements in the same group also show patterns in their atomic radius, ionization energy, and electronegativity.

From top to bottom in a group, the atomic radii of the elements increase. Since there are more filled energy levels, valence electrons are found farther from the nucleus.

7. Why do boiling points of HF and H_2O deviate from the expected trend?

    A. Cl and O are elements of the second and third period
    B. H_2O and HF are relatively small molecules
    C. H_2O and HF molecules are less polarizable
    D. H_2O and HF molecules form hydrogen bonds

D is correct.

For boiling point questions on the MCAT, consider hydrogen bonding as the strongest intermolecular force that accounts for increased temperatures (kinetic energy) for boiling points compared to expected values.

The presence of hydrogen bonding increases the strength of attractions between molecules and requires more energy (heat) to dissociate them from their neighbors.

8. Why are van der Waals interactions weaker than dipole-dipole interactions?

    A. dipole-dipole interactions occur only with ionic bonded compounds
    B. dipole-dipole is an electrostatic interaction between the molecules
    C. van der Waals interactions rely on temporary momentary flux of electron density
    D. van der Waals interactions require a large surface area of molecules

C is correct.

All intermolecular bonding occurs via electrostatic forces. The momentary flux of electron distribution density (i.e. dipoles) in van der Waals forces is temporary while dipole-dipole interactions result from permanent dipoles.

9. Which type of intramolecular forces binds the atoms within the molecule of $CaCl_2$?

    A. van der Waals   **B.** hydrogen   **C. ionic**   **D.** covalent

C is correct.

$CaCl_2$ uses forces of ionic bonding because alkaline earth metals form ionic bonds with halogens.

The alkaline earth metals are elements comprising Group 2 of the Periodic table and include beryllium (Be), magnesium (Mg), calcium (Ca), strontium (Sr), barium (Ba) and radium (Ra). The alkaline earth metals are soft metals of silver color which react with halogens to form ionic salts, and with water to form strong alkaline (basic) hydroxide solutions. These elements melt at very high temperatures and remain solid in fire and have distinguishable flame colors. Like other groups, the alkaline earth metals show patterns in electron configuration, especially the outermost valence shells that result in chemical behavior trends.

The halogens are nonmetal elements from Group 17 (formerly VII) of the Periodic table, comprising fluorine (F); chlorine (Cl); bromine (Br); iodine (I); and astatine (At). Halogens are the only group of the periodic table which contains elements in all three states of matter at standard temperature and pressure. The halogens show a number of trends such as decreasing electronegativity and reactivity, and increasing melting and boiling points when moving down the Periodic table.

An ionic bond is a type of chemical bond that involves metal and non-metal ions through electrostatic attraction. An ionic bond is formed by the attraction between two oppositely charged ions with low electronegativity metals and high electronegativity non-metals. The energy change of the reaction is most favorable when metals lose electrons and non-metals gain electrons. The larger the difference in electronegativity between two atoms, the more ionic the bond is.

A: van der Waals forces include attractions between atoms, molecules, and surfaces. They differ from covalent and ionic bonding because they are caused by correlations in fluctuating polarizations of nearby particles. Van der Waals forces define the chemical character of many organic compounds and the solubility of organic substances in polar and non-polar environments. Van der Waals forces are relatively weak compared to normal chemical bonds, but play an important role in structural biology, polymer science and nanotechnology.

D: in covalent bonding, atoms are bound by sharing electrons and the molecular geometry around each atom is determined by VSEPR rules, whereas, in ionic materials, the geometry follows maximum packing rules.

10. Which of the following best describes why boiling points are better indicators of the strength of intermolecular bonding than melting points?

  A. vaporization is easier to measure
  B. vaporization requires less energy than melting
  C. vaporization requires more energy than melting
  D. melting point involves factors such as crystalline lattice structures

D is correct.

Boiling point is strongly dependent upon intermolecular bond strength. Crystallization depends upon molecular symmetry as well as intermolecular bonding. A crystal structure is a unique arrangement of atoms in a crystal composed of a motif, a set of atoms arranged in a particular way, and a lattice. Motifs are located upon the points of a lattice, which is an array of points repeating periodically in three dimensions.

11. As the period increases, the boiling points of noble gases increase because the bonds are:

   A. weaker due to larger atoms being more polarizable
   B. stronger due to larger atoms being more polarizable
   C. weaker due to larger atoms being less polarizable
   D. stronger due to larger atoms being less polarizable

B is correct.

Boiling point increases because the strength intermolecular bonds increases. The intermolecular bonds in noble gases are due only to weak van der Waals forces.

If atoms are more polarizable, instantaneous dipoles can have greater strength. Larger atoms are more polarizable because the electrons can get farther from the nucleus and create a larger dipole moment.

The noble gases are a group of chemical elements with very similar properties and under standard conditions they are all odorless, colorless, monatomic gases with a very low chemical reactivity. The six naturally occurring noble gases are helium (He), neon (Ne), argon (Ar), krypton (Kr), xenon (Xe) and radioactive radon (Rn). The noble gases have weak intermolecular forces, and consequently have very low melting and boiling points. The properties of the noble gases are explained by theories of atomic structure where the outer valence electron shell is "full". The melting and boiling points for each noble gas are close together, differing by less than 10 °C (18 °F) and they are liquids in only a small temperature range.

Polarizability is the relative tendency of a charge distribution, like the electron cloud of an atom or molecule, to be distorted from its normal shape by an external electric field, caused by a nearby ion or dipole.

> Questions 12 through 15 are not based on any descriptive passage and are independent of each other

12. Which statement is true for bases?

   A. Strong bases are always corrosive
   B. Strong bases readily accept protons from weak acids
   C. Weak bases do not react with strong acids
   D. Weak bases completely dissociate into ions in H_2O

B is correct.

A strong base (e.g. KOH or NaOH) is fully ionic and dissociates into metal ions and hydroxide ions in solution. Each mole of sodium hydroxide dissociates into one mole of hydroxide ions in solution.

A weak base does not completely dissociate into hydroxide ions in solution. Ammonia (i.e. weak base) does not contain hydroxide ions but reacts with water to produce ammonium ions (NH4+) and hydroxide ions. $NH_3(aq) + H_2O(l) \rightleftharpoons NH_4^+ + {}^-OH(aq)$ This reaction is reversible with about 99% of ammonia still present; only about 1% has actually produced hydroxide ions.

The relative strength of the acid or base can be determined by the pK_a. Molecules with a lower pK_a are acidic (accepts protons / lone pair acceptors) while molecules with a higher pK_a are bases (lone pair donors). A strong base (higher pK_a) is stabilized when it accepts protons from the acid. In relative terms, a weak acid is more stable after donating a proton (exists as an anion) than the stability of the base (anion before accepting the proton).

13. Which of the following is the correct statement about the relationship between the temperature of hot water at 80°C and its heat content?

    A. Temperature measures the average potential energy of the molecules and heat measures the stability
    B. Temperature and heat and have no relationship
    C. Heat is the energy transferred due to the difference in their temperatures
    D. Temperature and heat mean the same measure but use different numerical scales

C is correct.

Heat is the transfer of thermal energy from high to low temperature regions.

Temperature is a measure of the average kinetic energy ($KE = \frac{1}{2} mv^2$) of the molecules, not the potential energy ($PE = mgh$) of the molecules.

14. Body 1 moves toward Body 2 which is at rest. The mass of Body 2 is twice the mass of Body 1.

After collision, the bodies stick together. What fraction of initial speed of Body 1 do the two bodies move at after the collision?

    A. 2/3   **B.** ½   **C. 1/3**   **D.** 1/4

C is correct.

In an inelastic collision, the colliding particles stick together and momentum is conserved but kinetic energy is not conserved.

Conservation of momentum: $m_1 v_1 + m_2 v_2 = (m_1 + m_2)v_f$
and final velocity: $v_f = (m_1 v_1 + m_2 v_2) / (m_1 + m_2)$

From conservation of momentum (inelastic collision):

$$P_{before} = P_{after}$$
$$mv = (m + 2m)v_f$$
$$v_f = 1/3v$$

An elastic collision conserves total kinetic energy (KE) and momentum of the colliding bodies. During the collision, kinetic energy is first converted to PE (e.g. repulsive force between particles) then PE is converted into KE. The collision of atoms is an example of an elastic collision.

15. Mike sits on a stationary sled (total mass of Mike + sled = 100 kg) on a skating rink with smooth ice and holds a 2 kg ball. If he throws the ball at a speed of 10 m/s, what is the speed at which Mike and the sled move?

A. 0.1 m/s   **B. 0.2 m/s**   **C.** 0.4 m/s   **D.** 0 m/s

B is correct.

From conservation of momentum, we get: $P_{before} = P_{after}$
$$0 = m_{ball}v'_{ball} + m_{Mike+sled}v'_{sled}$$
$$v'_{sled} = (-m_{ball}v'_{ball}) / (m_{Mike+sled})$$
$$v'_{sled} = -(2)(-10) / 100 = 0.2 \text{ m/s}$$

Passage 3
(Questions 16–20)

When light in the ultraviolet region of the electromagnetic spectrum shines on a phosphor, the phosphor fluoresces and emits light in the visible region of the spectrum. Fluorescent lamps utilize this principle and are very efficient light sources. The lamp is a glass tube with inside walls coated with a phosphor. The tube has a large length-to-diameter ratio (to reduce the power loss at each end of the tube) and is filled with argon gas mixed with mercury vapor. Inside both ends of the tube are tungsten electrodes covered with an emission material.

The two main parts in a fluorescent lamp are a gas-filled tube (bulb) and the magnetic (or electronic) ballast. An electrical current from the ballast flows through the gas (mercury vapor), causing emission of ultraviolet light. The ultraviolet light then excites a phosphor coating on the inside of the tube which emits visible light. Electrons are liberated at the cathode and accelerated by an applied electric field. These free electrons encounter the mercury gas, ionizing some mercury atoms and exciting others. Since it requires more energy to ionize atoms than excite electrons, more excitation than ionization occurs.

When the excited electrons revert to their ground state, they radiate ultraviolet photons which strike the phosphor coating electrons and excite them to higher energy states. The excited electrons in the phosphor return to their ground state in several steps, producing radiation in the visible region of the spectrum. Not every fluorescent lamp emits the same color of radiation and color depends on heavy metal compounds within the phosphor. New phosphor compositions have improved the color of the light emitted by fluorescent lamps and some light from new lamps is similar in color to standard incandescent lamps.

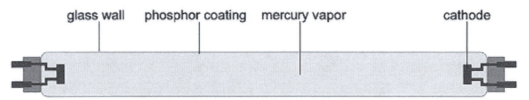

Figure 1. Fluorescent lamp

The fluorescent lamp shown operates at 100 volts and draws 400 milliamps of current during normal operation. Only 25% of the lamp's power is converted to light, while the remaining 75% dissipates as heat which keeps the lamp at its optimal working temperature of 40°C.

16. Which of the following best describes light emitted when excited electrons in the phosphor coating revert to the ground state in more than one step?

    A. greater energy than light absorbed   **C. longer wavelength than light absorbed**
    B. same wavelength as light absorbed   **D.** higher frequency than light absorbed

C is correct.

When electrons fall from an excited to lower energy state, light is emitted. The electrons in atoms of phosphor coating are excited to higher energy levels in a single step by absorbing ultraviolet light. When these electrons return to the lower energy state from which they were excited, the total energy emitted equals the energy of the excited level minus the energy of the lower level. If electrons return to the lower state in more than one transition, the energy for each transition is less than the total energy. The sum of the energies of all transitions equals the total energy of excitation due to the conservation of energy principle.

The energy of a photon equals hc/λ, where h is Planck's constant, c is speed of light, and λ is wavelength of light.

Since the energy emitted in each step of the multi-step transitions is smaller than energy absorbed, the wavelengths of photons emitted in multi-step transitions is longer than wavelength of light absorbed.

17. In addition to light emitted in the visible spectrum, the lamp also emits a small proportion of ultraviolet light. This ultraviolet light is incident on a metal that has a minimum energy necessary to free an electron (work function) of 3.0 eV. If the frequency of the incident light is 1.2×10^{15} Hz, what is the kinetic energy of an electron ejected from the metal? ($h = 4.14 \times 10^{-15}$ eV·s)

A. 1.83 eV   **B.** 4.13 eV   **C.** 7.96 eV   **D.** 9.66 eV

A is correct.

The photoelectric effect occurs when electrons are emitted from matter (metals, non-metallic solids, liquids, or gases) after the absorption of energy from electromagnetic radiation such as X-rays or visible light. The minimum frequency (f) of light that causes a metal to eject electrons is called threshold frequency and is determined from the work function of the metal. The work function is the minimum energy (electron volts) needed to remove an electron from a solid.

According to the question, an electron in this metal must receive at least 3.0 electron-volts of energy to be ejected and excess energy is converted to kinetic energy of the electron.

The energy of incident light equals Planck's constant (h) times its frequency (f).

$E = hf$
$E = (4.14 \times 10^{-15})(1.2 \times 10^{15}) \approx 4.8$ electron-volts.
4.8 electron-volts is the incomplete answer because the work function must be subtracted from total energy of incident light (energy needed by electron to escape the metal). Work function does not contribute to electron's kinetic energy.

The kinetic energy of the ejected electron equals energy of incident light minus work function of the metal, or 4.8 – 3 = 1.8 electron-volts. The closest answer is 1.83 electron-volts.

18. What is the explanation of why some fluorescent light bulbs glow for a short period after the power supply has been turned off?

    A. incandescence of hot ionic gas within the bulb surface
    B. emission of light stored as vibrational kinetic energy in the phosphor coating
    C. dissipation of electric charge built up on the bulb's surface
    D. electrons returning to the ground state from excited states

D is correct.

Time is needed for electrons to return to the ground state from excited states after the power is shut off.

A: incandescence of hot ionic gases in the bulb's surface sounds feasible, but is incorrect. Incandescence is light which is emitted due to heat, and since the fluorescent lamp operates at an optimum temperature of 40°C (from passage) and 40°C is not a high enough temperature for incandescence to occur.

B: even though moving charges can radiate light, the energy of vibration is too low to emit visible light.

C: a steady glow cannot be produced from the dissipation of electric charge.

19. How much light energy is emitted by the fluorescent lamp after 5 hours?

    A. 72 kJ   **C.** 1,800 kJ
    B. 180 kJ   **D.** 720 kJ

B is correct.

From passage, only 25% of lamp operating power is converted to light. The lamp has an operating voltage of 100 volts and draws 400 milliamps (or 0.4 amps) of current. Power = (voltage)(current) = $P = (V)(I) = (100$ volts$) (0.4$ watts$)$.

Since only 25% of power is converted to light, only 10 watts of power from the lamp is emitted as light.

From $E = Pt$, useful energy = (10 watts)(5 hours)(3600 sec/hr)

= 180,000 J = 180 kJ.

20. What is the wavelength of the light emitted by the fluorescent lamp when an electron of phosphor coating falls from an excited state to a lower energy state emitting a photon with energy of 3.04 eV? (Planck's constant $h = 4.14$ x 10^{-15} eV·s, and $c = 3$ x 10^8 m/s)

    A. 30 nm   **C.** 1200 nm
    B. 400 nm   **D.** 3600 nm

B is correct.

600 nanometers = 6 x 10^{-7} meters.

Energy = hc / λ.

Energy is given in electron-volts instead of joules, but Planck's constant (h) is given as 4.14 x 10^{-15} electron-volts·seconds (eV·s).

Therefore:

$$\lambda = hc \,/\, E$$

$$\lambda = (4.14 \text{ x } 10^{-15})(3 \text{ x } 10^8) \,/\, 3.04$$

Rounding to nearest integer: $\lambda \approx (12 \text{ x } 10^{-7}) \,/\, 3$

≈ 4 x 10^{-7} meters.

Passage 4
(Questions 21–26)

Electron configuration is the arrangement of electrons of an atom or molecule and describes the way electrons are distributed in orbitals of the atomic or molecular system. The periodic table of elements uses the electron configuration of atoms as a main principle, and electron configuration describes the sharing of electrons within chemical bonds.

The ground state of an atom refers to the state when all the electrons of an atom occupy orbitals of the lowest energy levels. For example, the ground state for fluorine is $1s^2 2s^2 2p^5$, for phosphorus is $1s^2 2s^2 2p^6 3s^2 3p^3$ and for chlorine is $1s^2 2s^2 2p^6 3s^2 3p^5$.

When an atom in the ground state absorbs energy, its electron is promoted to a higher energy level, and a dark band appears on its absorption spectrum. Absorption spectrum shows the fraction of incident electromagnetic radiation absorbed by the material over a range of frequencies. Every chemical element has absorption lines at several particular wavelengths corresponding to the differences between the energy levels of its atomic orbitals.

When the excited electron returns to the ground state, a photon is emitted and produces a bright band on the emission spectrum. Absorption and emission spectra provide important information about the energy levels of the electrons within atoms and ions.

Hydrofluoric acid (HF) is created by reacting hydrogen (H_2) and fluorine (F_2) gasses:

$$H_2(g) + F_2(g) \rightleftarrows 2\ HF(g) \quad \Delta H = -269 \text{ kJ/mol}$$

Reaction 1

In aqueous solutions of hydrofluoric acid (HF), the electron configuration of the conjugate base F^- may be determined by absorption spectroscopy. In the ground state, the fluoride ion's additional electron occupies the outer position in the 3s subshell as: $1s^2 2s^2 2p^4 3s^1$.

21. Gaseous hydrogen fluoride is formed by reacting hydrogen and fluorine in a closed container (Reaction 1). What is the result of increasing the reaction temperature when the reaction reaches equilibrium?

  A. [HF] increases due to increased rate of reaction
  B. [HF] increases due to a decrease in enthalpy of forward reaction
  C. [HF] decreases due to an exothermic forward reaction
  D. [HF] decreases due to an increase in molar quantity of gas of the forward reaction

C is correct.

Le Chatelier principle predicts that exothermic reactions shift to the left (reactants) when the temperature is increased and refers to thermodynamic equilibrium (K_{eq},) and not kinetics (k).

An exothermic reaction is a chemical reaction that releases energy in the form of heat. It is the opposite of an endothermic reaction.

Expressed in a chemical equation: reactants → products + energy

An exothermic reaction is a chemical reaction that is accompanied by the release of heat. In other words, the energy needed for the reaction to occur is less than the total energy released. As a result of this, the extra energy is released, usually in the form of heat. ΔG (Gibbs free energy) is negative for exothermic reactions and positive for endothermic reactions.

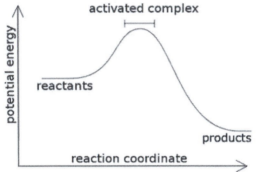

ΔH (enthalpy) is the difference in potential energy between reactants and products.

Temperature is a measure of the average kinetic energy of the molecules and kinetic energy is different than potential energy.

22. Which of the following is the conjugate base of the unknown hydrogen halide?

   A. Xe   **B.** Xe⁻   **C.** I   **D.** I⁻

D is correct.

Hydrogen halides (hydrohalic acids) are acids formed by chemical reactions of hydrogen with a halogen (Fl, Cl, Br, I and At) found in Group 7 of the Periodic table. They are acids because of their ability to release hydronium ions (H_3O^+) in aqueous solution.

Within the Bronsted-Lowry theory of acids and bases, a conjugate acid is the acid member (HX) of a pair of two compounds that transform into each other by gain (or loss) of a proton. A conjugate acid releases (donates) a proton (H^+) in the forward reaction.

The anion formed, X^-, is the conjugate base and it gains a proton in the reverse reaction. Xenon (Xe) is a noble gas, not a halogen.

23. Which of the following statements is true for the ground state electron configurations of conjugate bases of two hydrogen halides?

 A. electrons are absent   **C.** they are configurations of two metals
 B. electrons are excited   **D. they are configurations of two inert gases**

D is correct.

The conjugate bases (X^-) of hydrogen halides (HX) are anions with an additional electron, similar to the noble-gas configurations, which explains their stability.

24. Which of the following represents the electron configuration of a chlorine atom in excited state?

 A. $1s^22s^22p^43d^1$ **C.** $1s^22s^22p^63s^23p^44s^1$
 B. $1s^22s^22p^63p^1$ **D.** $1s^22s^22p^13s^23d^2$

C is correct.

From the periodic table, the atomic number for chlorine is 17 which represents the number of protons. In a neutral atom, the number of protons, neutrons and electrons are identical.

An excited state results when the electron is promoted to a higher orbital (3p to 4s). For example, in excited chlorine, the configuration changes from $1s^22s^22p^63s^23p^5$ to $1s^22s^22p^63s^23p^44s^1$ where one valence electron from the 3p orbital is promoted to the 4s orbital.

A: $1s^22s^22p^43d^1$ represents an atom with 9 electrons and not with the correct promotion into a higher orbital of an excited electron because 3s would be the correct orbital for a promoted electron to occupy.

B: $1s^22s^22p^63p^1$ represents an atom with 11 electrons.

D: $1s^22s^22p^13s^23d^2$ represents an atom with 9 electrons.

25. What does the absorption spectrum of an excited conjugate base (X^-) of the hydrogen halide (HX) show?

 A. red shift   **B. dark bands**   **C.** no absorption   **D.** bright bands

B is correct.

From the passage, dark bands indicate absorption and bright bands indicate emission. Excitation of electrons in any atom requires the absorption of light.

26. What is pH of 0.1 M solution of hydrogen bromide?

   A. 0.1   **B. 1.0**   **C.** 2.0   **D.** 7.0

B is correct.

Since hydrogen bromide (HBr) is a strong acid, it dissociates completely in water.

$[H^+]$ = original [HBr].
pH = $-\log[H^+]$
= $-\log(0.1)$ = 1.

Questions 27 through 31 are not based on any
descriptive passage and are independent of each other

---

27. Which of the following elements is the most electronegative?

   A. H   **B.** K   **C. Cl**   **D.** Mg

C is correct.

Electronegativity is higher for non-metals (right side of the periodic table) than for metals (left side of the periodic table). Electronegativity increases moving up the Periodic table and to the right whereby fluorine (F) is the most electronegative element and francium (Fr) at the bottom left side is the least electronegative. Noble gases are an exception and not the most electronegative. The most electronegative are halogens (F > Cl > Br > I).

Electronegativity is not strictly an atomic property, but rather a property of a bonding atom in a molecule. The equivalent property of a free atom is its electron affinity.

Electronegativity is a chemical property (within molecules) that describes the ability of an atom to attract electrons (or electron density) towards itself in a covalent bond. An element's electronegativity is affected by both its atomic weight and the distance of the valence (outermost) electrons to the charged nucleus. The higher the electronegativity, the more an element attracts electrons towards itself when bonded to another atom.

28. In a KCl molecule, how many electrons are shared in the potassium-chlorine bond?

   A. 1   **B.** 2   **C.** 3   **D. 0**

D is correct.

KCl (like NaCl) is an ionic compound and no electrons are shared in an ionic bond.

An ionic bond is a type of chemical bond that involves a metal and a non-metal ion (or polyatomic ions such as ammonium) through electrostatic attraction. Ionic bonds are formed by the attraction between two oppositely charged ions. The metal donates one or more electrons, forming a positively charged ion (cation) with a stable electron configuration. These electrons are transferred to the non-metal, causing it to form a negatively charged ion (anion) which also has a stable electron configuration. The electrostatic attraction between the oppositely charged cation and anion causes them to come together and form an ionic bond.

For example, common table salt is sodium chloride. When sodium (Na) and chlorine (Cl) are combined, the sodium atom loses an electron, forming a cation (Na^+), and the chlorine atom gains an electron to form an anion (Cl^-). These ions are then attracted to each other in a 1:1 ratio to form sodium chloride (NaCl).

$$Na + Cl \rightarrow Na^+ + Cl^- \rightarrow NaCl \qquad K + Cl \rightarrow K^+ + Cl^- \rightarrow KCl$$

29. What would be the molarity of a 2N concentration of H_2SO_4 completely dissociated in water?

A. 1 M   **B.** 2 M   **C.** 3 M   **D.** 4 M

A is correct.

Molarity (units of mol/L, molar, or M) denotes the number of moles of a substance per liter of solution. M is used to abbreviate units of mol/L.

The formula for molarity is: $\dfrac{\text{Moles of solute}}{\text{Liters of solution}}$ = Molarity of solution.

For instance, $\dfrac{2.0 \text{ moles of dissolved particles}}{4.0 \text{ liters of liquid}}$ = solution of 0.5 mol/L.

Normality = molar concentration / equivalence factor: $N = C_i / f_{eq}$. The definition of a gram equivalent depends on the type of chemical reaction. Normality measures a single ion. For example, the normality of hydroxide or sodium in an aqueous solution of NaOH, but the normality of NaOH itself has no meaning. Normality often describes solutions of acids or bases when it is implied that normality refers to H^+ or OH^- ions.

For example, 2 N sulfuric acid (H_2SO_4), means that the normality of H^+ ions is 2, or the molarity of sulfuric acid is 1.

For 1 molar H_3PO_4 the normality is 3 for three moles of H^+ ions for every mole of PO_4^{3-}. Normality highlights the chemical nature of salts. In solution, salts dissociate into distinct reactive species (ions such as H^+, Fe^{3+}, or Cl^-). Normality accounts for any discrepancy between the concentrations of the various ionic species in a solution. For example, in $MgCl_2$, there are two moles of Cl^- for every mole of Mg^{2+}, so Cl^- is 2 N.

Normality takes into account that acid dissociates to 2 moles of H^+ for each mole of H_2SO_4 that dissociates. Therefore:

$$\frac{2 \text{ equivalents}}{\text{liter}} \times \frac{1 \text{mole } H_2SO_4}{2 \text{ equivalents}} = 1M$$

30. The car, with its engine off, slows down as it coasts. Which of the following statements is true about the forces acting on the car?

    A. no forces are acting on the car
    B. net force is zero while there are forces acting on the car
    C. net force acting on car does not equal zero
    D. none of the above statements can be concluded

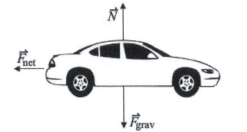

C is correct.

Because the car is slowing down, the car is not undergoing uniform motion and it has a net force acting on it. The net force points in the direction opposite to the car's motion.

31. Which of the following conclusions best describes each of the hydrogen halides and bonding between hydrogen and halide atoms?

    A. smaller halide atoms have stronger bonds
    B. smaller halide atoms have weaker bonds
    C. hybrids of smaller halide atoms have greater lengths
    D. hybrids of greater lengths are associated with stronger bonds

A is correct.

When the radius of the halide atom decreases, bond strength increases because the Coulomb force is inversely proportional to the square of the separation distance between the charges. Decreasing the distance increases the force of attraction.

Coulomb's law describes the electrostatic force between electric charges. The magnitude of the electrostatic force between two point electric charges is directly proportional to the product of the magnitudes of each of the charges and inversely proportional to the square of the total distance between the two charges.

The magnitude of the electrostatic force (F) on a charge (q_1) due to presence of a second charge (q_2), is given by:

$$F = k_e\,(q_1 q_2 / r^2),$$
$$\text{where } k_e \text{ (Coulomb's constant)} \approx 8.998 \times 10^9 \text{ N·m}^2\text{·C}^{-2}$$

Passage 5
(Questions 32–36)

In fluid dynamics, drag refers to forces that oppose the relative motion (resistance) of an object through a fluid (liquid or gas). Drag forces act in the direction opposite the oncoming flow velocity. Unlike other resistive forces (e.g. dry friction), drag forces depend on velocity. When an object moves through a fluid, the drag force retards its motion with a magnitude expressed by:

$$F_{drag} \approx -\tfrac{1}{2}\, CA\rho v^2,$$

Equation 1

where C, drag coefficient, is a dimensionless constant, A is cross-sectional area of object normal to flow direction, ρ is density of the fluid, and v is velocity of object relative to fluid.

Equation 1 applies to fluids with an onset of turbulence that develops whirls and eddies. For an undisturbed fluid, the drag force is actually greater than the value in Equation 1. Reynolds number, also a dimensionless constant, determines the extent to which a fluid is disturbed.

$$R_e = \rho v l / \eta,$$

Equation 2

where l is linear size of object and η is viscosity (stickiness) of fluid.

substance	$\rho\,(kg/m^3)$	$\eta\,(kg/m\ s)$
Air	1.3	1.8×10^{-5}
Water	1.0×10^{3}	1.0×10^{-3}
Mercury	1.36×10^{4}	1.5×10^{-3}
Methanol	0.9×10^{3}	5.7×10^{-4}
Benzene	0.8×10^{3}	6.0×10^{-4}

Table 1.

For R_e values greater than 100, Equation 1 for F_{drag} is relatively accurate. Reynolds number also determines the onset of turbulence in the fluid. When R_e is greater than 2×10^5, the fluid develops whirls and eddies that break off from the flow in an unpredictable manner and turbulence is observed.

Viscosity is a measure of the resistance of a fluid which is being deformed by stress (shear or extensional). Viscosity characterizes a fluid's internal resistance to flow and may be thought of as a measure of fluid friction and describes "thickness" of a fluid. Thus, water is "thin" with a lower viscosity, while molasses is "thick" with a higher viscosity. The less viscous a fluid is, the greater its ease of movement and flow.

32. What should be the minimum velocity of the car with the linear size of 3 m (l) for turbulence to develop behind it ($\rho = 1.3$ kg/m³, $\eta = 1.8$ x 10^{-5} kg/m·s)?

    A. 0.24 m/s   **B.** 0.5 m/s   **C.** 0.84 m/s   **D. 0.92 m/s**

D is correct.

The equation for viscous resistance (i.e. linear drag) is appropriate for bodies moving at relatively slow speeds through a fluid without turbulence ($R_e < 1$). Under these conditions, F_{drag} is approximately proportional to velocity, but opposite in direction.

The equation for viscous resistance is: $F_d = -bv$

where b is a constant depending on properties of the fluid and dimensions of object, and v is the velocity of the object.

For turbulence to develop, Reynolds number should be greater than 2 x 10^5

$R_e > 2$ x 10^5 (for turbulence)

$\rho v l / \eta > 2$ x 10^5

$\rho v l > (2$ x $10^5) (1.8$ x 10^{-5} kg/m·s)

$v > (2$ x $10^5) (1.8$ x 10^{-5} kg/m·s) / (1.3 kg/m³) (3 m)

$v > 3.6$ kg/m·s / 3.9 kg/m²

$v > 0.92$ m/s

33. What minimum velocity makes Equation 1 true for a cube with dimensions 2 x 2 x 2 m moving through the air ($\rho = 1.3$ kg/m³, $\eta = 1.8$ x 10^{-5} kg/m·s)?

    A. 1.1 x 10^2 m/s   **C.** 4.8 x 10^{-3} m/s
    B. 3.3 x 10^{-2} m/s   **D. 6.9 x 10^{-4} m/s**

D is correct.

Equation 1 is valid when the Reynolds number > 100

From Equation 2,

$R_e > 100$,
$\rho v l / \eta > 100$

$\rho v l > (100) (1.8$ x 10^{-5} kg/m·s)

$v > (100) (1.8$ x 10^{-5} kg/m·s) / (1.3 kg/m³) (2 m)

$v > 1.8$ x 10^{-3} kg/m·s / 2.6 kg/m²

$v > 6.9$ x 10^{-4} m/s

34. What thrust would be exerted by a fish swimming in the ocean at constant 3 m/s velocity with dimensions of $0.1 \times 0.1 \times 0.1$ m ($C = 0.2$, $\rho = 1.0 \times 10^3$ kg/m^3)?

A. 0.09 N   **B. 9 N**   **C.** 90 N   **D.** 3×10^5 N

B is correct.

From Equation 1, $F_{drag} \approx -\frac{1}{2} CA\rho v^2$,

$$= (0.5)(0.2)\,(0.01\text{ m}^2)(1 \times 10^3\text{ kg/m}^3)(3\text{ m/s})^2 = 9\text{ N.}$$

35. What is the drag force on the 1000 kg car with dimensions 1.5 m high, 2 m wide, and 3 m long if it is moving at 20 m/s ($\rho = 1.3$ kg/m^3, $C = 0.25$)?

A. 10 N   **B.** 100 N   **C. 195 N**   **D.** 1,950 N

C is correct.

From Equation 1, $F_{drag} \approx -\frac{1}{2} CA\rho v^2$,

$$= (0.5)(0.25)\,(3\text{ m}^2)(1.3\text{ kg/m}^3)(20\text{ m/s})^2 = 195\text{ N}$$

36. For solving Equation 1, what is the effective cross-sectional area (A) for a car with dimensions 1.5 m high, 2 m wide, and 3 m long?

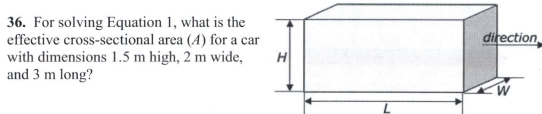

A. 3 m^2   **B.** 3.5 m^2 **C.** 6 m^2 **D.** 9 m^2

A is correct.

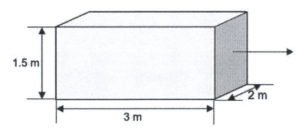

From the passage, A is cross-sectional area of object normal to flow direction.

The diagram models the shape of the car.

Arrow shows direction of car, and the shaded face of block is the cross section area.

$$A = (1.5\text{ m})(2\text{ m}) = 3\text{ m}^2.$$

The length of car is not used in the calculation.

Passage 6
(Question 37–42)

In an average household some very toxic substances may be found. For example, oven cleaners and drain cleansers dissolve organic substances such as grease, fat, hair, and skin because these substances contain concentrated solutions of sodium hydroxide (NaOH). Like all strong aqueous bases, NaOH hydrolyzes protein peptide and ester linkages.

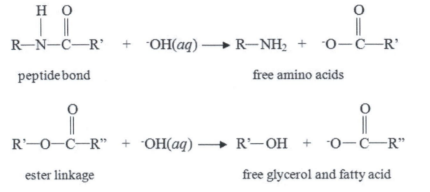

Household bleach is a 5% (by mass) solution of sodium hypochlorite (NaClO) and H_2O. The hypochlorite ion (^-ClO) is a mild oxidizing agent and toxic when ingested internally. Low concentrations of chlorine gas are also present within bleach solutions.

Another common household toxic substance is ammonia (NH_3). NH_3 is a strong ligand and gas at room temperature. If NH_3 is inhaled in high concentration, death can ensue due to irreversible exclusion of O_2 from the hemoglobin within the red blood cell. The same mechanism is observed for death caused by carbon monoxide (CO) poisoning.

$$4\ NH_3(g) + Hb\cdot 4\ O_2(aq) \rightarrow Hb\cdot 4\ NH_3(aq) + 4\ O_2(g)$$

NH_3 Poisoning

Most US deaths in the household caused by chemicals are due to toxic gases formed when ammonia and bleach come in contact with each other. Harmful insidious vapors containing hydrazine (H_2NNH_2), chloroamine ($ClNH_2$) and hydrogen chloride (HCl) are released from the reaction of bleach and ammonia solutions.

$$nNaOCl(aq) \quad + \quad nNH_3(aq)$$
$$\text{Bleach} \qquad\qquad \text{Ammonia}$$
$$\downarrow$$
$$H_2NNH_2(aq) \ + \ ClNH_2(aq) \ + \ HCl(aq)$$

For consumer safety, warning notices are required on the labels of these chemicals. A safety precaution is to never mix two substances with different active ingredients because a cloud of toxic fumes could result.

37. Which one of the following statements is true?

   A. N_2H_4 cannot act as a ligand
   B. N_2H_4 experiences dipole interactions, not hydrogen bonds
   C. O_2 is a better Lewis base than either NH_3 or CO
   D. vapor pressure of NH_3 at room temperature is greater than 760 torr

D is correct.

NH_3 is a gas at room temperature (see the passage) which means that the vapor pressure of NH_3 must be greater than atmospheric pressure (760 torr).

A: the N atoms in N_2H_4 have a lone pair of electrons and N_2H_4 is a strong ligand like NH_3.

B: molecules with large differences in electronegativity among the atoms such as N—H, O—H, or F—H experience hydrogen bonding.

C: the toxicity of NH_3 and CO is due to the fact that these compounds are better ligands (via lone pair attack) than O_2 – this accounts for why they replace O_2 in hemoglobin.

38. Which of the following statements is true for ammonia?

   A. NH_3 is a weak base and weak acid   **C.** NH_3 is a strong acid and weak base
   B. NH_3 is a strong acid and strong base   **D.** NH_3 is neither an acid nor a base

A is correct.

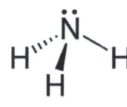

The nitrogen atom in ammonia has a lone electron pair, which makes ammonia a base (proton acceptor) with a pK_b of 4.75 (pK_a = 9.25). This trigonal planar shape gives the molecule a dipole moment and makes it polar so ammonia readily dissolves in water. The degree to which ammonia forms the ammonium ion increases with lowering the pH of the solution – at "physiological" pH (~7.3), about 67% of the ammonia molecules are protonated (NH_4^+).

Ammonia

A molecule that can function as both an acid and a base (e.g. H_2O) is amphipathic. Weak bases have lone pairs of electrons but are weak because they are stable molecules (or negatively charged anions) due to 1) resonance stability or 2) inductive stability due to the attachment of electronegative atoms to the molecule. Strong acids or bases are unstable molecules that become more stable. Bases abstract protons (i.e. Arrhenius or Bronsted-Lowry) or donate lone pairs of electrons (i.e. Lewis base). Acids donate protons (i.e. Arrhenius or Bronsted-Lowry) or accept lone pairs (i.e. Lewis acid).

39. The formal charges of atoms in the hypochlorite ion (ClO^-) are:

   A. 0 for Cl and –1 for O   **C.** –1 for Cl and 0 for O
   B. +1 for Cl and –2 for O   **D.** –1/2 for both the Cl and O atoms

A is correct.

In the hypochlorite ion, oxygen has a –1 formal charge, and chlorine has no formal charge.

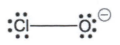 The choice +1 for Cl and –2 for O can be eliminated because a molecule will not develop separation of charge with integers greater than 1 if a more stable configuration is possible.

The electronegativity of atoms determines the distribution of electrons within the molecule. Oxygen is more electronegative than chlorine, so the electron density will be more on oxygen than chlorine.

The choice –1/2 for both the Cl and O atoms can be eliminated.

Due to electronegativity, oxygen attracts electron density, so –1 for Cl and 0 for O can be eliminated.

40. Ammonium chloride (NH_4Cl) is formed when bleach and ammonia are mixed together. What is the phase of ammonium chloride at room temperature?

  A. plasma   **B.** gas   **C. solid**   **D.** liquid

C is correct.

Ammonium chloride ($NH_4^+\,Cl^-$) is a clear white water-soluble crystalline salt of ammonia.

Like all ionic compounds, NH_4Cl is a salt and is a solid at room temperature.

A: plasma is one of the four fundamental states of matter (along with solid, liquid, and gas). Like gas, plasma does not have a definite shape or a definite volume unless enclosed in a container. Unlike gas, under the influence of a magnetic field, it may form structures such as filaments, beams and double layers. Plasma is found in stars and neon signs.

D: an ionic liquid is a salt in the liquid state. The term of ionic liquid is often restricted to salts whose melting point is below 100° C (212° F). While ordinary liquids (e.g. water and gasoline) are predominantly made of electrically neutral molecules, ionic liquids are largely made of ions and short-lived ion pairs.

41. The shapes of NH_3 and NH_2Cl are identical. Which one of the following molecules also has a trigonal pyramidal shape?

  A. iodine trifluoride (IF_3)   **C.** hypochlorous acid (HOCl)
  B. hydronium ion (H_3O^+)   **D.** hydrochloric acid (HCl)

B is correct.

Trigonal pyramidal shape molecules have three groups of bonding electrons and one pair of nonbonding (lone pair) electrons.

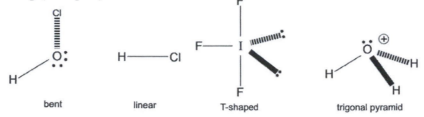

| bent | linear | T-shaped | trigonal pyramid |

42. Electrolytes dissociate into anions and cations in water. Which of the following compounds is/are NOT electrolytes?

    I. Chloramine   **II. Hydrazine**   III. Hydrogen chloride

  A. I only   **B.** II only   **C. I & II only**   **D.** I, II & III

C is correct.

Unlike hydrogen chloride (HCl), which completely dissociates into ions when dissolved in water, both, hydrazine (N_2H_4) and chloramine (NH_2Cl), are covalent compounds and therefore do not dissociate in water which makes them poor electrolytes.

Ionic compounds are formed between atoms of very different electronegativities. Except ammonium salts and a few strong acids (HI, HBr, HCl), compounds of all nonmetal elements are covalent compounds and therefore weak electrolytes because they do not dissociate within solution of H_2O.

> Questions 43 through 46 are not based on any descriptive passage and are independent of each other

43. A 1 kg block slides back and forth on a frictionless table while attached to the free end of an anchored spring. If the spring constant (k) is 9 N/m, what is the frequency of motion with a period ($T = 2\pi\sqrt{m/k}$)?

  A. 0.25 Hz   **B. 0.5 Hz**   **C.** 2 Hz   **D.** 4 Hz

B is correct.

Period, $T = 2\pi\sqrt{1/9}$ $T = 2\pi\,(1/3) = (2)(3.1)\,/\,3 \approx 2$ s,

frequency, $f = 1/T$ $f = 1/2 = 0.5$ Hz

In mechanics, a harmonic oscillator is a system that, when displaced from its equilibrium position, experiences a restoring force proportional to the displacement. If the restoring force is the only force acting on the system, the system is called a *simple harmonic oscillator*, and it undergoes simple harmonic motion (sinusoidal oscillations about the equilibrium point, with a constant amplitude and a constant frequency). If an external time dependent force is present, the harmonic oscillator is described as a *driven oscillator*. Mechanical examples of a driven oscillator include pendula (with small angles of displacement) and masses connected to springs.

A *spring* is an elastic object used to store mechanical energy. When a spring is compressed or stretched, the force it exerts is proportional to its change in length. In physics, a spring can be described as a device that stores potential energy (elastic potential energy) by straining the bonds between the atoms of an elastic material.

When a spring is stretched or compressed by a mass, the spring develops a restoring force – elastic potential energy, which then is transferred into kinetic energy. When the spring is stretched or compressed, kinetic energy of the mass gets converted into potential energy of the spring. By conservation of energy, when the spring reaches its maximum potential energy, the kinetic energy of the mass is zero. When the spring is released, it tries to return to equilibrium, and all its potential energy converts to kinetic energy of the mass.

44. The displacement of an object in simple harmonic motion is expressed as: $x = 3 \cos (\omega t + \pi/3)$ (t in sec and x in cm). At which of the following positions (x) will the block have the greatest speed?

A. 0 cm   **B.** 3/2 cm   **C.** 3 cm   **D.** $3\sqrt{3}/2$ cm

A is correct.

Speed is greatest when all energy of object is in kinetic form. Kinetic energy is greatest when potential energy = 0. The position where kinetic energy is greatest is equilibrium position, where $x = 0$.

Hooke's law is a principle of physics where the force (F) needed to extend or compress a spring by some amount X is proportional to that amount: $F = kX$, where k is a constant that is characteristic of the spring (i.e. stiffness).

Hooke's equation also applies (to some extent) in many other situations where an elastic body (i.e. internal forces oppose deformation) is deformed, such as wind blowing on a tall building, plucking a string of a violin, or the filling of a balloon.

Hookes's law is only a first order linear approximation to the real response of springs and other elastic bodies to applied forces and fails once the force exceeds some limit. No material can be compressed beyond a certain minimum size, or stretched beyond a maximum size, without some permanent deformation or change of state.

Hooke's law for a spring is applied under the convention that F is the restoring force exerted by the spring on whatever is pulling its free end. The equation becomes: $F = -kX$

since the direction of the restoring force is opposite to that of the displacement (X).

45. When the following equation is balanced, what is the sum of the coefficients?

$$Hg + HCl \rightarrow HgCl_2 + H_2$$

    A. 1   **B.** 4   **C.** 5   **D.** 7

C is correct.

The balanced equation is: $Hg + 2HCl \rightarrow HgCl_2 + H_2$, therefore the sum of coefficients is 5.

46. When the following equation is balanced, what is the coefficient of $Mg(OH)_2$?

$$(NH_4)_2SO_4 + Mg(OH)_2 \rightarrow NH_3 + H_2O + MgSO_4$$

    A. 1
    B. 2
    C. 3
    D. 4

A is correct.

The balanced equation is: $(NH_4)_2SO_4 + Mg(OH)_2 \rightarrow 2NH_3 + 2H_2O + MgSO_4$

Passage 7
(Questions 47–52)

Radio waves carry information by varying a combination of the amplitude, frequency and phase of the wave within a frequency band. The radio waves which carry information in a standard broadcast are an example of electromagnetic radiation. These waves are disturbance, not of a material medium, but of electric and magnetic fields. In linearly polarized wave, the electric field points perpendicular to propagation of the wave although its magnitude varies in space and time. The magnetic field points in a direction perpendicular to the wave propagation and to electric field, and two fields propagate in phase.

The electromagnetic radiation is generated by an antenna, which is a metal rod that points perpendicular to the wave propagation. An alternating current is generated in the antenna, whose frequency is the same as the radiation produced. The electric field of the resulting electromagnetic radiation points along the same axis as the current.

The electric field of the electromagnetic radiation encounters electrons on the receiving antenna, which is also a metal rod. The electric field creates a current along the receiving antenna. Transmission and reception can be enhanced by having the length of the antenna one quarter of the wavelength of the electromagnetic wave.

The following questions refer to a transmitting antenna which points vertically and a receiving antenna which points directly to the north. The speed of light (c) is 3×10^8 m/s.

47. According to the passage, what is the best orientation of the receiving antenna?

A. any orientation   **C. vertical**
B. east/west   **D.** north/south to point towards the transmitting antenna

C is correct.

The electric field points vertically (up/down), therefore the force on electrons in the antenna is also vertical (up/down). The electrons must move in this direction (up/down) for an alternating current to be established. Therefore, the orientation of the receiving antenna should be vertical (up/down).

The mechanical vibrations of sound are able to travel through all forms of matter (e.g. gas, liquid, solid and plasma) but cannot travel though a vacuum. The medium is the matter that supports the mechanical vibrations associated with sound.

Sound is transmitted through the medium as longitudinal waves (i.e. compression waves). However, through solids, sound can also be transmitted as transverse waves. Longitudinal sound waves are waves of alternating pressure deviations from the equilibrium pressure, causing local regions of compression. Transverse waves (in solids) are waves of alternating shear stress at the right angle to the direction of propagation.

Matter in the medium is periodically displaced by a sound wave, and thus oscillates. The energy carried by the sound wave converts back and forth between the potential energy of the extra compression (in case of longitudinal waves) or lateral displacement strain (in case of transverse waves) of the matter and the kinetic energy of the oscillations of the medium.

48. According to the passage, what is the reasonable length for an efficient antenna when the frequency of the alternating current in the transmitting antenna is 10^7 Hz?

   A. 150 m   **B.** 75 m   **C.** 30 m   **D. 7.5 m**

D is correct.

The frequency (f) of radiation equals frequency of alternating current (10^7 Hz).

Wavelength of radiation: $\lambda = c / f$

$\lambda = (3 \times 10^8$ m/s$) / (10^7$ Hz$) = 30$ m.

From the passage, a quarter-wave antenna: $(30$ m $\times 0.25) = 7.5$ m.

49. Which of the following statements is the best description of energy flow between two antennas?

   A. kinetic to electromagnetic to kinetic
   B. electrical to electromagnetic to electrical
   C. electromagnetic to electrical to electromagnetic
   D. mechanical to electromagnetic to mechanical

B is correct.

The energy starts as electrical, converted to electromagnetic and then to electrical.

Electric energy is energy newly derived from electrical potential energy. When loosely used to describe energy absorbed or delivered by an electrical circuit, "electrical energy" is the energy converted from electrical potential energy. This energy is supplied by the combination of electric current and electrical potential that is delivered by the circuit. At the point that this electrical potential energy has been converted to another type of energy, it ceases to be electrical potential energy. Therefore, all electrical energy is potential energy before it is delivered to the end-use. Once converted from potential energy, electrical energy can always be described as another type of energy (heat, light, motion, etc.).

Electromagnetic radiation (EMR) is a form of energy emitted and absorbed by charged particles and acts as a wave when it travels through space. EMR has both electric and magnetic field components, (in a fixed ratio of intensity to each other) which oscillate in phase perpendicular to each other and perpendicular to the direction of energy and wave propagation. In a vacuum, electromagnetic radiation propagates at the speed of light.

Electromagnetic radiation is a particular form of the more general electromagnetic field (EM field) which is produced by moving charges. EMR is produced when charged particles are accelerated by forces acting on them. Electrons are responsible for emission of most EMR because they have low mass, and are easily accelerated by a variety of mechanisms.

50. What is the direction of the electric field vector of the radiation for a point between the two antennas referenced in the passage?

A. east / west   C. north / south

B. up / down   D. north / south and east / west

B is correct.

According to passage, the electric field of the resulting electromagnetic radiation points along the same axis as the current. A vertical antenna carries vertical current, therefore the electric field is vertical and the electric field vector is up / down.

The *polarization* of an antenna is the orientation of the electric field of the radio wave with respect to the Earth's surface and is determined by the physical structure of the antenna and by its orientation. Polarization is the sum of the electric field orientations projected onto an imaginary plane perpendicular to the direction of motion of the radio wave. It is important that linearly polarized antennas be matched or the strength of the received signal is greatly reduced. So horizontal antennae should be used with horizontal waves and vertical antennae be used with vertical waves.

Polarization is a property of waves that can oscillate with more than one orientation. Electromagnetic waves (e.g. light and gravitational waves) exhibit polarization. Sound waves in a gas or liquid do not have polarization because the medium vibrates only along the direction in which the waves are travelling.

51. According to the passage, how is a current on the receiving antenna created by the electric field?

A. electrons are promoted to higher energy orbitals by the electric field

B. resistance of antenna is changed by the electric field

C. electrons are polarized by the electric field

D. force on electrons is exerted by the electric field

D is correct.

Electric field exerts a force on electrons because the force creates the current.

Electrons are not promoted to higher energy orbitals because electrons are not bound to individual atoms.

The electric field is a vector field (SI units of newtons per coulomb (N C^{-1}) or, volts per meter (V m^{-1}). The SI base units of the electric field are kg·m·s^{-3}·A^{-1}. The strength (i.e. magnitude) of the field at a given point is defined as the force that would be exerted on a positive test charge of 1 coulomb placed at that point; the direction of the field is given by the direction of that force.

The direction of the electric field is the same as the direction of the force it would exert on a positively charged particle, and opposite the direction of the force on a negatively charged particle. Since like charges repel and opposites attract, the electric field is directed away from positive charges and towards negative charges.

52. What is the direction of the magnetic field vector of the radiation for a point between the two antennas referenced in the passage?

   A. east / west   **C.** north / south
   B. up / down   **D.** north / south or east / west

A is correct.

The magnetic field is perpendicular to the direction of wave propagation (i.e. north/south) and magnetic field is perpendicular to direction of electric field (i.e. up/down). Therefore, the magnetic field points east/west.

A magnetic field is a mathematical description of the magnetic influence of electric currents and magnetic materials. The magnetic field at any given point is specified by both a direction and a magnitude (or strength); as such it is a vector field. The magnetic field can be defined in several equivalent ways based on the effects it has on its environment. Often the magnetic field is defined by the force it exerts on a moving charged particle (Lorentz force). Alternatively, the magnetic field can be defined in terms of the torque it produces on a magnetic dipole

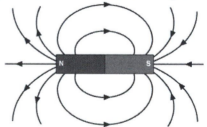

Magnetic fields are produced by moving electric charges and the intrinsic magnetic moments of elementary particles associated with a fundamental quantum property, their spin.

Magnetic field of an ideal cylindrical magnet

> Questions 53 through 59 are not based on any descriptive passage and are independent of each other

53. Which compound consists of only carbon and hydrogen?

A. carbohydrate   **B. hydrocarbon**   C. homolog   D. isomer

B is correct.

54. Which of the following statements is correct about naturally occurring monosaccharides?

A. The ratio of L and D-isomers varies widely depending on the source
B. The L and D-isomers occur in equal ratios
C. The D-isomers predominate
D. The L-isomers predominate

C is correct.

The 'D-' and 'L-' prefixes are used for monosaccharides to distinguish two particular stereoisomers that are mirror-images of each other.

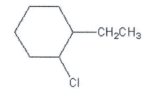

D-Glucose   L-Glucose

55. The following structure's IUPAC name is:

A. 2-chloro-1-ethylcyclohexane
B. Chloro-ethylcyclohexane
C. 1-chloro-2-ethylcyclohexane
D. 2-ethyl-l-chlorohexane

C is correct.

56. Which of the following is true for a reducing sugar?

A. It can reduce Cu^{2+} but not Ag^+ C. It contains a b(1→1) link
B. It has an acetal group   **D. It has a hemiacetal group**

D is correct.

A sugar can be classified as a reducing sugar only if it has a free hemiacetal group or an open-chain form with an aldehyde group. A reducing sugar is any sugar that either has an aldehyde group or is able to form one via isomerism. The aldehyde functional group allows the sugar to act as a reducing agent.

57. Which amino acid, unlike all others, does NOT contain a chiral carbon?

   A. Histidine   **B. Glycine**   **C.** Cysteine   **D.** Phenylalanine

B is correct.

58. Which of the following terms is used to describe the structure of the cell membrane?

   A. mosaic model   **C.** fluid model
   B. diffusion model   **D. fluid mosaic phospholipid bilayer model**

D is correct.

Cell membranes consists primarily of two thin layers (bilayer) of amphipathic phospholipids which spontaneously arrange so that the hydrophobic "tails" are isolated from the surrounding fluid, while the hydrophilic "heads" associate with the intracellular and extracellular surfaces of the bilayer. This arrangement forms a continuous spherical lipid bilayer which prevents polar solutes (e.g. amino acids, nucleic acids, carbohydrates, proteins, ions) from diffusing across the membrane, while allowing the passive diffusion of hydrophobic molecules. This membrane structure allows the cell to control the transport of these substances through transmembrane protein complexes (e.g. pores, channels and gates).

59. Which of the following molecules is a ketone?

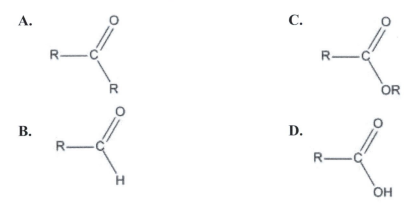

A is correct.

CHEMICAL & PHYSICAL FOUNDATIONS OF BIOLOGICAL SYSTEMS
MCAT® PRACTICE TEST #2 ANSWER KEY

Passage 1
1 : C
2 : B
3 : A
4 : D
5 : D
6 : A

Passage 2
7 : C
8 : C
9 : B
10 : A
11 : D

Independent questions
12 : B
13 : C
14 : C
15 : A

Passage 3
16 : D
17 : A
18 : B
19 : C
20 : C
21 : A
22 : D

Passage 4
23 : C
24 : B
25 : C
26 : A
27 : B

Independent questions
28 : A
29 : D
30 : A
31 : B
32 : A

Passage 5
33 : D
34 : A
35 : C
36 : B
37 : C
38 : D

Passage 6
39 : D
40 : A
41 : B
42 : C
43 : D

Independent questions
44 : B
45 : C
46 : C
47 : B

Passage 7
48 : B
49 : A
50 : B
51 : B
52 : C

Independent questions
53 : D
54 : C
55 : A
56 : B
57 : B
58 : B
59 : A

Passage 1
(Questions 1–6)

The combustion of fuel occurs with an oxidizer (usually air) in a combustion chamber of an internal combustion engine. The expansion of high temperature and pressure gases, produced by combustion, directly applies force to a movable component of the engine generating useful mechanical energy. Internal combustion engines form carbon monoxide (CO) and oxides of nitrogen including nitrogen monoxide (NO) and nitrogen dioxide (NO_2). These gases enter the atmosphere and undergo several reactions.

NO is a colorless gas which spontaneously reacts with oxygen forming NO_2. NO_2 is a reddish-brown gas and can react with H_2O to form nitric acid (HNO_3) which causes increased rain acidity. At low temperatures NO_2 molecules dimerize forming dinitrogen tetroxide (N_2O_4) molecules.

NO_2 and CO also react in the atmosphere in the following reaction:

$$NO_2(g) + CO(g) \rightarrow NO(g) + CO_2(g)$$

Reaction 1

The reaction mechanism involves two steps:

$$(1a) \quad NO_2(g) + NO_2(g) \rightarrow NO_3(g) + NO(g) \quad \textit{slow step}$$

$$(1b) \quad NO_3(g) + CO(g) \rightarrow NO_2(g) + CO_2(g) \quad \textit{fast step}$$

The Earth's atmosphere (stratosphere) contains an ozone (O_3) layer at relatively high concentrations which absorbs 93-99% of the sun's high frequency ultraviolet light. Ozone is created is by ultraviolet light striking oxygen molecules (O_2), and splitting them into atomic oxygen (O) which combines with O_2 to create ozone, O_3.

NO and CO gases are ozone-depleting compounds. Before NO and CO gases entered the atmosphere and reacted with ozone, the ozone level was in equilibrium maintained by a photochemical process. Self-propagating chain reactions disrupt the dynamics of the ozone layer by the mechanism below:

$$(2a) \quad NO(g) + O_3(g) \rightarrow NO_2(g) + O_2(g)$$

$$(2b) \quad NO_2(g) + O(g) \rightarrow NO(g) + O_2(g)$$

Net reaction:

$$O_3(g) + O(g) \rightarrow 2\ O_2(g)$$

Reaction 2

1. For ozone to be maintained in dynamic equilibrium, what must be true about the rate of the ozone-depleting process?

   A. equal to zero

   B. less than rate of ozone formation

   C. equal to rate of ozone formation

   D. greater than rate of ozone formation

C is correct.

Dynamic equilibrium exists when formation and destruction reactions are still occurring, so the rate is not equal to zero. In dynamic equilibrium, there is no net change in the amount of ozone and the rate of ozone formation equals the rate ozone destruction.

2. The ozone-depleting reactions described in the passage are noxious because the destructive chemical:

   A. is more reactive than ozone

   B. is repeatedly regenerated

   C. is produced in large quantities

   D. diffuses into stratosphere with ozone layer

B is correct.

Each NO molecule shown in both steps of Reaction 2 is regenerated from a reaction with ozone.

Therefore, NO is a repeatedly regenerated (e.g. catalyst) because there is no net change (loss or gain) during the reaction.

3. Which of the following is a true statement about the mechanism of Reaction 1?

   A. step 1a determines the overall rate of reaction

   B. step 1b is the rate-limiting step of reaction

   C. adding catalyst increases activation energy of reaction

   D. NO is an intermediate and not final reaction product

A is correct.

B: the rate-determining step is always the slowest step, so step 1a determines the overall rate of the reaction.

C: catalysts lower the activation energy.

D: NO is the product, not the reactant consumed in Step 1b and therefore not an intermediate. NO_3 is an intermediate in Reaction 1.

4. After adding more $NO_2(g)$ to Reaction 1:

   A. equilibrium constant decreases

   B. equilibrium constant increases

   C. reaction proceeds in the reverse direction

   D. reaction proceeds in the forward direction

D is correct.

The equilibrium constant (K) changes when the reaction temperature changes.

From the LeChatelier principle, adding more reactant (left side of equation) shifts the reaction towards products (right side of equation).

5. A 1 L vessel at 400°C contains the following equilibrium concentrations: $[NO] = 0.2$ M, $[CO_2] = 0.04$ M, $[NO_2] = 0.01$ M and $[CO] = 0.2$ M. What is the equilibrium constant of Reaction 1?

   A. 0.5   **B.** 1.0   **C.** 2.0   **D. 4.0**

D is correct.

For Reaction 1, the equilibrium expression: $K = [NO][CO_2] / ([NO_2][CO])$

Substituting known reactants' concentrations:

$K = [(0.2)(0.04)] / [(0.01)(0.2)]$

$= (0.008) / (0.002) = 4$

6. Which of the following is necessary for maintaining the ozone layer in absence of ozone depleting chemicals?

   A. electromagnetic radiation
   B. atmospheric pressure
   C. nitrogen oxides
   D. water vapor

A is correct.

From the passage, photochemical processes were responsible for maintaining ozone levels.

Photochemistry, a sub-discipline of chemistry, studies the interactions between atoms, small molecules, electromagnetic radiation and the effects of light on chemical reactions.

Passage 2
(Questions 7–11)

The speed of longitudinal waves (e.g. sound waves) through a fluid medium is expressed as:

$$v = \sqrt{\frac{\beta}{\rho}}$$

Equation 1

where B is bulk modulus and ρ is density of medium.

The formula for the speed of longitudinal waves moving through a solid is the same as for waves moving through fluid medium, except B is replaced by Young's modulus (Y). At constant temperature, an increased pressure of fluid medium results in a decreased volume. The bulk modulus is the ratio that describes this effect:

$$B = \frac{F/A}{\Delta V/V_0}$$

Equation 2

where F/A is external pressure, ΔV is the change in volume of the medium and V_0 is initial volume.

Because increased pressure always results in decreased volume, a minus sign is required for B to be positive. Fluids with a higher bulk modulus are less affected by changes in external pressure than fluids with a lower bulk modulus.

The Young's modulus of a solid expressed by the same ratio as for bulk modulus of fluids, except the denominator is replaced by $\Delta L/L_0$, where L is length of solid.

Material	Modulus (N/m^2)	Density (kg/m^3)
Air	$B = 1.4 \times 10^5$	1.2
Water	$B = 2.2 \times 10^9$	1,000
Aluminum	$Y = 7.0 \times 10^{10}$	2,700
Copper	$Y = 1.4 \times 10^{11}$	8,900
Lead	$Y = 1.6 \times 10^{10}$	11,340
Gold	$Y = 7.8 \times 10^{10}$	19,300

at 23°C and 1 atm

Table 1. Moduli and densities for various materials

7. From Equation 1 and Table 1, the speed of sound through water is approximately 1,500 m/s. What is the wavelength of a 50-kHz sound wave emitted by a humpback whale underwater?

A. 0.3 cm   **B.** 1.5 cm   **C. 3.0 cm**   **D.** 15.0 cm

C is correct.

Using $\lambda f = v$:
$$\lambda = v/f$$
$$= (1{,}500 \text{ m/s}) / (50{,}000 \text{ Hz})$$
$$= 0.03 \text{ m}$$
$$= 3.0 \times 10^{-2}$$
$$= 3 \text{cm}$$

8. What is the ratio of thr speed of sound moving through gold to the speed of sound moving through water?

    A. 0.0135   **B.** 0.135   **C.** 1.35   **D.** 13.3

C is correct.

Use Equation 1 and set the ratio:

$$\frac{v_{Au}}{v_{H_2O}} = \sqrt{\frac{Y_{Au}}{B_{H_2O}} \cdot \frac{\rho_{H_2O}}{\rho_{Au}}} \sqrt{\frac{7.8 \times 10^{10}}{2.2 \times 10^9} \cdot \frac{1000}{19{,}300}}$$

$$\frac{v_{Au}}{v_{H_2O}} = \sqrt{\frac{78 \times 10^9}{2.2 \times 10^9} \cdot \frac{1000}{19{,}300}}$$

$$\frac{v_{Au}}{v_{H_2O}} = \sqrt{\frac{78}{2.2} \cdot \frac{10}{193}}$$

$$\frac{v_{Au}}{v_{H_2O}} = \sqrt{\frac{780}{424.6}} = \sqrt{1.84} \qquad \frac{v_{Au}}{v_{H_2O}} = 1.35$$

9. At 0°C and 1 atm, the speed of sound in hydrogen gas is four times greater than the speed of sound in air. What is the reason for this difference between the speeds of sound in these two mediums?

    A. H_2 gas is significantly more compressible than air

    B. H_2 molecules have a lower mass and therefore move faster when subjected to sound wave

    C. H_2 molecules experience smaller London dispersion forces than N_2 and O_2

    D. H_2 gas is denser than air at STP (standard temperature and pressure)

B is correct.

The speed of sound through an ideal diatomic gas is expressed by the equation:

$$v = \sqrt{1.4 \, RT/M}$$

where R is gas constant, T is absolute temperature and M is molecular mass.

Assuming the diatomic gases hydrogen (H_2) and air (N_2 and O_2) are ideal, the difference in v (speed) is due to difference in M (mass):

v is inversely proportional to $\sqrt{M}$.

Since the molecular mass of H_2 is about 16 times less than the molecular mass of the air, sound travels $\sqrt{16} = 4$ times faster through H_2 than through air.

A: The statement that H_2 gas is significantly more compressible than air is incorrect because H_2 gas and air are similarly compressible (have similar bulk moduli).   Even if true, this answer choice would not explain why sound travels at a higher speed through H_2 than through air.

D: The statement that H_2 gas is denser than air at STP is incorrect because air consists mostly of N_2 and O_2 and both have greater molecular mass than H_2.

10. If a block of aluminum with volume (V_0) is taken to an underwater depth (d) of greater than 1,000 m, ρ is density of the water and B is the bulk modulus of aluminum, which of the following expressions describes the change in volume of the block?

A. $\dfrac{V_0\rho gd}{B}$ **B.** $\dfrac{V_0}{B\rho gd}$ **C.** $\dfrac{B\rho gd}{V_0}$ **D.** $\dfrac{B}{V_0\rho gd}$

A is correct.

From Equation 2, $F/A = P = \rho gd$

Use hydrostatic gauge pressure & ignore atmospheric pressure because at depths > 1000 m atmospheric pressure is < 1% of total pressure.

This expression simplifies to:
$$\frac{\Delta V}{V_0} = \frac{P}{B} \qquad\qquad \Delta V = \frac{V_0 P}{B} = \frac{V_0 \rho gd}{B}$$

11. In vulcanized rubber, the speed of sound is 45 m/s. How long does it take for a 650 Hz sound wave to pass through a 0.50 m cube of vulcanized rubber?

  A. 0.45 ms   **B.** 4.5 ms   **C.** 9.3 ms   **D. 11.1 ms**

D is correct.

Using $d = vt$, $t = d/v$
$$
\begin{aligned}
&= (0.5\ \text{m}) / (45\ \text{m/s}) \\
&= (5/450) = 1/90 \\
&= 0.011\ \text{s} \\
&= 11.1\ \text{ms}
\end{aligned}
$$

Questions 12 through 15 are not based on any descriptive passage and are independent of each other

12.

In a physics experiment, carts run along a level frictionless one-dimensional track. Cart A is 2 kg and cart B is 3 kg.

Initially cart A moves to the right at 0.4 m/s, and cart B moves to the left at 0.5 m/s. After cart A & B collide, they stick together.

Note: movement to the right is positive while movement to the left is denoted as negative.

Before collision, what is the total momentum of the system?

  A. 0.7 kg m/s   **B.** –0.7 kg m/s   **C.** 2.3 kg m/s   **D.** –2.3 kg m/s

B is correct.

The observation that, after collision, two objects stick together indicates conservation of momentum.

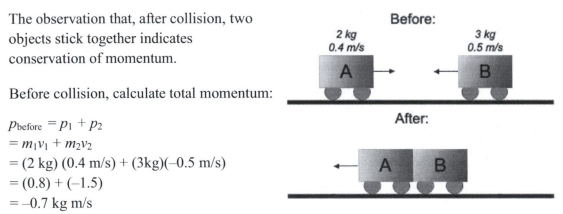

Before collision, calculate total momentum:

$p_{before} = p_1 + p_2$
$= m_1 v_1 + m_2 v_2$
$= (2 \text{ kg}) (0.4 \text{ m/s}) + (3 \text{kg})(-0.5 \text{ m/s})$
$= (0.8) + (-1.5)$
$= -0.7 \text{ kg m/s}$

where negative sign indicates momentum vector points left.

13. From question 12, what is the magnitude of the final velocity of the two carts?

  A. 3.5 m/s   **B.** 7.14 m/s   **C.** –0.14 m/s   **D.** –1.6 m/s

C is correct.

The external forces (gravity and the normal force) are balanced, so momentum is conserved. Therefore, momentum before the collision is equal to the momentum after the collision:

$p_{before} = p_{after},$
$-0.7 \text{ kg m/s} = (5 \text{kg}) v_f$
$v_f = (-0.7 \text{ kg m/s}) / 5 \text{ kg} = -0.14 \text{ m/s}$

where negative sign indicates velocity vector points left.

14. A hoisting mechanism pulls a 1,000 kg block on wheels at a slow speed up the hill with an incline Ø = 40°. The block starts at ground level, and the hoisting mechanism exerts a power 3,000 Watts, for 100 seconds, where g = 10 m/s^2.

With no friction and 100% efficiency, what is the height above horizontal that the mechanism pulls the block to?

    A. 10 meters   **B.** 20 meters   **C. 30 meters**   **D.** 40 meters

C is correct.

Energy expended: $\Delta E = P\Delta t$.

ΔE equals the increase of potential energy of the block because no heat is lost to friction and the system is 100% efficient.

Setting $P\Delta t = mgh$

    (3,000W)(100s) = (1,000kg)(10m/s^2)(h)
    (300,000) = 10,000 (h)
    h = 300,000 / 10,000 = 30/1 = 30 m.

Note that the 40° angle is not used to calculate the answer.

15. Which type of energy flow is the most efficient?

    A. electric energy to potential energy   **C. potential energy to kinetic energy**
    B. electric energy to kinetic energy   **D.** potential energy to electric energy

C is correct.

Potential energy ($PE = mgh$) is based on position, kinetic energy ($KE = \frac{1}{2} mv^2$) is based on motion.

The transformation of energy between different forms (e.g. electrical energy into potential or kinetic into potential and such) occurs with different efficiencies. How efficiently energy can be converted into other forms of energy via work and heat is subject to the second law of thermodynamics (i.e. entropy of an isolated system never decreases). The transformations of energy are often determined by entropy (i.e. measurement of disorder).

An example for this concept is a pendulum. The PE of the pendulum is greatest as its highest points (i.e. KE is zero) while its KE is maximum at its lowest point (i.e. PE is lowest). Ignoring air friction, the conversion of energy (PE ↔ KE) for a pendulum between these processes is perfect and the pendulum swings forever. Energy is transferred from PE ↔ KE (i.e. conservation of energy). In a closed system, energy can neither be created nor destroyed whereby the initial and final energies are equal.

Passage 3
(Questions 16–22)

The rate of reaction for reactants (starting material) or products in a particular reaction is defined as how fast the reaction takes place. Several laboratory techniques are used to determine the order of a reaction. The rate-determining step, not the overall equation, is necessary to predict the rate of the reaction.

For example, the following reaction occurs in three steps:

$$A + D \rightarrow F + G$$

Step 1 (*slow*)	$A \rightarrow B + C$
Step 2 (*fast*)	$B + D \rightarrow E + F$
Step 3 (*fast*)	$C + E \rightarrow G$

Reaction 1

In the reaction pathway above, the rate-determining step is the first step. Therefore, the overall reaction rate equals the rate of the first step, $k_1 [A]$, where k is rate constant. Rate constants are denoted as k_x, where *x* is step number.

Sometimes it is preferable to measure the rate of a reaction relative to one reactant or product. For second-order reaction, excess of one reactant is included in the reaction mixture. A pseudo first-order reaction is when only a small portion of excess reactant is consumed and its relative concentration remains constant. To analyze enzyme activity, a new rate constant k′ equals the product of the original rate constant k, and concentration of reactant in excess.

The reaction rate may depend on the concentration of the intermediates and is common if the rate-determining step is not the first step. In this case, the concentration of intermediates must be derived from the equilibrium constant of the preceding step.

In electrochemistry, the Nernst equation can be used (in conjunction with other information) to determine the equilibrium reduction potential of a half-cell in an electrochemical cell. For redox reactions at equilibrium, the reaction rate is proportional to voltage produced by two half-cells as expressed by equation:

$$E = E°_{tot} - (RT/zF) \ln([C]^c[D]^d / [A]^a[B]^b)$$

Equation 1

where, T = absolute temperature, R = 8.314 J/K·mol, z = # electrons transferred and F = 9.6485 x 10^4 C/mol.

16. Which of the following expressions is true for the reaction at equilibrium?

I. $E = E°$ II. $k_1/k_{-1} = 1$ **III. $\ln([C]^c[D]^d/[A]^a[B]^b) = zFE°/RT$**

A. I only **B.** II only **C.** I and III only **D. III only**

D is correct.

Statement III is true at equilibrium when the voltage is zero because the forward and reverse reactions occur at equal rates. Rearrange the equation to find that the standard potential equals $(\ln([C]^c[D]^d/[A]^a[B]^b)$, rearranging the equation, $zFE°/RT$.

Statement I: $E = E°$ might be true under certain conditions but equilibrium is not such a condition. Standard potential is defined as the reaction potential under standard conditions. Under standard conditions, the concentrations of reactants and products equal one, so the expression simplifies. The natural log of one is zero, which leaves the reaction potential equal to standard potential. This statement is true at standard conditions, but not at equilibrium, unless equilibrium occurs under standard conditions.

Statement II: $k_1/k_{-1} = 1$ seems correct because the reaction is at equilibrium and the rate of the forward reaction equals the rate of the reverse reaction. But the reaction constant is only part of the reaction rate. k_1/k_{-1} will not equal one at equilibrium, unless [reactants] and [products] are equal at equilibrium and not all reactions satisfy such condition.

17. What would be the electromotive force of the galvanic cell of the following system at 298K?

$$Zn(s)|Zn^{2+}(0.2M)\|Cu^{2+}(0.02M)|Cu(s)$$
$$E°_{cell} = +1.10V$$

A. 1.07V **B.** 1.13V **C.** 1.10V **D.** 0.05V

A is correct.

The Galvanic cell, named after Luigi Galvani, is a part of a battery consisting of an electrochemical cell with two different metals connected by a salt bridge (or porous disk) between the individual half-cells. Galvanic cells are also called Voltaic cells.

From Equation 1, cell potential (E) equals the standard cell potential ($E°$) minus the product of RT/zF times ln (natural log) [products] / [reactants].

The term $([C]^c[D]^d/[A]^a[B]^b)$ is defined as Q (mass action expression), where [reactants] and [products] are raised to a power equal to their stoichiometric coefficients in the balanced reaction equation.

The balanced reaction equation for the cell is as follows:

$$Cu^{2+}(aq) + Zn(s) \rightarrow Zn^{2+}(aq) + Cu(s)$$

Copper is reduced and zinc is oxidized because the standard cell potential is positive (+1.10V). A positive cell potential indicated a spontaneous reaction and the cell must be galvanic.

In galvanic cells, the anode undergoes oxidation (loss of electrons) and the cathode undergoes reduction (gain of electrons). Zn is oxidized (anode) and Cu is reduced (cathode).

From Equation 1, $E = +1.10 - [(8.314 \times 298) / (2 \times 96485)]$ ln ($[Zn^{2+}] / [Cu^{2+}]$).

$Zn(s)$ and $Cu(s)$ are part of the equation because solids have a molar concentration of 1.

Also z = 2 because electrons are exchanged in the reaction.

The ln (natural log) of 0.2/0.02 = 2.3, so the equation can be simplified to:

$E = +1.10 - [(8.314 \times 298) / (2 \times 96485)] \times 2.3$

$E = +1.07V$

To minimize calculations, the standard cell potential, +1.10, corresponds to $1M$ for $[Zn^{2+}]$ and $[Cu^{2+}]$.

The cell potential equals the standard cell potential, since RT/zF ln $[Zn^{2+}] / [Cu^{2+}] = 0$.

With $[Zn^{2+}]$ of $0.2M$ and $[Cu^{2+}]$ $0.02M$, the term RT/zF ln $[Zn^{2+}]/[Cu^{2+}]$ is greater than zero. Since this term is subtracted from the standard cell potential, the actual cell potential must be lower than +1.10V.

B: 1.13V would be the correct answer if copper was oxidized and zinc was reduced.

C: 1.10V is the cell potential under standard conditions of 1 atm and 1 molar concentration but the reaction takes place under non-standard conditions.

Common usage of the word battery has evolved to include a single Galvanic cell, but the first batteries had many Galvanic cells.

A Galvanic cell is different from electrolytic cell, which decomposes chemical compounds by means of electrical energy.

18. To test the rate of Step 3 in Reaction 1, a solution containing concentration of 0.1 M of E and 50 M of C was prepared. After the reaction was 50% complete, the rate was calculated. If the reaction was pseudo first-order, the calculated rate will differ from the true rate by:

    A. 0.2%   **B. 0.1%**   **C.** 0.05%   **D.** 0.02%

B is correct.

For pseudo first-order reaction, the excess of reactant C is so large that its concentration is considered constant and the reaction is first-order reaction with respect to E.

However, the rate predicted will be slightly higher than the actual rate because the absolute concentration of C is slightly reduced.

[E] = 0.1 mol/l and [C] = 50 mol/l.

When the reaction is 50% complete, [E] = 0.05 mol/l and [C] = 49.95 mol/l.
The reaction rate = k (0.05)(49.95), not = k (0.05)(50) as predicted by pseudo first-order.

The % difference between these two rates equals the difference divided by true rate:
The difference = [(k)(0.05)(50)] –[(k)(0.05)(49.95)] / [(k)(0.05)(49.95)].
Cancel common terms and simplify, 0.05 /49.95, or approximately 0.001.

Multiply by 100% for a percent, correct answer is 0.1 percent.

19. Catalysts are effective in increasing the rate of a reaction because they:

    A. increase the value of equilibrium constant
    B. increase the energy of activated complex
    C. lower activation energy
    D. decrease the number of collisions between reactant molecules

C is correct.

Activation energy is the minimum energy needed for a reaction to occur. Catalysts are effective because they lower the activation energy of the reaction. More reactant molecules with sufficient kinetic energy collide and react with each other. An increase in number of colliding molecules results in a faster reaction.

In chemical equilibrium, the rate of forward reaction is equal to the rate of reverse reaction. If a catalyst is added to increase the rate of the forward reaction, the system adjusts so that the reverse rate increases to match the forward rate. A catalyst, therefore, does not affect the value of the equilibrium constant, but does affect the speed at which equilibrium is reached.

B: Increasing the energy of the activated complex is the same as increasing the activation energy of the reaction. An activated complex forms when reactant molecules interact. These molecules combine to form products, or dissociate into original reactants. Naturally, if the energy barrier to form this complex is higher, reactant molecules have difficulty overcoming the barrier to product formation. Therefore, an increase in energy of the activated complex decreases the rate of reaction.

20. The reaction of A and B is catalyzed by enzyme P. With P in large excess, concentrations of A and B produced the following initial results.

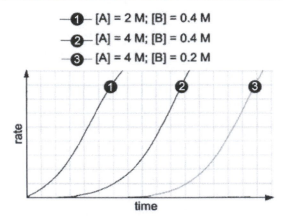

Which of the following rate expression best describes the reaction?

A. rate = $k'[A]^x$

B. rate = $k'[B]^y$

C. rate = $k'[A]^x[B]^y$

D. rate = $k'[A]^x[B]^y[P]^z$

C is correct.

Analyze the graph and determine if rate of reaction is proportional to concentration of A, or B, or both.

The rate of a reaction usually slows with increasing time because the reactants get depleted for product formation. However, in the graph above, this reaction is initially slow and rate increases with time. Lag period increases as A increases and B decreases which is opposite to expected because most reaction rates decrease as product formation increases.

The graph illustrates only a temporary lag period but not the ultimate rate of reaction. The length of the lag period is proportional to the ratio of A to B.

If the rate of reaction increase with a higher concentration of product, this suggests that product participates in the reaction. The more B present, the faster A reacts. Once the reaction gets started, more B is present and rate increases. At equal concentrations of B (curves 1 and 2), the reaction with higher concentration of A (curve 2) is slower to initiate because of lower relative concentration of B. It is unknown how A reacts with B but changing the concentration of either A or B affects the lag period and rate, so both must factor into the rate equation. Thus the best answer is rate = $k'[A]^x[B]^y$.

Exponents are X and Y because the actual effect of the two reactants on rate is unknown and accounts for a tentative, not an actual, rate equation.

C: the enzyme participates in the reaction, but because of its large excess the enzyme can be considered a constant and excluded from the rate equation. Therefore, $k[A]^x[B]^y[P]^z$ is incorrect.

Stoichiometry is the calculation of quantitative (measurable) relationships of the reactants and products in a balanced chemical reaction. It can be used to calculate quantities such as the amount of products that can be produced with the given reactants and percent yield.

21. In galvanic cells, what is the result of increasing the concentrations of reactants?

    A. both voltage and spontaneity increase
    B. voltage increases, while reaction spontaneity remains constant
    C. reaction rate increases, while voltage and reaction spontaneity remain constant
    D. reaction spontaneity increases, while the voltage remains constant

A is correct.

For reactions in galvanic (voltaic) cells, the oxidation reaction (anode) produces excess electrons. The reduction reaction (cathode) consumes electrons. For a continued reaction, cathode requires additional supplies of electrons. Two half-reactions result in a movement of electrons through the wire from anode to cathode. The faster the reaction rate, the greater the electrical force is, pushing electrons away from the anode and pulling them towards the cathode. This pressure on electrons is the electromotive force (EMF). EMF is measured in volts (voltage).

Voltage is different from current – voltage is pressure on electrons, while current is actual movement of electrons through wire. In addition to pressure exerted by EMF, the current also depends on the amount of resistance within the wire.

The voltage (or EMF) generated by a redox reaction depends on the number of electrons exchanged in the reaction and rate of reaction. A change in the rate of reaction results in change of the voltage (or potential). An increase in reactant concentration increases voltage because more electrons are produced (anode) and more electrons are consumed (cathode).

The spontaneity of a reaction is determined by Gibb's free energy (ΔG). There is a direct relationship between reaction potential and its free energy, expressed by the equation:

$$\Delta G = -nFE$$

where n is number of moles of electrons transferred in reaction, F is Faraday's constant and E is cell voltage. If ΔG is negative, the reaction is spontaneous; if ΔG is positive, the reaction is not spontaneous.

When reactant concentrations increase reaction rate increases, increasing flow of electrons and voltage and ΔG becomes more negative. As ΔG becomes more negative, the reaction becomes more spontaneous. Increased concentration of reactants increases both voltage and spontaneity of the reaction.

22. If Step 2 was the rate-determining step of Reaction 1, which of the following equations would be the correct expression for the rate?

    A. rate = k_1k_2 [D] / k_{-1}[C]   **C.** rate = k_1k_2 [A][D] / $k_{-1}k_{-2}$[C]
    B. rate = k_1k_2 [D] / $k_{-1}k_{-2}$[C]   **D. rate = k_1k_2 [A][D] / k_{-1}[C]**

D is correct.

The rate = k_2[B][D], where k_2 is rate constant of step 2.

[B] cannot be measured because it is an intermediate. But, from the passage, [B] can be calculated from the equilibrium constant (K_{eq}) of step 1.

Equilibrium constant for step 1: K_{eq} = [B][C] / [A], rearranging, [B] = K_{eq}[A] / [C].

Combining this expression with rate constant for step 2, rate = $k_1 k_2$ [A][D] / k_{-1}[C].

All answer choices are not expressed in terms of K_{eq} but as k_1, k_2 and k_{-1}; K_{eq} (step 1) = k_1; rate constant for reverse reaction: k_{-1}. Therefore, $K_{eq} = k_1 / k_{-1}$

Passage 4
(Questions 23–27)

A section of copper tubing has three cross sectional areas, A_1, A_2, A_3, which are decreasing in size. Fluid is moving through the tube at a constant rate. To measure hydrostatic pressure, narrow columns of identical diameter extend vertically from each of three sections of the tube.

Bernoulli's equation describes fluids in motion at the same elevation by the following equation:

$$P + \tfrac{1}{2}\rho v^2 = \text{constant}$$

where P is pressure, ρ is density and v is speed of the flow.

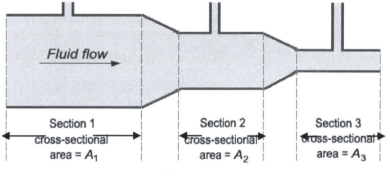

Figure 1.

Note: Assume the fluid flows in non-turbulent manner and the fluid is incomprehensible

23. If the ratio of A_1 to A_2 is tripled, then the v_1 to v_2 ratio of flow speeds will:

A. increase by a factor of 3
B. increase by a factor of 9
C. decrease by a factor of 3
D. decrease by a factor of 9

C is correct.

Flow rate: $f = Av$. Since flow rate is constant, from Bernoulli's equation:

$$A_1v_1 = A_2v_2, \text{ so } A_1/A_2 = v_2/v_1.$$

If A_1/A_2 increases by a factor of 3, then v_2/v_1 also increases by a factor of 3.

Therefore, the inverse ratio v_1/v_2 decreases by a factor of 3.

24. If the cross-sectional area of Section 2 is 12 cm^2 and the fluid is flowing through that section at a velocity of 10 cm/s, the velocity of the fluid flow in Section 1 with a cross-sectional area of 30 cm^2 will be:

A. 2 cm/s **B. 4 cm/s** **C.** 8 cm/s **D.** 10 cm/s

B is correct.

From Bernoulli's equation, flow rate through Section 1 equals flow rate through

Section 2: $f_1 = f_2$.

Since $f = Av$, $A_1v_1 = A_2v_2$.

Substituting values: $(30 \text{ cm}^2)v_1 = (12 \text{ cm}^2)(10 \text{ cm/s})$

$v_1 = 4$ cm/s.

25. Fluids A and B pass through Tubes 1 and 2 at equal rates of flow. The cross-sectional area of Tube 1 is greater than Tube 2. Which of the following would best explain the equal rate of flow?

    A. Fluid A has a greater viscosity than Fluid B
    B. Fluid A is less dense than Fluid B
    C. Fluid A has less velocity than Fluid B
    D. Fluid A has a greater vapor pressure than Fluid B

C is correct.

Tubes 1 and 2 carry equal flows ($f_1 = f_2$), therefore $A_1v_1 = A_2v_2$.

If $A_1 > A_2$, then $v_1 < v_2$.

26. Which of the following correctly describes the relationship of pressure readings from each cross-sectional area?

    A. $P_1 > P_2 > P_3$ **B.** $P_1 < P_2 < P_3$ **C.** $P_1 < P_2 = P_3$ **D.** $P_1 = P_2 < P_3$

A is correct.

From Figure 1, the tube narrows from Section 1 to Section 2, and from Section 2 to Section 3.

With a decrease in the tube cross-sectional area, the flow speed increases.

    $P + \frac{1}{2}\rho v^2 = $ constant.

Therefore, $v_1 < v_2 < v_3$ is consistent with Bernoulli's continuity equation.

As a constant, P and $\frac{1}{2}\rho v^2$ are inversely related. Since Bernoulli's equation predicts faster flow speed, inverse relationship implies lower fluid pressure, therefore $P_1 > P_2 > P_3$.

27. What is the pressure difference between Sections 1 and 3 if the fluid velocity in Section 1 is 0.4 m/s and in Section 3 it is 0.6 m/sec and the density is 1000 kg/m^3?

    A. 10 Pa   **B. 100 Pa**   **C.** 200 Pa   **D.** 1000 Pa

B is correct.

Applying Bernoulli's equation, $P_1 + \frac{1}{2} \rho v_1^2 = P_3 + \frac{1}{2} \rho v_3^2$

$$P_1 - P_3 = \frac{1}{2} \rho (v_3^2 - v_1^2)$$
$$= \frac{1}{2}(1000)[(0.6)^2 - (0.4)^2]$$
$$= \frac{1}{2}(1000)(0.2)$$
$$= 100 \text{ Pa}$$

Questions 28 through 32 are not based on any
descriptive passage and are independent of each other

---

28. A woman jumps from an airplane with a parachute. After an initial accelerating thrust, she falls at a constant speed (terminal velocity) in a straight vertical vector. Are the forces on the woman balanced during the latter portion of her fall?

   A. yes because she is falling at a constant velocity
   B. no because gravity is greater than drag force
   C. no because gravity is not balanced by other forces
   D. no because forces are balanced only for stationary objects

A is correct.

Newton's laws of motion are three physical laws that form the basis for classical mechanics.

1. Without a net external force, a body is either at rest or moves in a straight line with constant velocity.

2. Force is proportional to (mass) x (acceleration): $(F = ma)$. Alternatively, force is proportional to the time rate of change of momentum.

3. A first body exerts a force F on a second body and the second body exerts a force −F on the first body. F and −F are equal in magnitude and opposite in direction.

Newton's laws describe the relationship between forces acting on a body to the motion of the body. From the first law of motion, a force balance on an object implies it has a constant velocity. From this, the force of gravity and the drag force due to the air are exactly balanced.

In fluid dynamics, drag (air resistance or fluid resistance) refers to forces that oppose the relative motion of an object through a fluid (liquid or gas). Drag force acts in a direction opposite to the oncoming flow velocity. Unlike other resistive forces such as dry friction (independent of velocity), drag force depends on velocity.

29. When there is one force acting on an object, what can be concluded?

   A. object is moving in a straight line at a constant speed
   B. object is accelerating or decelerating
   C. object is moving ata constant speed but not necessarily in a straight line
   D. none of the above may be concluded

D is correct.

There must be a net force on the object because there is only one force and there are forces to be balanced. From first law of motion, the object is not undergoing uniform motion and the object is accelerating, decelerating or changing direction.
Therefore, none of the answers choices can be concluded.

30. Which one of these aqueous solutions has a pH greater than 7.0?

   A. 0.1 M KCN   **B.** 0.25 M HCN   **C.** 0.5 M NH_4Cl **D.** 1.0 M HClO

A is correct.

In addition to being highly poisonous, potassium cyanide is the salt of a strong base (potassium hydroxide) and a weak acid (hydrogen cyanide). When potassium hydroxide salt dissolves in water, the potassium ions do not react with water, but the cyanide ions pick up hydrogen ions from the water to establish an equilibrium with hydrocyanic acid resulting in the creation of excess hydroxide ions and a basic solution.

B: a weak acid.

C: is the salt of ammonia (a weak base) and hydrochloric acid (a strong acid). When dissolved in water, the chloride ion remains in solution, but the ammonium ion enters into a dissociation equilibrium with ammonia and hydrogen ion as products; the hydrogen ion concentration increases making the solution acidic.

D: is a weak acid, and while the solution would not be as acidic as in the case of an equal concentration of a strong acid, it would still be acidic.

31. A radio is producing 30 W of sound and the listener is 5 m away. What would be the intensity of sound energy at the listener's ear if the sound travels equally in all directions?

   A. 0.5 W/m^2 **B. 0.095 W/m^2**   **C.** 90 W/m^2 **D.** 9,000 W/m^2

B is correct.

The 30 W sound travels equally in all directions. If a listener is located 5 m from the sound source, imagine a sphere of a 5 m radius around the sound source.

The total surface area of the sphere is $4\pi r^2$. Since intensity is power per area, write:

$I = P / A$

$\quad = 30 \text{ W} / 4\pi \, (5\text{m})^2$

$\quad = 30 / 4 \times 3^* \times 25 \text{ W/m}^2$

$\quad = 30 / 300 = 0.1 \text{ W/m}^2$

*estimate $\pi \approx 3$

32. A massless meter stick is placed on a fulcrum at its 0.3 m mark. A 5 kg object is placed on the meter stick at its 0.2 m mark. An object of what mass must be placed at the 0.8 m mark to establish torque balance?

A. 1 kg   **B.** 2 kg   **C.** 5 kg   **D.** 10 kg

A is correct.

Figure below shows the forces on the meter stick.

For torque balance, the net force on the meter stick about fulcrum must be zero. Since the torque due to the force of the fulcrum is zero:

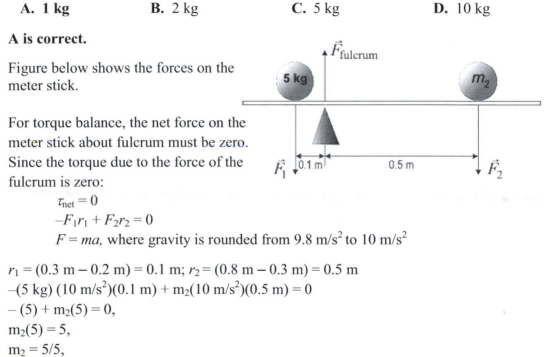

$\quad \tau_{net} = 0$

$\quad -F_1 r_1 + F_2 r_2 = 0$

$\quad F = ma$, where gravity is rounded from 9.8 m/s^2 to 10 m/s^2

$r_1 = (0.3 \text{ m} - 0.2 \text{ m}) = 0.1 \text{ m}$; $r_2 = (0.8 \text{ m} - 0.3 \text{ m}) = 0.5 \text{ m}$

$-(5 \text{ kg}) \, (10 \text{ m/s}^2)(0.1 \text{ m}) + m_2(10 \text{ m/s}^2)(0.5 \text{ m}) = 0$

$-(5) + m_2(5) = 0,$

$m_2(5) = 5,$

$m_2 = 5/5,$

$m_2 = 1.0 \text{ kg}$

Passage 5
(Questions 33–38)

The ideal gas law uses the following equation to describe the state of an ideal gas:

$$PV = nRT$$

where P is pressure, V is volume, n is number of moles of gas, R is the ideal gas constant, and T is the temperature of the gas.

The gas particles in a container are constantly moving at various speeds characterized by the Maxwell distribution shown in the figure below.

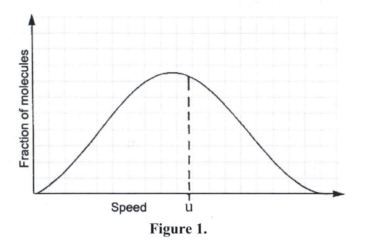

Figure 1.

When two particles collide, their velocities change. However, for a gas in thermal equilibrium, the velocity distribution of the gas as a whole remains unchanged.

The average kinetic energy (E) of the gas is:

$$E = (\tfrac{1}{2})mu^2$$

Equation 1

where m is mass of one particle and u is root mean square (rms) speed of gas particles.

$$u = [1/n(v_1^2 + v_2^2 + \ldots + v_n^2)]^{1/2}$$

Equation 2

where n is number of gas particles; rms is different than average speed.

For an ideal gas: $E = (3/2)\, nRT$

Equation 3

where n is number moles of gas.

Combining Equations 1 and 3:

$$u = (3RT/M)^{1/2}$$

Equation 4

where M is the molar mass of gas particles.

l is the mean free path (mfp) which is the average distance a particle travels between collisions. The mfp is expected to be larger for gases at a low pressure because of the greater space between gas particles and for gases where gas particles are small.

The following expression for the mfp supports these assumptions:

$$l = kT/(2^{(1/2)}\pi s^2 P)$$

Equation 5

where s is the atomic diameter (typically 10^{-8}), k is the Boltzmann constant and P is pressure.

In addition to colliding with each other, gas particles also collide with the container walls. If the container wall has a pinhole that is small compared to the mfp of the gas, and a pressure differential exists across the wall, gas particles escape (effusion) through the pinhole without affecting Maxwell's distribution.

The effusion rate is described by the equation:

$$dN_{eff}/dt = A(P-P_1) / (2\pi MRT)^{1/2}$$

Equation 6

where N_{eff} is the number of moles of effusing particles, A is the area of the pinhole, P and P_1 – pressure on the inside and outside of the container walls respectively, and $P > P_1$.

33. For a mixture of two noble gases, G_X and G_Y, which escape through the same pinhole, what is the relative rate of effusion?

A. 1   **B.** $P_Y (M_Y)^{1/2} / P_X (M_X)^{1/2}$ **C.** $A_Y (M_Y)^{1/2} / A_X (M_X)^{1/2}$ **D.** $(M_Y / M_X)^{1/2}$

D is correct.

Using the ratio of effusion rates for two gases, all the same factors cancel and remaining is the inverse of the square root of the masses.

Gases X and Y are mixed in the same container, at the same pressure (P) and effuse through the same pinhole with the same area (A), so P and A cancel from the equation.

A: the ratio of 1 would be the correct answer if G_X and G_Y had the same molar mass. For the two noble gases (G_X and G_Y), assume the two gases have different molar masses.

34. Which of the following conditions imply a shorter mean free path (mfp) of a gas?

   A. pressure of the gas is increased
   B. pressure of the gas is decreased
   C. number of gas particles per unit volume is decreased
   D. distance between collisions is increased

A is correct.

The mean free path (mfp) of a particle is the average distance the particle can travel before it collides with another gas particle or the wall of the container. The longer the distance that gas particles travel before colliding the greater the distance between the gas particles. With a fixed number of particles, the volume of gas must decrease to decrease mfp. Decreasing gas pressure results in increased volume.

An increase in pressure results in a decrease in volume along with mean free path. Decrease in mfp means that gas particles are closer together and collide more often.

Decreasing the number of gas particles per unit of volume decreases the likelihood of collision which implies greater mfp. This would also decrease the pressure because the number of particles per unit volume decreases.

35. For an ideal gas, the average kinetic energy can be directly related to:

A. Boltzmann constant   **C. temperature**
B. universal gas constant   D. rms speed

C is correct.

Equation 3 is the expression for the average kinetic energy (E) of an ideal gas.

Determine which factors are proportional to E.

D: the rms speed (u) cancels from the equation.

A and BBoltzmann constant (k) and universal gas constant (R) are the same for every value of E.

C: temperature is the only variable remaining.

In general, the temperature is a measure of average kinetic energy.

36. If a vessel contained the following gas mixture in equal amounts of NH_3, H_2, O_2 and Cl_2 and had a pinhole, which gas would have the highest rate of effusion?

A. NH_3 **B. H_2**   C. O_2 D. Cl_2

B is answer.

The hydrogen molecule (H_2) has the lowest molar mass and would have the highest rate of effusion.

From Equation 6, the rate of effusion depends on A (area) of the pinhole, P (pressure inside) and P_1 (pressure outside) of the container, M (molar mass of gas particles), R (gas constant) and T (temperature).

With all 4 gases mixed in one container, the difference among the gases is their molar mass. Since the rate of effusion is inversely proportional to the square root of the molar mass, the rate of effusion increases as molar mass decreases. Therefore, the particle with the least molar mass effuses at the highest rate.

Molecular hydrogen (H_2) has the lowest molar mass of the four gases mixed in the container and effuses at the greatest rate.

37. At 298K, which of the following gases will have the smallest rms speed?

A. N_2 **B.** O_2 **C. Cl_2**   **D.** CO_2

C is correct.

From Equation 4, u (rms speed) $= (3RT/M)^{1/2}$

u is proportional to $\sqrt{T}$ and $1/\sqrt{M}$. Since temperature is constant, consider the molar mass. Since u is proportional to $1/\sqrt{M}$, the gas with the greatest molar mass has the smallest rms speed. Chlorine, (Cl_2) has the greatest molar mass (71 g/mol) and is the correct answer. Oxygen (32 g/mol), carbon dioxide (44 g/mol) and nitrogen (28 g/mol) have greater rms than Cl_2.

38. Which of the following provides for a standard pressure and temperature?

A. 1 atm and 273 K   **C.** 760 mm Hg and 273 K

B. 760 Torr and 0°C   **D. All of the above**

D is correct.

Standard temperature is usually expressed in 2 different units: degrees Celsius (°C) and Kelvin (K).

Standard pressure is expressed in 3 different units: Torr, atmospheres (atm), and millimeters of mercury (mm Hg).

Knowing standard temperature and pressure in one set of units allows conversion into other standard units.

Conversion factors are not provided in this question.

To convert pressure units: 1 atm = 760 Torr = 760 mm Hg.

To convert temperature units from Celsius to Kelvin, add 273: 0°C = 273 K.

All values and units listed in the answers choices are correct.

Passage 6
(Questions 39–43)

A man stands on a scale at the surface of the Earth. The scale reading is the magnitude of the normal force which the scale exerts on the man. To a first approximation, there is a balance of forces and the magnitude of the gravitational force is the magnitude of the scale's force:

$$F_{grav} = \frac{GM_{Earth} m}{R_{Earth}^2}$$

Equation 1

where G is Newton's constant, M_E is the mass of Earth and R_E is the radius of Earth.

The force of gravity (F_{grav}) and the reading of the scale (g) is proportional and the mass (m) of object:

$$F_{grav} = mg$$

Equation 2

where g has the value $GM_E/R_E^2 = 9.8$ m/s^2.

There are several approximations made and to calculate the scale reading, idealizations need to be accounted for.

For example, consider the rotation of Earth. If a person is standing on a scale at the equator, there is a centripetal acceleration because he is moving in a circle. The scale will not give a reading equal to the force of gravity (Equation 1).

Because the Earth is not a perfect sphere, the distance from the center of the Earth to the equator is greater than the distance from the center of the Earth to a pole by about 0.1%.

Additionally, the contours of the Earth vary at different location so g would have to be measured at an exact location to determine an exact value of the effective acceleration due to gravity.

39. At the equator, if a man stood on a scale, how would the scale read compared to the reading for the same man standing on a non-rotating Earth?

A. the same as on a non-rotating Earth
B. depends on where the man is
C. greater than on a non-rotating Earth
D. **less than on a non-rotating Earth**

D is correct.

The scale would read less for the man on a rotating Earth than for the same man on a non-rotating Earth because the scale reading on a rotating Earth is less than the gravitational force.

40. Which of the following gives the best expression for the velocity of a man standing at the equator of a rotating Earth when T_{day} is the time of one rotation and equals 1 day?

A. $2\pi R_E/T_{day}$ **B.** $2\pi g T_{day}$ **C.** R_E/T_{day} **D.** $g T_{day}$

A is correct.

In 1 day the man travels a distance equal to the circumference of Earth:

$C = 2\pi R_E$ = distance.   Velocity = distance/time = $2\pi R_E/T_{day}$

41. How would the reading of the scale of a man standing at the South pole compare to the scale reading of the same man standing at the equator of an identical but not rotating Earth?

    A. readings would be the same
    B. reading at the South pole would be greater
    C. reading at the South pole would be less
    D. there is not enough information to answer this question

B is correct.

From the passage, the Earth is not a perfect sphere and the distance from the center of the Earth to the equator is greater than the distance from the center of the Earth to a pole by about 0.1%.

According to Newton's law of gravitation, when distance (denominator) decreases the gravitational force increases.

Rotation is a distracter in this question.

42. If the period of the man's motion is known, what variables are needed to calculate the centripetal force on him?

    A. radius of Earth   **C. mass of man and radius of Earth**
    B. velocity of man and radius of Earth   **D.** mass and velocity of man and radius of Earth

C is answer.

To calculate centripetal force, use equation: $F_{cent} = ma_{cent}$

The centripetal acceleration and mass of man are needed.

The centripetal acceleration $a_{cent} = v^2/R_E$ can be determined from radius and velocity of Earth.

The velocity of man can be calculated from the period and radius.

43. Which of the following force diagrams best describes a man standing on a scale at the equator of rotating Earth?

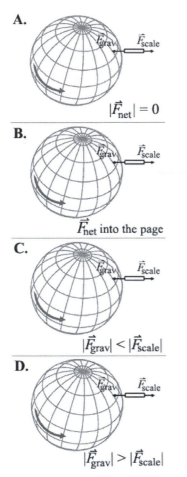

D is correct.

Since the man travels at a constant speed in a circle, both, his acceleration vector and net force vector, point towards the center of rotation. The magnitude of gravitational force must be greater than magnitude of force of scale for this to be true.

> Questions 44 through 47 are not based on any
> descriptive passage and are independent of each other

44. What will be the approximate pH after adding 0.7 moles NaOH to a buffer solution that contains 0.15 moles $NaNO_2$ and 1.5 moles HNO_2 with the initial pH of 2.4?

   A. 0.7   **B. 3.4**   **C.** 4.4   **D.** 5.4

B is correct.

Henderson-Hasselbach equation may be used to calculate the pH of a buffer solution where the pH of a buffer solution should be approximately equal to the pK_a of the acid plus the log of the amount of conjugate base to acid ratio:

$$pH = pK_a + \log \left(\frac{\text{[conjugate base]}}{\text{[undissociated acid]}} \right)$$

pK_a can be found by substituting in the pH and the values for the original solution.

$pK_a = 2.4 - \log (0.15 / 1.5) = 3.4$
The pK_a of nitrous acid 3.4, this is a constant and doesn't change.

After adding of 0.7 moles of NaOH, 0.7 moles of nitrous acid (HNO_2) is converted to 0.7 moles of nitrite ion ($NaNO_2$).

The new concentrations for both species is now a total of 0.8 moles of HNO_2 (1.5 – 0.7) and 0.85 moles of $NaNO_2$ (0.15 + 0.7).

Using the new values in the equation with the pK_a found to be 3.4, solve for the new pH.

$pH = 3.4 + \log (0.85 / 0.80) = 3.4$.

In a buffer solution the concentrations of the weak acid and its conjugate base are approximately the same and the pH is equal to the pK_a.

45. A calorimeter consisting of two nested Styrofoam cups with a lid is used to measure energy. What is the primary purpose of using two Styrofoam cups?

   A. increase the heat capacity of the calorimeter by increasing its mass
   B. reduce the likelihood of the cups tipping over by increasing their mass
   C. reduce conduction through Styrofoam due to a thicker barrier
   D. reduce convection through Styrofoam due to a thicker barrier

C is correct.

Styrofoam creates an insulation barrier between the substance in the calorimeter and the environment. It seems reasonable that a thicker substance reduces conduction.

Conduction is heat (energy) transfer between molecules from a region of higher temperature (kinetic energy) to a region of lower temperature. Convection is the movement of molecules within fluids (liquids and gases). Convection through a single Styrofoam cup effectively equals zero because it requires some fluid to pass through the surface.

46. Two balls of 500 grams each move in opposite directions after an isolated collision. Ball 1 moves at 0.3 m/s in the negative x direction and Ball 2 moves at 0.6 m/s in the positive x direction. What was the total momentum of this system before the collision?

  A. –0.15 kg·m/s   **B.** –0.45 kg·m/s   **C. 0.15 kg·m/s**   **D.** 0.45 kg·m/s

C is correct.

Momentum is conserved in the collision.

The total momentum before the collision equals total momentum after the collision:

$$p' = m_1 v'_1 + m_2 v'_2$$
$$= (0.5)(-0.3) + (0.5)(0.6)$$
$$= (-0.15) + (0.3)$$
$$= 0.15 \text{ kg·m/s}$$

47. A white billiard ball with a mass of 250 g moves at 0.9 m/s, strikes a purple billiard ball, at rest, with a mass 200 g. After the collision, the white ball moves with a velocity of 0.5 m/s. What is the velocity of the purple ball after collision?

  A. 1.0 m/s   **B. 0.5 m/s**   **C.** 1.25 m/s   **D.** 0.75 m/s

B is correct.

Using conservation of momentum, where w = white ball, p = purple ball and prime denotes "after collision", the following expression applies:

$$p_{before} = p_{after}$$

$$\rightarrow m_w v_w = m_w v'_w + m_p v'_p$$

$$\rightarrow v'_p = \frac{m_w (v_w - v'_w)}{m_p} = \frac{250 (0.9 - 0.5)}{200}$$

$$\rightarrow v'_p = \frac{250 (0.4)}{200} = 0.5 \text{ m/s}$$

Passage 7
(Questions 48–52)

Ionic compounds are solids composed of ions with opposing charges held together by strong electrostatic attraction (ionic bonds). Typically, the positively charged portion consists of metal cations and the negatively charged portion is an anion or polyatomic ion. Ionic compounds are usually hard, brittle and have relatively high melting and boiling points.

In the solid phase, ionic compounds are poor conductors because there are no mobile ions or electrons present. However, in aqueous solutions or molten state, the mobile ions are free to conduct electric current. When dissolved in water, ionic compounds establish equilibrium between the solid phase and free ions. Low solubility ionic compounds are known as *slightly soluble salts*.

Ionic compounds dissolve in polar solvents, especially one that ionize (e.g. water, ionic liquids). They are typically more soluble in other polar solvents (e.g. alcohols, acetone, dimethyl sulfoxide). Ionic compounds usually do not dissolve in nonpolar solvents (e.g. diethyl ether or petrol). The conjugate acid of the strong base has no tendency to combine with a H_2O to produce an OH^- ion.

When the oppositely charged ions in the solid ionic compound are surrounded by the opposite pole of a polar molecule, the solid ions are pulled out of the lattice into the liquid. When this force is greater than the electrostatic attraction of the lattice, the ions dissolve in the liquid.

Reaction 1 illustrates the example when solid silver chloride enters the following equilibrium:

$$AgCl(s) \rightleftarrows Ag^+(aq) + Cl^-(aq)$$

Reaction 1

This dissolution of a salt is a thermodynamic process which depends on temperature. At 25° C, the solubility constant of AgCl is 1.8×10^{-10}.

Solvation, *dissolution* and *solubility* are related concepts though distinct from one another. Solvation is an interaction of a solute with the solvent and leads to stabilization of the solute species in the solution. Dissolution is a kinetic process quantified by its rate. Solubility quantifies the dynamic equilibrium state achieved when the rate of dissolution equals the rate of precipitation.

To identify an unknown slightly soluble salt an experiment is conducted. It is known that the salt forms a cation when it is dissolved in water. The cation is a weak acid which can therefore be titrated with a strong base. By adding aliquots of NaOH to an aqueous solution of the unknown salt, the following titration curve is obtained:

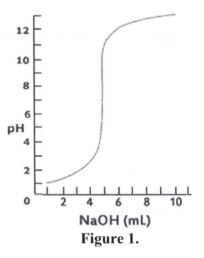

Figure 1.

According to the IUPAC (International Union of Pure and Applied Chemistry), an ionic compound's common name is written using two words. The name of the cation is first, the oxidation number in parentheses, followed by the name of the anion.

48. Which of the following statements is true, given that the K_{sp} of AgBr is 5.4×10^{-13}, and the K_{sp} of AgI is 8.5×10^{-17}?

    A. AgBr is less soluble than AgI
    B. AgBr is more soluble than AgI
    C. More energy is required for solvation of AgBr than of AgI
    D. The dissolution process of AgBr is more exothermic than that of AgI

B is correct.

The solubility equilibrium constant (K_{sp}) is directly related to solubility. Since the K_{sp} for AgBr is greater than for AgI ($10^{-13} > 10^{-17}$), AgBr is more soluble.

Solubility equilibrium is a *dynamic equilibrium* that exists when a chemical compound in the solid state is in chemical equilibrium with a solution of that compound. The solid may dissolve unchanged, with dissociation or with chemical reaction with another constituent of the solvent (e.g. acid or alkali). Each type of equilibrium is characterized by a temperature-dependent equilibrium constant.

Solubility equilibrium is considered as dynamic equilibrium because when some individual molecules move between the solid and solution phases the rates of dissolution and precipitation are equal. When equilibrium is established, the solution is called *saturated*. The concentration of the solute in a saturated solution is known as the solubility and it is temperature dependent. The solubility units may be molar (mol dm^{-3}) or mass per unit volume (μg ml^{-1}).

If a solution contains a higher concentration of solute than the known solubility, it is called *supersaturated*. Such solution can be induced to come to equilibrium by adding a "seed" (a small crystal of the solute or solid particle), which initiates precipitation.

There are three main types of solubility equilibria:

- Simple dissolution.
- Dissolution with dissociation (characteristic of salts). The equilibrium constant is known in this case as a solubility product.
- Dissolution with reaction. This is characteristic of the dissolution of weak acids or weak bases in aqueous media of varying pH.

49. From the titration curve for the unknown salt (Figure 1), the unknown salt is most likely:

A. monoprotic   **C.** amphiprotic
B. diprotic   **D.** amphoteric

A is correct.

Since the titration curve has one inflection point (the steepest portion of the curve), the unknown salt must be a monoprotic acid.

A weak acid only partially dissociates from its salt and the pH rises at first. As it reaches the zone where the solution seems to be buffered, the slope of the curve levels out. After this zone, the pH rises sharply through its equivalence point and levels out again.

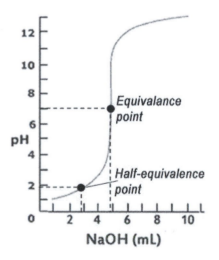

There are two significant points in this curve:

1) the *half-equivalence point* - occurs halfway through a buffered region where the pH barely changes for a lot of base added. This point signifies the stage when just enough base is added for half of the acid to be converted to the conjugate base. When this happens, the concentration of H^+ ions equals the K_a value of the acid and the pH = pK_a.

2) the *equivalence point* – occurs when the acid is neutralized (the pH is 7). When a weak acid is neutralized, the solution that remains is basic because the acid's conjugate base remains in solution.

B: *diprotic acid* is an acid that contains within its molecular structure two hydrogen atoms per molecule capable of dissociating in water (e.g. sufuric acid, oxalic acid). The dissociation doesn't happen all at once, but in two stages because of two different K_a values. In titration graphs, the curve will clearly show two equivalence points for the acid because the two hydrogen atoms in the acid molecule do not leave the acid at the same time.

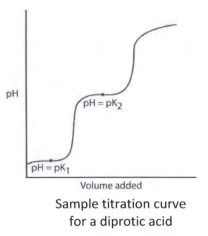

Sample titration curve
for a diprotic acid

C: *amphiprotic* molecules (i.e. can either donate or accept a H^+) include amino acids and proteins (i.e. an amine and carboxylic acid groups) and self-ionizable compounds such as H_2O and NH_3.

D: *amphoteric* species are molecules (or ions) that can react as an acid as well as a base. Many metals (e.g. tin, zinc, aluminum, lead, and beryllium) and most metalloids (e.g. boron, silicon, germanium, arsenic, antimony and tellurium) form amphoteric oxides or hydroxides. Amphoteric property depends on the oxidation state of the oxide.

50. What is the hydrogen ion concentration, when 4 mL of NaOH is added to the aqueous solution of the unknown salt?

   A. 1.0×10^{-2} M   **B.** 1.0×10^{-3} M   **C.** 1.0×10^{-4} M   **D.** 1.0×10^{-5} M

B is correct.

From Figure 1, after adding 4 mL of NaOH the pH of the solution is 3.

Therefore, $[H^+] = 10^{-ph} = 10^{-3}$ M.

51. Which of the following buffers would best maintain a solution at pH 7.35 at 23°C?

   A. SSC ($pK_a = 7.0$)   **C.** Tricene ($pK_a = 8.05$)
   B. K_2HPO_4 (aq) ($pK_a = 7.2$)   **D.** Citric acid ($pK_a = 4.76$)

B is correct.

A buffer is an aqueous solution of a weak acid/its conjugate base or a weak base/its conjugate acid mixture. Its pH changes very little when a small amount of strong acid or base is added to it and therefore it is used to prevent changes in the pH of a solution. Select a buffer system with the pK_a as close as possible to the pH of the solution. Buffering solutions are effective within one pK_a unit from the pH that the solution is being maintained at.

If the desired pH is 7.35, then, among the given choices, the best buffer to use is dipotassium phosphate, K_2HPO_4 which has the closest pK_a to the desired pH.

A: SSC is saline sodium citrate and is used as a hybridization buffer to control stringency for washing steps in protocols for Southern blotting, Northern blotting, DNA Microarray or *in situ* hybridization.

C: tricene, N-tris(hydroxymethyl)methylglycine, is a zwitterionic amino acid commonly used as an electrophoresis buffer and in resuspension of cell pellets.

D: citric acid's dominant use is as a flavoring and preservative in food and beverages (especially soft drinks). The buffering properties are used to control pH in household cleaners and pharmaceuticals.

52. Which of the following occurs when KBr is added to a solution of AgBr(*s*) that is at equilibrium at 23°C?

    A. Increase of the solubility constant
    B. Decrease of the solubility constant
    C. Formation of more AgBr(*s*)
    D. More AgBr(*s*) goes into solution

C is correct.

Increasing the concentration of Br⁻(*aq*) by adding KBr (product) shifts the reaction to the left (reactants), resulting in the formation of more AgBr(*s*). This is the *common ion effect* and is responsible for the reduction in solubility of an ionic precipitate when a soluble compound containing one of the ions of the precipitate is added to the solution in equilibrium with the precipitate.

According to Le Chatelier's principle, if the concentration of any one of the ions is increased, the ions in excess should combine with the oppositely charged ions. Some of the salt will be precipitated until the ionic product is equal to the solubility of the product. In summary, common ion effect is the suppression of the degree of dissociation of a weak electrolyte containing a common ion.

The only way to change the value of the equilibrium constant (K_{sp}) is to change the temperature.

Questions 53 through 59 are not based on any
descriptive passage and are independent of each other

53. Which statement correctly explains why enzymes are very effective catalysts?

   A. Enzyme can convert a normally endergonic reaction into an exergonic reaction
   B. Enzymes release products very rapidly
   C. Enzymes bind very tightly to substrates
   D. Enzyme stabilizes the transition state

D is correct.

54. How many carbon atoms are in a molecule of heptane?

   A. 4   **B.** 5   **C. 7**   **D.** 9

C is correct.

Heptane is the straight-chain alkane with the chemical
formula $H_3C(CH_2)_5CH_3$ or C_7H_{16}. It has 9 isomers (11
if enantiomers are counted).

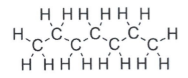

55. In the presence of a competitive inhibitor, what changes are expected in kinetics?

   A. K_M appears to increase while V_{max} remains the same
   B. K_M appears to increase while V_{max} decreases
   C. K_M appears to decrease while V_{max} remains the same
   D. K_M appears to decrease, while V_{max} decreases

A is correct.

56. Two compounds that consist of the equal number of the same atoms but have a
different molecular structure are:

   A. hydrocarbons   **B. isomers**   **C.** homologs   **D.** isotopes

B is correct.

Isomers are molecules with the same molecular formula (i.e. contain the same number of
atoms of each element), but different arrangements of these atoms in space. Isomers do
not necessarily have the same or similar properties, unless they have the same functional
groups. There are two main forms of isomerism (stereoisomerism and structural
isomerism) and many classes of isomers (e.g. positional isomers, enantiomers, *cis-
trans* isomers etc.).

57. What agent causes the formation of a cyclobutane thymine dimer?

A. Propylmethanesulfonate

B. Ultraviolet radiation

C. *N*-ethyl-*N*′nitro-*N*-nitrosoguanidine

D. DNP

B is correct.

58. In relation to each other, α-D-fructofuranose and β-D-fructofuranose are:

A. conformational isomers

B. anomers

C. epimers

D. enantiomers

B is correct.

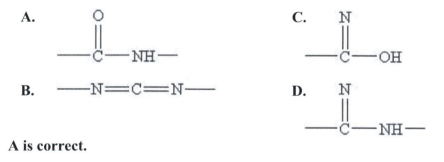

Depending on the direction of the anomeric hydroxy group, the furanose ring can have either alpha or beta configuration. In a D-configuration furanose, α configuration has the hydroxy pointing down, and β has the hydroxy pointing up.

α-D-fructofuranose

β-D-fructofuranose

59. Which of the following structures represents an amide (protein) bond?

A.

C.

B. ——N≡C≡N——

D.

A is correct.

CHEMICAL & PHYSICAL FOUNDATIONS OF BIOLOGICAL SYSTEMS
MCAT® PRACTICE TEST #3 ANSWER KEY

Passage 1
1 : B
2 : C
3 : D
4 : A
5 : D

Passage 2
6 : B
7 : D
8 : C
9 : B
10 : A
11 : C

Independent questions
12 : C
13 : C
14 : D
15 : C

Passage 3
16 : A
17 : D
18 : B
19 : C

Passage 4
20 : D
21 : B
22 : B
23 : C
24 : C

Independent questions
53 : A
54 : B
55 : A
56 : A
57 : B
58 : D
59 : C

Independent questions
25 : C
26 : B
27 : D
28 : A
29 : B

Passage 5
30 : A
31 : B
32 : B
33 : D
34 : C
35 : C
36 : D

Passage 6
37 : B
38 : B
39 : D
40 : C
41 : A

Independent questions
42 : C
43 : A
44 : A
45 : B

Passage 7
46 : B
47 : A
48 : A
49 : C
50 : C
51 : C
52 : D

Passage 1
(Questions 1–5)

Geological time scale is a system for measuring change occurring on wide-ranging time scales. This system helps scientists describe the timing and connections between events that took place throughout Earth's history. Isotopic dating shows that the Earth is about 4.5 billion years old.

Eon is a time period of over one-half billion years. Some ecological changes (like the slow building of mountain ranges) take eons or can occur during extremely brief periods when dramatic geologic changes (e.g. earthquakes) make a significant impact. Physical effects account for much of the geologic changes, but many geological processes are based on chemical reactions. For example, the formation of limestone caves involves aqueous carbonic acid interacting with limestone rock strata (layers with consistent composition).

This process is illustrated by the following reactions:

$$CO_2(g) + \text{pressure} \overset{H_2O}{\longleftrightarrow} CO_2(aq)$$

Reaction 1

$$CO_2(aq) + H_2O(l) \longleftrightarrow H_2CO_3(aq)$$

Reaction 2

$$H_2CO_3(aq) \longleftrightarrow H^+(aq) + HCO_3^-(aq)$$

Reaction 3

$$CaCO_3(s) + H^+(aq) \longleftrightarrow Ca^{2+}(aq) + HCO_3^-(aq)$$

Reaction 4

Atmospheric carbon dioxide dissolves in water (Reaction 1). The concentration of dissolved carbon dioxide (at atmospheric pressure and 25°C temperature) is low. However, the concentration would be much higher in the fissures and cracks of the limestone because they may have higher pressure. Then, the dissolved carbon dioxide reacts with water and forms carbonic acid (Reaction 2) which then dissociates (Reaction 3) and the acidic hydrogens enter into reaction with limestone (Reaction 4) and dissolve it.

Eventually, water drains from the caves leaving a web of cracks filled with dissolved limestone which then exits the cracks and gets exposed to the lower pressure within the cave interior. Reactions 1 through 4 reverse resulting in the calcium carbonate precipitation. Stalactites (mineral formations that hang from the cave ceiling) form when this precipitation occurs before a drop of dissolved limestone leaks out of the cave ceiling; stalagmites (formations that rise from the floor) form if the precipitate builds-up on the cave floor.

1. Which of the following statements is true for this reaction?

$$HCO_3^- + HCl \leftrightarrow H_2CO_3 + Cl^-$$

  A. HCO_3^- is a base and Cl^- is its conjugate acid
  B. HCO_3^- **is a base and** H_2CO_3 **is its conjugate acid**
  C. Cl^- is an acid and HCl is its conjugate base
  D. HCl is an acid and HCO_3^- is its conjugate base

B is correct.

A conjugate acid loses an H^+ and becomes its conjugate base. Therefore a conjugate acid has one more H^+ than the compound of the base. Conversely, a base gains an H^+ to become its conjugate acid.

Bicarbonate (HCO_3^-) is a base and carbonate (H_2CO_3) is the conjugate acid.

2. Which of these compounds is a strong acid?

  A. H_2CO_3 **B.** CF_3CO_2H **C.** HNO_3 **D.** H_3PO_4

C is correct.

Nitric acid (HNO_3) is a strong acid, while phosphoric acid (H_3PO_4), carbonic acid (H_2CO_3) and trifluoroacetic acid (CF_3CO_2H) are weak acids.

Learn the few common strong acids and assume that all other acids are weak acids. Some common strong acids are: sulfuric acid (H_2SO_4), nitric acid (HNO_3), hydrochloric acid (HCl), hydrobromic acid (HBr), hydroiodic acid (HI), chloric acid ($HClO_3$) and perchloric acid ($HClO_4$). Organic acids (e.g. carboxylic acids) are weak acids.

3. The main component of stalagmites is:

  A. H_2CO_3 **B.** $Ca(HCO_3)$ **C.** Ca_2CO_3 **D.** $CaCO_3$

D is correct.

Limestone caves form when solid limestone rock strata come in contact with aqueous carbonic acid. Limestone is calcium carbonate ($CaCO_3$) as shown in Reaction 4 where acidic hydrogens react with limestone. As stated in the passage, the reactions reverse when dissolved limestone exits the cracks and calcium carbonate precipitates. The stalagmite is composed of the precipitate – calcium carbonate or $CaCO_3$.

A: carbonic acid (H_2CO_3) is also a name given to a solution of carbon dioxide in water and is an intermediate in respiratory gas exchange for the transport of CO_2 (waste product of cellular respiration) to the lungs. Red blood cells contain the enzyme, carbonic anhydrase that increase the rate of the reaction and dissociates the H^+ and yields the bicarbonate (HCO_3^-) dissolved in the blood plasma. This catalyzed reaction is reversed in the lungs where bicarbonate is converted back to CO_2 which is expelled. This reaction plays an important role as a buffer in mammalian blood (pH 7.35).

B: $Ca(HCO_3)_2$, calcium hydrogen carbonate (aka calcium bicarbonate) only exists in aqueous solutions (soluble) that contain calcium and bicarbonate (HCO_3^-) and is the soluble product of the chemical reaction of limestone.

C: calcium is an alkaline earth metal element and forms +2 ions. Because the carbonate ion has a –2 charge (molecule is neutral), the charge on calcium would be +. A +1 on Ca is not likely because the valence shell would have one remaining electron and therefore be less stable than the vacant valence shell when Ca is +2.

4. Given that many acids contain an H^+ ion and many bases contain OH^- ions, how is BCl_3 (containing neither H^+ nor OH^-) classified?

   A. Lewis acid   **C.** Brønsted-Lowry acid
   B. Lewis base   **D.** Brønsted-Lowry base

A is correct.

A Lewis acid is defined as a compound which has fewer electrons than an octet and therefore can accept a pair of electrons from another compound. BCl_3 has a central boron atom with only 6 valence electrons.

A Lewis base is defined as a compound which has a pair of unshared (i.e. lone pair) electrons and can donate a pair of electrons. Lewis acids and bases are defined in terms of their ability to accept (for acids) or donate (for bases) an electron pair.

The Brønsted-Lowry definition of acids and bases is different from the Lewis definition. Brønsted acids and bases are defined in terms of their ability to donate or receive a proton. A Brønsted acid is able to donate a proton (H^+) while a Brønsted base is a proton acceptor. A hydronium ion (H_3O^+) is a Brønsted acid (H^+ donor) and it does not have an available lone pair of electrons (cannot accept H^+). Boron trichloride (BCl_3) is not able to do either and therefore is not a Brønsted acid or a Brønsted base.

Boron is an unusual element for it has four orbitals yet only three valence electrons – less electrons than orbitals. In boron trichloride, boron has only 6 electrons around it (all bonded to chlorine) and no electrons around boron are available to form a boron-hydrogen bond. Therefore, without available electrons, boron trichloride cannot be an acid (proton donor) and is not a Brønsted base (proton acceptor).

5. What would be an approximate pH of a 1.0 M solution of $CaCO_3$ if it was water soluble?

    A. 1   **B.** 4   **C.** 6   **D.** 8

D is correct.

Since calcium carbonate ($CaCO_3$) is a salt of the strong base aqueous calcium hydroxide ($Ca(OH)_2$) and a salt of the weak acid (i.e. carbonic acid H_2CO_3), it is basic. The hydroxides of all Group I and II metals are strong bases. From Reaction 3, carbonic acid (a weak acid) is in equilibrium with its ions and does not dissociate completely.

There are many weak acids (e.g. organic acids in organic chemistry) but only a few strong acids.

Learn the strong acids (pK_a is less than 2) and assume all others to be weak (pK_a between 2 and 12). Some examples of strong acids and their approximate pK_a: HI ($pK_a = -9.3$), HBr ($pK_a = -8.7$), $HOCl_4$ ($pK_a = -8$), HCl ($pK_a = -6.3$), H_2SO_4 ($pK_a = -3$), H_3O^+ ($pK_a = -1.74$), HNO_3 ($pK_a = -1.64$).

For predicting whether a salt in solution is acidic or basic a simple rule is used: the salt will have the characteristics of the acid or the base from which it was produced, whichever is stronger.

If calcium carbonate dissolved, the calcium ions would not react with the water but the carbonate ions abstract H^+ from the water to reestablish the carbonate-hydrogen carbonate-carbonic acid equilibrium. When H^+ is removed from water the product is OH^- and the solution becomes basic. A basic pH means the pH is greater than 7 and therefore the correct answer has a pH greater than 7.

Passage 2
(Questions 6–11)

During the winter Olympics, a ski jumper travels down an inclined track. He comes to the end of the track, leaves the take off ramp, passes through the air and lands on the slope.

The skier's trajectory through the air is shown in Figure 1. The take off ramp from which he left the track is at a 30° angle to the horizontal. The track is at an angle of θ to the horizontal and the slope is inclined at a 45° angle.

A ski jumper starts off stationary at the top of the track, but once he pushes off, he accelerates down the track, and then takes off from the ramp. The vertical height between the top of the track and its lowest point is 65 m, and the vertical height between the top of the ramp and its lowest point is 15 m.

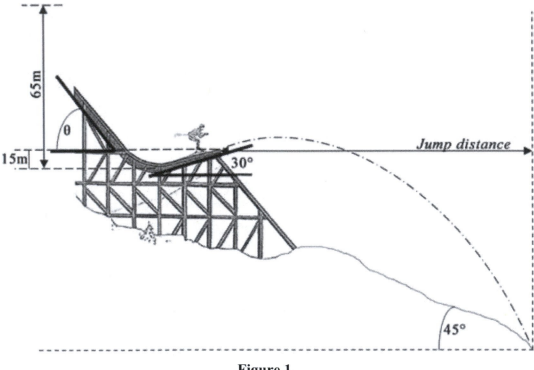

Figure 1

The jump distance is the distance traveled by the skier in the air from leaving the ramp to landing on the slope. Sometimes, a skier may slightly jump when leaving the jump ramp to increase the jump distance by increasing the vertical velocity.

Assume that the friction between the skis and the slope is negligible and ignore air resistance. Acceleration (due to gravity) = 9.8 m/s^2

Note: $\cos 30° = \dfrac{\sqrt{3}}{2}$, $\sin 30° = 0.5$, $\cos 45° = \dfrac{\sqrt{2}}{2}$

6. If θ is 45°, what is the acceleration of a 90 kg skier going down the track?

A. 3.4 m/s²   **B. 6.9 m/s²**   **C.** 9.8 m/s²   **D.** 14.7 m/s²

B is correct.

This is an incline/plane problem. Disregarding friction and air resistance, the only force parallel to the track is the component of the skier's weight parallel to the track, which is W sin θ (or mg sin θ) = ma, where m = skier's mass, and a = acceleration down the track.

Therefore, mg sin θ = ma.

Note: the m terms cancel so the result does not depend on the mass and is the same for all skiers and the equation simplifies to a = g sin θ

From the question, θ = 45°. Substituting, a = g sin θ, a = g sin 45°

$$a = 9.8 \frac{\sqrt{2}}{2} = 4.9\sqrt{2}$$

Approximate √2 is less than 2 but greater than 1, acceleration (a) is between 4.9 and 9.8 m/s².

7. Which of these factors would increase a ski jumper's jump distance?

     I. increased angle of incline θ of the track
     II. increased vertical height h of the track
     III. increased total mass of the ski jumper

     A. I only   **B.** II only   **C.** III only   **D. I and II only**

D is correct.

Statement I: increasing the incline angle (of a fixed distance track) does increase the maximum potential energy necessary to increase the kinetic energy of a ski jumper at the end of the ramp because it increases the vertical component of height. The take off speed is increased and the jump distance is increased because potential energy (converted to kinetic energy) depends on vertical height (h).

Statement II: increasing the vertical height (h) of the track increases the initial potential energy and the overall change in potential energy. This means that the ski jumper's kinetic energy (i.e. speed) at the point of take off is greater. Increasing the take off speed increases the jump distance.

Statement III: the mass term cancels because all objects (irrespective of their mass) accelerate at the same rate. A ski jumper with a mass of 70 kg has the same take-off speed as one with a mass of 95 kg.

8. If the vertical height of the jump ramp was increased from the original 15 meters while the skier's starting point on the track is unaffected, how would the speed of a skier leaving the ramp change?

A. remains the same   **C. decreases**

B. increases   D. depends on the ramp's incline angle

C is correct.

This question is about conservation of energy. At the top of the track, the skier is stationary and all his energy is potential energy (PE = mgh). When he leaves the jump ramp, he has velocity in the form of kinetic energy (KE = $1/2\ mv^2$). The height difference between the top of the track and the take off point on the jump ramp is proportional PE converted to KE.

At the top of the track, h equals the height of the platform minus the height of the top of the jump ramp. h is the vertical drop from the top of the track to the top of the ramp. If the height of the ski jump ramp is increased, h is decreased and the skier's travel distance (i.e. vertical height) is less.

As h decreases, less potential energy gets converted into kinetic energy, and the skier's speed is lower when he jumps.

Neglecting friction and air resistance, PE = KE, $mgh = 1/2\ mv^2$

$gh = 1/2v^2$, $v^2 = 2gh$

solving $v = (2gh)^{1/2}$.   Therefore, a decrease in h results in a decrease in v.

9. What would occur if a skier used skis of a greater surface area?

A. pressure exerted on the slope by the skis increases

B. pressure exerted on the slope by the skis decreases

C. normal force of the slope on the skier increases

D. normal force of the slope on the skier decreases

B is correct.

The normal force of the slope exerted on the skier depends only on mass (m), acceleration due to gravity (g) and the angle of the slope (θ). Therefore, changing the surface area of the skies has no affect on the normal force.

The pressure exerted on the slope by the skis does depend on the surface area of the skis: P = F/A, where P = pressure on the slope due to the skis, F = force exerted by the skis on the slope, and A = surface area over which the force acts (e.g. surface area of the skis).

The force exerted by the skis is the component of the weight of the skier normal to the slope (i.e. normal force) which is constant.

Therefore, the pressure exerted on the slope by the skis is inversely proportional to the surface area of the skis.

10. When the skier skis down the track or if he fell the same vertical height, how would the work done by gravity on the skier in each case compare?

    A. Equal amounts of work would be done
    B. More work would be done on the skier when he falls
    C. Less work would be done on the skier when he falls
    D. Depends on the track incline angle

A is correct.

Work done by gravity equals W ($= mgh$); where W = weight of object, m = mass of object, g = acceleration due to gravity, and h = vertical distance.

Work depends only on the vertical distance and is independent of the actual path taken. Gravity is a conservative force because work done by gravity is independent of the path taken. Therefore, since the vertical distance is the same, the work done by gravity is the same.

11. Another skier takes off from a point farther down the ramp and leaves it at a speed of 12 m/s traveling in the air for 5 s. What is the total horizontal distance traveled by the ski jumper between take off and landing on the slope?

    A. 12 m   **B.** 6√3 m   **C. 30√3 m**   **D.** 60 m

C is correct.

The information about the skier's speed (12 meters per second) and time in the air (5 seconds) can be used to calculate the horizontal distance traveled. If the skier was moving in the horizontal flat line, with no forces acting on him, the horizontal distance traveled would equal the horizontal speed (12 m/s) times the total time (5 s) in flight. But the ski jumper is traveling through the air at a trajectory shown in Figure 1. The total time in flight is given, but there is no value given for the horizontal velocity.

However, the total velocity and the angle at which he leaves the jump ramp are given.

Using the equation $v_h = v_t \cdot \cos \phi$, where v_h = horizontal component of velocity, v_t = total velocity, and ϕ = angle measured with respect to the horizontal.

Substituting, horizontal velocity $v_h = 12 \cdot \cos 30°$, which equals $12\frac{\sqrt{3}}{2}$, or $6\sqrt{3}$ meters per second.

The horizontal distance traveled equals $6\sqrt{3}$ times 5 seconds, or $30\sqrt{3}$ meters.

Questions 12 through 15 are not based on any descriptive passage and are independent of each other

---

12. There are two poles (X and Y) of cylindrical shape where pole X has a greater cross sectional area than pole Y. Both poles at their bases experience a force of their weight. If the poles themselves are of equal weight, the pressure at the base of which pole will be greater?

    A. pressure will be equal for pole X and Y
    B. pressure will be greater for pole X than for pole Y
    C. pressure will be greater for pole Y than for pole X
    D. pressure will depend on the relative height of the two poles

C is correct.

$P = F / A$

The pressure (P) at the pole's base is equal to that pole's force (F = mg) divided by its cross-sectional area ($A = \pi r^2$). Because both poles have the same mass, the pole with the smaller cross-sectional area (Pole Y) experiences the greater pressure (P) at its base.

---

13. Which of these aqueous solutions has the lowest pH?

    A. 0.5 M HF   **B.** 1.5 M NaClO   **C. 0.4 M HBr**   **D.** 1.0 M KCl

C is correct.

Hydrobromic acid (HBr) is a strong acid which would ionize completely at 0.4 M concentration.

A: hydrofluoric acid (HF) is a weak acid and although has a higher concentration than HBr, it would produce a lower hydrogen ion concentration and, therefore, a higher pH.

B: sodium hypochlorite (NaClO), commonly known as bleach, is the salt of a strong base and a weak acid and has a pH greater than 7, as the hypochlorous ion picks up hydrogen ions from the water and forms its conjugate acid and hydroxide ion.

D: the salt solution is the salt of a strong acid and a strong base, which is neutral because no ions react with water to produce conjugates.

14. Given that the penetration depth difference for *gamma* rays and *beta* particles is about two $\log_{10}$ units, how many times deeper does a *gamma* ray penetrate lead compared to a *beta* particle?

A. 2 **B.** 4 **C.** 20 **D. 100**

D is correct.

Two $\log_{10}$ units: $10^2 = 100$ times;

$10^2 = 100$ times (10×10); $10^4 = 10{,}000$ times ($10 \times 10 \times 10 \times 10$); $10^{-2} = 0.01$ times (0.1×0.1); $10^{-3} = 0.001$ times ($0.1 \times 0.1 \times 0.1$).

Logarithmic scales are defined by either a ratio of the referenced quantity or as a measure of the quantity in fixed units. A log scale is a scale of measurement that displays the value of a physical quantity (e.g. pH, decibel) using intervals corresponding to orders of magnitude.

For example, a solution of pH 2 is 10 times more acidic than a solution of pH 3 (one log unit); a solution of pH of 3 is 1,000 times more acidic than a solution of pH 6 (three log units).

15. Given that the cornea has a larger refractive index for violet light than for yellow light, where would the focus for a beam of violet light land considering that the yellow light is focused on the retina?

A. at the same place
B. behind the retina and the yellow light focus
C. in front of the retina and yellow light focus
D. both in front of and behind the retina

C is correct.

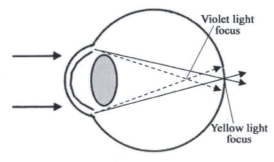

The figure shows that the eye refracts violet light more than yellow light and focuses violet light in front of the yellow focus.

Passage 3
(Questions 16–19)

The transition metals are defined by valence electrons that have d subshells. These elements in the fourth through seventh period of the periodic table undergo sequential filling of the d subshell. For example, in the third period, elements like Cr, Mn, Fe and Co, undergo sequential filling of orbitals in the $3d$ subshell. They have a general electron configuration [Ar] $4s^x 3d^y$ where [Ar] is the electron configuration for the noble gas argon, x is the number of electrons in the $4s$ subshell and y is the number of electrons in the $3d$ subshell.

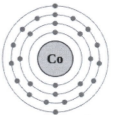

For cobalt in the +2 oxidation state (Co^{2+}) the electron configuration is [Ar] $3d^7$. In transforming from a neutral (+0) to an oxidized (+2) state, the cobalt atom must first lose two electrons from the $4s$ subshell.

Generally, transition metals may assume multiple oxidation states. Even though metals usually form basic oxides (e.g., Na_2O) and nonmetals usually form acidic oxides (e.g., SO_3), transition metal oxides, depending on the oxidation state of the metal, may be either acidic or basic. For example, Mn_2O_7 is highly acidic while MnO is basic.

This behavior of the oxides (i.e. anhydrides) may be better explained in terms of the elemental hydroxides.

Reactions of the manganese oxides, Mn_2O_7 and MnO, with H_2O are as follows:

$$
\begin{array}{ll}
1) & Mn_2O_7 + H_2O \rightarrow 2\ \overset{\displaystyle O}{\underset{\displaystyle O}{\overset{\|}{\underset{\|}{H-O-Mn-O}}}}
\end{array}
$$

$$
\begin{array}{ll}
2) & MnO + H_2O \rightarrow Mn(OH)_2
\end{array}
$$

The difference in behavior between the two oxides and their hydroxides is the result of the relative sizes of the metal-oxygen (M-O) electronegativity difference ($\Delta\chi_{M-O}$). Electronegativity (χ) is the propensity by atoms within a molecule to attract electrons towards their nuclei. An atom's χ is affected by both its atomic number and the distance of its valence electrons from the positively charged nucleus.

When $\Delta\chi_{M-O}$ is less than $\Delta\chi_{O-H}$, the oxygen-hydrogen (O-H) bond has ionic character and the proton may dissociate. Therefore, the metal hydroxide is an acid. This behavior is observed in metal anhydrides where the metal has a high oxidation state (greater than +5).

Conversely, when $\Delta\chi_{M-O}$ is greater than $\Delta\chi_{O-H}$, the metal-hydroxide (M-OH) bond has ionic properties, and the hydroxide is basic. Generally, metal anhydrides are basic when the oxidation state of the metal is less than or equal to +4.

16. After two oxides of the same transition metal, Compound A and Compound B, are placed separately into two vessels of aqueous media, Compound A produced an acidic solution while Compound B produced a basic solution. From this observation, what can be concluded about the metal-oxide bonding in these compounds?

    A. The bonding in Compound A is more covalent and the bonding in Compound B is more ionic

    B. The bonding in Compound A is more ionic and the bonding in Compound B is more covalent

    C. The bonding in Compound A is more polar than the bonding in Compound B

    D. The bonding in both compounds is nonpolar

A is correct.

From the passage, acidic compounds are those where the O-H bond is ionic and basic compounds are those where the M-OH bond is ionic. Given that Compound A is acidic and compound B is basic, the metal-oxide bond in compound A is not ionic (because the O-H bond is) but the metal-oxide bond in Compound B must be ionic.

17. Knowing that manganese is a transition metal that is able to assume the oxidation states 0, +1, +2, +3, +4, +5, +6 or +7, a chemist attempted to identify the oxidation state of manganese in an oxide of an unknown formula of Mn_xO_y. He dissolved the compound in water completely and measured the pH of the solution to be 6.0. Which of the following empirical formulas is the most likely one for the Mn_xO_y?

    A. MnO **B.** MnO_2 **C.** Mn_2O_3 **D.** Mn_2O_7

D is correct.

From the passage, in an acidic transition metal oxide the metal has an oxidation state of greater than +5. For reference, oxygen is often in a –2 oxidation state. The possible oxidation states of Mn are 0 and +7.

In Mn_2O_7, manganese(VII) oxide, Mn in a +7 oxidation state because the molecule is neutral.

At pH of 6, the solution is acidic and therefore the oxidation state for manganese must equal +5, +6 or +7.

A: MnO (manganese(II) oxide): oxygen (–2 x 1 = –2), Mn has a +2 oxidation state.

B: MnO_2 (manganese dioxide): oxygen (–2 x 2 = –4), Mn has a +4 oxidation state.

C: Mn_2O_3 (manganese(III) oxide): oxygen (–2 x 3 = –6), Mn has +3 oxidation state.

18. Which of the following would NOT be paramagnetic based on the provided electronic configurations?

A. Co^{2+} — [Ar] $3d^7$

C. Si — [Ne] $3s^2 3p^2$

B. Cd — [Kr] $5s^2 4d^{10}$

D. Mn — [Ar] $4s^2 3d^6$

B is correct.

An atom/ion is considered paramagnetic if at least one electron is unpaired, so an atom with an odd number of electrons must be paramagnetic.

There are five d orbitals. When filling orbitals, 1 electron goes into each orbital before they pair. Therefore, the 7 d-orbital electrons in Co^{2+} would be placed as follows: the first 5 electrons are unpaired into the five available d orbitals, and the sixth and seventh electrons pair with two unpaired electron in the d orbital. Since this ion has unpaired electrons, it is paramagnetic.

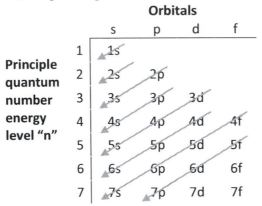

Orbitals

Order of filling valence shells: 1s 2s 2p 3s 3p 4s 3d 4p 5s 4d 5p 6s 4f 5d 6p 7s 5f 6d 7p

19. Which of these metals is the LEAST reactive considering the closed-shell and half-closed shell characteristics?

A. Sc(s)

B. Na(s)

C. Ag(s)

D. Rb(s)

C is correct.

Silver (Ag) has a closed valence d subshell ([Kr] $5s^1 4d^{10}$) that gives silver greater stabilization, making it much less reactive.

A: scandium ([Ar] $4s^2 3d^1$) does not have a complete valence d subshell.

B: sodium ([Ne] $3s^1$) does not have a complete valence s subshell.

D: rubidium ([Kr] $5s^1$) does not have a complete valence s subshell.

Passage 4
(Questions 20–24)

When a light wave passes slantingly from one medium to another, the angle at which it emerges from the boundary between the media is different from the angle at which it strikes it. The change is called refraction and is caused by change in the medium composition.

The relationship between the angle of refraction (θ_2) and the angle of incidence (θ_1) is described by Snell's law.

$$n_1 \sin \theta_1 = n_2 \sin \theta_2$$

Snell's law

n_1 = the refractive index of medium 1, n_2 = the refractive index of medium 2.

Refractive index = c/v, where c = speed of light (vacuum) and v = speed of light (medium). For air, $n \approx 1$.

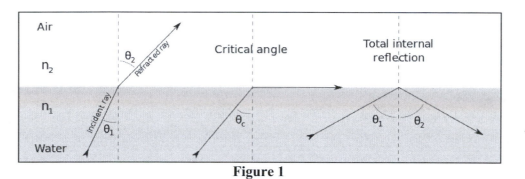

Figure 1

When a light wave encounters a medium with a refractive index smaller than that of the medium it was traveling through, it may exhibit the phenomenon of total internal reflection. This happens when the angle the wave strikes at is greater than or equal to the critical angle θ_c for the two media.

For any two media where $n_1 > n_2$, $\sin \theta_c = n_2/n_1$.

Figure 2 shows a classic experiment where white light passes through a prism with a 1.67 refractive index and the emerging light strikes a screen opposite the light source as a color spectrum.

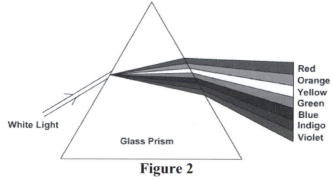

Figure 2

For each material medium, n slightly varies depending on the frequency of light wave going through it and the n value increases with increasing frequency. For instance, with any change in medium, violet light has greater refraction than yellow light.

Variability in n causes a prism to disperse white light into its component wavelengths of different colors. The various wavelengths that come out of the prism at different angles appear as a spectrum.

20. To determine the relative magnitude of the wavelengths emitted from yellow and violet light sources, the likely conclusion is that the shorter of the two wavelengths is emitted from the:

    A. yellow light source because yellow light's refraction is lower than the violet light's
    B. violet light source because violet light's refraction is lower than the yellow light's
    C. yellow light source because yellow light's refraction is greater than the violet light's
    D. violet light source because violet light's refraction is greater than the yellow light's

D is correct.

From the passage: "violet light has greater refraction than yellow light," therefore choices B and C can be eliminated.

From the passage: the refractive index (n) "increases with increasing frequency", the violet light must have the higher frequency, and therefore the shorter wavelength.

The order of the colors (of increasing frequency and decreasing wavelength) in the visible spectrum is:

ROY G BIV (red, orange, yellow, green, blue, indigo and violet).

21. What is the approximate velocity of light as it passes through the prism shown in Figure 2?

    A. 0.6×10^8 m/s   **B. 1.8×10^8 m/s**   C. 5.0×10^8 m/s   D. 9.0×10^8 m/

B is correct.

The speed of the light through a medium with refractive index n is given by the equation $v = c/n$.

The prism has an index of 1.67, which is approximately 5/3, the speed of light through the prism is:

$$v = c/n = c / \frac{5}{3} = c\,\frac{3}{5}$$
$$= (3 \times 10^8 \text{ m/s})\,\frac{3}{5} = 1.8 \times 10^8 \text{ m/s}$$

22. When indigo light passes through a nesosilicate medium and strikes the silicate-air border, the smallest angle that results in a total internal reflection is approximately 25°. Based on this information, what is the refractive index of nesosilicate? *Note:* sin 25° = 0.4.

A. 4.0   **B. 2.5**   **C.** 0.4   **D.** 0.25

B is correct.

The critical angle for total internal reflection (TIR) θ_c is provided for by the equation sin θ = n_2 / n_1.

$n_1 = n_2 / \sin\theta_c$, therefore: $n_1 = n_2 / \sin 25°$

$n_1 = 1 / (0.4) = 2.5$.

23. A ray of light travelling through the air hits the surface of a transport medium at a 65° angle to the normal and continues though the medium at an angle of 30° to the normal. What is the approximate refractive index of this medium? *Note:* sin 30° = 0.5, sin 65° = 0.9

A. 0.55   **B.** 1.4   **C. 1.8**   **D.** 4.5

C is correct.

Using Snell's law,

$n_1 \sin\theta_1 = n_2 \sin\theta_2$,

$(1)(0.9) = n_2(0.5)$,

$n_2 = 9/5 \approx 2 = 1.8$

24. If green light has a wavelength of 5.1×10^{-7}m in air, what is its frequency?

A. 1.6×10^{14} Hz   **C. 5.9 x 10^{14} Hz**
B. 5.1×10^{14} Hz   **D.** 1.6×10^{15} Hz

C is correct.

Frequency and wavelength are related: $v = \lambda f$, where v is the wave speed.
Light travels through air with almost the same speed as the speed of light through vacuum.

Therefore, $v \approx c$ and $c = \lambda f$

$$f = c/\lambda = (3 \times 10^8 \text{ m/s}) / (5.1 \times 10^{-7} \text{ m})$$

$$\approx \frac{3}{5} \times 10^{15} \text{Hz}$$

$$\approx 5.9 \times 10^{14} \text{ Hz}$$

$1 \text{ Hz} = 1 \text{ s}^{-1}$

Questions 25 through 29 are not based on any
descriptive passage and are independent of each other

25. The air streams that provide frictionless sliding along the track for two carts are shut off while the carts are moving. What is the ratio of the frictional force exerted on the heavier cart to the frictional force exerted on the lighter cart, given that the heavier cart is twice the mass of the lighter one?

A. 1 : 2   C. 2 : 1
B. 1 : 4   D. 4 : 1

C is correct.

Force of friction: $F_f \leq \mu F_n$

where,

F_f = force of friction exerted by each surface on the other. The force of friction is parallel to the surface and is a force in the direction *opposite* to the net applied force.

μ = the coefficient of friction (i.e. empirical property of the materials in contact).

F_n = the normal force exerted by each surface on the other. The normal force is *perpendicular* to the surface: N = mg cos θ or N = mg, (where θ is zero: cos 0° = 1).

Since the heavier cart is twice the mass of the lighter one, the normal force on the heavier cart is twice the normal force on the lighter one.

Since the force of sliding friction is proportional to the strength of the normal force, the friction force acting on the heavier cart must also be twice the force acting on the lighter one.

26. Susan and Mike are playing on a 4 meter seesaw with a fulcrum in the middle. Susan is 30 kg and sits on the end, while Mike, 40 kg, sits so that they balance. The seesaw itself is uniform and balanced. How far from the end should Mike sit in order to achieve balance?

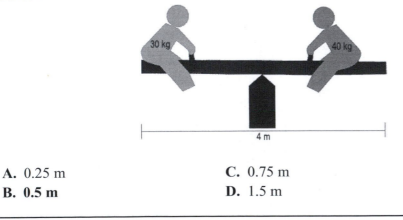

A. 0.25 m   C. 0.75 m
B. 0.5 m   D. 1.5 m

B is correct.

The figure below shows all forces on the seesaw.

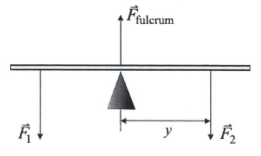

Since there is a torque balance about the fulcrum,
$-F_1r_1 + F_2r_2 = 0$, $\tau_{net} = 0$,

$F = ma$, $r_1 = 2$ m, $r_2 = (y)$

$F_1(2 \text{ m}) - F_2(y) = 0$,

$(30 \text{ kg}) (10 \text{ m/s}^2) (2 \text{ m}) - (40 \text{ kg}) (10 \text{ m/s}^2) (y) = 0$

$(600) - (400) (y) = 0$,

$y = 600/400 = 1.5 \text{meters}$

$y = 1.5$ m is the distance from Mike to the fulcrum. Thus, he sits 0.5 m from end.

27. What is the pH of a 0.05 *M* solution of acetic acid? *Note:* The K_a for acetic acid is 2×10^{-5}.

   A. 0.05   **B.** 0.1   **C.** 1.0   **D.** 3.0

D is correct.

The pH of the solution can be found from knowing how the acidity constant K_a is defined. The K_a is a constant defined as the equilibrium constant for the dissociation process of an acid. Therefore the acidity constant of acetic acid is the equilibrium constant for the equilibrium between the undissociated acetic acid (CH_3COOH) on the left and the proton (H^+) and acetate (CH_3COO^-) on the right.

The equilibrium constant K_a equals the product of the concentrations of H^+ and CH_3COO^- divided by the concentration of CH_3COOH. Since the H^+ and the acetate come from the same source in equal amounts their concentrations must be equal. Since the concentrations of acetate and hydronium ion are unknown, they can be x. The numerator in the K_a expression becomes x · x or x^2.

The concentration of undissociated acetic acid in the denominator is 0.05 moles per liter minus x (the amount that dissociates) making the expression: $K_a = \dfrac{x^2}{0.05\text{-}x}$.

The K_a for acetic acid is 2×10^{-5}.

To solve this difficult equation in a more simple way, make an approximation. The x in the denominator should be small compared to 0.05 because acetic acid is a weak acid and only dissociates to a small extent.

This approximation reduces the expression to $\dfrac{x^2}{0.05} = 2 \times 10^{-5}$.

Solve for x by multiplying both sides of the equation by 0.05 and taking the square root of both sides. X equals to 1×10^{-3}. This value represents the approximate concentration of both H^+ and acetate. To get a more accurate answer, substitute this value of x into the denominator and resolve the equation for the value of x in the numerator. As pH is the negative log of the hydronium ion concentration, the solution's pH is 3.

28. Charge Q is at a distance of 15 cm from a charge q_1 and 60 cm from charge q_2. What is the ratio of q_1 to q_2 if Q experiences an attractive force of 0.4 mN (milliNewtons) to q_1 and a repulsive force of 0.8 mN to q_2?

A. −1/32   B. −1/8   C. −1   D. −2

A is correct.

q_1 and q_2 must have opposite signs because the question states that the force between Q and q_1 is attractive while the force between Q and q_2 is repulsive. If q_1 and q_2 had the same sign, the forces would both be either attractive (q_1 and q_2 have the same sign but the opposite to Q) or repulsive (same sign for all three). Therefore, the ratio of q_1 to q_2 is negative.

Coulomb's law describes the electrostatic interaction between electrically charged particles. It states that the force of attraction (or repulsion) between two charged particles is directly proportional to the product of the magnitude of each particle and inversely proportional to the square of the distance between them.

If the two charges have the same sign (e.g. +/+ or −/−), the electrostatic force between them is repulsive. If the two charges have opposite signs the force between them is attractive.

Using Coulomb's law:

$$|F| = k_e \frac{|q_1 q_2|}{r^2} \text{ and } F = k_e \frac{|q_1 q_2 r_{21}|}{r_{21}^2}$$

$$\frac{F_1}{F_2} = \left(\frac{kq_1 Q}{r_1^2} \right) / \left(\frac{kq_2 Q}{r_2^2} \right)$$

$$\frac{F_1}{F_2} = \frac{q_1}{q_2} \times \left(\frac{r_2}{r_1} \right)^2$$

$$\frac{q_1}{q_2} = \frac{F_1}{F_2} \times \left(\frac{r_2}{r_1} \right)^2$$

$$= -\frac{0.4}{0.8} \times \left(\frac{15}{60} \right)^2$$

$$= -\frac{1}{2} \times \left(\frac{1}{4} \right)^2$$

$$= -\frac{1}{2} \times \left(\frac{1}{16} \right)$$

$$= -\frac{1}{32}$$

29. Given that a wave with a period of 0.006 seconds is traveling at 36 m/s, what is the wavelength?

A. 0.166 m   **B. 0.216 m**   **C.** 0.432 m   **D.** 2.16 m

B is correct.

The equation for waves: $v = f\lambda$, where v is the speed, f is the frequency and λ is the wavelength.

However, the question did not provide the frequency but provides the period of the wave.

The period is the inverse of frequency: $T = \frac{1}{f}$, therefore $f = \frac{1}{T}$

The wave equation becomes: $v = \frac{1}{T} \lambda$

Solving for wavelength: $\lambda = v / \frac{1}{T} = vT = 36$ m/s $\times 0.006$ s $= 0.216$ m

Wavelength is measured in units of length (meters). The question stem provides the speed of the wave in meters per second, and the period in seconds. Multiplying the two values gives a quantity in meters.

Passage 5
(Questions 30–36)

Thermochemistry is the study of energy and heat related to chemical reactions and/or physical transformations. A reaction may release (i.e. exothermic) or absorb (i.e. endothermic) heat or release (i.e. exergonic) or absorb (i.e. endergonic) energy to predict (along with considerations to entropy) if the reaction is spontaneous (i.e. energetically favorable) or non-spontaneous (i.e. energetically unfavorable). A phase change may also release heat (e.g. melting and boiling).

Thermochemistry focuses on these energy changes with particular focus on the system's energy exchange with its surrounding. Thermochemistry is useful in predicting relative reactant and product quantities throughout the course of a reaction. In combination with entropy (i.e. a measure of disorder), it is also used to predict whether a reaction is spontaneous (i.e. products are more stable than reactants) or non-spontaneous (i.e. reactants are more stable than products), favorable or unfavorable. Thermochemistry integrates the concept of thermodynamics with concepts of energy in the formation of chemical bonds. It can be used to calculate heat capacity, heat of formation, entropy, enthalpy, free energy and calories.

During the heating of 504 g of water to boiling, 4 g of it was lost to vaporization. Most of this water was lost near the boiling point.

In a 23°C room, a 250 g pewter pot was filed with 500 g of the boiling water. The pot and water were allowed to cool to 75°C and 100 g of water was transferred from the pot into an insulated thermos.

The specific heat of the pewter pot is 0.17 J/g·K and that of water is 4.2 J/g·K. The entire procedure was done under a pressure of 1.0 atm.

Note: heat of fusion of water = 80cal/g, heat of vaporization of water = 540cal/g, heat capacity of water = 4.184 J/K and 4.184 J = 1 calorie.

30. The heat transferred from the boiling water to the pewter pot is called:

A. enthalpy
B. entropy
C. heat capacity
D. specific heat

A is correct.

For any system at constant pressure, the heat lost or gained is equal to the enthalpy (ΔH) and has the same unit as heat or energy.

Enthalpy is a measure of the total energy within a thermodynamic system. It includes the internal energy which is the energy needed to create a system and the energy required to make room for it by displacing its environment and establishing its volume and pressure. Enthalpy is a thermodynamic potential. The unit of measurement for enthalpy is the joule, but it also can be measured in calories. The total enthalpy (*H*), of a system cannot be measured directly therefore, change in enthalpy (Δ*H*) is a more useful measure. The change Δ*H* is positive in endothermic reactions, and negative in exothermic (heat-releasing) reactions. Δ*H* of a system is equal to the sum of non-mechanical work done on it and the heat supplied to it.

For processes under constant pressure, Δ*H* is equal to the change in the internal energy of the system, plus the work that the system has done on its surroundings. The change in enthalpy under these conditions is the heat absorbed (or released) by a chemical reaction. Enthalpies for chemical substances at constant pressure assume standard state – usually 1 bar pressure. Standard state does not specify a temperature, but expressions for enthalpy generally reference the standard heat of formation at 25 °C.

B: entropy (Δ*S*) is a measure of the disorder of a system.

C: heat capacity is the amount of heat required to raise the temperature of a substance one degree centigrade.

D: specific heat is a property of a substance and is defined as the amount of heat (energy) required to raise the temperature of one unit mass of a substance one degree centigrade.

31. During boiling, how much energy is necessary to evaporate 4 g of water?

A. 0.74 kJ   **B. 9.0 kJ**   **C.** 13.5 kJ   **D.** 135 kJ

B is correct.

The passage states that the heat of vaporization of water is 540 calories per gram of water.

540 cal/g x 4 g = 2,160 cal (not kilocalories).

The answer choices are in joules: 2,160 cal x 4.184 J/cal ≈ 9,000 J or 9 kJ.

32. Given that after the water is transferred to the thermos, its temperature falls quickly from 75°C to 71.8°C as it achieves thermal equilibrium with the thermos flask, what is the heat capacity of the thermos?

A. 10.8 J/K   **B. 27.3 J/K**   **C.** 38.3 J/K   **D.** 54.6 J/K

B is correct.

Heat capacity (C), also known as thermal capacity, is a measurable physical quantity indicating the amount of heat (Q) required to change the temperature of a substance. The units of heat capacity are expressed in Joules per Kelvin (J/K).

Derived quantities that specify heat capacity as an intensive property (i.e., independent of sample size) are the *molar heat capacity*, (i.e. heat capacity per mole of a pure substance) and the *specific heat* (i.e. heat capacity per unit mass) of a material.

Given the mass of the water (100 g) poured into the thermos, and the temperature change (e.g. 3.2° C), the heat lost by the water is:

$$Q = mC\Delta T:$$

$$Q_{water} = (100 \text{ g})(4.184 \text{ J/g}\cdot\text{K})(71.8°C – 75°C)$$

$$\approx (100 \text{ x } 4 \text{ x } –3) \text{ J}$$

$$\approx –1200 \text{ J (exact value is 1,338.9 J)}$$

Since the magnitude of one degree Celsius equals the magnitude of one Kelvin, the two scales can be used interchangeably because the calculation is for changes in temperature.

The heat lost by water is gained by the thermos:
$$Q_{thermos} = –Q_{water} \approx +1200 \text{ J}$$

The thermos had an initial temperature of 23°C (same as the room), and must have a final temperature equal to the water inside since the two reach thermal equilibrium.

The heat capacity of the thermos can be determined through $Q = mC\Delta T$:

$$1200 \text{ J} = (mC)(71.8°C – 23°C)$$

$$1200 \text{ J} = (mC)(49°C)$$

$$\approx (mC) \ 49°C = (mC)(49 \text{ K})$$

$$1200 \text{ J} = (mC)(49 \text{ K})$$

$$mC = 1200 \text{ J} / 49 \text{ K}$$

$$C = (1200 \text{ J} / 49 \text{ K}) / m$$

$$C = (1200 \text{ J} / 49 \text{ K}) \text{ x } \frac{1}{m}$$

Heat capacity is an intrinsic property independent of sample size: ignore m

$$C = m\frac{1200 \text{ J}}{50 \text{ K}} \approx 24 \text{ J/K (approximation)}$$

$$C = m\frac{1338.9 \text{ J}}{49 \text{ K}} = 27.3 \text{ J/K (precise values)}$$

33. Which of these graphs best represents the cooling curve for the pewter pot contents when placed in a cooler set at –25°C?

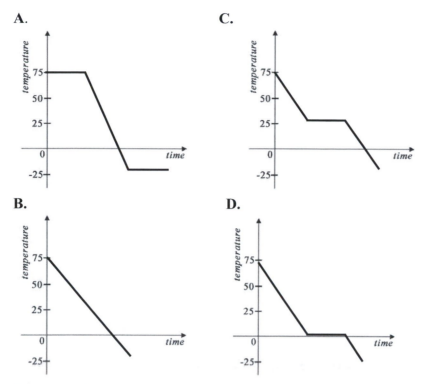

D is correct.

The contents of the pewter pot cool from 75°C to –25°C when placed in a cooler set to –25°. Under these conditions, the temperature of the water initially decreases (negative sloping line) to the freezing point (0° C), it remains constant (horizontal line) as it changes from the liquid to the solid phase.

After the entire contents freeze, the temperature of the solid water decreases (negative sloping line) until it reaches thermal equilibrium with its surroundings (–25°C).

The cooling curve must show a negative slope initially, then a flat line at 0° C, and then another negative slope as the line approaches –25°C.

A: graph shows that temperature remains constant at 75°C for a period of time even when exposed to a surrounding with a very low temperature.

B: graph shows only the sloping line of decreasing temperature without the constant temperature (horizontal line) region when freezing.

C: graph shows the constant temperature (horizontal line) region, but at 25°C and not at 0°.

34. Which of the following systems has the lowest entropy?

A. Water at 100°C   **C. Ceramic plate at 70°C**

B. Steam at 100°C   D. Water at 50°C

C is correct.

Entropy (ΔS) is a measure of disorder (randomness) of a thermodynamic system. The more disordered a system, the greater its entropy. Gases have the highest entropy, followed by liquids, then – solids (as they are the most ordered of the three phases). A ceramic plate is a solid, so it has the lowest entropy.

35. After 100 g of the water has been transferred to the thermos, the pewter pot with its contents at a temperature of 75°C was placed on the insulated warmer that transfers 500 cal/min to the water. What is the water's temperature after being placed on the warmer for 10 minutes? *Note:* assume no significant heat transfer with the surroundings.

   A. 79.2°C
   B. 83.1°C
   C. 87.2°C
   D. 91.5°C

C is correct.

If the insulated warmer transfers the heat to the pewter pot and its contents for 10 minutes at a rate of 500 cal/min, the total heat transferred is:

$$Q = 500 \text{ cal/min} \times 10 \text{ min} = 5{,}000 \text{ cal}$$

The heat absorbed by both the pewter pot and the water is equal to the heat given off by the warmer.

The water and the pewter pot have a common initial temperature of 75°C and final temperature (same ΔT).

Because the specific heats for the water and the pewter pot are expressed in J/g·K, the calorie units must be converted to joules:

$Q = mC\Delta T$

$$m_{pot} \, C_{pot}\Delta T + m_{water} \, C_{water}\Delta T = Q_{pot+water} \cdot 4.184 \text{ J/ cal}$$

$$m_{pot} \, C_{pot}\Delta T + m_{water} \, C_{water}\Delta T = 5{,}000 \text{ cal} \cdot 4.184 \text{ J/ cal}$$

$$m_{pot} \, C_{pot}\Delta T + m_{water} \, C_{water}\Delta T = 20{,}920 \text{ J}$$

Precise values: $= (250 \text{ g} \times 0.17 \text{ J/g·K} + 400 \text{ g} \times 4.184 \text{ J/g·K})\Delta T = 20{,}920 \text{ J}$

$$= (42.5 \text{ J/K} + 1673.6 \text{ J/K})\Delta T = 20{,}920 \text{ J}$$

$$\Delta T \approx \frac{20{,}920}{1716.1} = 12.19$$

75°C (initial) + 12.19°C (transfer from warmer) = 87.19°C (temperature after 10 minutes).

Approximation: $= (250 \text{ g} \times 0.17 \text{ J/g·K} + 400 \text{ g} \times 4.184 \text{ J/g·K})\Delta T = 20{,}920 \text{ J}$

$$\approx (50 \text{ J/K} + 1600 \text{ J/K})\Delta T \approx 21{,}000 \text{ J}$$

$$\Delta T \approx \frac{21{,}000}{1{,}650} \approx 12.5$$

75°C (initial) + 12.5°C (transfer from warmer) = 87.5°C (approximate temperature after 10 minutes).

36. As an alternative for keeping the water hot, the pewter pot can be placed on a block heated in an oven to 250°C. A block of which of the following substances is best able to keep the water hot?

A. silver (specific heat = 0.23 J/g·K)
B. titanium (specific heat = 0.52 J/g·K)
C. glass (specific heat = 0.84 J/g·K)
D. aluminum (specific heat = 0.90 J/g·K)

D is correct.

To best be able to keep the water hot, the heated object must be able to transfer large amounts of heat (energy) to the pewter pot as they reach thermal equilibrium. The substance with the highest specific heat transfers the most heat to the pewter pot and water per degree drop in its temperature. Aluminum would be the best choice because it has the highest specific heat.

Specific heat is the heat capacity per unit mass of a material.

Heat capacity (C) is the amount of heat required to change the temperature of a substance by a given amount and is expressed in units of Joules (J) per Kelvin (K). Heat capacity is an intensive property and independent of the size of the sample.

Heat is the transfer of thermal energy from high to low temperature regions.

Temperature is the average kinetic energy of the particles in matter.

Thermal energy transmitted by heat is stored in kinetic energy of atoms as they move or molecules as they rotate.

Passage 6
(Questions 37–41)

The circulatory system in the body functions to distribute blood, lymph, nutrients and hormones to and from the cells within the organism. Several factors control the flow of blood through the human vascular system. The rate of flow (Q) is directly proportional to the pressure difference (ΔP) between different points along the system and inversely proportional to the resistance (R) of the system:

$$Q = \Delta P/R$$

Equation 1

The resistance (R) is determined by the length (L) of the blood vessel, the viscosity (η) of blood and the radius (r) of the blood vessel:

$$R = \frac{8\eta L}{\pi r^4}$$

Equation 2

Under normal conditions, the length of the blood vessel and the viscosity of the blood are negligible and therefore, the resistance is insignificant. However, certain conditions cause changes in the blood composition which alters the viscosity. Veins are more compliant (expand and contract in response to pressure changes) since there is less smooth muscle surrounding them in contrast to arteries which are surrounded by thick muscularity. The flow of blood through the major arteries can be approximated by the equations of ideal flow.

The dynamics of blood and fluid movement from capillaries to body tissue (i.e. interstitial space) and back to capillaries are driven by the differences in pressure. The net movement depends on the difference between the hydrostatic pressure of the blood in the capillaries (P_c) and that of interstitial fluid outside the capillaries (P_i). The difference between the osmotic pressure of the capillaries (π_c) of approximately 25 mmHg and the osmotic pressure of the interstitial tissue fluids (π_I) (which is negligible) is called *oncotic* pressure. The difference in hydrostatic and oncotic pressure determines the direction of fluid movement (whether the fluid moves into or out of the capillary) and is calculated as:

$$\Delta P = (P_c + \pi_I) - (P_i + \pi_c)$$

Equation 3

The sum of $P_c + \pi_I$ is the force acting to move fluid into the interstitial space from the capillaries, while the sum of $P_i + \pi_c$ is the force acting to move fluid into the capillaries from the interstitial space.

Note: 1 atm = 760 Torr = 760 mmHg.

37. The body increases red blood cell count as the art of adaptation to living at high altitudes. Ignoring other physiological compensating factors, what effect will this change have on the flow of blood?

A. increased due to increased viscosity   **C.** increased due to decreased viscosity
B. decreased due to increased viscosity   **D.** decreased due to decreased viscosity

B is correct.

Increasing RBCs count in the blood increases the blood's viscosity. Since Q is inversely proportional to η (*Poiseuille's* Law), increasing the viscosity decreases the flow rate.

The Hagen-Poiseuille equation of fluid dynamics determines the pressure drop in a fluid moving through a long cylindrical pipe (such as vascular system). The assumptions are: 1) the fluid is viscous (i.e. internal friction) and incompressible, 2) the flow is laminar (i.e. streamline flow where fluid flows in a parallel layers with no disruption between the layers) through a pipe of a constant circular cross-section that is much longer than its diameter, and 3) there is no acceleration of the fluid in the pipe.

However, the flow of actual fluid is turbulent, not laminar, for velocities and pipe diameters above a threshold which produces a greater pressure drop than the value calculated by Poiseuille's equation.

38. According to the diagram of systemic circulation below, which of the following is true?

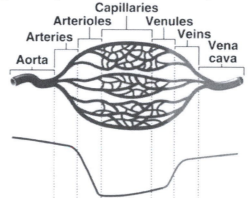

Vascular architecture of organs is in:

A. parallel, total peripheral resistance is greater than the resistance of individual organs
B. parallel, total peripheral resistance is less than the resistance of individual organs
C. series, total peripheral resistance is greater than the resistance of individual organs
D. series, total peripheral resistance is less than the resistance of individual organs

B is correct.
With various parallel branches (e.g. arteries and arterioles) the architecture is in parallel. By the analogy with electrical circuits, the total resistance of a collection of parallel resistors is *less* than that of any of the individual resistances.

39. The dilation and constriction of the blood vessels regulates the blood flow to the various systems in the body. For example, after ingesting a large meal, the blood vessels supplying the digestive system will dilate to increase their radii by 25% and the flow of blood to the digestive system will be about:

    A. 25% of the original flow   **C.** 125% of the original flow

    B. 75% of the original flow   **D. 250% of the original flow**

D is correct.

Combining equations 1 and 2: $Q = \Delta P \pi r^4 / 8 \eta L$

The flow rate (Q) is proportional to r^4

If r increases by 25% to $1.25r$

then Q increases by a factor of $(1.25)^4 = (5/4)^4$

$= 625/256$

$\approx 2.5 = 250\%$

40. Given that the cross sectional area of the aorta is approximately 5 cm^2 and the speed of the blood in the aorta is 20 cm/sec, what is the average blood speed in the major arteries if their cross sectional area is 4 cm^2?

    A. 2 cm/sec   **B.** 8 cm/sec   **C. 25 cm/sec**   **D.** 100 cm/sec

C is correct.

Use the equation: $A_1 v_1 = A_2 v_2$ and substitute the values given:

$(5 \text{ cm}^2)(20 \text{ cm/sec}) = (4 \text{ cm}^2) v_2,$

$\dfrac{(5 \text{ cm}^2)(20 \text{ cm/sec})}{(4 \text{ cm}^2)} = v_2,$

$v_2 = 25$ cm/sec.

41. The hydrostatic pressure of the capillary at the venular end of skeletal muscle capillaries is 15 mmHg, hydrostatic pressure of the interstitial fluid is 0 mmHg and oncotic pressure in the interstitial fluid is 3 mmHg. Under these conditions, blood moves from the:

    A. interstitial to the capillary, with a pressure of 7 mmHg
    B. interstitial to the capillary, with a pressure of 13 mmHg
    C. capillary to the interstitial, with a pressure of 7 mmHg
    D. capillary to the interstitial, with a pressure of 13 mmHg

A is correct.

Since the osmotic pressure of the interstitial fluid is negligible ($\pi_1 = 0$), the total pressure force to move fluid *out* of the capillaries is: $P_c + \pi_1 = 15 + 3 = 18$ mmHg.

The total pressure moving the fluid *into* the capillaries is greater: $P_1 + \pi_c = 0 + 25 = 25$ mmHg.

Therefore, the fluid moves *into* the capillaries at a rate proportional to $25 - 18 = 7$ mmHg.

The Starling equation provides for the relationship between hydrostatic (i.e. blood pressure) and oncotic (i.e. osmotic pressure due to plasma proteins) forces in the movement of fluids across capillary membranes:

$$J_v = K_f([P_c - P_i] - \sigma[\pi_c - \pi_i])$$

Capillary fluid movement occurs via diffusion, filtration and pinocytosis.

Location	P_c (mmHg)	P_i (mmHg)	π_c (mmHg)	π_i (mmHg)
Arteriolar end of capillary	+35	0	+25	+0.1
Venular end of capillary	+15	0	+25	+3

P_c (mmHg) is hydrostatic pressure in the capillary
P_i (mmHg) is hydrostatic pressure in the interstitial space
π_c (mmHg) is oncotic pressure in the capillary
π_i (mmHg) is oncotic pressure in the interstitial space

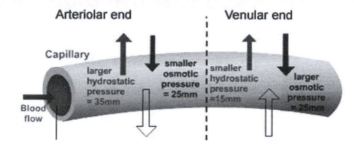

Questions 42 through 45 are not based on any descriptive passage and are independent of each other

42. What is the K_b value of ⁻OH, given that the K_a of H_3O^+ is 1.75 x 10⁻⁵ ?

  A. 3.3 x 10⁻⁷   **B.** 5.3 x 10⁻⁸   **C. 5.7 x 10⁻¹⁰**   **D.** 10

C is correct.

In any aqueous solution, the K_a of any acid x the K_b of its conjugate base = 1 x 10⁻¹⁴. This relationship is always valid for hydroxide and hydrogen ions, as well as for all other acids and bases in aqueous solutions.

The acidity constant for an acid x the base constant for the conjugate base = the water constant.

Substituting the K_a of hydronium ion H_3O^+:
(1.75 x 10⁻⁵) x K_b = 1 x 10⁻¹⁴ K_b = (1 x 10⁻¹⁴) / (1.75 x 10⁻⁵) = 5.71 x 10⁻¹⁰

43. The two lowest notes on the piano are A_0 (28.6 Hz) and $A\#_0$ (30.1 Hz). If the notes are played simultaneously, the resulting sound seems to repeatedly turn off and on. How much time exists between the successive "on" sounds?

  A. 0.66 s   **B.** 1.5 s   **C.** 28.6 s   **D.** 30.1 s

A is correct.

The beat frequency is: f_{beat} = (30.1 Hz) – (28.6 Hz) = 1.5 Hz.
Since the period is $T = 1/f$, $T = 1/1.5 = 0.66$ s.

44. In the Hubble Space Telescope (HST) the incoming light is focused by the primary mirror ofa 2.4 m diameter onto the detection apparatus. Considering that the HST is used to observe galaxies in visible light, which of the following is the closest estimation for the resolution?

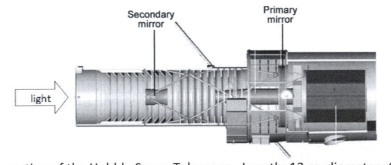

Cross section of the Hubble Space Telescope. Length: 13 m; diameter: 4.3 m

  A. 2.4 x 10⁻⁷ radians   **C.** 13.56 x 10⁻⁷ radians
  B. 24.0 x 10⁻⁷ radians   **D.** 1356.0 x 10⁻⁷ radians

A is correct.

Using the wavelength of yellow light as representative for visible light, solve for diffraction:

$$\theta_{diff} = \frac{\lambda}{d} = (565 \times 10^{-9} \text{ m}) / (2.4 \text{ m})$$

$$= 2.35 \ 10^{-7} \text{ rad}$$

$$\approx 2.4 \times 10^{-7} \text{ rad}$$

45. The Hubble Space Telescope is also equipped with ultraviolet light detectors. Assuming diffraction limitation, how would the resolution for the ultraviolet compare to the one for visible light?

    A. About the same as for visible light
    B. Higher than for visible light
    C. Lower than for visible light
    D. Sometimes lower and sometimes higher than for visible light

B is correct.

Ultraviolet (UV) light has a shorter wavelength (λ) than visible light (10-400nm versus 400-750nm).

From the equation $\theta_{diff} = \lambda/d$, the diffraction angle for UV light is lower and therefore provides for better resolution (assuming the detection apparatus is diffraction limited).

Passage 7
(Questions 46–52)

Explosive is a reactive substance containing a large amount of potential energy which may be chemical energy (e.g. nitroglycerin), pressurized gas (e.g. gas cylinder) or nuclear energy (e.g. uranium-235 or plutonium-239). An explosion occurs when this potential energy is released suddenly. Explosions often produce light, sound, heat and pressure. Explosive materials are categorized by the speed at which they expand where materials that detonate at speeds faster than the speed of sound are *high explosives* and the others are *low explosives*.

Oxidation-reduction reactions are the most common type of chemical reactions. Redox reactions that result from strong oxidizing and strong reducing agents are highly exothermic. The amount of heat produced from these reactions is directly proportional to the strengths of the oxidant and the reductant.

Compounds that contain an electropositive atom (e.g., C, H, alkali earth metals) in a nonpositive (i.e. charged) oxidation state are reducing agents. Alternatively, a reducing agent has two or more electropositive atoms that are covalently bonded together. A reductant's strength is proportional to the eletropositivity and the oxidation state of the atom. Some mild reducing agents are $H_2(g)$, $C(s)$, $S(s)$, metal powders and butane. Strong reducing agents like alkali metals are rarely used to make explosives because it is difficult to prevent the spontaneous detonation that takes place when they are exposed to atmospheric oxygen.

Compounds which contain a highly electronegative atom (such as F, O, N, Cl) in a nonnegative (i.e. charged) oxidation state are oxidizing agents. Alternatively, an oxidizing agent has two or more highly electronegative elements that are covalently bonded together. An oxidant's strength is proportional to the electronegativity and oxidation state of the atoms. Some *strong* oxidizing agents are Cl_2, H_2O_2, $NaNO_3$, $KMnO_4$ and $NaClO_4$.

46. Which of these compounds is one of the components of gun powder, in addition to charcoal (pure carbon) and elemental sulfur?

 A. LiCl   **B. NaNO₃**   **C.** Manganese   **D.** CaF_2

B is correct.

Being an explosive, gunpowder must consist of an oxidant and a reductant. Since both elemental carbon and sulfur are moderate reductants, an oxidizing agent is needed to provide for potential energy in the mix. Sodium nitrate ($NaNO_3$) is a strong oxidizing agent because the electronegative nitrogen is in a +5 oxidative state: Na = +1, O = (–2 x 3) = –6

A: is neither an oxidizing nor a reducing agent.

C: a good reducing agent.

D: is neither an oxidizing nor a reducing agent.

47. With the reaction mechanism below, Zn metal is attacked by hydrochloric acid. Why Cu metal would not be affected by HCl?

$$Zn(s) + 2HCl\ (aq) \rightarrow ZnCl_2\ (aq) + H_2\ (g)$$

   A. Cu^+ is a stronger oxidant than H^+
   B. Zn is a stronger oxidant than H^+
   C. Zn is a stronger oxidant than Cu
   D. Cl^- is a stronger oxidant than Zn, but is a weaker oxidant than Cu

A is correct.

With redox questions, determine which element is gaining (pulling on) electrons from the other element. $HCl(aq)$ and $ZnCl_2(aq)$ are effectively H^+, Cl^-, and Zn^{2+} in solution.

The H^+ ion is oxidizing (pulling) the Zn's electrons but it is too weak to pull away Cu's electrons. H^+ is a stronger oxidant than Zn^{2+}, but not as strong as the Cu^+ ion.

D: Cl is a spectator ion and not involved in redox.

48. All of these compounds, when mixed with lithium metal, will make it explode EXCEPT:

   A. argon gas   **B.** nitric oxide   **C.** chlorine liquid   **D.** sulfuric acid

A is correct.

Lithium metal is a strong reductant which, in the presence of an oxidizing agent, reacts and explodes. The alkali metals sodium, potassium, lithium, rubidium and cesium are the most reactive class of metals. They are highly combustible, react with water to generate hydrogen gas and are easily ignited.

Argon is a noble gas inert to all chemical reactions. According to the passage, an oxidizing agent is a compound that has two or more highly-electronegative atoms covalently bonded together.

B: nitric oxide (HNO_3) is a strong oxidizing agent.
C: chlorine liquid is a strong oxidizing agent.

D: sulfuric acid (H_2SO_4) is a strong oxidizing agent.

49. In which of these compounds oxygen atom is most highly oxidized?

   A. O_2^- **B.** H_2O_2 **C. F_2O**   **D.** N_2O

C is correct.

Determine which molecule has an oxygen atom in the most positive oxidation state. Oxygen would only have a positive oxidation state when ionized or when bonded to a more electronegative atom. Only fluorine is an element with a greater electronegativity than oxygen's.

Even without determining the atom's individual oxidation states, the oxidation state for O in oxygen difluorine (F_2O) = +2.

A: in superoxide ion (O_2^-), the oxidation state for O = –1/2.

B: in peroxide ion (H_2O_2 with O_2^{2-}), the oxidation state for each O = –1.

D: in nitrous oxide (N_2O), the oxidation state for O = –2.

50. The chemical rockets of a space shuttle use a liquid fuel that is a mixture of liquid hydrogen and oxygen which produce highly exothermic reactions. Which of these fuel mixtures is most likely to release more energy than H_2 and O_2?

   A. H_2 and Cl_2 **B.** H_2 and I_2 **C. H_2 and F_2**   **D.** H_2 and Br_2

C is correct.

According to the passage, the energy released by a redox reaction is directly proportional to the strengths of the oxidant and the reductant. An exothermic reaction with a greater energy output than H_2 and O_2 must utilize a stronger oxidizing agent, or stronger reducing agent or both.

All answer choices offer the same reductant (H_2). F_2 is among the most powerful oxidants because it has the highest electronegativity of all the elements, but it is not used by NASA because of the environmental concerns associated with the release of hydrofluoric acid into the atmosphere as opposed to steam (H_2O).

Cl_2, I_2 and Br_2 are all weaker oxidants than the highly electronegative F in F_2.

51. Which of the following compounds is used in household bleach which consists of 94-97% water and 3-6% of a mild oxidizing agent that contains electronegative atoms with a +1 or +2 oxidation state?

   A. KCl   **B.** $NaClO_3$ **C. NaClO**   **D.** $NaIO_4$

C is correct.

Given that household bleach contains an oxidizing agent with an electronegative atom with a +1 or +2 oxidation state, determine the oxidation state of each answer choice.

In NaClO, Cl has an oxidation state +1. The oxidant in bleach must be sodium hypochlorite, NaClO.

A: KCl is not an oxidant because Cl has an oxidation state of –1.

B: Na has a +1 oxidation state, each O atom has a –2 oxidation state (3 x –2 = –6) and the oxidation state of iodine in $NaIO_3$ is: Cl = +5, Na = +1, O = – 6. Therefore, I is: +5+1–6 = 0

D: in $NaIO_4$, I has an oxidation state +7.

52. Which one of these mixtures would produce an explosion when heated?

   A. RbF and Cu powder   **C.** H_2O_2 and Cl_2
   B. CH_4 and NH_3 **D. $KMnO_4$ and Mn powder**

D is correct.

A +7 oxidation state of the Mn atom in the permanganate ion (MnO_4^-) makes it one of the strongest oxidizing agents. Manganese metal (like all metals) is a reducing agent.

The other choices are not mixtures of a reductant and an oxidant and therefore are not explosives.

A: a non-reactive salt and a mild reducing agent.

B: two strong reducing agents (methane & ammonia).

C: two very strong oxidizing agents.

> Questions 53 through 59 are not based on any
> descriptive passage and are independent of each other

53. Given that enzyme is a catalyst, which of the following statements is correct?

    A. The enzyme is not changed over the course of an enzyme-catalyzed reaction
    B. Reaction that is normally catalyzed by the enzyme will not take place without an enzyme
    C. Enzyme-catalyzed reaction is always exergonic
    D. Enzymes increase the rate of a reaction though a mechanism different than in uncatalyzed reaction

A is correct.

54. Which statement best explains how the inhibitor binds to the enzyme in noncompetitive inhibition?

    A. The inhibitor binds to a site other than the active site only after the substrate binds
    B. Either before or after the substrate binds, the inhibitor binds to a site other than the active site
    C. The inhibitor binds to the active site only after the substrate binds
    D. The inhibitor binds to a site other than the active site only before the substrate binds

B is correct.

Non-competitive inhibition is an enzyme inhibition whereby the inhibitor binds equally well to the enzyme (whether or not it has already bound the substrate) and reduces the activity of the enzyme. The most common mechanism for non-competitive inhibition is reversible binding of the inhibitor to an allosteric site.

55. Which enzyme activity is associated with the termination factor ρ?

    A. Helicase   **B.** Exonuclease   **C.** Endonuclease   **D.** Topoisomerase

A is correct.

56. Monomers of a polysaccharide are linked together by:

    A. Glycosidic bond   **C.** Phosphate ester bond
    B. Peptide bond   **D.** Glucotide bond

A is correct.

Glycosidic bond is a covalent bond that joins a sugar molecule to another group (which may or may not be a carbohydrate).

57. In animal cell membranes, cholesterol:

    A. acts as a receptor site for hormones on the surface of membranes
    B. broadens the temperature range of optimum membrane fluidity
    C. blocks the association of the fatty acyl chains of phospholipids at high temperature
    D. aids in the transport of small hydrophobic molecules across the membrane

B is correct.

58. Why are triacylglycerols NOT found in cell membranes?

    A. Because they are not abundant in cells
    B. Because they are charged at biological pH
    C. Because they are amphipathic
    D. Because they are not amphipathic

D is correct.

Membrane fluidity refers to the viscosity of the lipid bilayer of a cell membrane. Cholesterol acts as a bidirectional regulator of membrane fluidity. At high temperatures, it stabilizes the membrane and raises its melting point, while at low temperatures, it intercalates between the phospholipids and prevents them from clustering together and stiffening.

59. Which of these molecules is aromatic?

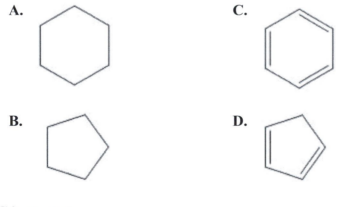

C is correct.

CHEMICAL & PHYSICAL FOUNDATIONS OF BIOLOGICAL SYSTEM
MCAT® PRACTICE TEST #4 ANSWER KEY

Passage 1
1 : A
2 : C
3 : D
4 : D

Passage 2
5 : C
6 : A
7 : B
8 : B
9 : C

Independent questions
10 : B
11 : D
12 : D
13 : B

Passage 3
14 : B
15 : D
16 : C
17 : D
18 : C

Passage 4
19 : B
20 : D
21 : B
22 : D
23 : A

Independent questions
53 : B
54 : B
55 : B
56 : D
57 : A
58 : C
59 : B

Independent questions
24 : C
25 : B
26 : C
27 : A
28 : C

Passage 5
29 : B
30 : C
31 : B
32 : C
33 : B
34 : D
35 : C

Passage 6
36 : D
37 : B
38 : B
39 : B
40 : D
41 : C

Independent questions
42 : C
43 : A
44 : A
45 : B

Passage 7
46 : B
47 : C
48 : A
49 : C
50 : D
51 : A
52 : B

Passage 1
(Questions 1–4)

A cylindrical pole stands vertically with one end attached securely to the ground. The pole is made of a homogeneous material with a density of 6000 kg/m³, its length is 12 m and cross sectional area is 0.03 m². Figure 1 shows the pole and three hypothetical cross sections at 4-meter intervals.

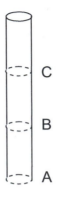

Figure 1.

The pole can be considered a very rigid spring that follows *Hooke's Law* which states that stress is directly proportional to strain:

$$F = -kx$$

Equation 1

where F is the restoring force exerted by the spring on that end (N or kg·m/s²), k is a constant referred to as the *rate* or *spring constant* (N/m or kg/s²) and x is displacement of the spring's end from its equilibrium position (a distance in meters).

If some object is placed at the top of the pole, the pole gets compressed by an amount proportional to that object's weight. But if the object's mass is significant enough to bend the pole, Hooke's law no longer applies. Assume that the pole above acts as a Hooke's Law spring until it collapses.

Young's modulus of elasticity (*E*) is the ratio of stress (units of pressure) to strain (dimensionless). Therefore, Young's modulus has units of pressure (*p*). Pressure is the ratio of the force over the area to which that force is applied.

Young's modulus is similar to the spring constant in Hooke's Law and Equation 1 shows that *E* depends on the stress (σ) exerted on an object.

$$E = \frac{\text{tensile stress}}{\text{tensile strain}} = \frac{\sigma}{\varepsilon} = \frac{F/A_o}{\Delta L/L_o}$$

Equation 2

where E = Young's modulus (modulus of elasticity);
F = force exerted on an object under tension;
A_0 = original cross-sectional area through which the force is applied;
ΔL = amount by which the length of the object changes;
L_0 = original length of the object.

Strain (ε), the fractional change in length the body undergoes is defined as:

$$\varepsilon = \frac{\Delta L}{Lo}$$

Equation 3

One also must consider that in reality, a pole needs to be able to support its weight. If the diameter of a pole is fixed, there is a limit to the pole's height. The stress (σ) on the pole exerted by its own weight is $\sigma = \rho gh$ at any point, where ρ is the density of the pole, h is the height of the pole above that point and g is acceleration due to gravity.

Note: for the pole above, $E = 945$ N/m^2; the acceleration due to gravity, $g = 9.8$ m/s^2.

1. What is the relative value of the Young's modulus for a metal pole if it undergoes minimal fractional change in length while subject to significant stress?

A. large & positive   C. small & positive
B. large & negative   **D.** small & negative

A is correct.

From Equation 2,

$$E = \frac{\sigma}{\varepsilon}$$

if σ is "significant", but ε is "minimal" their ratio is large & positive.

2. Which of the following expressions best represents the pressures at each of the pole's cross sections A, B, and C?

A. $\sigma_A = \sigma_B = \sigma_C$ **B.** $\sigma_A < \sigma_B > \sigma_C$ **C.** $\sigma_A > \sigma_B > \sigma_C$ **D.** $\sigma_A < \sigma_B < \sigma_C$

C is correct.

According to the passage, the pressure at any given point on the pole is given as $\sigma = \rho gh$, where h is the height of the pole above that point. Therefore, the lower the point on the pole, the greater the pressure is.

Since cross section A is located lower on the pole than B, which is lower than C, the stress (σ) exerted on the pole by its own weight is: $\sigma_A > \sigma_B > \sigma_C$.

3. Which expression corresponds with how tall the pole could get before buckling under its own weight if it collapses when compressed by more than a factor of ε_c?

A. $\dfrac{\varepsilon_c}{E}$ **B.** $\dfrac{\varepsilon_{cg}}{E}$ **C.** $\dfrac{Eg}{\rho\varepsilon_c}$ **D.** $\dfrac{E\varepsilon_c}{\rho g}$

D is correct.

Check units: E (N/m^3), g (m/s^2), ρ (kg/m^3) and ε has no units. Note: $N = kg\,\dfrac{m}{s^2}$

Only expression D has units of meters.

For example, B: $\dfrac{\varepsilon_c g}{E} = \dfrac{m/s^2}{N/m^3}$

For example, D: $\dfrac{E\varepsilon_c}{\rho g} = \dfrac{N/m^3}{\dfrac{kg}{m^3}\cdot\dfrac{m}{s^2}}$

Mathematical solution: let σ_c denote critical stress (i.e. stress at the buckling point) where ε becomes the critical strain (ε_c).

Then $\sigma_c/E = \varepsilon_c$.

$\sigma_c = \rho g h_c$,

where h_c denotes critical height (i.e. maximum height before buckling).

Combining these two equations: $\varepsilon_c = \dfrac{\rho g h_c}{E}$ or $E\varepsilon_c = \rho g h_c$ or $\dfrac{E\varepsilon c}{\rho g} = h_c$

4. What is the pressure of the pole's weight (Figure 1) at cross section B?

A. 8.0×10^2 Pa   **B.** 1.3×10^3 Pa   **C.** 4.8×10^4 Pa   **D.** 4.8×10^5 Pa

D is correct.

The stress at any point of the pole, $\sigma = \rho g h$ where h is the pole's height above that point:

$$\sigma = (6000 \text{ kg/m}^3)\,(9.8 \text{ N/kg})\,(8 \text{ m}) = 4.8 \times 10^5 \text{ Pa}$$

where, 1 Pa = 1 N/m^2 = 1 kg/m·s^2

Passage 2
(Questions 5–9)

Energy is an indirectly observed quantity of matter that comes in many forms such as potential energy, kinetic energy, radiant energy and so on. In physics and chemistry, heat is energy transferred from one body to another by thermal interactions. The transfer of energy can occur in a variety of ways, among them conduction (i.e. collision of particles), radiation, (i.e. propagation of energy without matter) and convection (i.e. transfer of heat with any fluid or gas movement). Heat is not a property of a system or body, but is associated with a process of some kind, and is synonymous with heat flow and heat transfer.

Heat flows from hotter to colder systems, occurs spontaneously and is always accompanied by an increase in entropy. The second law of thermodynamics states that the entropy of an isolated system never decreases because isolated systems spontaneously evolve towards thermodynamic equilibrium – the state of maximum entropy where there is no net flow of matter or energy. The second law of thermodynamics prohibits heat flow directly from cold to hot systems.

Several thermodynamic definitions are very useful in thermochemistry. A system is the specific portion of the universe that is being studied. Everything outside the system is considered the surrounding or environment. A system may be an *isolated system* – when it cannot exchange energy or matter with the surroundings (e.g. an insulated bomb calorimeter), a *closed system* – when it can exchange energy but not matter with the surroundings (e.g. a steam radiator), or an *open system* – when it can exchange both matter and energy with the surroundings (e.g. a pot of boiling water).

A system undergoes a process when one or more of its properties changes. A process relates to the change of state. An *isothermal* (i.e. same temperature) process occurs when the temperature of the system remains constant. An *isobaric* (i.e. same pressure) process occurs when the pressure of the system remains constant. An *adiabatic* (i.e. no heat exchange) process occurs when no heat exchange occurs.

To produce acetic acid (i.e. table vinegar) in a lab from inexpensive starting materials, a researcher can use carbon dioxide and water. Reaction 1 shows how these two compounds react to produce carbonic acid:

$$H_2O(l) + CO_2(g) \rightarrow H_2CO_3(aq) \quad \Delta G° = 8.5 \text{ kJ/mol}$$

Reaction 1

If the researcher can find the correct catalyst, the following reaction produces acetic acid:

$$2CO_2(g) + 2H_2O(l) \rightarrow CH_3COOH(l) + 2O_2(g)$$

$$\Delta H° = 873 \text{ kJ/mol}$$

$$\Delta S° = 3 \text{ J/mol·K}$$

Reaction 2

Substance	$\Delta H°f$ (kJ/mol)	$\Delta G°f$ (kJ/mol)
$H_2CO_3(aq)$	–700	–623
$H_2O(g)$	–241.8	–237.1
$CO_2(g)$	–393.5	–394.4
$CH_3COOH(l)$	–484	–389
$C_6H_{12}O_6(aq)$	–1271	–917

Table 1. Enthalpies and free energies of formation for several compounds

5. What is the $\Delta G°f$ value for $H_2O(l)$?

A. 0 kJ   **B.** –229.0 kJ   **C.** –237.5 kJ   **D.** –246.0 kJ

C is correct.

This value cannot be taken from Table 1 because the table only provides the value for water vapor and not for liquid water. Instead, Reaction 1 is applied to the following relationship:

$$\Delta G° = \text{free energy of product formation} - \text{free energy of formation of reactants}$$

8.5 kJ = (free energy of carbonic acid formation) – (free energy of liquid water formation + free energy of carbon dioxide formation)

8.5 kJ = –623 kJ – [(free energy of liquid water formation + (– 394 kJ)]

free energy of liquid water formation + (– 394 kJ) = –623 kJ – 8.5 kJ

$$\Delta G°f\,H_2O(l) + (- 394 \text{ kJ}) = -623 \text{ kJ} - 8.5 \text{ kJ}$$

$$\Delta G°f\,H_2O(l) = -623 - 8.5 + 394$$

$$\Delta G°f\,H_2O(l) = -237.5 \text{ kJ}$$

A: since liquid water is the most stable form under standard conditions, it has a $\Delta G°f = 0$. This only applies to elements and not to compounds.

6. For Reaction 2 to occur spontaneously, what condition must be satisfied (assuming that ΔH and ΔS are independent of temperature)?

    A. The temperature is sufficiently high
    B. It never occurs spontaneously because $\Delta G°$ is positive
    C. The correct catalyst is found
    D. The temperature is sufficiently low

A is correct.

Since both the $\Delta H°$ and $\Delta S°$ for Reaction 2 are positive, the reaction is spontaneous only at high temperatures because only then the free energy change ($\Delta H° - T\Delta S°$) is negative.

B: while $\Delta G°$ (i.e. free energy change) is positive (at 298° K), its value changes as T changes.

C: a catalyst would not affect the spontaneity of the reaction.

D: a reaction that is spontaneous only at low temperatures will have negative $\Delta H°$ and $\Delta S°$.

7. For Reaction 1, what is the value of the thermodynamic equilibrium constant at 298 K? *Note:* ln x = 2.3 log$_{10}$ x; the universal gas constant (R) is 8.3145 J/mol·K.

A. 2×10^{-17} B. 4×10^{-2} C. 1 D. 25

B is correct.

Determine the value of K_{eq}:

$\Delta G° = -RT\ln K_{eq}$

$\Delta G°$ (given) for reaction 1 = 8.5 kJ/mol or 8,500 J/mol.

Therefore:

$$\Delta G° = -RT\ln K_{eq}$$

$$\ln K_{eq} = \Delta G° / -RT$$

$$\ln K_{eq} = -\frac{8500 \text{ J/mol}}{8.3145\frac{\text{J}}{\text{mol·K}} \text{ x } 298 \text{ K}}$$

$$= -\frac{8500}{8.5 \text{ x } 300} = -3.3$$

$$2.3 \log_{10} K_{eq} = -3.3$$

$$\log_{10} K_{eq} = -3.3 / 2.3$$

$$\log_{10} K_{eq} = -1.4$$

$$K_{eq} = 10^{-1.4}$$

The thermodynamic equilibrium constant is between 10^{-2} (0.01) and 10^{-1} (0.1). Alternatively, (qualitatively), ΔG is positive (thermodynamically not favored) so $K_{eq} < 1$.

8. What is the entropy change (ΔS) for the formation of acetic acid from its elements under standard conditions?

A. –3.19 kJ/mol·K C. 0.319 kJ/mol·K
B. –0.319 kJ/mol·K D. 3.19 kJ/mol·K

B is correct.

$\Delta G = \Delta H - T\Delta S$. Under standard conditions, formation reaction is $\Delta G°f = \Delta H°f - T\Delta S°f$.

According to Table 1, the fourth compound acetic acid formed from its elements.

$$-389 \text{ kJ/mol} = -484 \text{ kJ/mol} - (298°K)\,\Delta S°f$$

$$\Delta S°f = \frac{-389 + 484}{-298}$$

$$= -\frac{95}{298} \text{ kJ/mol·K}$$

which equals $\approx -1/3$ kJ/mol·K or -0.319 kJ/mol·K.

9. Under standard conditions, would $H_2O(g)$ decompose into its elements spontaneously?

    A. Yes, H_2O cannot exist in the gaseous phase at 25°C
    B. Yes, entropy increases
    C. No, $\Delta G°$ for the reaction is positive
    D. No, the reaction is endothermic

C is correct.

Decomposition of water vapor into its elements is the reverse of the second line in Table 1. If the equation is reversed, the signs of ΔG and ΔH change.

Since in the reverse reaction $\Delta G°$ is positive (i.e. energy of the products is higher than energy of reactants), decomposition is nonspontaneous.

> Questions 10 through 13 are not based on any descriptive passage and are independent of each other

10. Which element has the electronic configuration [Ar] $4s^2\, 3d^3$?

    A. titanium   **B. vanadium**   **C.** chromium   **D.** molybdenium

B is correct.

Count the number of electrons: the Nobel gas argon [Ar] = 18 electrons, $4\,s^2 = 2$ electrons, and $3d^3 = 3$ electrons. $18 + 2 + 3 = 23$ electrons.

The element with atomic number (Z) 23 is vanadium.

11. The energy of photons emitted by the mercury vapor is:

A. equal to the energy of electric current
B. equal to the voltage across the fluorescent tube
C. less than the energy difference between electron orbitals of mercury atoms
D. equal to the energy difference between electron orbitals of mercury atoms

D is correct.

Photon is an elementary particle, quantum of electromagnetic field and the basic "unit" of light and all other forms of electromagnetic radiation and carrier of electromagnetic force. The energy of emitted photons equals the energy difference between electron orbitals in the mercury atom. Photons are emitted from an atom when its electrons fall from an excited state to a lower energy state. The conservation of energy principle indicates that energy of an emitted photon equals energy of an excited state minus lower state.

The energy of electric current is not related to this process.

Voltage is unrelated to the physical process of atoms emitting photons.

Choice C violates conservation of energy and therefore is a false statement.

12. Isocyanic acid is not an oxidizing agent. Therefore the structure of HCNO is:

A. $H-N=O-N$ C. $N-O=C-H$
B. $C=N-O-H$ D. $O=C=N-H$

D is correct.

Given that HCNO is not an oxidizing agent, it can be concluded that the electronegative atoms N and O are not bonded directly to each other.

Additionally, the other choices would not meet the valence requirements of hydrogen, carbon, nitrogen or oxygen.

13. How many molecules are present in Y grams of a compound with a molecular mass of X, assuming the Avogadro's constant is A?

A. $\dfrac{XY}{A}$ B. $\dfrac{YA}{X}$ C. $\dfrac{Y}{XA}$ D. XYA

B is correct.

First, find the number of moles of the compound: $Y \text{ grams} \cdot \dfrac{1 \text{ mole}}{X \text{ grams}} = \dfrac{Y}{X} \text{ moles}$

Multiply the number of moles by Avogadro's number $\dfrac{Y}{X} \cdot A = \dfrac{YA}{X}$

The molecular mass is the mass of a molecule. It is sometimes called "molecular weight", but it is incorrect because weight is a different property.

The Avogadro constant is the number of constituent particles (atoms or molecules) in one mole of a given substance. The Avogadro constant value is $6.02 \times 10^{23} \text{ mol}^{-1}$

Passage 3
(Questions 14–18)

Elastic collision is a collision between two bodies where the sum of their linear momenta ($P_1 + P_2$) has the same value before and after the collision. The total kinetic energy (KE) of the system remains unchanged because none of the system's kinetic energy is converted into other forms (e.g. heat, light, sound) of energy.

The conservation of the total momentum demands that the total momentum before and after the collision is the same, and is expressed by the equation:

$$m_1 \vec{u}_1 + m_2 \vec{u}_2 = m_1 \vec{v}_1 + m_2 \vec{v}_2.$$

Likewise, the conservation of the total kinetic energy is expressed by the equation:

$$\frac{m_1 u_1^2}{2} + \frac{m_2 u_2^2}{2} = \frac{m_1 v_1^2}{2} + \frac{m_2 v_2^2}{2}.$$

where m_1 and m_2 are the masses, u_1 and u_2 the velocities before the collision, and v_1 and v_2 are the velocities after collision.

The main condition that makes a collision perfectly elastic is the absence of friction. This condition usually exists at atomic and subatomic levels whereby atoms and nuclear particles often undergo ideal elastic collisions. This condition is not achievable for macroscopic bodies on the earth and all such bodies produce collisions that are not perfectly elastic because some of the kinetic energy of each body gets converted into other energy forms.

To simulate motion and contact free of friction, researchers run experiments that involve miniature carts sliding along a track. Carts are supported by air streams projecting from the track's surface and this allows them to slide almost free of friction.

Physicists set up an experiment involving the collision of two such carts whereby light springs are attached to the front and back of each cart. These springs undergo compression and extension and obey Hooke's law. The masses of the carts are 2 kg and 4 kg. When the air streams are turned off, the coefficient of kinetic friction is less than 0.01, therefore frictional effects can be disregarded. When the carts slide toward each other, immediately prior to the collision, the speed of the lighter cart is 4 m/s and that of the heavier one is 2 m/s.

14. Which of the following sequences represents corresponding energy transfers when the two carts approach each other, collide and separate?

   A. elastic potential → kinetic → elastic potential
   B. kinetic → elastic potential → kinetic
   C. kinetic → heat → gravitational potential → heat → kinetic
   D. heat → kinetic → heat → gravitational potential

B is correct.

First, the carts have kinetic energy as they move toward each other. When they collide and momentarily come to rest, the springs between them experience maximum compression which means they are given maximum elastic potential energy.

Then the springs expand back, converting their stored elastic potential energy back into the kinetic energy of the carts which are now separating and moving in the opposite directions.

Given that friction is negligible, there is no heat transfer.

15. What is the total kinetic energy of the system immediately before the collision?

A. 8 J   **B.** 12 J   **C.** 16 J   **D. 24 J**

D is correct.

The sum of the carts' individual kinetic energies = total kinetic energy:

$$KE_{total} = \frac{1}{2} m_i v_1^2 + \frac{1}{2} m_2 v_2^2$$

$$= \frac{1}{2}(2)(4)^2 + \frac{1}{2}(4)(2)^2 = 16 + 8 = 24 \text{ J}$$

16. If the experiment is conducted on an elevated platform inclined at an angle of 50° to the horizontal, what is the magnitude of the component of the sliding cart's weight (i.e. *mg*) normal to the plane?

A. *mg* sin 50°   **B.** *mg* cos 40°   **C. *mg* sin 40°**   **D.** None of the above

C is correct.

If $w = mg$ is the magnitude of the cart's weight, then the component of this force which is normal ($N = mg \cos\theta$) to the inclined platform is $mg \cos\theta$, where θ is the incline angle.

cos 50° = sin 40° (because the angles 50° and 40° are complementary).

17. If the experiment was designed in a way that the collision between carts was perfectly inelastic, what would be the energy dissipation for the collision?

A. 0 J   **B.** 2 J   **C.** 12 J   **D. 24 J**

D is correct.

Elastic collision is defined as a collision where there is no loss of kinetic energy. However, in reality, some amount of the kinetic energy is converted to internal energy. Inelastic collision is a collision where there is a change of kinetic energy to other energy forms.

Momentum ($\rho = mv$) is always conserved in both inelastic and elastic collisions, but the kinetic energy cannot be tracked because some energy is converted to other energy forms (e.g. heat, light, sound).

In a perfectly inelastic collision, two carts would come to a halt after they collide, because they go into the collision with equal but opposite momenta:

$m_1v_1 = (2 \text{ kg})(+4 \text{ m/s})$

$= +8 \text{ kg·m/s}$, while m_2v_2

$= (4 \text{ kg})(-2 \text{ m/s}) = -8 \text{ kg·m/s}$

Therefore, the total momentum after the collision is zero which means that their final common velocity is zero. That is why their final total kinetic energy is also zero.

Before the collision, the total kinetic energy is 24 J,

$$KE_{total} = \frac{1}{2} m_i \, v_1^2 + \frac{1}{2} m_2 \, v_2^2 \; \frac{1}{2}$$

$$= \frac{1}{2} (2) (4)^2 + \frac{1}{2} (4) (2)^2$$

$$= 16 + 8 = 24 \text{ J}$$

In this perfectly inelastic collision, the dissipated energy is the entire 24 J.

18. In a system where two objects undergo an ideal elastic collision, which of the following statements is valid?

    I.   **Momentum (ρ) is conserved**
    II.   **Kinetic energy (KE) is conserved**
    III.   Velocity of each object remains unchanged

  A. I only   **B.** II only   **C. I and II only**   **D.** II and III only

C is correct.

Kinetic energy ($KE = \frac{1}{2} mv^2$) is conserved in an elastic collision by definition.

In an isolated collision (e.g. elastic or inelastic collision), momentum ($\rho = mv$) is always conserved.

Statement III: when the two objects collide, the velocity of each object cannot remain the same because the objects have different mass.

Passage 4
(Questions 19–23)

Alpha (α), beta (β) and gamma (γ) particles are destructive to biological molecules because they are able to ionize atoms they collide with. In living organisms, ionization of compounds ultimately results in some type of biochemical dysfunction because ionized molecules typically lose all their useful activity. Limited exposure to these particles on the cellular level is typically not fatal because the majority of the damaged molecules can be replaced. However, if cellular DNA is struck by several decay particles, the damage to the DNA molecule is usually fatal for the cell.

Occasionally, a nonessential (e.g. non-coding) region of the DNA may be damaged causing the genome of the cell to be altered (mutated) but not resulting in phenotypic changes or in cell death. If the damaged gene affects cell replication (i.e. tumor suppressor gene or oncogene), that cell may become cancerous and replicate uncontrollably.

The destructiveness of ingested radioisotopes may be graded as alpha > beta > gamma rays. External exposure hazards vary significantly, with the potential biohazard depending on the penetrability of the particle. Figure 1 illustrates the average penetration depth of alpha, beta and gamma rays through various media. Alpha radiation consists of a helium nucleus and would not penetrate through a sheet of paper. Beta radiation consists of electrons and is not able to penetrate an aluminum plate. Gama radiation consists of atomic nuclei decay and requires over 1cm of dense shielding such as lead.

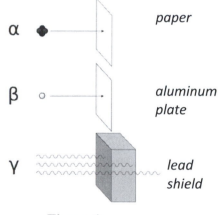

Figure 1.

In 1986, the catastrophe at the Chernobyl nuclear power plant released into the atmosphere vast amounts of highly toxic radioisotopes such as cesium-137, strontium-90, and iodine-131. All of them are short-lived radioisotopes, with half-lives of 30 years, 28 years and 8 days, respectively, and all are beta (β⁻) emitters. As these radionuclides settled from the atmosphere, they contaminated the soil and water over hundreds of thousands of square kilometers within Ukraine and Scandinavia. Today, nearly one million people in the countries of the former Soviet Union may be suffering from some physiological effects associated with chronic exposure to radiation from the Chernobyl nuclear power plant accident.

19. Why was strontium-90 (^{90}Sr) responsible for the high occurrence of bone marrow cancer following the Chernobyl disaster?

    A. ^{90}Sr is chemically similar to Be, a major component of bone matrix

    B. ^{90}Sr is chemically similar to Ca and is incorporated into the bone matrix

    C. ^{90}Sr is an essential component of hemoglobin synthesized in the bone marrow

    D. ^{90}Sr decays into ^{90}Y, a stable isotope and is a heavy metal that gets incorporated into the bone matrix

B is correct.

Sr and Ca (calcium) are both alkaline earth metals and are chemically compatible.

A: Be (beryllium) is extremely toxic and therefore is not normally present in living organisms.

C: hemoglobin is synthesized in the bone marrow, but lacks Sr.

D: while heavy metals do get incorporated into the bone matrix, heavy-metal induced cancers require long-term exposure to a metal source and may take years to develop.

20. The daughter nucleus of ^{137}Cs is:

    A. ^{136}Xe   **B.** ^{137}Xe   **C.** ^{136}Ba   **D.** ^{137}**Ba**

D is correct.

Cesium-137 has a half-life of 30 years and decays *via* gamma (γ) emission. During this process, a neutron (n) is converted into a proton (p) and an electron (e) which is violently ejected.

Therefore, the atomic number increases by one but the mass number remains constant – this corresponds with barium-137.

Note, for *beta* decay, the mass number doesn't change.

21. In constructing a barrier to penetration by *gamma* radiation, which material would be the best substitute for lead?

    A. Neon   **B. Platinum**   C. Radon   D. Silicon

B is correct.

For *gamma* radiation, the best barriers are the densest. Pt has a density of 21.45 g·cm^{-3}.

Silicon ($\rho = 2.33 \text{ g·cm}^{-3}$), neon ($\rho$ is negligible; gas at room temperature) and radon ($\rho = 5.58 \text{ g·cm}^{-3}$) are not dense elements and therefore would not stop *gamma* rays from penetrating.

Normally, lead is used for shielding from radiation because it is a relatively dense, accessible and inexpensive material, not because it has any special chemical or physical properties. Other substances with sufficient density include the less-dense Fe (i.e. weaker barrier) or the dense element of Au (but gold is not practical in many applications because of the cost).

22. Which of the following statements is true about the depth of penetration of radioactive decay in products?

   A. It increases with the increase in magnitude of the particle's charge
   B. It decreases with the increase in magnitude of the particle's charge
   C. It increases with the increase of the particle's mass
   D. It decreases with the increase of the particle's mass

D is correct.

While, like all photons, *gamma*-ray photons don't have mass, they have the greatest penetration depth.

Gamma (γ) rays are high-energy electromagnetic radiation given off by an atomic nucleus undergoing radioactive decay. Because the wavelengths of *gamma* rays are shorter than those of x-rays, *gamma* rays have greater energy and greater penetrating power than x-rays.

Alpha (α) particles have greater mass and less penetrability than *beta* (β) particles.

There is an inverse relationship between mass and depth of penetrability.

23. Considerable radiation burns on the skin, throat and lungs of a patient indicate that this person had been recently exposed to high concentrations of:

   A. ^{210}Po, an *alpha* emitter   **C.** ^{59}Ni, decay by electron capture
   B. ^{137}Cs, a *gamma* emitter   **D.** ^{15}O , a positron emitter

A is correct.

Since the radiation burns affect the epithelial surface exposed to the environment, the radiation must not penetrate tissues very well. Polonium (Po) is an α emitter.

Alpha decay is a type of radioactive decay whereby an atomic nucleus emits an alpha particle (He^{2+}) consisting of two protons and two neutrons. The parent atom decays into a daughter atom of 2 less for the atomic number (i.e. number of protons) and 4 less for the mass number (i.e. number of protons and neutrons).

Alpha decay most often occurs in the heaviest nuclides – often with mass numbers greater than 106 (e.g. ^{52}Te). Because of their relatively large mass, +2 charge and relatively low velocity, alpha particles interact with other atoms and lose their energy. Therefore, their motion penetrating distance is less than a few centimeters in air.

A *gamma* emitter is not the cause because *gamma* rays cause equal damage to all tissues, especially dense tissues like bone.

Electron capture is a process whereby a *proton-rich* nuclide absorbs an inner atomic electron.

Positron (β^+) decreases the proton number relative to the neutron number; usually occurs in *proton-rich* radionuclides.

> Questions 24 through 28 are not based on any descriptive passage and are independent of each other

24. If three moles of Cu_2S are consumed in the following reaction, how many moles of solid copper are produced?

$$Cu_2S \rightarrow 2Cu + S$$

A. 2 **B.** 3 **C.** 6 **D.** 9

C is correct.

In copper sulfide (cuprous sulfide), for each mole of Cu_2S consumed, 2 moles of Cu are produced. For three moles of Cu_2S consumed, 6 moles of Cu are produced.

25. What is the best expression for the K_{eq} in the following reaction:

$$H_2(g) + Cl_2(g) \rightleftarrows 2HCl(g)?$$

A. $[H_2][Cl_2] / [HCl]$ **C.** $[HCl] / [H_2][Cl_2]$
B. $[HCl]^2 / [H_2][Cl_2]$ **D.** $[H_2][Cl_2] / [HCl]^2$

B is correct.

K_{eq} (equilibrium expression) is derived from [products] / [reactants] with exponents equal to stoichiometric coefficients.

Stoichiometry calculates quantities of reactants and products in balanced chemical reactions. Stoichiometry can be used to calculate quantities such as the amount of products that can be produced with the given reactants and percent yield.

Knowledge of equilibrium constants is necessary for the understanding of many biological processes such as hemoglobin transport of oxygen and acid-base homeostasis in the human body. Types of equilibrium constants include stability constant, formation constant, binding constant, association constant and dissociation constant.

Equilibrium constants quantify chemical equilibria and are expressed as:

$wA + xB \rightleftarrows yC + zD$

$K_{eq} = [C]^y[D]^z / [A]^w[B]^x$

The K_{eq} is a function of concentrations [A], [B] etc. of the chemical species in equilibrium.

26. All of the following statements about chemical formulas are true EXCEPT:

    A. Molecular formula can be derived from the empirical formula and molecular weight
    B. Molecular formula can be identical to the empirical formula
    C. Molecular formula cannot be identical to the empirical formula
    D. Empirical formula can be derived from the molecular formula

C is correct.

Empirical formulas are the simplest type of chemical formulas and use only letters and numbers indicating atomic proportional ratios (the numerical proportions of atoms of one type to those of other types).

Molecular formulas indicate the simple numbers of each type of atom in a molecule of a molecular substance and therefore are sometimes the same as empirical formulas (for molecules that only have one atom of a particular type). At other times molecular formulas require larger numbers than empirical ones.

An example of this difference is the empirical formula for glucose, which is CH_2O, while its molecular formula requires all numbers to be increased by a factor of six, giving $C_6H_{12}O_6$.

A: Molecular formula (i.e. true formula) can be derived from the empirical formula and the molecular weight of the compound because the empirical formula is the simplest formula for a compound.

D: Molecular formula can be reduced to the empirical formula. For example, a molecular formula $C_3H_6O_6$ reduces to an empirical formula CH_2O_2.

27. What type of intermolecular bonding occurs between C_5H_{12} molecules?

    A. van der Waals   **C.** ionic
    B. hydrogen   **D.** covalent

A is correct.

Pentane is a nonpolar hydrocarbon, so the only intermolecular bonding between molecules is van der Waals forces.

Van der Waals forces include attractions between atoms, molecules, and surfaces. They differ from covalent and ionic bonding because they are caused by correlations in fluctuating polarizations of nearby particles. Van der Waals forces define the chemical character of many organic (e.g. hydrocarbons) compounds and the solubility of organic substances in polar and non-polar environments. Van der Waals forces are relatively weak compared to normal chemical bonds, but play an important role in structural biology, polymer science and nanotechnology.

B: hydrogen bonding is the strongest of the three intermolecular bonds. Hydrogen bonding requires a hydrogen to be bonded directly to an electronegative atom (e.g. F, O, N & Cl). Note the electronegativity of chlorine is at the bounds of sufficient electronegativity as measured in Pauling units (i.e. F = 4.0 to Fr – 0.7).

C: an ionic bond is a type of chemical bond that involves metal and non-metal ions through electrostatic attraction. An ionic bond is formed by the attraction between two oppositely charged ions with low electronegativity metals and high electronegativity non-metals. The energy change of the reaction is most favorable when metals lose electrons and non-metals gain electrons. The larger the difference in electronegativity between two atoms, the more ionic the bond is.

D: covalent bonding, where atoms are bound by sharing electrons, occurs between atoms of the same (or similar) electronegativity.

28. All of the following conditions are correct for ionic bond formation EXCEPT:

    A. transfer of electrons between two atoms
    B. valence orbitals need to be filled
    C. sharing of pairs of electrons between atoms
    D. electronegativity difference between the two atoms is greater than 1.7

C is correct.

Ionic bond is a chemical bond formed through an electrostatic attraction between two oppositely charged ions. Ionic bonds are formed between a cation (usually a metal) and an anion (usually a non-metal). Pure ionic bonding does not exist, all ionic compounds have some degree of covalent bonding. Therefore, an ionic bond is considered a bond where the ionic character is greater than the covalent character.

The larger the difference in electronegativity between the two atoms involved in the bond, the more ionic the bond is. Bonds with partially ionic and partially covalent character are called *polar covalent bonds*. Ionic bonding is a form of non-covalent bonding.

Covalent bond is the chemical bond that involves the sharing of pairs of electrons between atoms resulting in a stable balance of attractive-repulsive forces between atoms. For many molecules, the electron sharing allows each atom to attain the equivalent of a full outer shell, corresponding to a stable electronic configuration.

Covalent bonds are affected by the electronegativity of the connected atoms. Two atoms with equal electronegativity will make *non-polar covalent bonds* (e.g. H–H) while an unequal relationship creates a *polar covalent bond* (e.g. H–Cl).

Passage 5
(Questions 29–35)

In all types of collisions (assuming no external forces acting), the total momentum vector p_{total} is conserved and expressed by the equation $p'_{total} = p_{total}$, where prime denotes *after* the collision and no prime – *before*. Each component of momentum (p_x and p_y) is conserved separately. For an object of nonzero mass m, including an atom, $p = mv$. Under conditions where an external force F exists and acts for a time interval Δt, the resulting change in momentum is expressed as $\Delta p = F\Delta t$.

A photon is the quantum of light and other electromagnetic waves. Photons do not have a mass. For a photon, the magnitude of the momentum is expressed by $p = E/c$, where E is the photon's energy and c is the speed of light. The photon's energy is:

$$E = hv$$

Equation 1.

where h is Planck's constant and f is the frequency of the light.

The photon's frequency f and wavelength λ are related by the equation:

$$\lambda f = c.$$

Equation 2.

The constant $h = 4.1 \times 10^{-15}$ eV·sec $= 6.6 \times 10^{-34}$ J·sec, and the speed of light c $= 3 \times 10^8$ m/sec $= 3 \times 10^{17}$ nm/sec.

When an atom absorbs a photon, an electron can be excited to a higher energy level. The difference in energy between the original and the higher levels is equal to the energy of the photon (E). If no higher level exists so that the difference in energy equals E, the photon will not be absorbed, which means the atom will be transparent to photons of energy E. Likewise, when an electron falls from a higher to a lower energy level, a photon is emitted.

When an atom absorbs or emits a photon, momentum (p) is conserved:

$$p'_{atom} = p_{atom} + p_{photon}$$

Equation 3. Conservation of momentum

29. If a stationary atom with a mass of 3×10^{-27} kg absorbs a photon of energy 3.0×10^{-19} J, what is the magnitude of the atom's velocity after the absorption?

A. 0.1. m/s   **B. 0.3 m/s**   **C.** 3.0 m/s   **D.** 27 m/s

B is correct.

The photon's momentum, which is momentum given to the atom is $p = E/c$

Velocity of the atom $p = mv$,

Therefore,

$$v = \frac{p}{m} = \frac{E/c}{m}$$

$$= \frac{(3 \times 10^{-19})/(3 \times 10^8)}{3 \times 10^{-27}}$$

$$= 0.3 \text{ m/s}$$

30. If a 7.2 eV photon is in the vicinity of an atom that is in its ground state and the next energy level is 8.7 eV above the ground state, then the:

    A. atom's momentum changes in proportion to the energy of the photon
    B. atom absorbs the photon, but no electron will move to a different energy level
    C. photon passes the atom and has no effect
    D. photon causes one of the electrons to be ejected from the atom

C is correct.

The passage states that atoms are transparent to photons that don't have enough energy to cause a transition.

A photon is an elementary particle, the quantum of light and all other forms of electromagnetic radiation. It is the force carrier for the electromagnetic force. The effects of this force are easily observable at both the microscopic and macroscopic level because the photon has no rest mass. Like all elementary particles (e.g. neutron, protons), photons are best explained by quantum mechanics and exhibit wave–particle duality (i.e. exhibiting properties of both waves and particles). For example, a single photon may be refracted by a lens or exhibit wave interference with itself, but also act as a particle giving a definite result when its position is measured.

31. Given that the photon's wavelength is 600 nm, what is its frequency?

    A. 1.8×10^{19} sec^{-1} **C.** 1.8×10^{14} sec^{-1}
    B. 5.0×10^{14} sec^{-1} **D.** 5.0×10^{20} sec^{-1}

B is correct.

Using the equation $\lambda f = c$, $f = \frac{c}{\lambda}$

$$= \frac{3.0 \times 10^{17} \text{nm/sec}}{6 \times 10^2 \text{nm}} = 5.0 \times 10^{14} \text{ sec}^{-1}$$

32. An atom experiences a head-on collision with a photon that travels in the opposite direction and which has twice the magnitude of the momentum. The atom absorbs the photon and, as a result:

    A. moves along the initial path with increased speed   **C. reverses direction**

    B. moves along te=he initial path with decreased speed   **D.** ceases motion

C is correct.

Since the photon has twice the magnitude of the momentum and that momentum points in the opposite direction, the photon's momentum gets added to the atom's, $p + (-2p) = -p$; the atom reverses direction.

33. An atom has the magnitude of momentum p and the velocity vector perpendicular to a heavy barrier. What is the magnitude of the change in the atom's momentum after it strikes the barrier in elastic collision?

    A. p **B. 2p**   **C.** $4p$ **D.** $8p$

B is correct.

No kinetic energy is lost in the elastic collision. Since the barrier doesn't move, it didn't absorb any kinetic energy. The atom bounced off the barrier with the same speed as when it approached the barrier.

Since momentum is a vector,

$\Delta p = p_{final} - p_{initial}$

$= (-p) - p$

$= -2p.$

34. Which of the following is/are measure of momentum?

    I. N·sec

    II. kg·m/sec

    III. J·sec/m

    A. I only   **C.** II & III only

    B. I & II only   **D. I, II, & III**

D is correct.

I: $\Delta p = F\Delta t$, $[p] = $ N·sec.

II: $p = mv$, $[p] = $ kg·m/sec.

III: $p = E/c$, $[p] = $ J/(m/sec) $= $ J·sec/m.

35. If an initially stationary atom with a mass of 4.5×10^{-26} kg emits a photon of energy 4.0×10^{-19} J, what is the magnitude of the atom's momentum after the emission?

   A. 1.2×10^{-11} kg·m/s
   B. 1.2×10^{-27} kg·m/s
   C. 1.3×10^{-27} kg·m/s
   D. 7.5×10^{-11} kg·m/s

C is correct.

Momentum is conserved: the initially stationary atom gains the photon's momentum.

From the passage,

$p = E/c$:

$$p = \frac{E}{c}$$
$$= \frac{4.0 \times 10^{-19} J}{3.0 \times 10^{8} m/s}$$
$$= 1.3 \times 10^{-27} \text{ kg·m/s}$$

Passage 6
(Questions 36–41)

The first modern definition of acids and bases was proposed by Svante Arrhenius and resulted in Arrhenius receiving the Nobel Prize in Chemistry in 1903. According to Arrhenius, an acid is a substance that dissociates in water to form hydrogen (H^+) ions. Thereby, an acid increases the concentration of H^+ ions in an aqueous solution. This protonation of water yields hydronium (H_3O^+). The use of H^+ is regarded as shorthand for H_3O^+, because a bare proton (H^+) does not exist as a free species in an aqueous solution. An *Arrhenius base* is a substance that dissociates in water to form hydroxide (OH^-) ions. Thereby, a base increases the concentration of OH^- ions in an aqueous solution.

The Arrhenius definitions of acidity and alkalinity apply only to aqueous solutions and refer to the concentration of the solvent ions. By this definition, pure H_2SO_4 and HCl dissolved in toluene are not acidic, and molten KOH and solutions of sodium amide in liquid ammonia are not alkaline.

The *universal aqueous acid–base definition* of the Arrhenius concept is described as the formation of a water molecule from a proton and hydroxide ion. This leads to the definition that in Arrhenius acid–base reactions, a salt and water are formed from the reaction between an acid and a base. This is a neutralization reaction where:

$$acid + base \rightarrow salt + water$$

Arrhenius definition defines acids as compounds that dissociate a proton when mixed with water or when reacting with another substance. The proton is always closely associated with at least one water molecule, therefore sometimes it's identified as H_3O^+. In the past it was believed that all acids contained oxygen (in Greek "oxygen" means "acid-forming"), but the elemental analysis of hydrochloric acid refuted this proposition.

Acids with the low ionization percentage are weak acids and acids that are almost 100% dissociated are considered strong acids. There are thousands of compounds that are technically acids, majority of which are weak organic acids.

The acid's relative strength is identified by its K_a value (a dissociation constant). The following table provides dissociation constants for some common acids.

Name	Formula	Acidity constant (K_a)		
Acetic acid	$HC_2H_3O_2$	1.8×10^{-5}		
Carbonic acid	H_2CO_3	$K_{a1} = 4.5 \times 10^{-7}$	$K_{a2} = 4.7 \times 10^{-11}$	
Citric acid	$C_6H_8O_7$	$K_{a1} = 7.1 \times 10^{-4}$	$K_{a2} = 1.7 \times 10^{-5}$	$K_{a3} = 6.4 \times 10^{-6}$
Hydrochloric acid	HCl	1.3×10^6		
Hydrocyanic acid	HCN	6.2×10^{-10}		
Lactic acid	$H_6C_3O_3$	1.4×10^{-4}		
Nitric acid	HNO_3	2.4×10^1		
Nitrous acid	HNO_2	7.1×10^{-4}		
Oxalic acid	$H_2C_2O_4$	$K_{a1} = 5.4 \times 10^{-2}$	$K_{a2} = 6 \times 10^{-5}$	
Phosphoric acid	H_3PO_4	$K_{a1} = 7.25 \times 10^{-3}$	$K_{a2} = 6.31 \times 10^{-8}$	$K_{a3} = 3.98 \times 10^{-13}$
Sulfuric acid	H_2SO_4	$K_{a1} = 2.4 \times 10^6$	$K_{a2} = 1.2 \times 10^{-2}$	

Table 1.

36. To neutralize 20 mL of 1.0 M HNO$_2$, what is the necessary volume of 0.5 M NaOH?

A. 4 mL   **B.** 10 mL   **C.** 20 mL   **D. 40 mL**

D is correct.

The amount of H$^+$ dissociated by the nitrous acid (HNO$_2$) must be equal to the amount of $^-$OH in the potassium hydroxide. Since nitrous acid provides one H$^+$ per molecule and sodium hydroxide provides one $^-$OH per molecule, the number of moles of both compounds must be equal to completely neutralize nitrous acid.

The volume of sodium hydroxide x [NaOH] = the volume of nitrous acid x [HNO$_2$].

Since the concentration of nitrous acid is twice of that of sodium hydroxide, two times the volume of sodium hydroxide (40 mL) is needed to completely neutralize 20 mL of 1.0 M solution of nitrous acid.

37. Which of these mixtures can be used as a buffer solution?

A. HBr and NaBr   **C.** HNO$_3$ and NaNO$_2$
B. KHCO$_3$ and Na$_2$CO$_3$ **D.** H$_4$C$_2$O$_2$ and KCN

B is correct.

A buffer solution must contain a weak base and its conjugate acid or a weak acid and its conjugate base, preferably in approximately equal concentrations.

A mixture of KHCO$_3$ and Na$_2$CO$_3$ would be a buffer because it consists of a weak acid (from Table 1, bicarbonate can act as a weak acid) and its conjugate base, the carbonate ion from potassium carbonate. The fact that the carbonate comes from potassium carbonate and the bicarbonate comes from sodium carbonate is irrelevant as neither sodium nor potassium participate in the reactions – they are spectator ions.

A: while bromide is the conjugate base of hydrobromic acid, the acid is too strong and cannot be a buffer.

C: a weak base and a strong acid, but wouldn't make a buffer since nitric acid is not the conjugate acid.

D: a weak acid and the salt of another acid – the necessary conjugate base of the weak acid is absent.

38. Which ion is the conjugate base of oxalic acid (H$_2$C$_2$O$_4$)?

A. C$_2$O$_4^{2-}$ **B.** HC$_2$O$_4^-$ **C.** H$_2$C$_2$O$_4^+$ **D.** H$_3$C$_2$O$_4^+$

B is correct.

The conjugate base of an acid is a compound that has one less hydrogen ion and therefore one unit greater negative charge than its counterpart. In other terms, it has one less H^+ in its formula. $HC_2O_4^-$ meets these conditions for oxalic acid.

A: $C_2O_4^{2-}$ is the conjugate base of $HC_2O_4^-$ but not of oxalic acid because the difference is two hydrogen ions.

C: $H_2C_2O_4^+$ does not exist.

D: $H_3C_2O_4^+$ would be the conjugate acid for oxalic acid because it has one more hydrogen ion than oxalic acid.

39. Which curve correctly reflects the titration curve for oxalic acid when it is completely titrated with NaOH?

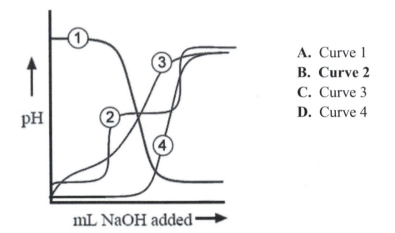

A. Curve 1
B. Curve 2
C. Curve 3
D. Curve 4

B is correct.

Since oxalic acid is an acid, a solution of it initially (before sodium hydroxide is added) is acidic and becomes more basic as the basic sodium hydroxide is added.

While weak acids begin at a higher pH than strong acids, they usually have a buffering region where the pH changes slowly but remains relatively constant as base is added because the acid and its conjugate base are in equilibrium.

As more base is added and reacts with the hydrogen ion in solution, the equilibrium is disturbed and more undissociated acid ionizes, releasing more hydrogen ion. The concentration of hydrogen ion remains relatively constant as long as a significant amount of undissociated acid species remains.

The titration curve for oxalic acid would have two breaks as each of the acidic hydrogens is titrated (curve 2) as it shows two breaks characteristic of a diprotic acid combined with a gradual pH change for a weak acid.

A: curve 1 begins at a basic pH and becomes more acidic.

C: curve 3 is a typical curve of titration of a weak acid with a strong base, but not for oxalic acid because it is *diprotic* (two K_a values in Table 1).

D: the titration curve 4 is characteristic of a strong acid titrated by a strong base because the pH stays low until it changes rapidly near the equivalence point. Since oxalic acid is a weak acid (Table 1 of the passage), the equivalence point is not as sharp and pronounced as for a strong acid shown in curve 4.

40. Which of the following acids is the strongest?

A. Acetic acid   **B.** Carbonic acid   **C.** Citric acid   **D. Lactic acid**

D is correct.

The acid with the highest K_a value is the strongest because the greater the K_a value the greater extent to which the acid dissociates.

Multiprotic acids are those that have more than one acidic hydrogen that can be removed. From Table 1, oxalic acid and carbonic acid are multiprotic. For these acids only the first K_a's significantly contribute to the total acidity of the acid.

Since the K_a values for oxalic acid differ by a factor of a thousand (Table 1), the second proton is a thousand times less acidic and the first proton that comes off is the major contributor to the acidity of oxalic acid. Because the K_a for the first deprotonation is greater than in the other acid choices, oxalic acid is the strongest acid among them.

41. When 0.2 moles of NaOH is added to 0.4 moles HCN (hydrocyanic acid), what is the approximate pH?

A. 4.3   **B.** 5.7   **C. 9.2**   **D.** 12.1

C is correct.

Hydrocyanic acid is a weak acid. When 0.4 moles of the acid is added to 0.2 moles of NaOH, half of the acid is converted into the salt sodium cyanide which means that there are approximately equal amounts of the undissociated acid (HCN) and its conjugate base, the cyanide ion ($^-$CN) from the salt.

A solution with approximately equal amounts of an acid and its conjugate base is a buffer solution and the Henderson-Hasselbach equation can be used to find the buffer solution's approximate pH.

According to the Henderson-Hasselbach equation, the pH of a buffer solution is about equal to the pK_a of the acid plus the log of the ratio of the concentration of the conjugate base to the acid.

$$pH = pK_a + \log \left([\text{conjugate base}] / [\text{undissociated acid}] \right)$$

The pK_a of HCN is 9.2. Since half of the hydrocyanic acid reacted with the sodium hydroxide, the amount of acid and conjugate base are both 0.2 mol, so the ratio of conjugate base to acid is 1.

The log of 1 is zero, therefore the pH is approximately equal to pKa, 9.2.

Questions 42 through 45 are not based on any descriptive passage and are independent of each other

---

42. On a distant planet, rain consists of sulfuric acid droplets in a carbon dioxide atmosphere. Compare a raindrop on Earth to the same size and mass drop of sulfuric acid on the distant planet. The acceleration due to gravity is the same on both planets. Which of these factors affects the terminal velocity of the rain drop?

> I. Chemical composition of the drop
> **II. Temperature of the atmosphere**
> **III. Pressure of the atmosphere**

A. I only   B. I & II   C. II & III   D. I, II & III

C is correct.

Below is the force diagram for the rain drop at terminal velocity:

The two forces are equal in magnitude,

$$Mg = C\rho A v^2$$

where,

$$v = \sqrt{Mg/C\rho A}$$

Compare the terminal velocity for the planets. Mass of the drop (M), g and A are the same and C is constant, but the density of the atmospheres of the two planets is different. Eliminate the statement about chemical composition of the drop because it is not a factor to determine terminal velocity.

The density of the atmosphere depends on temperature and pressure.

---

43. Why are intermolecular forces in dry ice (CO_2) weaker than intermolecular forces in frozen water?

    A. carbon dioxide is nonpolar while water is polar
    B. carbon dioxide molecules have more kinetic energy than water molecules
    C. carbon dioxide cannot exist in the liquid phase at one atmosphere while water can
    D. carbon dioxide has a much higher molecular weight than water

A is correct.

The intermolecular force for hydrogen bonding is strong, but this answer is not among the choices. Polarity due to electronegativity differences is a prerequisite for hydrogen bonding, an answer referring to polarity is the best choice.

44. Which of the following family of elements do lithium, sodium and potassium belong to?

    A. alkali metals
    B. alkaline earth metals
    C. transition elements
    D. lanthanides

A is correct.

The MCAT requires familiarity with the Periodic table. Lithium (Li), sodium (Na) and potassium (K) are alkali metals.

Alkali metals, comprising Group 1 of Periodic table, are all highly reactive and are never found in nature in their elemental form. Therefore they are stored under mineral or paraffin oil in the laboratory. Alkali metals easily tarnish and have low densities and melting points.

45. In a chemical reaction, a compound accepts a pair of electrons from:

    A. oxidant
    B. reductant
    C. proton acceptor
    D. oxidant and reductant

B is correct.

A compound is reduced when it accepts electrons. Reducing agents reduce other compounds by donating electrons and themselves become oxidized.

Redox (reduction-oxidation) reactions are chemical reactions where an atoms' oxidation state is changed. They include simple redox processes (e.g. oxidation of carbon to yield carbon dioxide, CO_2, or reduction of carbon by hydrogen to yield methane, CH_4) and complex processes (e.g. oxidation of glucose in the human body through a series of complex electron transfer processes).

Generally, redox reactions are reactions associated with the transfer of electrons between species. The term comes from the two concepts of reduction and oxidation.

Oxidation is the loss of electrons or an increase in oxidation state by a molecule, atom, or ion.

Reduction is the gain of electrons or a decrease in oxidation state by a molecule, atom, or ion.

An *oxidizing agent* (also called an oxidant) is a substance that removes electrons from another reactant in a redox chemical reaction. The oxidizing agent is "reduced" by taking electrons onto itself and the reactant is "oxidized" by having its electrons taken away. Oxygen is a common example of an oxidizing agent, but it is only one of many.

A *reducing agent* (also called a reductant) is a substance that donates an electron to another species in a redox reaction. Since the reductant loses an electron it becomes "oxidized."

A *proton acceptor* is a base, an anionic substance that accepts a proton during an acid-base reaction.

Passage 7
(Questions 46–52)

The eye of a mammal collects light and focuses it onto the retina which consists of a multitude of cells that are able to detect that light. The interface between air and the cornea is where most of the refraction and focusing of incoming light rays occurs. The eye lens changes the focal length so the image projects precisely on the retina for the eye to be able to focus light from objects that are very close and very far.

The eye's ability to distinguish waves coming from different directions is known as *spatial resolution*. If a distant object emits two separate light beams, the human eye can distinguish the two separate lights because the light from the two sources approaches the eye from two directions, but if the light source is too far away from the eye, it lacks the resolution (i.e. ability to distinguish two separate lights) and they appear as one.

Resolution is measured in degrees or radians. For example, if a human eye can distinguish two lights emitted by two sources 1.5 m apart from each other and 1 km away from the observer, the angular separation of the lights is approximately 1.5 m/1000 m = 1.5×10^{-3} radians. The resolution of the eye is 1.5×10^{-3} rad or 0.09 degrees (since 1 rad = 57°) or 5 seconds of an arc. To a good approximation, the angular separation of two light sources (or any objects) is the ratio of spatial separation (Δx) to distance from the point of reference (L). Therefore, the smaller the resolution angle the better the resolution.

The spatial resolution of the eye (and any other detector) is limited by *diffraction,* which is essentially the spreading of waves. When waves pass through an aperture, they spread on the other side forming an angle given by:

$$\theta_{\text{diff}} = \frac{\lambda}{d}$$

Equation 1.

where θ_{diff} is measured in radians, λ = wavelength, and d = the diameter of the hole through which the waves pass. Diffraction is the physical limit of the resolution. The actual resolution of a detector may be much lower than given by Equation 1 if it is designed poorly.

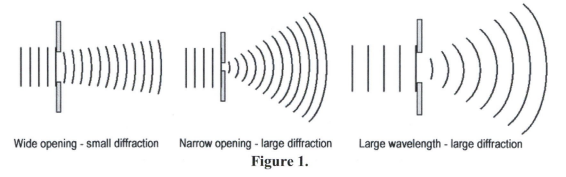

Wide opening - small diffraction   Narrow opening - large diffraction   Large wavelength - large diffraction

Figure 1.

The properly functioning human eye is limited by diffraction.

Color	Wavelength (nm)
Red	625 - 740
Orange	590 - 625
Yellow	565 - 590
Green	520 - 565
Blue	500 - 520
Indigo	435 - 500
Violet	380 - 435

* 1 nm = 10^{-9} m

Table 1. The visible light spectrum

46. What should be the approximate power of the appropriate corrective lens for an eye that does not focus correctly if the front to back length of the eye is 0.025 m, but the focusing power of the resting eye is 30 diopters?

   A. 5 diopters   **B. 10 diopters**   **C.** –5 diopters   **D.** –10 diopters

B is correct.

The desired power of the combination of corrective lens plus eye lens is 1/0.025 m = 40 D.

Since, $P_{combo} = P_{eye} + P_{correct}$, $P_{40} = P_{30} + P_{correct} = 10$ D.

Lenses are classified as concave and convex by the curvature of their two optical surfaces. A *convex* (converging) lens has a greater diameter in the center compared to the edges and a *concave* (diverging) lens has a smaller diameter at the center compared to the edges.

Corrective lenses used in optometry often have one convex and one concave side.

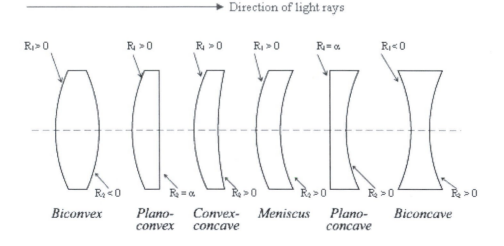

In a convex lens, a beam of light travelling parallel to the lens' axis and passing through the lens converges to a spot on the axis at a certain point behind the lens (focal point) and this lens is referred to as a positive or converging lens.

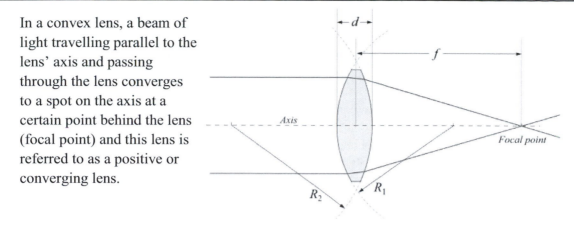

Positive (converging) lens

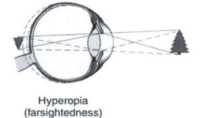

In a concave lens, a beam of light diverges and appears to be emanating from a particular point on the axis in front of the lens. The distance from this point to the lens is known as the focal length and the lens is referred to as a negative or diverging lens.

Negative (diverging) lens

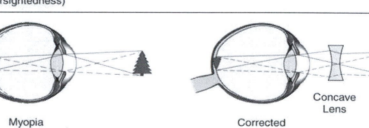

Hyperopia (farsightedness) — Corrected — Convex lens

Myopia (nearsightedness) — Corrected — Concave Lens

47. Being adapted to seeing at night, a cheetah's eye has a much larger lens than a human eye and a larger pupil. However, a cheetah's eye resolution is not superior to that of almost diffraction limited human eye. Which of these statements is the most likely explanation for a cheetah's eye lack of resolution?

 A. The larger pupil limits the amount of directional information entering the eye
 B. The larger pupil allows more light to enter the eye
 C. The large lens causes spherical aberration
 D. The large lens causes chromatic aberration

C is correct.

Spherical aberration is an optical effect in an optical device (lens, mirror) caused by the increased refraction of light rays when they strike a lens. The term can also mean a reflection (the change in direction of a wavefront at an interface between two different media where the wavefront returns into the medium it originated from) of light rays when they strike a mirror near its edge (as compared to the center). Spherical aberration determines a device's deviation from the norm (e.g. imperfections of the image produced).

A: a larger pupil actually allows more directional information to enter the eye, which would improve resolution in the absence of another limiting factor.

B: while a larger pupil does allow more light to enter the eye, this doesn't explain a decrease in resolution.

D: both cats and humans have issues with chromatic aberration which is a type of distortion when a lens fails to focus all colors to the same convergence point. Chromatic aberration manifests itself as "fringes" of color along boundaries that separate dark and bright parts of the image, because each color in the optical spectrum cannot be focused at a single common point.

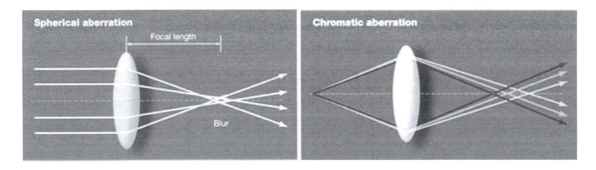

48. What is the frequency of yellow light?

 A. 5.3 x 10^{14} Hz **B.** 1.9 x 10^{13} Hz **C.** 1.7 x 10^{15} Hz **D.** 1695 Hz

A is correct.

$c = v\lambda$ where,

$c = 3.0 \times 10^8$ m/s (the speed of light),

v = frequency in Hertz (1/s or s^{-1}),

λ = wavelength in meters

Solving for frequency:

$v = c/\lambda$

$= (3 \times 10^8 \text{ m/s}) / (565 \times 10^{-9} \text{ m})$

$= 5.3 \times 10^{14}$ Hz.

49. A painting of Camille Pissarro consists of a multitude of pure color dots of 0.002 m diameter. When a viewer looks at the painting from a far enough distance, the dots blend together and a coherent image is visible. Given that the resolution of an observer's eye limited by diffraction is 2×10^{-4} radians, how far away must he or she stand to be able to make out the image?

A. 2 m away   **B.** 4 m away   **C. 10 m away**   **D.** 20 m away

C is correct.

The exercise is similar to trying to distinguish two distant lights in the third paragraph of the passage. The resolution of the eye is the ratio of dot separation to standing distance, therefore:

$$\theta_{diff} = \frac{\lambda}{d}$$

$$2 \times 10^{-4} = \frac{0.002\text{m}}{d}$$

$d = (0.002\text{m}) / (2 \times 10^{-4})$

$d = 10$ m

50. When the human eye with the front to back length of 0.024 m focuses on a 0.02 m bead located 0.25 m away, what is the size of the image on the retina?

A. 10^{-4} m   **B.** 10^{-3} m   **C.** 0.0002 m   **D. 0.002 m**

D is correct.

Magnification is the process of enlarging something in appearance, but not in physical size. The factor of enlargement is quantified by a calculated number also called "magnification".

To calculate magnification:

$$M = -\frac{d_i}{d_o}$$

where M = magnification, d_i = distance from the lens to the image and d_o = the distance from the lens to the object.

$$M = -\frac{0.024m}{0.25m} = -0.1$$

Since magnification = –0.1, the size of the image is (magnification) x (object size)

= (–0.1) (0.02 m)

= 0.002 m and *inverted* (because value is negative).

51. To photograph distant landscapes, an engineer designed a camera with a lens that focuses the light on a detector. While the camera is diffraction limited, the resolution is not good enough. Which solution would improve the camera's resolution?

   A. Make the lens bigger
   B. Design the lens from a more transparent material
   C. Change the lens shape
   D. Decrease the distance from the lens to the detector

A is correct.

The passage states that, if the detector (eye, camera etc.) is diffraction limited, the resolution depends on the size of the hole through which the light passes (in this case it's the lens) and the wavelength of the light.

Increasing the size of the lens decreases the resolution angle (as shown in Figure 1) and therefore increases the resolution.

52. When the human eye with the front to back length of 0.025 m focuses on a 0.02 m bead located 0.25 m away, what angle is subtended by the bead in the view of the eye?

   A. 2.3°   **B. 4.6°**   **C.** 10.3°   **D.** 20.6°

B is correct.

The subtended angle is the ratio of the spatial separation of the top and bottom of the bead to the distance from the bead to the eye.

$$\theta_{diff} = \frac{\lambda}{d} = \frac{0.02}{0.25} = 0.08 \text{ radians}$$

Convert 0.08 radians to degrees:

1 rad = 180°/π = 57°

0.08 × 57° ≈ 4.6°

> Questions 53 through 59 are not based on any
> descriptive passage and are independent of each other

53. If glucose provides the anomeric carbon atom in a glycosidic link, the resulting compound is a:

   A. glucosamine   **B. glucoside**   **C.** glycan   **D.** glycoside

B is correct.

54. The impaired synthesis of sphingomyelins or cerebrosides most likely affects the proper formation of:

   A. blood groups   **C.** cell to cell communication
   B. nerve cells   **D.** cell surfaces

B is correct.

55. Which of these molecules is a tertiary amine?

   A. R_2NH^+ **B. R_3N**   **C.** R_2NH **D.** RNH_2

B is correct.

In tertiary amines, all three hydrogen atoms are replaced by organic substituents. Examples of tertiary amines include trimethylamine and ortriphenylamine. Cyclic amines can be either secondary or tertiary amines. Examples of cyclic tertiary amines are N-methylpiperidine and N-phenylpiperidine.

56. The disaccharide below is formed by joining two monomers of D-glucose. Its name is:

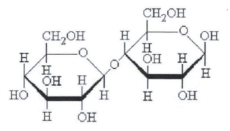

   A. α-D-glucopyranosyl-(1→3)-β-D-glucopyranose
   B. β-D-glucofuranosyl-(1→4)-β-D-glucofuranose
   C. α-D-glucopyranosyl-(1→4)-α-D-glucopyranose
   D. β-D-glucopyranosyl-(1→4)-β-D-glucopyranose

D is correct.

57. Which amino acid is the C-terminal group in the peptide Gly–Ala–Val–Phe–Tyr ?

    A. Tyr   **B.** Val   **C.** Ala   **D.** Gly

A is correct.

58. Sterols are steroids with:

    A. 5 fused rings compared to the 4 fused rings of cholesterol
    B. hydroxyl groups at both position C-3 and C-17
    C. hydroxyl group at position C-3
    D. hydroxyl group at position C-17

C is correct.

Sterols are steroids with a hydroxyl group at the 3-position of the A-ring. They are amphipathic lipids with a relatively flat molecule. The hydroxyl group on the A ring is polar while the rest of the aliphatic chain is non-polar. Sterols (also called steroid alcohols) occur naturally in plants, animals and fungi, with the most well-known type of animal sterol being cholesterol.

59. Which of the following molecules is cis-2,3-dichloro-2-butene?

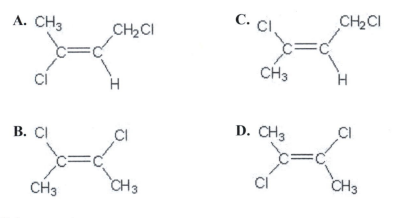

B is correct.

BIOLOGICAL & BIOCHEMICAL FOUNDATIONS OF LIVING SYSTEMS

PART II.I

MCAT® Practice Tests

Biological & Biochemical Foundations of Living Systems

Practice Test #1

59 questions

For explanatory answers see pgs. 375-416

For CBT online format of this test that provides Diagnostics Report with performance statistics, difficulty rating of each question and other features visit:

www.MasterMCAT.com

Most questions in the Biological Sciences test are organized into groups, each containing a descriptive passage. After studying the passage select the one best answer to each question in the group. Some questions are not based on a descriptive passage and are also independent of each other. If you are not certain of an answer, eliminate the alternatives you know to be incorrect and then select an answer from the remaining alternatives. Indicate your selected answer by marking the corresponding answer on your answer sheet. A periodic table is provided for your use. You may consult it whenever you wish.

Periodic Table of the Elements

1 H 1.0																	2 He 4.0
3 Li 6.9	4 Be 9.0											5 B 10.8	6 C 12.0	7 N 14.0	8 O 16.0	9 F 19.0	10 Ne 20.2
11 Na 23.0	12 Mg 24.3											13 Al 27.0	14 Si 28.1	15 P 31.0	16 S 32.1	17 Cl 35.5	18 Ar 39.9
19 K 39.1	20 Ca 40.1	21 Sc 45.0	22 Ti 47.9	23 V 50.9	24 Cr 52.0	25 Mn 54.9	26 Fe 55.8	27 Co 58.9	28 Ni 58.7	29 Cu 63.5	30 Zn 65.4	31 Ga 69.7	32 Ge 72.6	33 As 74.9	34 Se 79.0	35 Br 79.9	36 Kr 83.8
37 Rb 85.5	38 Sr 87.6	39 Y 88.9	40 Zr 91.2	41 Nb 92.9	42 Mo 95.9	43 Tc (98)	44 Ru 101.1	45 Rh 102.9	46 Pd 106.4	47 Ag 107.9	48 Cd 112.4	49 In 114.8	50 Sn 118.7	51 Sb 121.8	52 Te 127.6	53 I 126.9	54 Xe 131.3
55 Cs 132.9	56 Ba 137.3	57 La* 138.9	72 Hf 178.5	73 Ta 180.9	74 W 183.9	75 Re 186.2	76 Os 190.2	77 Ir 192.2	78 Pt 195.1	79 Au 197.0	80 Hg 200.6	81 Tl 204.4	82 Pb 207.2	83 Bi 209.0	84 Po (209)	85 At (210)	86 Rn (222)
87 Fr (223)	88 Ra (226)	89 Ac† (227)	104 Rf (261)	105 Db (262)	106 Sg (266)	107 Bh (264)	108 Hs (277)	109 Mt (268)	110 Ds (281)	111 Uuu (272)	112 Uub (285)		114 Uuq (289)		116 Uuh (289)		

	58 Ce 140.1	59 Pr 140.9	60 Nd 144.2	61 Pm (145)	62 Sm 150.4	63 Eu 152.0	64 Gd 157.3	65 Tb 158.9	66 Dy 162.5	67 Ho 164.9	68 Er 167.3	69 Tm 168.9	70 Yb 173.0	71 Lu 175.0
*														
†	90 Th 232.0	91 Pa (231)	92 U 238.0	93 Np (237)	94 Pu (244)	95 Am (243)	96 Cm (247)	97 Bk (247)	98 Cf (251)	99 Es (252)	100 Fm (257)	101 Md (258)	102 No (259)	103 Lr (260)

BIOLOGICAL & BIOCHEMICAL FOUNADTIONS OF LIVING SYSTEMS
MCAT® PRACTICE TEST #1 ANSWER SHEET

Passage 1
1 : A B C D
2 : A B C D
3 : A B C D
4 : A B C D
5 : A B C D

Passage 2
6 : A B C D
7 : A B C D
8 : A B C D
9 : A B C D
10 : A B C D

Independent questions
11 : A B C D
12 : A B C D
13 : A B C D
14 : A B C D

Passage 3
15 : A B C D
16 : A B C D
17 : A B C D
18 : A B C D
19 : A B C D
20 : A B C D

Passage 4
21 : A B C D
22 : A B C D
23 : A B C D
24 : A B C D
25 : A B C D
26 : A B C D

Independent questions
27 : A B C D
28 : A B C D
29 : A B C D

Passage 5
30 : A B C D
31 : A B C D
32 : A B C D
33 : A B C D
34 : A B C D
35 : A B C D

Passage 6
36 : A B C D
37 : A B C D
38 : A B C D
39 : A B C D
40 : A B C D

Independent questions
41 : A B C D
42 : A B C D
43 : A B C D
44 : A B C D
45 : A B C D
46 : A B C D

Passage 7
47 : A B C D
48 : A B C D
49 : A B C D
50 : A B C D
51 : A B C D
52 : A B C D

Independent questions
53 : A B C D
54 : A B C D
55 : A B C D
56 : A B C D
57 : A B C D
58 : A B C D
59 : A B C D

This page is intentionally left blank

Passage 1
(Questions 1–5)

An antibiotic is a soluble substance derived from a mold or a bacterium that inhibits the growth of other microorganisms. Despite the absence of the bacterial beta-lactamase gene that typically confers penicillin resistance, there is a strain of penicillin-resistant pneumococci bacteria. Additionally, some of the cells in this strain are unable to metabolize the disaccharides of sucrose and lactose. A microbiologist studying this strain discovered that all of the cells in this strain were infected with two different types of bacteriophage: phage A and phage B. Both, phage A and phage B, insert their DNA into the bacterial chromosome. The researcher infected wildtype pneumococci with the two phages to determine if the bacteriophage infection could give rise to this new bacterial strain.

Experiment 1

Two separate 25ml nutrient broth solutions containing actively growing wild-type pneumococci were mixed with 15µl of phage A and 15µl of phage B. In addition, another 25ml broth solution containing only wild-type pneumococci was used as a control. After 30 minutes of room temperature incubation, the microbiologist diluted 1µl of the broth solutions in separate 1ml aliquots of sterile water. These dilutions were plated on three different agar plates containing glucose, sucrose, and lactose, respectively. The plates were incubated at 37°C for 12 hours and the results are summarized in Table 1.

Plates	phage A infected cells	phage B infected cells	wild-type cells
glucose	+	+	+
sucrose	+	–	+
lactose	+	–	–

(+) plates show bacterial growth; (–) plates show no growth

Table 1.

Experiment 2

10µl of each of the broth solutions from experiment 1 was again diluted in separate 5ml aliquots of sterile water. These dilutions were plated on three different agar plates containing tetracyne, ampicillin, and no antibiotic, respectively. The plates were incubated at 37°C for 12 hours and the results are summarized in Table 2.

Plates	phage A infected cells	phage B infected cells	wild-type cells
Tetracyne	–	–	–
Ampicillin	+	+	–
No antibiotic	+	+	+

(+) plates show bacterial growth; (–) plates show no growth

Table 2.

1. Which of the following best accounts for the results of Experiment 2?

    I.   wild-type bacteria has no natural resistance to either ampicillin or tetracyne
    II. phage A DNA and phage B DNA encode for beta-lactamase
    III. phage A and phage B disrupted the wild-type bacteria's ability to resist ampicillin
    IV. phage A DNA and phage B DNA encode for enzymes that inhibit tetracyne's harmful effects

    A. II only
    B. I & II only

    C. III & IV only
    D. I, II & IV only

2. Plaques are transparent areas within the bacterial lawn caused by bacterial cell death. In which of the following cycles must phage A be able to produce plaques?

    A. S phase
    B. translocation

    C. lytic
    D. lysogenic

3. Which of the following best describes the appearance of pneumococci, a streptococcal bacteria, when stained and then viewed with a compound light microscope?

    A. spherical   **B.** rod   **C.** helical   **D.** cuboidal

4. Based on the results of the experiments, which statement is most likely true of phage A?

    A. phage A reduced the ampicillin on the agar plates and therefore allows bacterial growth
    B. phage A inserted its DNA into the bacterial chromosome rendering ampicillin ineffective against the bacterial cell wall
    C. phage A inhibited the growth of the bacteria
    D. phage A contained the viral gene that encoded for beta-lactamase

5. Which of the following conclusions is consistent with the data in Table 1?

    A. phage A inserted its DNA into the bacterial chromosome region that encodes for the enzymes of glycolysis
    B. phage A prevented larger molecules such as lactose and sucrose from passing through the bacterial cell wall
    C. phage B utilized all of the sucrose and lactose and starved out the bacteria
    D. phage B inserted its DNA into the bacterial chromosome region that encodes for enzymes that digest disaccharides

Passage 2
(Questions 6–10)

Water is the most abundant compound in the human body and comprises about 60% of total body weight. The exact contribution of water to total body weight within a person varies with gender and also decreases with age. Daily water needs are about 2.7 liters for women and about 3.7 liters for men.

Total body water (TBW) in the body is distributed between two fluid compartments. These compartments comprise the intracellular fluid (ICF) and extracellular fluid (ECF). The sum of ICF and ECF volumes equals the TBW:

TBW volume = ECF volume + ICF volume

There are approximately 100 trillion cells in the human body. Intracellular fluid is the fluid contained within the membrane of each cell. ICF accounts for about 65% or about 2/3 of TBW. Extracellular fluid is the fluid surrounding the individual cells within the body. ECF, present outside of body cells, can be further divided into: interstitial fluid (IF), lymph fluid and blood plasma. Interstitial fluid and lymph fluid together comprise about 27% of the TBW. Blood plasma accounts for another 8% of the TBW.

Other extracellular fluids are found in specialized compartments such as the urinary tract, digestive tract, bone and synovial fluids lubricating the joints and organs.

Total body water (TBW) can be measured with isotope dilution. After ingesting a trace dose of a known isotopic marker, saliva samples are collected from the patient over several hours. The measurements are compared between experimental and baseline data. The calculation of body mass before and after the experiment provides a ratio of TBW to total body mass. The data is analyzed using the following formula:

Volume = Amount (g) / Concentration

6. In periods of low water intake, the rennin-angiotensin feedback mechanism is used to minimize the amount of water lost by the system. The kidney works in conjunction with which of the following organs to excrete acidic metabolites and regulate acid-base buffer stores?

    A. brain   **C.** heart

    B. lungs   **D.** liver

7. In isotope dilution technique, a dose of approximately 7 milligrams of O^{18} labeled water was used as a tracer. If 21.0 M/L was the estimated particle concentration, what is the estimate of TBW?

    A. 0.33   **C.** 0.33×10^{-2}

    B. 33.3   **D.** 33.3×10^{-5}

8. The movement of water into the cell from the interstitial space to the cytosol is an example of:

    A. facilitated transport

    B. active transport

    C. osmosis

    D. passive transport

9. Edema is characterized by the presence of excess fluid forced out of circulation and into the extracellular space of tissue or serous cavities. Often edema is due to circulatory or renal difficulty. Which of the following could be a direct cause of edema?

    A. decreased permeability of capillary walls

    B. increased osmotic pressure within a capillary

    C. decreased hydrostatic pressure within a capillary

    D. increased hydrostatic pressure within a capillary

10. An experiment is conducted to estimate total body water. According to the passage, which of the following must be true?

    A. ECF comprises 35% of TBW and is estimated at 1/3 of body water

    B. ECF comprises 65% of TBW and is estimated at 2/3 of body water

    C. ICF comprises 50% of TBW and is estimated at 1/2 of body water

    D. ICF comprises 35% of TBW and is estimated at 1/3 of body water

Questions 11 through 14 are not based on any
descriptive passage and are independent of each other

11. Which of the following compounds would be most likely to produce color?

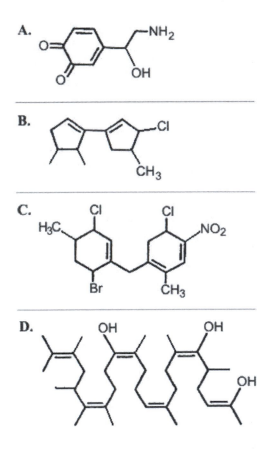

12. Which of the following molecules of digestion is NOT transported by a specific carrier in the intestinal cell wall?

    A. fructose

    B. sucrose

    C. alanine

    D. tripeptides

13. Which of the following answer choices would be a major product in the reaction of the molecule shown below with chloride anion in carbon tetrachloride (CCl_4)?

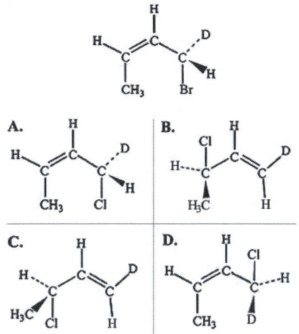

14. The nucleus of a tadpole myocardial cell is removed and transplanted into an enucleated frog zygote. After transplant, the frog zygote develops normally. The experimental results suggest that:

A. the zygote cytoplasm contains RNA for normal adult development
B. cell differentiation is controlled by irreversible gene repression
C. cell differentiation is controlled by selective gene repression
D. the ribosomes in the zygote nucleus are the same as in an adult frog

Passage 3
(Questions 15–20)

The earth's atmosphere absorbs the energy of most wavelengths of electromagnetic energy. However, significant amounts of radiation reach the earth's surface through two regions of non-absorption. The first region transmits ultraviolet and visible light, as well as infrared light or heat. The second region transmits radio waves. Organisms living on earth have evolved a number of pigments that interact with light. Some pigments capture light energy, some provide protection from light-induced damage, some serve as camouflage and some serve signaling purposes.

Polyenes are poly-unsaturated organic compounds that contain one or more sets of conjugation. Conjugation is alternating double and single bonds, which results in an overall lower energy state of the molecule. Polyenes are important photoreceptors. Without conjugation, or conjugated with only one or two other carbon-carbon double bonds, the molecule normally has enough energy to absorb within the ultraviolet region of the spectrum. The energy state of polyenes with numerous conjugated double bonds can be lowered so they enter the visible region of the spectrum and these compounds are often yellow or other colors.

Certain wavelengths of light (quanta) possess exactly the correct amount of energy to raise electrons with the molecule from their ground state to higher-energy orbitals. For most organic compounds, these wavelengths are in the UV range. However, conjugated double bond systems stabilize the electrons, so that they can be excited by lower-frequency photons with wavelengths in the visible spectrum. Such pigments are known as chromophores and transmit the complimentary color to the one absorbed. Carotene is a hydrocarbon compound with eleven conjugated double bonds that absorbs blue light and transmits orange light. The wavelength absorbed generally increases with the number of conjugated bonds. The presence of rings and side-chains within the molecule also affect the wavelengths of energy that the molecule absorbs.

Nucleic acids are biological molecules affected by light. DNA absorbs ultraviolet light and is damaged by UVC (electromagnetic energy with wavelength less that 280 nm), UVB (280-315 nm) and UVA (315-400 nm). UVA also stimulates the melanin cells during tanning and there is increasing evidence that UVA damages skin.

Wavelength	Color
390 - 460 nm	violet
460 - 490 nm	blue
490 - 580 nm	green
580 - 600 nm	yellow
620 - 790 nm	red

15. The color-producing quality of conjugated polyenes is dependent upon:

A. resonance   **C.** optical activity

B. polarity   **D.** antibonding orbitals

16. The four compounds represented by the electronic spectra below were evaluated as potential sunscreens. From strongest to weakest, what is the correct sequence of sunscreen effectiveness among these four absorption profiles?

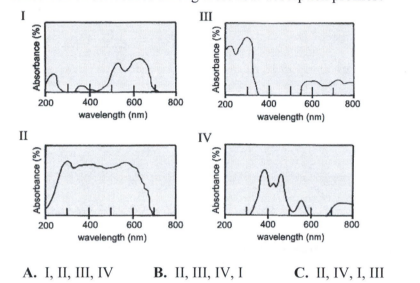

A. I, II, III, IV   **B.** II, III, IV, I   **C.** II, IV, I, III   **D.** IV, I, II, III

17. A chromophore is the moiety of a molecule responsible for its color. Two pigments differ in the lengths of the conjugated polyene chains. The first pigment transmits yellow light and the second transmits red light. What can be said about the sizes of the chromophores?

A. first chromophore is shorter

B. second chromophore is shorter

C. one of the chromophores must be a dimer

D. comparative lengths of chromophores cannot be determined

18. Many exoskeleton organisms produce a blue or green carotene-protein complex. What is the most likely cause of the color change from green to red when a lobster is boiled?

A. the protein is separated from the carotenoid pigment

B. increase in temperature permits the prosthetic group to become partially hydrated

C. heat causes the prosthetic group to become oxidized

D. the prosthetic group spontaneously disassociates

19. Why is a solution of benzene colorless?

    A. benzene does not absorb light
    B. benzene is not conjugated
    C. absorption energy is too high for a frequency to be visible
    D. absorption energy is too low for a frequency to be visible

20. The electrons that give color to a carotene molecule are found in:

    A. *d* orbitals
    B. *f* orbitals
    C. *s* orbitals
    D. *p* orbitals

Passage 4
(Questions 21–26)

Adenosine triphosphate (ATP) is the energy source for many biochemical reactions within the cell including many membrane transport processes. However, several membrane transport processes do not use the energy liberated from the hydrolysis of ATP. Instead, these transport processes are coupled to the flow of cations and/or anions down their electrochemical gradient. For example, glucose is transported into some animal cells by the simultaneous entry of Na^+. Sodium ions and glucose bind to a specific transport protein and, together, both molecules enter the cell. A symport is a protein responsible for the concerted movement (in the same direction) of two such molecules. An antiport protein carries two species in opposite directions. The rate and extent of the glucose transport depends on the Na^+ gradient across the plasma membrane. Na^+ entering the cell along with glucose, via symport transport, is pumped out again by the Na^+/K^+ ATPase pump.

A medical student investigated a type of bacteria that transports glucose across its cell membrane by use of a sodium-glucose cotransport mechanism. She performed two experiments in which bacterial cells were placed in glucose-containing media that differed with respect to relative ion concentration and ATP content. Glycolysis was inhibited in the cells during these experiments.

Experiment 1:

Bacterial cells with relatively low intracellular Na^+ concentration were placed in a glucose-rich medium. The medium had a relatively high Na^+ concentration but lacked ATP. At regular time intervals, the glucose and sodium concentrations were analyzed from the medium (Figure 1).

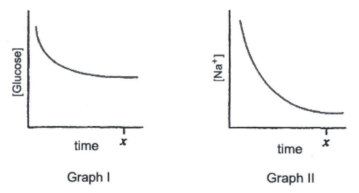

Graph I   Graph II

Figure 1. Glucose and Na+ concentrations in ATP-deficient medium

Experiment 2:

Bacterial cells with relatively low intracellular Na^+ concentration were placed in a glucose-rich medium. The medium had relatively high concentrations of both, Na^+ and ATP. At regular time intervals, the medium was analyzed for the concentration of glucose, Na^+ and ATP (Figure 2). Overtime, if radiolabeled ATP is used for the experiment, the majority of the radiolabel will be inside the cells in the form of ADP.

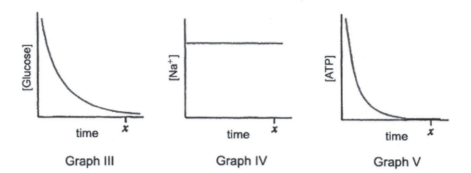

Figure 2. Glucose, Na⁺ and ATP concentrations in medium

21. Experiments 1 & 2 provide evidence that the cells take up glucose:

    A. in exchange for Na⁺, if the ATP concentration is zero
    B. in exchange for ATP, if the extracellular Na⁺ concentration remains constant
    C. together with Na⁺, if the extracellular ATP concentration gradient is increasing
    D. together with Na⁺, if a favorable sodium concentration gradient is maintained

22. From experiments 1 & 2, the student hypothesized that the cells being investigated ultimately depend on energy to operate the sodium-glucose cotransport mechanism. Is this hypothesis supported by the data?

    A. yes, because Figures 1 & 2 show that glucose crosses the cell membrane in exchange for phosphate
    B. yes, because Figure 1 shows that a Na⁺ gradient drives glucose transport and Figure 2 shows that ATP maintains the Na⁺ gradient
    C. no, because Figure 2 shows extracellular glucose and ATP concentrations are independent
    D. no, because Figure 1 shows glucose crosses the cell membrane indefinitely in the absence of exogenous energy

23. Based on the passage, the initial event in the transport of glucose and sodium into a cell is:

    A. direct hydrolysis of ATP in the cytoplasm by the sodium-glucose cotransporter
    B. direct hydrolysis of ATP on the extracellular surface by the sodium-glucose cotransporter
    C. binding of Na⁺ to specific secreted proteins in the surrounding medium
    D. binding of Na⁺ and glucose in the surrounding medium to specific membrane proteins

24. The result of experiments 1 & 2 indicate that ATP promotes the cellular uptake of glucose by serving as a source of:

   A. monosaccharide   **C.** metabolic energy

   B. enzymes   **D.** inorganic phosphate

25. Within animal cells, the transport of Na^+/K^+ ATPase pump involves:

   A. facilitated diffusion   **C.** osmosis

   B. active transport   **D.** passive transport

26. According to Figure 1, as Na^+ concentration in the medium approaches the same concentration found in the cells, glucose concentration in the medium would:

   A. level off because a sodium gradient is not available to drive cotransport

   B. remain at its original level because sodium concentration does not affect glucose concentration

   C. approach zero because glucose and sodium are transported together

   D. increase because less glucose is transported into the bacterial cells

> Questions 27 through 29 are not based on any descriptive passage and are independent of each other

27. Which one of the following structures is found in bacterial cells?

   A. nucleolus   **C.** ribosome

   B. mitochondria   **D.** smooth endoplasmic reticulum

28. Exocrine secretions of the pancreas:

   A. lower blood serum glucose levels

   B. raise blood serum glucose levels

   C. aid in protein and fat digestion

   D. regulate metabolic rate of anabolism and catabolism

29. What type of protein structure describes two alpha and two beta peptide chains within hemoglobin?

   A. primary   **B.** secondary   **C.** tertiary   **D.** quaternary

Passage 5
(Questions 30–35)

Thrombosis is the formation or presence of a blood clot which may cause infarction of tissue supplied by the vessel. Although the coagulation factors necessary to initiate blood clotting are present in the blood, clot formation in the intact vascular system is prevented by three properties of the vascular walls. First, the endothelial lining, which is sensitive to vascular damage, is smooth enough to prevent activation of the clotting system. Second, the inner surface of the endothelium is covered by a mucopolysaccharide (glycocalyx) that repels the clotting factors and platelets in the blood. Third, an endothelial surface protein known as thrombomodulin binds thrombin, the enzyme that converts fibrinogen into fibrin in the final stage of clotting. The binding of thrombin to thrombomodulin reduces the amount of thrombin that can participate in clotting. Also, the thrombin-thrombomodulin complex activates protein C, a plasma protein that hinders clot formation by acting as an anticoagulant.

If the endothelial surface of a vessel has been roughened by arteriosclerosis or infection, and the glycocalyx-thrombomodulin layer has been lost, the first step of the intrinsic blood clotting pathway (Figure 1) will be triggered. The Factor XII protein changes shape to become "activated" Factor XII. This conformational change within the protein initiates a cascade of reactions that result in the formation of thrombin and the subsequent conversion of fibrinogen to fibrin. Simultaneously, platelets release platelet factor 3, a lipoprotein that helps to activate the coagulation factors. A thrombus is an abnormal blood clot that develops in blood vessels and may impede or obstruct vascular flow.

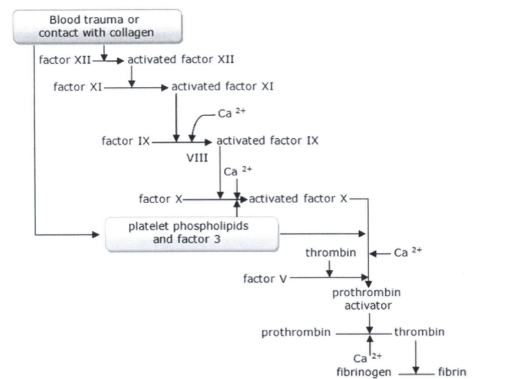

An embolus is a thrombus that dislodges and travels in the bloodstream. Typically, an embolus will travel through the circulatory system until it becomes trapped at a narrow point, resulting in vessel blockage.

30. All of the following would cause prolonged clotting time in a human blood sample EXCEPT:

A. addition of activated Factor X

B. removal of platelets or fibrinogen

C. addition of a calcium chelating agent

D. removal of Factor VIII

31. A physician injects small quantities of heparin in patients with pulmonary emboli histories to inhibit further thrombus formation. Heparin increases the activity of antithrombin III, the blood's primary inhibitor of thrombin. One possible adverse side effect of heparin administration is:

A. dizziness

B. minor bleeding

C. degradation of existing emboli

D. blood pressure increase

32. From the picture of the passage, the function of Factor VIII in the activation of Factor X is that of:

A. zymogen   **B.** substrate   **C.** enzyme   **D.** cofactor

33. The initial formation of thrombin in the intrinsic clotting pathway:

A. deactivates the blood factors

B. increases conversion of Factor XII to activated Factor XII

C. has a positive feedback effect on thrombin formation

D. causes a platelet reduction within plasma

34. Based on information in the passage, which of the following is the most likely mechanism of action of protein C?

A. activation of Factors XII and X

B. deactivation of activated Factors V and VIII

C. accelerates formation of prothrombin

D. negative feedback effect of thrombomodulin

35. Which of the following is most likely the origin of a pulmonary embolus that blocks thepulmonary artery?

A. left side of the heart

B. aorta

C. pulmonary veins

D. veins within the lower extremities

Passage 6
(Questions 36–40)

Fermentation is an anaerobic process that results in the conversion of high-energy substrates to various waste products. Fermentation harvests only a small amount of the energy stored in glucose. There are two common types: alcoholic fermentation and lactic acid fermentation.

Alcoholic fermentation (also called ethanol fermentation) is a biological process whereby sugars (e.g. glucose, fructose and sucrose) are converted into cellular energy and produce ethanol and carbon dioxide as metabolic waste products. Because yeasts perform this conversion in the absence of oxygen, alcoholic fermentation is considered an anaerobic process. Anaerobic respiration is a form of respiration that uses electron acceptors other than oxygen.

Lactic acid fermentation is a biological metabolic process where glucose, fructose, and sucrose are converted into cellular energy and the metabolite lactate. It is also an anaerobic fermentation that occurs in some bacteria and animal cells (e.g. muscle cells). In homolactic fermentation, one molecule of glucose is converted to two molecules of lactic acid. By contrast, heterolactic fermentation yields carbon dioxide and ethanol in addition to lactic acid via a process called the phosphoketolase pathway.

In alcoholic fermentation, the conversion of pyruvic acid to ethanol is a two-step process. In heterolactic acid fermentation, the conversion of pyruvic acid to lactic acid is a one-step process.

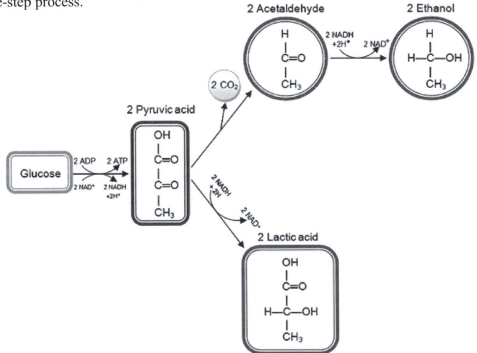

Figure 1. Alcoholic fermentation and lactic acid fermentation pathways.

36. Lactic acid accumulates in muscles and is carried by the blood and transported to the liver. What is the effect of lactic acid on the respiratory rate?

    A. decreases respiratory rate
    B. increases respiratory rate
    C. no effect on respiratory rate
    D. respiratory rate initially decreases and then quickly level off

37. In lactic acid fermentation, pyruvate functions as an:

    A. electron acceptor for the reduction of NAD^+
    B. electron acceptor for the oxidation of NADH
    C. electron donor for the reduction of NAD^+
    D. electron donor for the oxidation of NADH

38. Fermentation differs from glycolysis because in fermentation:

    A. glucose is oxidized
    B. NAD^+ is regenerated
    C. high-energy electrons transferred to NAD^+
    D. ATP is produced

39. During alcoholic fermentation, pyruvic acid and acetaldehyde are, respectively:

    A. decarboxylated and oxidized
    B. decarboxylated and reduced
    C. reduced and decarboxylated
    D. decarboxylated and phosphorylated

40. During fermentation, the final electron acceptor from NADH is:

    A. organic molecule
    B. alcohol
    C. NAD^+
    D. $\frac{1}{2} O_2$

Questions 41 through 46 are not based on any descriptive passage and are independent of each other

41. Which two atomic orbitals interact to form the D—D bond in D_2?

A. s and s
B. p and p
C. sp and sp
D. sp^3 and sp^3

42. During skeletal muscle contraction, which bands of the sarcomere shorten?

A. I and H bands
B. A and H bands
C. I bands and Z discs
D. Z discs

43. Human muscle cells behave in a manner similar to:

A. anaerobes
B. obligate aerobes
C. facultative anaerobes
D. strict aerobes

44. During the production of urine, the nephron controls the composition of urine by all of the following physiological processes EXCEPT:

A. reabsorption of H_2O
B. counter current exchange with blood
C. secretion of solutes into urine
D. filtration for Na^+ to remain in blood

45. Which of the following molecules is NOT transported via Na^+ dependent transport?

A. bile acids
B. galactose
C. proteins
D. fatty acids

46. Which of the following characteristics of water make it the most important solvent on earth?

I. water is non-polar
II. water is a Bronsted-Lowry Base
III. water is a Bronsted-Lowry Acid
IV. water forms hydrogen bonds

A. I & II only
B. II & III only
C. II, III & IV only
D. I, II, III & IV

This page is intentionally left blank

Passage 7
(Questions 47–52)

The reaction between alkyl bromide and chloride anion may proceed via any one of four possible reaction mechanisms. The observed pathway is a function of the solvent polarity. Although all four reactions involve substitution, each mechanism produces a distinct product.

Researchers calculated the free energies of activation (ΔG) in kcal mol^{-1} for the different mechanisms in two different solvents.

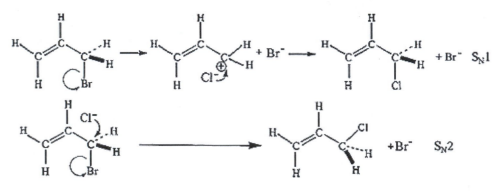

Figure 1.

Experiments demonstrated that the preferred pathway for the molecules in non-polar organic solvents is S_N2. However, as the solvent polarity increases, the difference in energy between the pathways narrows. In water, the preferred pathway, with a lower energy of activation, is S_N1.

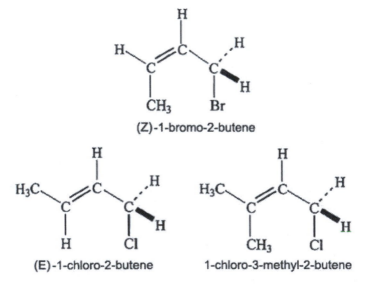

(Z)-1-bromo-2-butene

(E)-1-chloro-2-butene   1-chloro-3-methyl-2-butene

Figure 2.

47. Which of the following is true regarding the reaction of (Z)-1-bromo-2-butene with the chloride anion in carbon tetrachloride?

    A. reaction is unimolecular
    B. reaction produces a racemic mixture of products
    C. reaction is a concerted mechanism
    D. reaction rate is increased by increasing [Cl⁻]

48. Which of the following molecules forms the most stable carbocation following the dissociation of the halide ion?

    A. (E)-1-chloro-2-butene
    B. (Z)-1-bromo-2-butene
    C. 1-chloro-3-methyl-2-butene
    D. no difference is expected

49. Regarding the reaction of 1-chloro-3-methyl-2-butene with Cl⁻ in water, which of the following statements is supported by the passage?

    A. strong nucleophile is required for the reaction to proceed
    B. carbocation is formed
    C. reaction occurs with an inversion of stereochemistry
    D. reaction occurs with a single ΔG in the reaction profile

50. What hypothesis explains the difference in the mechanism pathway (Figure 1) when the solvent is changed from CCl_4 to H_2O?

    A. hydrogen bonding of the H_2O solvent stabilizes the transition state of the S_N2 pathway
    B. hydrogen bonding of the H_2O solvent stabilizes the intermediate of the S_N2 pathway
    C. hydrogen bonding of the H_2O solvent stabilizes the nucleophile of the S_N2 pathway
    D. hydrogen bonding of the H_2O solvent stabilizes the carbocation intermediate of the S_N1 pathway

51. Which of the following reagents must be reacted with (E)-1-chloro-2-butene for a saturated alkyl halide to be formed?

    A. H_2, Pd
    B. BH_3, THF / H_2O_2, ⁻OH
    C. $Hg(OAc)_2$, H_2O / $NaBH_4$
    D. concentrated H_2SO_4

52. Which of the following reagents, when reacted with 1-chloro-3-methyl-2-butene will produce an alcohol with the hydroxyl group on C2?

    A. Lindlar
    C. $Hg(OAc)_2$, H_2O / $NaBH_4$
    B. BH_3, THF / H_2O_2, ⁻OH
    D. Grignard

> Questions 53 through 59 are not based on any
> descriptive passage and are independent of each other

53. How many amino acids are essential in the human diet?

   A. 4   **B.** 9   **C.** 11   **D.** 12

54. In eukaryotic cells, most of the ribosomal RNA are transcribed by RNA polymerase [ ], major structural genes are transcribed by RNA polymerase [ ], and tRNAs are transcribed by RNA polymerase [ ].

   A. II; I; III   **B.** II; III; I   **C.** I, II, III   **D.** I; III; II

55. Cellulose is not highly branched because it does not have:

   A. β (1→4) glycosidic bonds   **C.** a polysaccharide backbone
   B. α (1→4) glycosidic bonds   **D.** α (1→6) glycosidic bonds

56. Which formula represents palmitic acid?

   A. $CH_3(CH_2)_8COOH$ **C.** $CH_3(CH_2)_{16}COOH$
   B. $CH_3(CH_2)_{18}COOH$ **D.** $CH_3(CH_2)_{14}COOH$

57. Lipids can be either:

   A. hydrophobic or hydrophilic   **C.** amphipathic or hydrophilic
   B. hydrophobic or amphipathic   **D.** amphipathic or amphoteric

58. Given that K_M measures the affinity of enzyme and substrate, then:

   A. k_{cat} is much smaller than k_{-1} **C.** k_{cat} must be smaller than K_M
   B. k_{cat} is about equal to k_1 **D.** k_{cat} must be larger than K_M

59. Which amino acid-derived molecule transports amino acids across the cell membrane?

   A. S-adenosylmethionine   **C.** Glutathione
   B. Insulin   **D.** γ-aminobutyric acid

Biological & Biochemical Foundations of Living Systems

Practice Test #2

59 questions

For explanatory answers see pgs. 417-458

For CBT online format of this test that provides Diagnostics Report with performance statistics, difficulty rating of each question and other features visit:

www.MasterMCAT.com

Most questions in the Biological Sciences test are organized into groups, each containing a descriptive passage. After studying the passage select the one best answer to each question in the group. Some questions are not based on a descriptive passage and are also independent of each other. If you are not certain of an answer, eliminate the alternatives you know to be incorrect and then select an answer from the remaining alternatives. Indicate your selected answer by marking the corresponding answer on your answer sheet. A periodic table is provided for your use. You may consult it whenever you wish.

Periodic Table of the Elements

1 H 1.0																	2 He 4.0
3 Li 6.9	4 Be 9.0											5 B 10.8	6 C 12.0	7 N 14.0	8 O 16.0	9 F 19.0	10 Ne 20.2
11 Na 23.0	12 Mg 24.3											13 Al 27.0	14 Si 28.1	15 P 31.0	16 S 32.1	17 Cl 35.5	18 Ar 39.9
19 K 39.1	20 Ca 40.1	21 Sc 45.0	22 Ti 47.9	23 V 50.9	24 Cr 52.0	25 Mn 54.9	26 Fe 55.8	27 Co 58.9	28 Ni 58.7	29 Cu 63.5	30 Zn 65.4	31 Ga 69.7	32 Ge 72.6	33 As 74.9	34 Se 79.0	35 Br 79.9	36 Kr 83.8
37 Rb 85.5	38 Sr 87.6	39 Y 88.9	40 Zr 91.2	41 Nb 92.9	42 Mo 95.9	43 Tc (98)	44 Ru 101.1	45 Rh 102.9	46 Pd 106.4	47 Ag 107.9	48 Cd 112.4	49 In 114.8	50 Sn 118.7	51 Sb 121.8	52 Te 127.6	53 I 126.9	54 Xe 131.3
55 Cs 132.9	56 Ba 137.3	57 La* 138.9	72 Hf 178.5	73 Ta 180.9	74 W 183.9	75 Re 186.2	76 Os 190.2	77 Ir 192.2	78 Pt 195.1	79 Au 197.0	80 Hg 200.6	81 Tl 204.4	82 Pb 207.2	83 Bi 209.0	84 Po (209)	85 At (210)	86 Rn (222)
87 Fr (223)	88 Ra (226)	89 Ac† (227)	104 Rf (261)	105 Db (262)	106 Sg (266)	107 Bh (264)	108 Hs (277)	109 Mt (268)	110 Ds (281)	111 Uuu (272)	112 Uub (285)		114 Uuq (289)		116 Uuh (289)		

	58 Ce 140.1	59 Pr 140.9	60 Nd 144.2	61 Pm (145)	62 Sm 150.4	63 Eu 152.0	64 Gd 157.3	65 Tb 158.9	66 Dy 162.5	67 Ho 164.9	68 Er 167.3	69 Tm 168.9	70 Yb 173.0	71 Lu 175.0
†	90 Th 232.0	91 Pa (231)	92 U 238.0	93 Np (237)	94 Pu (244)	95 Am (243)	96 Cm (247)	97 Bk (247)	98 Cf (251)	99 Es (252)	100 Fm (257)	101 Md (258)	102 No (259)	103 Lr (260)

BIOLOGICAL & BIOCHEMICAL FOUNDATIONS OF LIVING SYSTEMS
MCAT® PRACTICE TEST #2: ANSWER SHEET

Passage 1

1 : A B C D
2 : A B C D
3 : A B C D
4 : A B C D
5 : A B C D
6 : A B C D
7 : A B C D

Passage 2

8 : A B C D
9 : A B C D
10: A B C D
11 : A B C D
12 : A B C D
13 : A B C D

Independent questions

14 : A B C D
15 : A B C D
16 : A B C D
17 : A B C D

Passage 3

18 : A B C D
19 : A B C D
20 : A B C D
21 : A B C D
22 : A B C D
23 : A B C D

Passage 4

24 : A B C D
25 : A B C D
26 : A B C D
27 : A B C D
28 : A B C D

Independent questions

29 : A B C D
30 : A B C D
31 : A B C D
32 : A B C D
33 : A B C D

Passage 5

34 : A B C D
35 : A B C D
36 : A B C D
37 : A B C D
38 : A B C D

Passage 6

39 : A B C D
40 : A B C D
41 : A B C D
42 : A B C D
43 : A B C D

Independent questions

44 : A B C D
45 : A B C D
46 : A B C D
47 : A B C D

Passage 7

48 : A B C D
49 : A B C D
50: A B C D
51 : A B C D
52 : A B C D

Independent questions

53 : A B C D
54 : A B C D
55 : A B C D
56 : A B C D
57 : A B C D
58 : A B C D
59 : A B C D

This page is intentionally left blank

Passage 1
(Questions 1–7)

Researchers are studying a eukaryotic organism that has a highly active mechanism for DNA replication, transcription and translation. The organism has both a haploid and a diploid state. In the haploid state, only one copy of each chromosome complement is present. In the diploid state, two copies of each chromosome complement, usually homozygous for most traits, are present. To investigate this organism, two mutations were induced and the resulting cell lines were labeled as mutants #1 and #2, and these mutants demonstrated unique phenotypes.

To elucidate the events of transcription and translation, a wild-type variant of the organism was exposed to standard mutagens, including intercalating agents such as Ethidium bromide, which resulted in the creation of the two mutants. The researchers analyzed the exact sequence of events leading from DNA to RNA, and from RNA to protein products. Figure 1 illustrates this sequence of the wild-type and the sequences of the two mutant organisms.

Wild Type **Figure 1**

| GAC | TCA | CGA | ATG | GTA | | ← | DNA - sense strand |

| CTG | AGT | GCT | TAC | CAT | | ← | DNA - template strand |

| 1 2 3 | 4 5 6 | 7 8 9 | 10 11 12 | 13 14 15 | | ← | Nucleotide position number |

transcription

| GAC | UCA | CGA | AUG | GUA | | ← | RNA strand |

Asp — Ser — Arg — Met — Val   ← Amino acids

Mutant #1

| GAC | TCA | CGA | GTG | GTA | | ← | DNA - sense strand |

| CTG | AGT | GCT | CAC | CAT | | ← | DNA - template strand |

| GAC | UCA | CGA | GUG | GUA | | ← | RNA strand |

Asp — Ser — Arg — Val — Val   ← Amino acids

Mutant #2

| GAC | TCA | TGA | ATG | GTA | | ← | DNA - sense strand |

| CTG | AGT | ACT | TAC | CAT | | ← | Template DNA strand |

| GAC | UCA | UGA | AUG | GUA | | ← | RNA strand |

Asp — Ser — stop codon   ← Amino acids

Asp = asparagines, Ser = Serine, Arg = Arginine, Met = Methionine, Val = Valine

Experiment A:

Mutant #1 was plated onto a Petri dish and grown with a nutrient broth. The mutant #1 organism showed growth and reproduction patterns similar to the wild type, including the generation of a haploid stage. Mutant #2 was similarly treated and this organism also displayed stable growth and reproductive patterns.

Experiment B:

Mutants #1 and #2 were exposed to a virus to which the wild type is resistant. Mutant #1 was also found to be resistant, while the virus infected and destroyed mutant #2. The haploid form of mutant #2 was then fused with the haploid form of the wild type. The diploid fused organisms were protected against virus infection. The diploid forms of mutant #2 were not protected against virus infection.

1. Mutant #2 codon aberrations eventually results in a nonfunctioning and nonproductive polypeptide due to:

- **A.** termination of translation
- **B.** aberration of centriole reproduction
- **C.** initiation of DNA replication
- **D.** repression of RNA replication

2. If mutants #1 and #2 are separated within individual Petri dishes and subsequent mutations arise where the two mutant strains are no longer able to reproduce sexually with each other, the process can be described as:

- **A.** population control resulting from genetic variation
- **B.** population control resulting from random mating
- **C.** niche variability resulting in phenotypic variation
- **D.** speciation arising from geographic isolation

3. Consistent with Darwin's views about evolution, mutant #2 represents a less "fit" organism than mutant #1 because:

- **A.** mutant #1 and #2 produce protein products of variable length
- **B.** mutant #1 is immune against a naturally-occurring virus, while mutant #2 is susceptible
- **C.** mutant #1 is endogenous in humans, while mutant #2 is found in amphibians
- **D.** mutant #1 replicates at a different rate than mutant #2

4. In Experiment B, how many copies of mutant #2 were present in the surviving diploid?

    A. 0
    B. 1
    C. 2
    D. 4

5. From Figure 1, a biomedical researcher concluded that a single point mutation in DNA altered the size of the translated product. What observations supported this conclusion?

    A. valine is encoded by two different codons
    B. mutant #2 translated a longer polypeptide than mutant #1
    C. DNA point mutations created a stop codon which terminated the growing polypeptide
    D. point mutations within the DNA increased the length of the RNA molecule

6. In labeling the RNA in mutants #1 and #2, which of the following labeled radioactive molecules would be most useful to label the RNA?

    A. thymine
    B. uracil
    C. D-glucose
    D. phosphate

7. In Figure 1, the mutation in mutant #2 is caused by a defect in:

    A. RNA transcription
    B. protein translation
    C. DNA replication
    D. post-translational modification

Passage 2
(Questions 8–13)

Phenols are compounds containing a hydroxyl group attached to a benzene ring. Derivatives of phenols, such as naphthols (II) and phenanthrols (III), have chemical properties similar to many substituted phenols. Like other alcohols, phenols have higher boiling points than hydrocarbons of similar molecular weight. Like carboxylic acids, phenols are more acidic than their alcohol counterparts. Phenols are highly reactive and undergo several reactions because of the hydroxyl groups and the presence of the benzene ring. Several chemical tests distinguish phenols from alcohols and from carboxylic acids.

Thymol (IUPAC name: 2-isopropyl-5-methylphenol) is a phenol naturally occurring from thyme oil and can also be synthesized from *m*-cresol in Reaction A. Reaction B illustrates how thymol can be converted into menthol, another naturally-occurring organic compound.

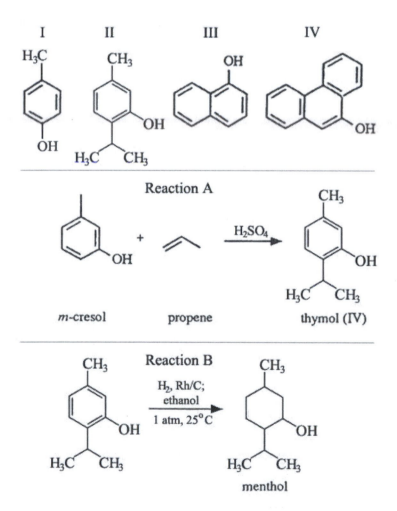

8. Which of the following is the sequence of decreasing acidity among the four compounds below?

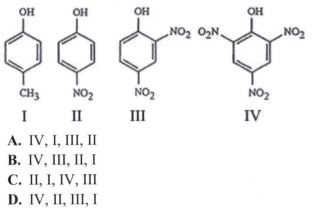

I   II   III   IV

A. IV, I, III, II
B. IV, III, II, I
C. II, I, IV, III
D. IV, II, III, I

9. Which of the following structures corresponds to Compound Y ($C_{10}H_{14}O$) that dissolves in aqueous sodium hydroxide but is insoluble in aqueous sodium bicarbonate. The proton nuclear magnetic resonance (NMR) spectrum of Compound Y is as follows:

chemical shift	integration #	spin-spin splitting
δ 1.4	(9H)	singlet
δ 4.9	(IH)	singlet
δ 7.3	(4H)	multiplet

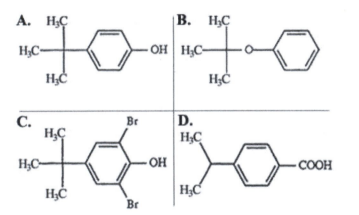

10. Which of the following compounds is the product of the reaction of phenol with dilute nitric acid?

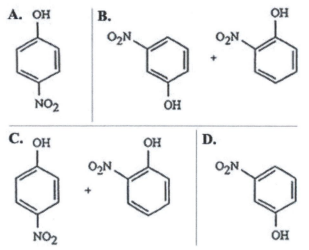

11. Comparing the pK$_a$ values for cyclohexanol (pK$_a$ = 16) to phenol (pK$_a$ = 9.95), phenol is more acidic than cyclohexanol. Which of the following explains the greater acidity of phenol compared to cyclohexanol?

I.   phenoxide delocalizes the negative charge on the oxygen atom over the benzene ring
II. phenol is capable of strong hydrogen bonding which increases the ability of phenol to disassociate a proton, making it more acidic than cyclohexanol
III. phenoxide, the conjugate base of phenol, is stabilized by resonance more than for cyclohexanol

   A. I only   **B.** I and II only   **C.** I and III only   **D.** I, II and III

12. Reaction A is an example of:

   A. free radical substitution   **C.** electrophilic aromatic substitution
   B. electrophilic addition   **D.** nucleophilic aromatic substitution

13. Which chemical test could distinguish between the two following compounds?

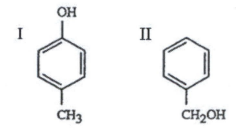

   A. compound I is soluble in NaHCO$_3$
   B. compound I is soluble in NaOH
   C. compound II decolorizes a solution of Br$_2$
   D. compound II is soluble in NaHCO$_3$

Questions 14 through 17 are not based on any descriptive passage and are independent of each other

14. In thin layer chromatography (TLC), a sheet of absorbent paper is partially immersed in a non-polar solvent. The solvent rises through the absorbent paper through capillary action. Which of the following compounds demonstrates the greatest migration when placed on the absorbent paper near the bottom and the solvent is allowed to pass?

A. $CH_3CH_2CH_3$ **B.** CH_3Cl **C.** NH_3 **D.** R-COOH

15. During meiosis, in which phase of oogenesis development does anaphase I occur?

A. 1
B. 2
C. 3
D. 4

oogonium ──1──▶ primary oocyte

primary oocyte ──2──▶ secondary oocyte

secondary oocyte ──3──▶ fertilized egg

fertilized egg ──4──▶ zygote

16. Why do acetoacetate and other ketone bodies form during low carbohydrate availability?

A. Because acetyl-CoA is converted into glucose

B. Because acetoacetate spontaneously decarboxylates into acetone

C. Because citrate cannot be formed due to low level of oxaloacetate that binds to acetyl-CoA

D. Because acetyl-CoA cannot combine with citrate because of a low level of citrate

17. In DiGeorge syndrome, caused by a deletion of a large portion of chromosome 22, there is defective embryonic development of the parathyroid glands. A patient with this syndrome would be expected to have:

A. low serum calcium   **C.** low serum thyroid hormone
B. high serum calcium   **D.** high serum PTH

This page is intentionally left blank

Passage 3
(Questions 18–23)

The parathyroid glands are part of the endocrine system. The parathyroid glands are two small endocrine glands that detect low plasma calcium levels and respond by releasing parathyroid hormone (i.e. PTH). The parathyroid hormone affects bone, kidneys and intestine to regulate serum calcium levels.

PTH acts on the bone to release stored calcium into the bloodstream. Osteoclasts dissolve bone matrix by secreting acid and collagenase onto the bone surface to release calcium. In the presence of PTH and 1,25-$(OH)_2$ D, the maturation of osteoclasts is accelerated, resulting in increased resorption and release of calcium from the bone mineral compartment.

In the kidneys, PTH acts within the nephron to increase calcium reabsorption in the thick ascending loop of Henle and in the distal tubule. These modifications to mechanisms within the kidneys recapture some calcium that was filtered by the kidney and reduce the amount of calcium excreted in the urine. PTH also upregulates the conversion of 25-hydroxyvitamin D (25-OH D) to 1,25-dihydroxyvitamin D (1,25-OH_2 D) in renal cells.

Additionally, Vitamin D stimulates calcium absorption within the intestine. 1,25-dihydroxyvitamin D is the active form of vitamin D, which promotes the active transport of calcium through the mircovilli of intestinal epithelium. Thus, PTH works indirectly in the intestines, via 1,25-$(OH)_2$ D to maximize dietary calcium absorption.

18. Although converted from 25-hydroxyvitamin D to 1,25-$(OH)_2$ D in the kidneys, the sites of action of 1,25-$(OH)_2$ D include cells within the intestine and within peripheral bone. Based on its mode of action, 1,25-$(OH)_2$ D may be classified as:

A. hormone
B. neuropeptide
C. coenzyme
D. enzyme

19. Hormone secretion is often regulated by negative feedback inhibition. Which of the following signals is used to decrease PTH secretion for homeostasis?

A. high serum PTH
B. low bone density
C. high serum calcium
D. high serum phosphate

20. The precursor to 1,25-(OH)$_2$ D is 7-dehydrocholesterol. Cholesterol derivatives are also precursors of:

   A. epinephrine and norepinephrine
   B. cortisol and aldosterone
   C. adenine and guanine
   D. prolactin and oxytocin

21. Homeostasis regulation of serum calcium is necessary for the proper function of nervous system. Low blood Ca^{2+} levels may result in numbness and tingling in the hands and feet. Insufficient serum calcium would have the greatest effect on which of the following neuronal structures?

   A. axon
   B. dendrites
   C. axon terminal
   D. axon hillock

22. PTH most likely acts on target cells by:

   A. increasing Na$^+$ influx into the cell
   B. decreasing Na$^+$ influx into the cell
   C. increasing synthesis of secondary messenger cAMP
   D. increasing 1,25-(OH)$_2$D transcription

23. McCune-Albright syndrome is a hereditary disease of precocious puberty and results in low serum calcium levels, despite elevated serum PTH levels. Which of the following is the most likely basis of the disorder?

   A. G$_s$-protein deficiency which couples cAMP to the PTH receptor
   B. defective secretion of digestive enzymes by osteoclast
   C. absence of nuclear receptor which couples PTH to the parathyroid transcription factor
   D. osteoblast autostimulation

Passage 4
(Questions 24–28)

The kidneys regulate hydrogen ion (H^+) concentration in extracellular fluid primarily by controlling the concentration of bicarbonate ion (HCO_3^-). The process begins inside the epithelial cells of the proximal tubule, where the enzyme carbonic anhydrase catalyzes the formation of carbonic acid (H_2CO_3) from CO_2 and H_2O. The H_2CO_3 then dissociates into HCO_3^- and H^+. The HCO_3^- enters the extracellular fluid, while the H^+ is secreted into the tubule lumen via a Na^+/H^+ counter-transport mechanism that uses the Na^+ gradient established by the Na^+/K^+ pump.

Since the renal tubule is not very permeable to the HCO_3^- filtered into the glomerular filtrate, the reabsorption of HCO_3^- from the lumen into the tubular cells occurs indirectly. Carbonic anhydrase promotes the combination of HCO_3^- with the secreted H^+ to form H_2CO_3. The H_2CO_3 then dissociates into CO_2 and H_2O. The H_2O remains in the lumen while the CO_2 enters the tubular cells.

From Figure 1, inside the cells, every H^+ secreted into the lumen is countered by an HCO_3^- entering the extracellular fluid. Thus, the mechanism by which the kidneys regulate body fluid pH is by the titration of H^+ with HCO_3^-.

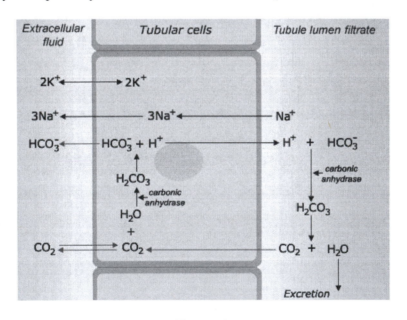

Figure 1.

The drug Diamox (i.e. acetazolamide) is a potent carbonic anhydrase inhibitor. Acetazolamide is available as a generic drug and used as a diuretic because it increases the rate of urine formation and thereby increases the excretion of water and other solutes from the body. Diuretics can be used to maintain adequate urine output or excrete excess fluid.

24. Spironolactone (an adrenocorticosteroid) is a competitive aldosterone antagonist and functions as a diuretic. Administering this drug to a patient would most likely result in:

A. Na^+ plasma concentration increase and blood volume increase
B. Na^+ plasma concentration increase and blood volume decrease
C. Na^+ plasma concentration decrease and blood volume increase
D. Na^+ plasma concentration decrease and blood volume decrease

25. Excretion of acidic urine by a patient results from:

A. more H^+ transported into the glomerular filtrate than HCO_3^- secreted into the tubular lumen
B. more H^+ secreted into the tubular lumen than HCO_3^- transported into the glomerular filtrate
C. more HCO_3^- secreted into the tubular lumen than H^+ transported into the glomerular filtrate
D. more HCO_3^- transported into the glomerular filtrate than H^+ secreted into the tubular lumen

26. What mechanism described in the passage is used to transport Na^+ into the tubular cells?

A. endocytosis   **C.** facilitated diffusion
B. exocytosis   **D.** active transport

27. Acetazolamide administration increases a patient's excretion of:

I. H_2O II. H^+ III. HCO_3^- IV. Na^+

A. III only   **C.** I, III & IV only
B. III & IV only   **D.** I, II, III & IV

28. Which of the following hormones would affect the patient's blood volume to oppose the effect of administering acetazolamide?

A. ADH
B. somatostatin
C. LH
D. calcitonin

> Questions 29 through 33 are not based on any
> descriptive passage and are independent of each other

29. Which of the following functions describes the purpose of the lysosome membrane?

   A. creating a basic environment for hydrolytic enzymes of the lysosome within the cytoplasm

   B. creating an acidic environment for hydrolytic enzymes of the lysosome within the cytoplasm

   C. serving as an alternative site for peptide bond formation during protein synthesis

   D. the lysosome membrane is a continuation of the nuclear envelope

30. How many σ bonds and π bonds are there in ethene?

   A. 1 σ and 2 π   **C.** 6 σ and 2 π

   B. 1 σ and 5 π   **D.** 5 σ and 1 π

31. Why is PCC a better oxidant for the conversion of an alcohol into an aldehyde compared to other oxidizing agents?

   A. PCC is a less powerful oxidant which does not oxidize the alcohol to a carboxylic acid

   B. PCC is a less powerful oxidant which does not oxidize the aldehyde to an alcohol

   C. PCC is a more powerful oxidant which oxidizes the alcohol to a carboxylic acid

   D. PCC is a more powerful oxidant which oxidizes the carboxylic acid to an alcohol

32. Which of the following describes the reaction of acyl-CoA to enoyl-CoA conversion?

   A. oxidation   **C.** hydrogenation

   B. reduction   **D.** hydrolysis

33. For breeding, salmon travel from saltwater to freshwater. The salmon maintain solute balance by reversing their osmoregulatory mechanism when entering a different solute environment. Failure to reverse this mechanism results in:

   A. no change because movement between saltwater and freshwater does not affect osmotic pressure in salmon

   B. metabolic activity increase due to an increase in enzyme concentration

   C. death because water influx causes cell lysis

   D. death because cells become too concentrated for normal metabolism

This page is intentionally left blank

Passage 5
(Questions 34–38)

Simple acyclic alcohols are an important class of alcohols. Their general formula is $C_nH_{2n+1}OH$. An example of simple acyclic alcohols is ethanol (C_2H_5OH) – the type of alcohol found in alcoholic beverages.

The terpenoids (aka isoprenoids) are a large and diverse class of naturally occurring organic chemicals derived from five-carbon isoprene units. Plant terpenoids are commonly used for their aromatic qualities and play a role in traditional herbal remedies. They are also being studied for antibacterial, antineoplastic (i.e. a chemotherapeutic property that stops abnormal proliferation of cells) and other pharmaceutical applications. Terpenoids contribute to the scent of eucalyptus; menthol and camphor are well-known terpenoids.

Citronellol is an acyclic alcohol and natural acyclic monoterpenoid that is found in many plant oils, including (-)-citronellol in geraniums and rose. It is used in synthesis of perfumes, insect repellants and moth repellants for fabrics. Pulegone, a clear colorless oily liquid, is a related molecule found in plant oils and has a camphor and peppermint aroma.

Below is the synthesis of pulegone from citronellol.

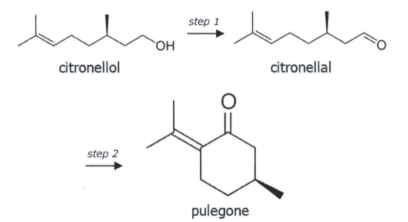

Figure 1. Synthesis of pulegone from citronellol

34. Pulegone has the presence of the following functional groups:

A. aldehydes and an isopropyl alkene
B. ketone and isobutyl alkene
C. ketone and isopropyl alkene
D. hydroxyl and tert-butyl alkene

35. What is the absolute configuration of pulegone?

    A. *R*
    B. *S*
    C. *cis*
    D. *trans*

36. Which of the following structures is the most likely product when HBr is added to citronellol?

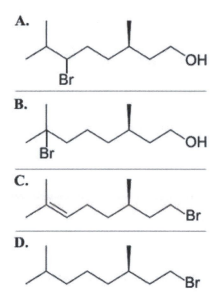

37. PCC promotes conversion of citrinellol to which molecule?

    A. citrinellone
    B. citrinellal
    C. citric acid
    D. no reaction

38. What is the relationship between citronellol and citronellal?

    A. enantiomers
    B. diastereomers
    C. geometric isomers
    D. constitutional isomers

Passage 6
(Questions 39–43)

Beta-oxidation is the process when fatty acids are broken down in the mitochondria. Before fatty acids are oxidized, they are covalently bound to coenzyme A (CoA) on the mitochondrion's outer membrane. The sulfur atom of CoA attacks the carbonyl carbon of the fatty acid and H_2O dissociates. The hydrolysis of two high-energy phosphate bonds drives this reaction producing acyl-CoA.

Special transport molecules shuttle the acyl-CoA across the inner membrane and into the mitochondria matrix. Further fatty acids beta-oxidation involves four recurring steps whereby acyl-CoA is broken down by sequential removal of two-carbon units in each cycle to form acetyl-CoA. Acetyl-CoA is the initial molecule that enters the Krebs cycle.

The beta-carbon of the fatty acyl-CoA is oxidized to a carbonyl that is attacked by the lone pair of electrons on the sulfur atom of another CoA. The CoA substrate molecule and the bound acetyl group dissociate. The acetyl-CoA, produced from fatty acid oxidation, enters the Krebs cycle and is further oxidized into CO_2. The Krebs cycle yields 3 NADH + 1 $FADH_2$ + 1 GTP, which are converted into ATP.

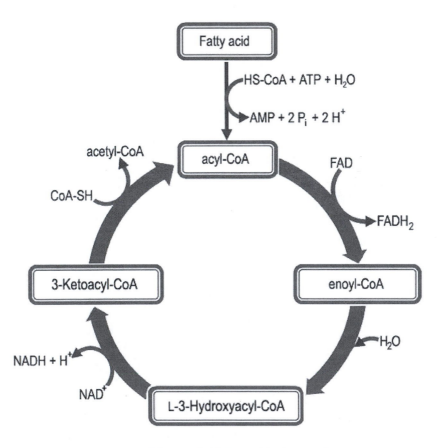

Figure 1. Beta-oxidation cycle

39. For an 18-carbon fatty acid to be completely oxidized, how many turns of the beta-oxidation cycle must be completed?

A. 1
B. 8
C. 9
D. 18

40. How many ATP would be produced if a 12-carbon fatty acid was completely oxidized to CO_2 and H_2O?

A. 5ATP
B. 51 ATP
C. 78 ATP
D. 80 ATP

41. Which of the following enzymes is involved in the conversion of acyl-CoA to enoyl-CoA?

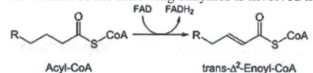

A. reductase
B. ketothiolase
C. isomerase
D. dehydrogenase

42. The equation for one turn of the fatty acid degradation cycle is:

A. C_n-acyl-CoA + H_2O → acetyl-CoA
B. C_n-acyl-CoA → C_{n-2}-acyl-CoA + acetyl-CoA
C. C_n-acyl-CoA + NAD^+ + FAD + H_2O → C_{n-2}-acyl-CoA + NADH + $FADH_2$ + acetyl-CoA
D. C_n-acyl-CoA + NAD^+ + FAD + H_2O + CoA → C_{n-2}-acyl-CoA + NADH + $FADH_2$ + acetyl-CoA + H^+

43. Which of the following traits are shared by the reactions of beta-oxidation and fatty acid biosynthesis?

A. both biochemical pathways use or produce NADH
B. both biochemical pathways use or produce acetyl alcohol
C. both biochemical pathways occur in the mitochondrial matrix
D. both biochemical pathways use the same enzymes

Questions 44 through 47 are not based on any
descriptive passage and are independent of each other

44. The deletion of nucleotides occurs during DNA replication. For mutations involving
the addition or deletion of three base pairs, the protein encoded for by the mutated gene is
relatively normal. A reasonable explanation for this observation is that:

A. cellular function is not affected by most DNA mutations
B. the size of amino acid codons often varies
C. the original reading frame is retained after removal of three nucleotide multiples
D. non-mutated mRNA are translated successfully by ribosome one-third of the time

45. Which sequence is the correct cycle of spermatogenesis?

A. spermatids → spermatogonia → spermatocytes → spermatozoa
B. spermatids → spermatogonia → spermatozoa → spermatocytes
C. spermatogonia → spermatids → spermatozoa → spermatocytes
D. spermatogonia → spermatocytes → spermatids → spermatozoa

46. What is the IUPAC name for the molecule shown below?

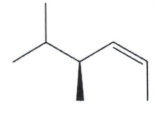

A. (S)-4,5 dimethyl-(Z)-2-hexene
B. (S)-4,5 dimethyl-(E)-2-hexene
C. (R)-4,5 dimethyl-(Z)-2-hexene
D. (R)-4,5 dimethyl-(E)-2-hexene

47. Which of the following is the site for collagen polypeptide synthesis?

A. lysosome
B. mitochondrion
C. smooth endoplasmic reticulum
D. rough endoplasmic reticulum

This page is intentionally left blank

Passage 7
(Questions 48–52)

With the advent of recombinant biology, *gene therapy* is a technique used to insert foreign genes into cells. Researchers are now able to introduce DNA into cells to treat genetic defects. One technique for gene therapy uses a small bore pipette to microinject a gene into a target cell. This technique worked in many cases but is very time consuming and requires high technical skills. Another method is electroporation whereby cells undergo electric shock to increase the permeability of the plasma membrane and DNA can enter cells. However, this procedure can destroy the cell. Alternative and highly effective gene therapy technique is when foreign genes are introduced into cells via a viral vector where foreign genes enter the cell through the mechanism of normal viral infection.

Viral genomes consist of DNA or RNA and the nucleic acid can be either single- or double-stranded. Simple RNA viruses use a mechanism where their genome is directly translated into mRNA (by the RNA *replicase* enzyme) without integration into hosts's DNA. On the other hand, when a DNA virus enters a cell, its DNA may be inserted into the host's genome via the lysogenic cycle. After integration into the host's genome, viral genes can be transcribed into mRNA and, subsequently, into proteins.

Retroviruses contain an RNA (either single- or double-stranded) genome and viral genome is transcribed into DNA by the enzyme *reverse transcriptase*. The newly synthesized DNA is then inserted into the host's genome, and viral genes can then be expressed to synthesize viral RNA and proteins. Retroviruses consist of a protein core that contains viral RNA and reverse transcriptase and are surrounded by an outer protein envelope. The RNA of a retrovirus is made up of three coding regions – *gag, pol* and *env* – which encode for core proteins, reverse transcriptase and the coat protein, respectively.

Retroviruses present a more promising gene therapy technology than simple RNA viruses or DNA viruses. A retrovirus, carrying a specific gene, enters a target cell by receptor-mediated endocytosis. Its RNA gets transcribed into DNA which then randomly integrates into the host's DNA, forming a provirus. The provirus would be copied along with the chromosomal DNA during the S phase of cell division. Retroviral vectors are constructed in a way that the therapeutic gene replaces *gag* or *env* coding region.

However, there are some practical problems associated with retroviral vector gene therapy because of the risk of random integration leading to activation of *oncogenes*. Oncogenes arise when newly integrated fragments of nucleic acids stimulate the cell to divide and increase protein production beyond desirable levels. A major limitation is that due to the randomness of the virus vector integration into the host's genome, gene expression of desired genes can't be controlled. Future research is underway to target integration of the virus vector into specific regions of the host's genome; similar to transposons in maze described by Nobel laureate Barbara McClintock. Additionally, integration can take place only in the cells that can divide.

48. To successfully integrate a retrovirus into the cell's genome, which of the following events must take place?

- **A.** New virions must be produced
- **B.** The retroviral proteins encoded by *gag*, *pol* and *env* must be translated after integration
- **C.** Reverse transcriptase must translate the retroviral genome
- **D.** The retroviral protein envelope must bind to the cell's surface receptors

49. All of these cells would be good targets for retroviral gene therapy EXCEPT:

- **A.** hepatocytes
- **B.** neuronal cells
- **C.** bone marrow cells
- **D.** epidermal cells

50. From in vitro gene therapy experiments, retroviral delivery system is preferred over physical techniques (i.e. microinjection or electroporation) of introducing therapeutic genes into cells. Which of the following statements is the most likely explanation for this?

- **A.** Retroviral gene delivery allows more control over the site of integration
- **B.** Retroviral gene delivery results in more cells that integrate the new gene successfully
- **C.** Retroviral gene delivery is less damaging to the cells and less labor-intensive
- **D.** Retroviral gene delivery permits the insertion of therapeutic genes into all cell types

51. Simple RNA viruses are not suitable for gene therapy vectors because:

- **A.** therapeutic gene introduced within a viral RNA cannot be replicated
- **B.** RNA genome becomes unstable due to an insertion of a therapeutic gene
- **C.** their genome size is not sufficient to carry a therapeutic gene
- **D.** only specific cell types can be infected by simple RNA viruses

52. Following an integration of a therapeutic gene into a cell's DNA, the retroviral DNA:

- **A.** causes nondisjunction to correct the genetic defect
- **B.** is deemed "foreign" by the host's immune system and degraded
- **C.** replicates and produces infectious virions
- **D.** remains in the cell in a noninfectious form

Questions 53 through 59 are not based on any
descriptive passage and are independent of each other

53. Incomplete proteins lack one or more:

A. essential amino acids

B. nonpolar amino acids

C. sulfur-containing amino acids

D. polar amino acids

54. Which statement regarding the number of initiation and STOP codons is correct?

A. There are multiple initiation codons, but a single STOP codon

B. There are two STOP codons and four initiation codons

C. There is a single STOP codon and single initiation codon

D. There are multiple STOP codons, but a single initiation codon

55. How many carbon atoms are in a molecule of stearic acid?

A. 12   **B.** 14   **C.** 16   **D.** 18

56. Fatty acids that mammals must obtain from nutrition are:

A. essential

B. saturated

C. dietary

D. esters

57. What type of amino acid is phenylalanine?

A. Basic

B. Acidic

C. Polar

D. Hydrophobic aromatic

58. The simplest lipids that can also be either a part of or a source of many complex lipids are:

A. Fatty acids

B. Terpenes

C. Waxes

D. Triglycerols

59. What type of macromolecule is a saccharide?

A. protein

B. nucleic acid

C. carbohydrate

D. lipid

Biological & Biochemical Foundations of Living Systems

Practice Test #3

59 questions

For explanatory answers see pgs. 459-496

For CBT online format of this test that provides Diagnostics Report with performance statistics, difficulty rating of each question and other features visit:

www.MasterMCAT.com

Most questions in the Biological Sciences test are organized into groups, each containing a descriptive passage. After studying the passage select the one best answer to each question in the group. Some questions are not based on a descriptive passage and are also independent of each other. If you are not certain of an answer, eliminate the alternatives you know to be incorrect and then select an answer from the remaining alternatives. Indicate your selected answer by marking the corresponding answer on your answer sheet. A periodic table is provided for your use. You may consult it whenever you wish.

Periodic Table of the Elements

1 H 1.0																	2 He 4.0
3 Li 6.9	4 Be 9.0											5 B 10.8	6 C 12.0	7 N 14.0	8 O 16.0	9 F 19.0	10 Ne 20.2
11 Na 23.0	12 Mg 24.3											13 Al 27.0	14 Si 28.1	15 P 31.0	16 S 32.1	17 Cl 35.5	18 Ar 39.9
19 K 39.1	20 Ca 40.1	21 Sc 45.0	22 Ti 47.9	23 V 50.9	24 Cr 52.0	25 Mn 54.9	26 Fe 55.8	27 Co 58.9	28 Ni 58.7	29 Cu 63.5	30 Zn 65.4	31 Ga 69.7	32 Ge 72.6	33 As 74.9	34 Se 79.0	35 Br 79.9	36 Kr 83.8
37 Rb 85.5	38 Sr 87.6	39 Y 88.9	40 Zr 91.2	41 Nb 92.9	42 Mo 95.9	43 Tc (98)	44 Ru 101.1	45 Rh 102.9	46 Pd 106.4	47 Ag 107.9	48 Cd 112.4	49 In 114.8	50 Sn 118.7	51 Sb 121.8	52 Te 127.6	53 I 126.9	54 Xe 131.3
55 Cs 132.9	56 Ba 137.3	57 La* 138.9	72 Hf 178.5	73 Ta 180.9	74 W 183.9	75 Re 186.2	76 Os 190.2	77 Ir 192.2	78 Pt 195.1	79 Au 197.0	80 Hg 200.6	81 Tl 204.4	82 Pb 207.2	83 Bi 209.0	84 Po (209)	85 At (210)	86 Rn (222)
87 Fr (223)	88 Ra (226)	89 Ac† (227)	104 Rf (261)	105 Db (262)	106 Sg (266)	107 Bh (264)	108 Hs (277)	109 Mt (268)	110 Ds (281)	111 Uuu (272)	112 Uub (285)		114 Uuq (289)		116 Uuh (289)		

	58 Ce 140.1	59 Pr 140.9	60 Nd 144.2	61 Pm (145)	62 Sm 150.4	63 Eu 152.0	64 Gd 157.3	65 Tb 158.9	66 Dy 162.5	67 Ho 164.9	68 Er 167.3	69 Tm 168.9	70 Yb 173.0	71 Lu 175.0
*														
†	90 Th 232.0	91 Pa (231)	92 U 238.0	93 Np (237)	94 Pu (244)	95 Am (243)	96 Cm (247)	97 Bk (247)	98 Cf (251)	99 Es (252)	100 Fm (257)	101 Md (258)	102 No (259)	103 Lr (260)

BIOLOGICAL & BIOCHEMICAL FOUNDATIONS OF LIVING SYSTEMS
MCAT® PRACTICE TEST #3: ANSWER SHEET

Passage 1
1 : A   B   C   D
2 : A   B   C   D
3 : A   B   C   D
4 : A   B   C   D
5 : A   B   C   D
6 : A   B   C   D

Passage 2
7 : A   B   C   D
8 : A   B   C   D
9 : A   B   C   D
10 : A   B   C   D
11 : A   B   C   D

Independent questions
12 : A   B   C   D
13 : A   B   C   D
14 : A   B   C   D
15 : A   B   C   D

Passage 3
16 : A   B   C   D
17 : A   B   C   D
18 : A   B   C   D
19 : A   B   C   D
20 : A   B   C   D
21 : A   B   C   D
22 : A   B   C   D

Passage 4
23 : A   B   C   D
24 : A   B   C   D
25 : A   B   C   D
26 : A   B   C   D
27 : A   B   C   D
28 : A   B   C   D

Independent questions
29 : A   B   C   D
30 : A   B   C   D
31 : A   B   C   D
32 : A   B   C   D
33 : A   B   C   D

Passage 5
34 : A   B   C   D
35 : A   B   C   D
36 : A   B   C   D
37 : A   B   C   D
38 : A   B   C   D
39 : A   B   C   D

Passage 6
40 : A   B   C   D
41 : A   B   C   D
42 : A   B   C   D
43 : A   B   C   D

Independent questions
44 : A   B   C   D
45 : A   B   C   D
46 : A   B   C   D
47 : A   B   C   D

Passage 7
48 : A   B   C   D
49 : A   B   C   D
50 : A   B   C   D
51 : A   B   C   D
52 : A   B   C   D

Independent questions
53 : A   B   C   D
54 : A   B   C   D
55 : A   B   C   D
56 : A   B   C   D
57 : A   B   C   D
58 : A   B   C   D
59 : A   B   C   D

This page is intentionally left blank

Passage 1
(Questions 1–6)

Aerobic respiration is the major process that provides cellular energy for oxygen requiring organisms. During cellular respiration, glucose is metabolized to generate chemical energy in the form of ATP:

$$C_6H_{12}O_6 + 6O_2 \rightarrow 6CO_2 + 6H_2O + 36 \text{ ATP}$$

Mitochondrion is the biochemical machinery within the cell utilized for cellular respiration. Mitochondria are present in the cytoplasm of most eukaryotic cells. The number of mitochondria per cell varies depending on tissue type and individual cell function.

Mitochondria have their own genome independent from the cell's genetic material. However, mitochondrial replication depends upon nuclear DNA to encode essential proteins required for replication of mitochondria. Mitochondria replicate randomly and independently of cell cycle.

The mitochondrial separate genome and the ribosomes of the protein synthesizing machinery became the foundation for the endosymbiotic theory. Endosymbiotic theory proposes that mitochondria originated as a separate prokaryotic organism that was engulfed by a larger anaerobic eukaryotic cell millions of years ago. The two cells formed a symbiotic relationship and eventually became dependent on each other. The eukaryotic cell sustained the bacterium, while the bacterium provided additional energy for the cell. Gradually the two cells evolved into the present-day eukaryotic cell, with the mitochondrion retaining some of its own DNA. Mitochondrial DNA is inherited in a non-Mendelian fashion because mitochondria, like other organelles, are inherited from the maternal gamete that supplies the cytoplasm to the fertilized egg. The study of individual mitochondria is used to investigate evolutionary relationships among different organisms.

1. Which of the following statements distinguishes the mitochondrial genome from the nuclear genome?

  A. most mitochondrial DNA nucleotides encode for protein
  B. specific mitochondrial DNA mutations are lethal
  C. mitochondrial DNA is a double helix structure
  D. some mitochondrial genes encode for tRNA

2. In which phases of the eukaryotic cell cycle does mitochondrial DNA replicate?

I. G_1 II. S   III. G_2 IV. M

A. I only   **C.** II & IV only
B. II only   **D.** I, II, III & IV

3. A wild-type strain of cyanobacteria (algae) is crossed with the opposite mating type of a mutant strain of cyanobacteria. All mitochondrial functions of the mutant strain are lost because of deletions within mitochondrial genome and all progeny also lack mitochondrial functions. From the passage, which of the following best explains this observation?

A. presence of genetic material in mitochondria distinct from nuclear DNA
B. recombination of mitochondrial DNA during organelle replication
C. non-Mendelian inheritance of mitochondrial DNA
D. endosymbiotic hypothesis

4. Four human cell cultures (colon cells, epidermal cells, erythrocytes and skeletal muscle cells) were grown in a radioactive adenine medium. After several days of growth, centrifugation was used to isolate the mitochondria. The radioactivity level of the mitochondria was measured by a liquid scintillation counter. Which of the following cell types would have the highest level of radioactivity?

A. colon cells   **C.** erythrocytes
B. epidermal cells   **D.** skeletal muscle cells

5. Which of the following facts does NOT support the endosymbiotic theory?

A. mitochondrial DNA is circular and not enclosed by a nuclear membrane
B. mitochondrial DNA encodes for its own ribosomal RNA
C. mitochondrial ribosomes resemble eukaryotic ribosomes more than prokaryotic ribosomes
D. many present day bacteria live within eukaryotic cells and digest nutrients within the hosts

6. Experimental data shows that mitochondrial DNA of humans mutates at a relatively low frequency. Due to mitochondria having an important role in the cell, these mutations are most likely:

A. nondisjunctions   **C.** frameshift mutations
B. point mutations   **D.** lethal mutations

Passage 2
(Questions 7–11)

Protons adjacent to a carbonyl functional group are referred to as α and are significantly more acidic than protons adjacent to carbon atoms within the hydrocarbon chain. The increased acidity characteristic for α hydrogens results from the electron withdrawing effect of the neighboring carbon-oxygen double bond. In addition, the resulting anion is stabilized by resonance shown below:

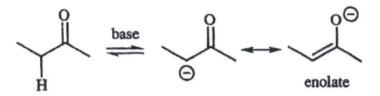

A reaction of the enolate anion with an alkyl halide or carbonyl compound forms a carbon-carbon bond at the α position. Condensation of an enolate with an aldehyde or ketone forms an unstable alcohol which is a reaction intermediate and not an isolated product. The intermediate spontaneously reacts, via dehydration, to form an α,β-unsaturated compound.

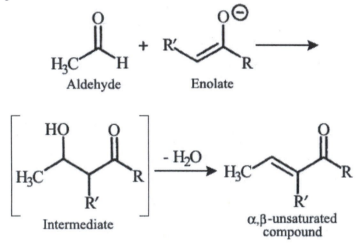

7. Which of the following ketones would NOT react with the strong base LDA?

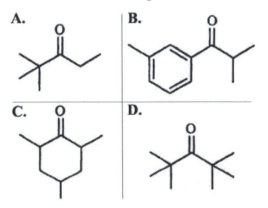

8. Which one of the following compounds would be the intermediate alcohol from the condensation reactions shown below?

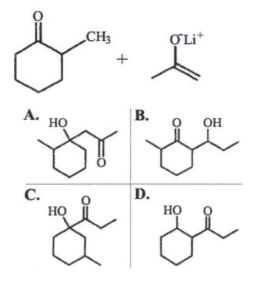

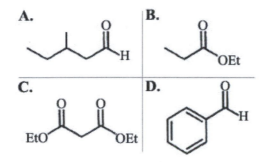

9. What is the order of decreasing basicity for the following reagents?

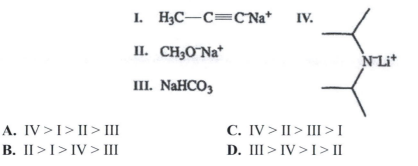

I. H_3C—C≡C^-Na^+ IV.

II. $CH_3O^-Na^+$

III. $NaHCO_3$

N^-Li^+

A. IV > I > II > III
B. II > I > IV > III

C. IV > II > III > I
D. III > IV > I > II

10. Which carbonyl compounds has the most acidic proton?

A.

B.

C.

D.

11. Which set of the following reactants would result in the formation of ethyl-2-hexanoate?

A. step 1: propanol, ethyl acetate & LDA; step 2: H^+
B. step 1: butanal, ethyl acetate & LDA; step 2: H^+
C. step 1: pentanal, ethyl acetate & LDA; step 2: H^+
D. step 1: hexanal, ethyl acetate & LDA; step 2: H^+

Questions 12 through 15 are not based on any descriptive passage and are independent of each other

12. In the graph below, the solid line represents the reaction profile A + B → C + D in the absence of a catalyst. Which dotted lines best represents the reaction profile in the presence of a catalyst?

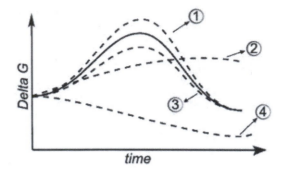

A. 1   **C.** 3
B. 2   **D.** 4

13. How would the beta-oxidation cycle be effected by depleting oxygen of the cell?

A. NADH and $FADH_2$ accumulate and the cycle slows
B. Krebs cycle replaces beta-oxidation
C. CoA availability decreases
D. beta-oxidation accelerates to satisfy energy needs

14. Rank the C–O bond length from shortest to longest for the following compounds:

A. $CO < CO_2 < CO_3^{2-}$ **C.** $CO_3^{2-} < CO < CO_2$
B. $CO < CO_3^{2-} < CO_2$ **D.** $CO_3^{2-} < CO_2 < CO$

15. Which of the following properties distinguish fungal and animal cells from bacterial cells?

    I.   presence of cell walls   III. asexual reproduction
    II. presence of ribosomes   IV. presence of membrane bound organelles

A. I & II only   **C.** IV only
B. III & IV only   **D.** I, II & IV only

This page is intentionally left blank

Passage 3
(Questions 16–22)

Viruses are classified into two major groups: DNA viruses and RNA viruses. Herpes simplex virus type 1 (HSV-1) infection, also known as Human Herpes Virus 1 (HHV-1) is almost universal among humans.

HSV-1 infects humans and hides in the nervous system via retrograde movement through afferent sensory nerve fibers. During latency period, the nervous system functions as a viral reservoir from which infection can recur and this accounts for virus's durability in a human body. Reactivation of the virus is usually expressed by watery blisters commonly known as cold sores or fever blisters. During this phase, viral replication and shedding occur as the most common way of herpes simplex transmission.

Following initial contact, production of the herpes virus growth mediators takes place. Viral growth factors bind axon terminal receptors and are related to tumor necrosis factors.

The structure of herpes viruses consists of a relatively large double-stranded, linear DNA genome encased within an icosahedral protein cage called the capsid, which is wrapped in a lipid bilayer called the envelope. The envelope is joined to the capsid by means of a tegument. This complete particle is known as the virion. Replication and assembly of the virus takes place via nuclear machinery.

HSV-1 infection is productive if the cell is permissive to the virus and allows viral replication and virion release. HSV-1 cell infection is often not productive due to a viral genome integration block that occurs upstream. However, stimulation of an infected cell will eliminate this block and allow for virion production. Abortive infection results when cells are non-permissive. In this case restrictive attacks occur when a few virion particles are produced. Viral production then ceases, but the genome integration persists.

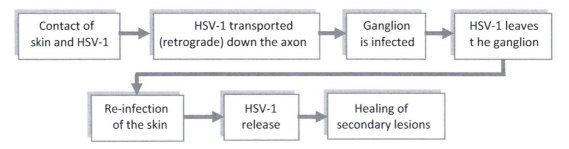

Figure 1. Steps of HSV-1 infection

16. Where in the nervous system will the latent virus of herpes simplex be localized?

A. neurotransmitter

B. axon hillock

C. lower motor neuron dendrites

D. afferent nervous system ganglion

17. The spreading of HSV-1 virus occurs during shedding by direct contact with the lesion. Which of the following locations is the source for the virus to acquire its glycoprotein-covered envelope?

A. nuclear membrane after transcription

B. storage vacuoles during lysis

C. outer cell wall during lysis

D. rough ER during protein synthesis

18. Which infection type results in the integration of the viral genome into the host cell chromosome?

I. restrictive   II. productive   III. abortive

A. I only   **B.** II only   **C.** I & II only   **D.** I, II & III

19. If the infectivity/particle ratio of picornaviruses is about 0.1%, what is the number of infectious particles present in a culture of 25,000 virions?

A. 5   **B.** 25   **C.** 250   **D.** 2500

20. Which of the following statements is NOT the cause of the abortive viral cycle?

A. infected esophagus cells lack DNA replication machinery

B. hepatitis C patients lack the majority of viral liver cell receptors

C. host autoimmune antibodies bind to the viral antigen and prevent infection

D. random mutations of influenza virus plasma membrane antigens causes genetic drift

21. Where will radioactive tegument dye be localized?

A. protein-filled area between capsid and envelope

B. protein-filled area between envelope and extracellular glycoprotein

C. protein-filled area between DNA core and nucleosome

D. protein-filled area between capsid and DNA core

22. From the information provided in the passage, which statement must be true for tumor necrosis factors (TNF)?

A. TNF are taken up by dendrites and transported toward the neuron cell body

B. TNF are produced following a malignant cancerous spread through the basement membrane

C. TNF uptake and transport are inhibited following an injury to the axon terminal

D. TNF function with nerve growth factors to stimulate voltage gated Na^+ channels

Passage 4
(Questions 23–28)

Translation is the mechanism of protein synthesis. Proteins are synthesized on ribosomes that are either free in the cytoplasm or bound to the rough endoplasmic reticulum (rough ER). The *signal hypothesis* states that about 8 initial amino acids (known as a leader sequence) are joined initially to the growing polypeptide. In the absence of a leader sequence, the ribosomes remain free in the cytosol. If the leader sequence is present, translation of the nascent polypeptide pauses and the ribosomes, along with the attached mRNA, migrate and attach to the ER.

Proteins used for transport to organelles, the plasma membrane, or to be secreted from the cell have *N-terminus signal peptide* of about 8 amino acids which are responsible for the insertion of the nascent polypeptide through the membrane of the ER. After the leading end of the polypeptide is inserted into the lumen of the ER, the leader sequence (i.e. signal peptide) is cleaved by an enzyme within the ER lumen.

With the aid of chaperone proteins in the endoplasmic reticulum, proteins produced for the secretory pathway are foldedinto tertiary and quaternarystructures. Those that are folded properly are packaged into transport vesicles that bud from the membrane of the ER via endocytosis. This packaging into a vesicle requires a region on the polypeptide that is recognized by a receptor of the Golgi membrane. The receptor-protein complex binds to the vesicle and then brings it to its destination where it fuses to the cis face (closest to the ER) of the Golgi apparatus.

A pathway of vesicular transport from the Golgi involves lysosomal enzymes that carry a unique mannose-6-phosphate (M6P) marker that was added in the Golgi. The marker is recognized by specific M6P-receptor proteins that concentrate the polypeptide within a region of the Golgi membrane. This isolations of the M6P-receptor proteins facilitates their packaging into secretory vesicle and after vesicle buds from the Golgi membrane, it moves to the lysosome and fuses with the lysosomal membrane. Because of the low pH of the lysosome, the M6P-receptor releases its bound protein. The lysosomal high H^+ concentration also produces the conformation change of the lysosomal enzymes.

23. The lumen of the endoplasmic reticulum most closely corresponds to:

   A. cytoplasm
   B. ribosome
   C. intermembrane space of the mitochondria
   D. extracellular environment

24. If a protein destined to become a lysosomal enzyme was synthesized lacking a signal peptide, where in the cell is the enzyme targeted?

    A. Golgi apparatus

    B. lysosome

    C. cytosol

    D. plasma membrane

25. In a cell that failed to label proteins with the M6P marker, which of the following processes would be disrupted?

    A. oxidative phosphorylation

    B. intracellular digestion of macromolecules

    C. Lysosomal formation

    D. protein synthesis

26. Within the cell, where is the M6P receptor transcribed?

    A. nucleolus

    B. smooth ER

    C. ribosome

    D. nucleus

27. Which of these enzymes functions in an acidic environment?

    A. pepsin

    B. lingual lipase

    C. signal peptidase

    D. salivary amylase

28. Which of the following is required for the transport of proteins to the lysosome?

    A. endocytosis

    B. absence of leader sequence

    C. acidic pH of the Golgi

    D. vesicular transport from the rough ER to the Golgi

Questions 29 through 33 are not based on any
descriptive passage and are independent of each other

29. Which of the following properties within a polypeptide chain determines the globular conformation of a protein?

   A. number of individual amino acids
   B. linear sequence of amino acids
   C. relative concentration of amino acids
   D. peptide optical activity measured in the polarimeter

30. In the Newman projection shown below, what does the circle represent?

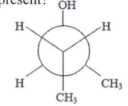

   A. first carbon along the C_1–C_2 axis of the bond
   B. first carbon along the C_2–C_3 axis of the bond
   C. second carbon along the C_2–C_3 axis of the bond
   D. second carbon along the C_3–C_4 axis of the bond

31. What is the degree of unsaturation for a molecule with the molecular formula $C_{18}H_{20}$?

   A. 2
   B. 9
   C. 18
   D. 36

32. If distillation was used to separate hexanol from butanol, which product would distill first?

   A. hexanol
   B. butanol
   C. they distill simultaneously
   D. cannot be determined

33. All of the following are involved in energy production within the mitochondrion EXCEPT:

   A. glycolysis
   B. Krebs cycle
   C. electron transport chain
   D. oxidative phosphorylation

Passage 5
(Questions 34–39)

Acetylsalicylic acid (known by the brand name Aspirin) is one of the most commonly used drugs. It has analgesic (pain relieving), antipyretic (fever-reducing) and anti-inflammatory properties. The drug works by blocking the synthesis of *prostaglandins*. A prostaglandin is any member of a lipid compound group enzymatically derived from fatty acids. Every prostaglandin is a 20-carbon (including a 5-carbon ring) unsaturated carboxylic acid.

Prostaglandins are involved in a variety of physiological processes and have important functions in the body. They are mediators and have strong physiological effects (e.g. regulating the contraction and relaxation of smooth muscle). These *autocrine* or *paracrine* hormones (i.e. messenger molecules acting locally) are produced throughout the human body with target cells present in the immediate vicinity of the site of their secretion.

Acetylsalicylic acid is a white crystalline substance that is an acetyl derivative and is a weak acid with a melting point of 136 °C (277 °F) and a boiling point of 140 °C (284 °F). Acetylsalicylic acid can be produced through acetylation of salicylic acid by acetic anhydride in the presence of an acid catalyst and is shown in the following reaction:

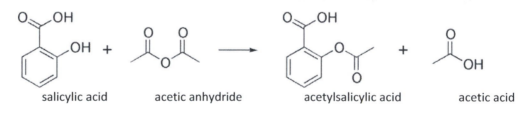

salicylic acid   acetic anhydride   acetylsalicylic acid   acetic acid

Reaction 1. Synthesis of acetylsalicylic acid

The acetylsalicylic acid synthesis is classified as an *esterification* reaction. Salicylic acid is treated with acetic anhydride, an acid derivative, which causes a chemical reaction that turns salicylic acid's hydroxyl group into an ester group (R-OH → R-OCOCH$_3$). This process yields acetylsalicylic acid and acetic acid, which for this reaction is considered a byproduct. Small amounts of sulfuric acid (and sometimes phosphoric acid) are almost always used as a catalyst.

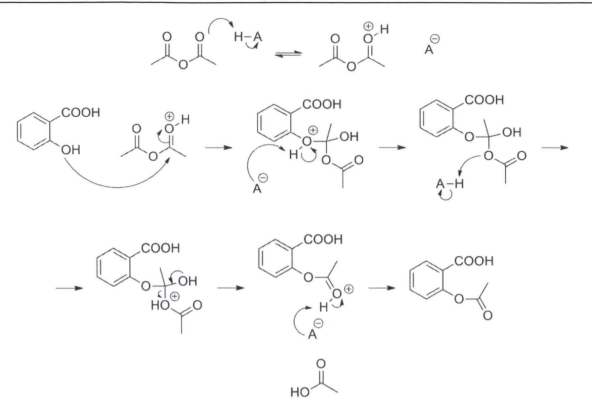

Reaction 2. Mechanism of acetylsalicylic acid synthesis

In a college lab, this synthesis was carried out via the following procedure:

10 mL of acetic anhydride, 4 g of salicylic acid and 2 mL of concentrated sulfuric acid were mixed and the resulting solution was heated for 10 minutes. Upon cooling the mix in an ice bath, a crude white product X precipitated. 100 mL of cold distilled water was added to complete the crystallization. By suction filtration the product X was isolated and then washed with several aliquots of cold water.

Product X was dissolved in 50 mL of saturated sodium bicarbonate and the solution was filtered to remove an insoluble material. Then, 3 *M* of hydrochloric acid was added to the filtrate and product Y precipitated. It was collected by suction filtration and recrystallized in a mixture of petroleum ether (benzine) and common ether.

After analyzing product X, it showed the presence of acetylsalicylic acid, trace levels of salicylic acid and a contaminate of a high molecular weight.

34. In the experiment described in the passage, salicylic acid primarily acts as an alcohol. What is the likely product when salicylic acid is reacted with an excess of methanol in the presence of sulfuric acid?

    A. methyl salicylate   **B.** benzoic acid   **C.** phenol   **D.** benzaldehyde

35. When acetylsalicylic acid is exposed to humid air, it acquires a vinegar-like smell because:

   A. moist air reacts with residual salicylic acid to form citric acid
   B. it undergoes hydrolysis into salicylic and acetic acids
   C. it undergoes hydrolysis into salicylic acid and acetic anhydride
   D. it undergoes hydrolysis into acetic acid and citric acid

36. What is the purpose of dissolving product X in saturated $NaHCO_3$ in the experiment conducted in a college lab?

   A. precipitate any side product contaminants as sodium salts
   B. remove water from the reaction
   C. form the water-soluble sodium salt of aspirin
   D. neutralize any remaining salicylic acid

37. Phenyl salicylate is a molecule different from acetylsalicylic acid that also possesses analgesic properties. Which of the following could be reacted with salicylic acid in the presence of sulfuric acid to produce phenyl salicylate?

   A. $PhCH_2OH$
   B. $PhCO_2H$
   C. PhOH
   D. Benzene

38. For the synthesis of acetylsalicylic acid, what is the reaction mechanism?

   A. Nucleophilic addition
   B. Nucleophilic acyl substitution
   C. Nucleophilic aromatic substitution
   D. Electrophilic aromatic substitution

39. Which of the following is the likely structure of the high-molecular weight contaminant in product X?

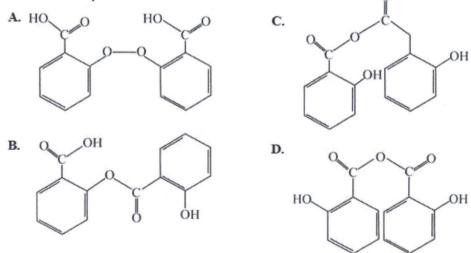

Passage 6
(Questions 40–43)

A female at birth contains on average 300,000 follicles (with a range from 35,000 to 2.5 million). These follicles are immature (*primordial*) and each contains an immature primary oocyte. By the time of puberty the number decreases to an average of 180,000 (the range is 25,000-1.5 million). Only about 400 follicles ever mature and produce an oocyte. During the process of *folliculogenesis* (i.e. maturation), a follicle develops from a *primary follicle* to a *secondary follicle*, to a *vesicular* (Graafian) follicle. The whole process of folliculogenesis, from primordial to a preovulatory follicle, belongs to the stage of *ootidogenesis* of *oogenesis*. A secondary follicle contains a secondary oocyte with a reduced number of chromosomes. The release of a secondary oocyte from the ovary is called *ovulation*.

Unlike male *spermatogenesis*, which can last indefinitely, folliculogenesis ends when the remaining follicles in the ovaries are incapable of responding to the hormonal signals that previously prompted some follicles to mature. The depletion in follicle supply sets the beginning of menopause in women.

The ovarian cycle is controlled by the *gonadotropic hormones* released by the pituitary: follicle-stimulating hormone (FSH) and luteinizing-hormone (LH). Imbalances of these hormones may often cause infertility in females. For treatment of many female reproductive disorders, therapies that act similar to FSH and LH are often used successfully.

In a pharmaceutical laboratory, scientists test two of such drugs. Drug X binds to LH receptors, while drug Y binds to FSH receptors. The scientists separated 15 mice with fertility disorders into three experimental groups. Mice in group I were administered drug Y, while mice in group II were administered drug X, and mice in group III received a placebo. After 1 month, the scientists performed an *ovariectomy* (i.e. surgical removal of ovaries in laboratory animals) and counted the number of developing follicles in the mice ovaries.

Note: a normal female mouse has on average 10-12 developing follicles at any point in the menstrual cycle.

Mice	Group I	Group II	Group III
#1	5	6	6
#2	11	4	5
#3	8	16	6
#4	11	11	4
#5	8	5	9

Table 1. Number of developing follicles per mouse

40. From the data, which of the following conditions is most likely the cause of infertility observed in mice #3 in all three groups given that they all are affected by the same reproductive disorder?

    A. inability of FSH to bind FSH receptors
    B. benign tumor of the pituitary
    C. elevated levels of LH
    D. gene mutation LH hormone

41. Which of the following conditions is LEAST likely to result in female infertility?

    A. downregulation of LH receptors
    B. inflammation of oviducts
    C. release of multiple follicles
    D. FSH gene mutation

42. Overstimulation of follicular development during reproductive therapies increases the probability of multiple ovulations often resulting in multiple pregnancies. Which of the test subjects is the best example for this case?

    A. mouse #2 of group I
    B. mouse #3 of group II
    C. mouse #4 of group II
    D. mouse #5 of group III

43. Which treatment is most likely responsible for the number of maturing follicles observed in the mouse #5 in group III?

    A. stimulation of the pituitary
    B. FSH receptor inhibition
    C. LH receptor stimulation
    D. no relationship to treatment

> Questions 44 through 47 are not based on any
> descriptive passage and are independent of each other

44. During DNA replication, individual dNTP nucleotides are joined by bond formation that releases phosphate. Which of the following describes the bond type between two dNTP nucleotides?

    A. covalent bond
    B. peptide bond
    C. van der Waals bond
    D. ionic bond

45. Which of the following is true about polar amino acids?

    A. side chains project towards the exterior of the protein chain
    B. side chains contain only hydrogen and carbon atoms
    C. side chains are hydrophobic
    D. side chains have neutral moieties

46. What is the net number of ATP produced per glucose in an obligate anaerobe?

    A. 2 ATP
    B. 4 ATP
    C. 36 ATP
    D. 38 ATP

47. All of the following hormones are released by the anterior pituitary gland EXCEPT:

    A. luteinizing hormone
    B. prolactin
    C. thyroid stimulating hormone
    D. Vasopressin

This page is intentionally left blank

Passage 7
(Questions 48–52)

The genome of all cells of the human body except germ line cells (i.e. gametes of either sperm or egg) and mature red blood cells (i.e. erythrocytes) contain identical DNA on chromosomes. Even with the same genetic material, cells of different tissue are diverse and specialized. This diversity of cellular function is due primarily to cell-specific variations in protein expression which is regulated mostly at the transcriptional level. Different genes are expressed by transcriptional controls that determine cellular function and growth.

Specifically, gene transcription is controlled by upstream regulatory sequences which include regulatory genes and promoters. Regulators and promoters are controlled by extracellular signals (e.g. hormones) and intracellular signals (e.g. calcium or glucose). Regulators stimulate or inhibit gene transcription of a gene while activated promoters only increase transcription.

A major cause of cancer is the cell's inability to regulate the cell cycle. Genetic mutations may occur at any level of the cell growth regulation system. There are two gene categories that, if mutated, often result in cancer: *oncogenes* and *tumor suppressor genes*. Oncogenes regulate cell growth and division and a mutation of the oncogene itself or its promoters can result in uncontrolled cell growth and division. Tumor suppressor genes regulate the cell cycle and may induce cell death when a cell has abnormal function. Mutations of tumor suppressor genes impair this regulatory ability and, without this control mechanism, the malfunctioning cells are able to proliferate.

When regulators or promoter sequences for genes involved in oncogenesis (also called carcinogenesis or tumorigenesis) are identified, it is possible to use drug treatments to regulate transcription of these genes. Certain drugs are effective at controlling the growth of cancerous cells, but have significant side effects that include diarrhea, significant hair loss, decreased immunity and kidney damage.

48. Given that oncogenes and tumor suppressor genes mutations usually arise during DNA replication, which phase of the cell cycle is most likely the phase for cancerous mutations?

A. S
B. metaphase
C. cytokinesis
D. G_0

49. What is the likely action mechanism of the cancer drugs mentioned in the passage?

    A. changes at the nucleotide level of an oncogene
    B. upregulation of the activator for an oncogene
    C. increased expression of a tumor suppressor gene
    D. blocking the promoter of a tumor suppressor gene from binding transcription factors

50. A new cancer drug with the brand name Colcrys acts to prevent cell division by inhibiting microtubule formation. In what stage of mitosis this drug would be most effective?

    A. prophase
    B. metaphase
    C. anaphase
    D. telophase

51. Along with its corresponding gene, a promoter sequence may be transcribed in one mRNA transcript. The mRNA sequence containing the transcribed promoter must be cleaved to make translation possible. Which cell region is most likely the site of this cleavage?

    A. Golgi apparatus
    B. nucleus
    C. cytoplasm
    D. nucleolus

52. A novel approach to cancer treatment employs modified tRNA molecules that carry inappropriate combinations of amino acids and anticodons. The tRNA molecule with the nucleotide triplets on one end is *charged* with mismatched amino acids on the other end. What is the likely mechanism of the anticancer action of these modified tRNA molecules?

    A. inhibition of cancer cells to translate protein
    B. inhibition of cancer cells to transcribe protein
    C. inhibition of ribosomes to bind to the mRNA
    D. change in the tertiary structure of the translated protein

Questions 53 through 59 are not based on any descriptive passage and are independent of each other

53. How many carbon atoms are in a molecule of oleic acid?

    A. 14   **B.** 16   **C.** 18   **D.** 20

54. Amylose is different from amylopectin because amylose:

    A. forms a helix with no branch points
    B. is highly branched while amylopectin is linear
    C. has more glucose residues than amylopectin
    D. is composed of a different monomer than is amylopectin

55. What value is expressed by the slope in a Lineweaver-Burke plot?

    A. V_{max} / K_m **B.** K_m / V_{max} **C.** K_m **D.** $1 / [S]$

56. Which statement about the initiation codon is correct?

    A. It is part of the TATA box
    B. It binds a protein complex that begins replication
    C. It specifies methionine
    D. It specifies uracil

57. Which tyrosine-derived molecule has the correct relationship?

    A. Norepinephrine – thyroid hormone
    B. Thyroxine – catecholamine
    C. Dopaquinone – precursor of melanin
    D. Dopamine – thyroid hormone

58. Which statement is correct about essential amino acids?

    A. They are not synthesized *de novo* by the body and must be part of the diet
    B. They are not synthesized by the body in sufficient amounts
    C. There are twelve essential amino acids
    D. They are plentiful in all animal protein

59. A term used for a carbohydrate polymer is:

    A. Multimer
    B. Oligosaccharide
    C. Glycan
    D. Polycarb

Biological & Biochemical Foundations of Living Systems

Practice Test #4

59 questions

For explanatory answers see pgs. 497-543

For CBT online format of this test that provides Diagnostics Report with performance statistics, difficulty rating of each question and other features visit:

www.MasterMCAT.com

Most questions in the Biological Sciences test are organized into groups, each containing a descriptive passage. After studying the passage select the one best answer to each question in the group. Some questions are not based on a descriptive passage and are also independent of each other. If you are not certain of an answer, eliminate the alternatives you know to be incorrect and then select an answer from the remaining alternatives. Indicate your selected answer by marking the corresponding answer on your answer sheet. A periodic table is provided for your use. You may consult it whenever you wish.

Periodic Table of the Elements

1 H 1.0																	2 He 4.0
3 Li 6.9	4 Be 9.0											5 B 10.8	6 C 12.0	7 N 14.0	8 O 16.0	9 F 19.0	10 Ne 20.2
11 Na 23.0	12 Mg 24.3											13 Al 27.0	14 Si 28.1	15 P 31.0	16 S 32.1	17 Cl 35.5	18 Ar 39.9
19 K 39.1	20 Ca 40.1	21 Sc 45.0	22 Ti 47.9	23 V 50.9	24 Cr 52.0	25 Mn 54.9	26 Fe 55.8	27 Co 58.9	28 Ni 58.7	29 Cu 63.5	30 Zn 65.4	31 Ga 69.7	32 Ge 72.6	33 As 74.9	34 Se 79.0	35 Br 79.9	36 Kr 83.8
37 Rb 85.5	38 Sr 87.6	39 Y 88.9	40 Zr 91.2	41 Nb 92.9	42 Mo 95.9	43 Tc (98)	44 Ru 101.1	45 Rh 102.9	46 Pd 106.4	47 Ag 107.9	48 Cd 112.4	49 In 114.8	50 Sn 118.7	51 Sb 121.8	52 Te 127.6	53 I 126.9	54 Xe 131.3
55 Cs 132.9	56 Ba 137.3	57 La* 138.9	72 Hf 178.5	73 Ta 180.9	74 W 183.9	75 Re 186.2	76 Os 190.2	77 Ir 192.2	78 Pt 195.1	79 Au 197.0	80 Hg 200.6	81 Tl 204.4	82 Pb 207.2	83 Bi 209.0	84 Po (209)	85 At (210)	86 Rn (222)
87 Fr (223)	88 Ra (226)	89 Ac† (227)	104 Rf (261)	105 Db (262)	106 Sg (266)	107 Bh (264)	108 Hs (277)	109 Mt (268)	110 Ds (281)	111 Uuu (272)	112 Uub (285)		114 Uuq (289)		116 Uuh (289)		

	58 Ce 140.1	59 Pr 140.9	60 Nd 144.2	61 Pm (145)	62 Sm 150.4	63 Eu 152.0	64 Gd 157.3	65 Tb 158.9	66 Dy 162.5	67 Ho 164.9	68 Er 167.3	69 Tm 168.9	70 Yb 173.0	71 Lu 175.0
†	90 Th 232.0	91 Pa (231)	92 U 238.0	93 Np (237)	94 Pu (244)	95 Am (243)	96 Cm (247)	97 Bk (247)	98 Cf (251)	99 Es (252)	100 Fm (257)	101 Md (258)	102 No (259)	103 Lr (260)

BIOLOGICAL & BIOCHEMICAL FOUNDATIONS OF LIVING SYSTEMS
MCAT® PRACTICE TEST #4: ANSWER SHEET

Passage 1

1 : A   B   C   D
2 : A   B   C   D
3 : A   B   C   D
4 : A   B   C   D
5 : A   B   C   D
6 : A   B   C   D
7 : A   B   C   D

Passage 2

8 : A   B   C   D
9 : A   B   C   D
10 : A   B   C   D
11 : A   B   C   D
12 : A   B   C   D

Independent questions

13 : A   B   C   D
14 : A   B   C   D
15 : A   B   C   D
16 : A   B   C   D

Passage 3

17 : A   B   C   D
18 : A   B   C   D
19 : A   B   C   D
20 : A   B   C   D
21 : A   B   C   D

Passage 4

22 : A   B   C   D
23 : A   B   C   D
24 : A   B   C   D
25 : A   B   C   D
26 : A   B   C   D

Independent questions

27 : A   B   C   D
28 : A   B   C   D
29 : A   B   C   D
30 : A   B   C   D

Passage 5

31 : A   B   C   D
32 : A   B   C   D
33 : A   B   C   D
34 : A   B   C   D
35 : A   B   C   D

Passage 6

36 : A   B   C   D
37 : A   B   C   D
38 : A   B   C   D
39 : A   B   C   D
40 : A   B   C   D
41 : A   B   C   D

Independent questions

42 : A   B   C   D
43 : A   B   C   D
44 : A   B   C   D
45 : A   B   C   D
46 : A   B   C   D

Passage 7

47 : A   B   C   D
48 : A   B   C   D
49 : A   B   C   D
50 : A   B   C   D
51 : A   B   C   D
52 : A   B   C   D

Independent questions

53 : A   B   C   D
54 : A   B   C   D
55 : A   B   C   D
56 : A   B   C   D
57 : A   B   C   D
58 : A   B   C   D
59 : A   B   C   D

Passage 1
(Questions 1–7)

There are two proteins that are involved in transporting O_2 in vertebrates. Hemoglobin (Hb) is found in red blood cells and myoglobin (Mb) is found in muscle cells. The hemoglobin protein accounts for about 97% of the dry weight of red blood cells. In erythrocytes, the hemoglobin carries O_2 from the lungs to the tissue undergoing cellular respiration. Hemoglobin has an oxygen binding capacity of 1.3 ml O_2 per gram of hemoglobin which increases the total blood oxygen capacity over seventy-fold compared to dissolved oxygen in blood.

When a tissue's metabolic rate increases, carbon dioxide production also increases. In addition to O_2, Hb also transports CO_2. Of all CO_2 transported in blood, 7-10% is dissolved in blood plasma, 70% is bicarbonate ions (HCO_3^-) and 20% is bound to the globin to Hb as carbaminohemoglobin.

CO_2 combines with water to form carbonic acid (H_2CO_3), which quickly dissociates. This reaction occurs primarily in red blood cells, where *carbonic anhydrase* reversibly and rapidly catalyzes the reaction:

$$CO_2 + H_2O \leftrightarrow H_2CO_3 \leftrightarrow H^+ + HCO_3^-$$

Hb of vertebrates has a quaternary structure comprised of four individual polypeptide chains: two α and two β protein polypeptides each with a heme group bound as a prosthetic group. The four polypeptide chains are held together by hydrogen bonding.

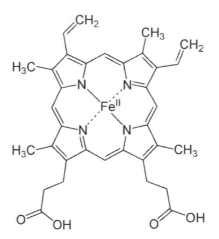

Figure 1. Hemoglobin

The binding of O_2 to Hb depends on the cooperativity of the Hb subunits. Cooperativity means that the binding of O_2 at one heme group increases the binding of O_2 at another heme within the Hb molecule through conformational changes of the entire hemoglobin molecule. This shape (conformational) change means it is energetically favorable for subsequent binding of O_2. Conversely, the unloading of O_2 at one heme increases the unloading of O_2 at other heme groups by a similar conformational change of the molecule.

Oxygen's affinity for Hb varies between different species and within species depending on multiple factors like blood pH, developmental stage (i.e. fetal versus adult), and body size. For example, small animals dissociate O_2 at a given partial pressure more readily than large animals because they have a higher metabolic rate and require more O_2 per gram of body mass.

Figure 2 represents the O_2-dissociation of Hb shown as sigmoidal curves B, C and D and myoglobin as hyperbolic curve A where saturation is the percent of O_2-binding sites occupied at specific partial pressures of O_2.

The *utilization coefficient* is the fraction of O_2 diffusing from Hb to the tissue as blood passes through the capillary beds. A normal value for the *utilization coefficient* is about 0.25.

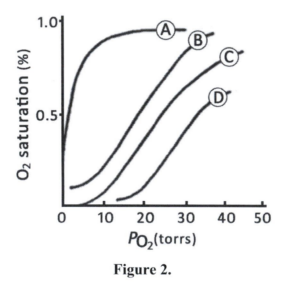

Figure 2.

In 1959, Max Perutz determined the molecular structure of myoglobin by x-ray crystallography which led to his sharing of the 1962 Nobel prize with John Kendrew. Myoglobin is a single-chain globular protein made up from 154 amino acids that transports and stores O_2 in muscle. Mb contains a heme (i.e. iron-containing porphyrin) prosthetic group with a molecular weight of 17.7 kd (kilodalton where 1 dalton is defined as 1/12 the mass of a neutral unbound carbon atom). As seen in Figure 2, Mb (curve A) has a greater affinity for O_2 than Hb. Unlike the blood-borne hemoglobin, myoglobin does not exhibit cooperative binding because cooperativity is present only in quaternary proteins that undergo allosteric changes. A high concentration of myoglobin in muscle cells allows organisms to hold their breath for extended periods of time. Diving mammals such as whales and seals have muscles with abundant myoglobin levels.

1. The mountain goat has developed a type of hemoglobin adapted to the unusually high altitudes. If curve C represents the O_2 dissociation curve for a cow's Hb, which curve most closely resembles the the O_2 dissociation curve for the mountain goat's Hb?

    A. curve A   **B.** curve B   **C.** curve C   **D.** curve D

2. If curve C represents the O_2-dissociation curve for a hippopotamus's Hb, which curve would most closely correspond with the Hb of a squirrel?

    A. curve A   **B.** curve B   **C.** curve C   **D.** curve D

3. If curve C represents the O_2-dissociation curve for Hb of an adult human, which of the following best explains why curve B most closely corresponds with the curve for fetal Hb?

    A. O_2 affinity of fetal Hb is lower than adult Hb
    B. O_2 affinity of fetal Hb is higher than adult Hb
    C. metabolic rate of fetal tissue is lower than adult tissue
    D. metabolic rate of fetal tissue is higher than adult tissue

4. Which of the following best explains the sigmoidal shape of the Hb O_2-dissociation curve?

    A. conformational changes in the polypeptide subunits of the Hb molecule
    B. heme groups within the Hb are being reduced and oxidized
    C. changing $[H^+]$ in the blood
    D. changing $[CO_2]$ transported by Hb in the blood

5. A sample of adult human Hb was placed in an $6M$ urea solution which resulted in the disruption of nonconvalent bonds. After that, the Hb α chains were isolated. If curve C represents the O_2-dissociation curve for adult human Hb *in vivo,* which curve most closely corresponds with the curve of the isolated α chains?

    A. curve A   **B.** curve B   **C.** curve C   **D.** curve D

6. In response to physiological changes, the utilization coefficient of an organism is constantly being adjusted. What value most closely represents the utilization coefficient for human adult Hb during strenuous exercise?

    A. 0.0675   **B.** 0.15   **C.** 0.25   **D.** 0.60

7. The Mb content in muscle of a humpback whale is about 0.005 moles/kg. Approximately how much O_2 is bound to Mb of a humpback that has 10,000 kg of muscle (assuming the Mb is saturated with O_2)?

    A. 12.5 moles   **B.** 50 moles   **C.** 200 moles   **D.** 2×10^7 moles

Passage 2
(Questions 8–13)

Corpus luteum (from the Latin "yellow body") is a temporary endocrine structure (yellow mass of cells) in female mammals involved in the production of relatively high levels of progesterone and moderate levels of estradiol (predominant potent estrogen) and inhibin A. The estrogen it secretes inhibits the secretion of LH and FSH by the pituitary which prevent future ovulation.

The corpus luteum is essential for establishing and maintaining pregnancy in females. It is typically very large relative to the size of the ovary (in humans, the size ranges from under 2 cm to 5 cm in diameter) and its color results from concentrating carotenoids from the diet.

The corpus luteum develops from an ovarian follicle during the luteal phase of the menstrual cycle or estrous cycle, following the release of a secondary oocyte from the follicle during ovulation. While the *oocyte* (subsequently the *zygote* if fertilization occurs) traverses the *oviduct* (Fallopian tube) into the uterus, the corpus luteum remains in the ovary.

Progesterone secreted by the corpus luteum is a steroid hormone responsible for the development and maintenance of the endometrium – thick lining of the uterus that provides area rich in blood vessels in which the zygote(s) can develop. If the egg is fertilized and implantation occurs, by day 9 post-fertilization the cells of the blastocyst secrete the hormone called *human chorionic gonadotropin* (hCG) which signals the corpus luteum to continue progesterone secretion. From this point on, the corpus luteum is called the *corpus luteum graviditatis*. The presence of hCG in the urine is the indicator used by home pregnancy test kits.

If the egg is not fertilized, the corpus luteum stops secreting progesterone and decays after approximately 14 days in humans. If fertilization occurred, throughout the first trimester, the corpus luteum secretes hormones at steadily increasing levels. In the second trimester of pregnancy, the placenta (in placental animals, including humans) eventually takes over progesterone production and the corpus luteum degrades without embryo/fetus loss.

8. Could high estrogen levels be used in home pregnancy tests to indicate possible pregnancy?

    A. No, because estrogen levels also rise prior to ovulation
    B. Yes, because estrogen is secreted at high levels during pregnancy
    C. No, because antibodies in the pregnancy test kit only recognize epitopes of proteins
    D. No, because estrogen is a steroid hormone and is not excreted into the urine by kidneys

9. All of these methods, if administered prior to ovulation, could theoretically be used as a method of female birth control, EXCEPT injecting:

    A. monoclonal antibodies for progesterone and estrogen
    B. antagonists of LH and FSH
    C. agonists that mimic the actions of estrogen and progesterone
    D. agonists that mimic the actions of LH and FSH

10. How would pregnancy be affected by the removal of the ovaries in the fifth month of gestation?

    A. Not affected because LH secreted by ovaries is not necessary in the 5th month of gestation
    B. Not affected because progesterone secreted by ovaries is not necessary in the 5th month of gestation
    C. Terminated because LH secreted by ovaries is necessary in the 5th month of gestation
    D. Terminated because progesterone secreted by ovaries is necessary in the 5th month of gestation

11. Very low levels of circulating progesterone and estrogen:

    A. inhibit the release of LH and FSH, thereby not inhibiting ovulation
    B. inhibit the release of LH and FSH and thereby inhibiting ovulation
    C. do not inhibit the release of LH and FSH, thereby not inhibiting ovulation
    D. do not inhibit the release of LH and FSH and thereby inhibiting ovulation

12. Which of these hormones must be present at high levels in a blood sample of a female patient who suspects to be 10 week pregnant to confirm the pregnancy?

    I.   Estrogen and progesterone
    II. FSH and LH
    III. hCG

    A. I only
    B. I and II only
    C. II and III only
    D. I and III only

Questions 13 through 16 are not based on any
descriptive passage and are independent of each other

13. Which of the following molecules is the site of NMR spin-spin coupling?

A. CH_4

B. FCH_2CH_2F

C. $(CH_3)_3CCl$

D. CH_3CH_2Br

14. Which of the following is correct about the hybridization of the three carbon atoms in the following molecule indicated by arrows?

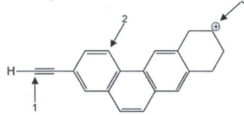

A. C_1 is sp hybridized, C_2 is sp^2 hybridized and C_3 is sp^3 hybridized

B. C_1 is sp^2 hybridized, C_2 is sp^2 hybridized and C_3 is sp hybridized

C. C_1 is sp hybridized, C_2 is sp^2 hybridized and C_3 is sp^2 hybridized

D. C_1 is sp^2 hybridized, C_2 is sp^2 hybridized and C_3 is sp^2 hybridized

15. The extracellular fluid volume depends on the total sodium content in the body. The balance between Na^+ intake and Na^+ loss regulates Na^+ levels. Which of the following will occur following the administration of digoxin, a poison that blocks the Na^+/K^+ ATPase?

A. increased intracellular $[H_2O]$

B. increased intracellular $[Cl^-]$

C. increased extracellular $[Na^+]$

D. increased intracellular $[K^+]$

16. To selectively function on ingested proteins and avoid digestion of a body's proteins in the digestive system, pancreatic peptidases must be tightly regulated. Which mechanism activates pancreatic peptidases?

A. osmolarity

B. coenzyme binding

C. carbohydrate moieties

D. proteolytic cleavage

This page is intentionally left blank

Passage 3
(Questions 17–21)

In pharmacology, a natural product is a chemical compound or substance produced by a living organism found in nature that usually has a pharmacological or biological activity for pharmaceutical drug discovery and drug design. However, a natural product can be classified as such even if it can be prepared by laboratory synthesis. Not all natural products can be fully synthesized because many have very complex structures making it too difficult or expensive to synthesize on an industrial scale. These compounds can only be harvested from their natural source - a process which can be tedious, time consuming, expensive, and wasteful on the natural resource.

Enediynes are a class of natural bacterial products characterized by either nine- or ten-membered rings containing two triple bonds separated by a double bond. Many enediyne compounds are extremely toxic to DNA. They are known to cleave DNA molecules and appear to be quite effective as selective agents for anticancer activity. Therefore, enediynes are being investigated as antitumor therapeutic agents.

Classes of enediynes target DNA by binding with DNA in the minor groove. Enediynes then abstract hydrogen atoms from the deoxyribose (sugar) backbone of DNA which results in strand scission. These small molecules are active ingredient of the majority of FDA-approved agents and continue to be one of the major biomolecules for drug discovery. This enediyne molecule is proven to be a potent antitumor agent:

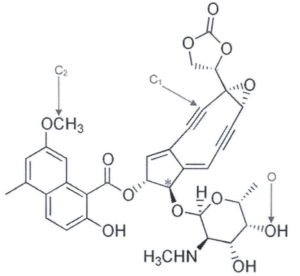

Figure 1. Neocarzinostatin

Neocarzinostatin is a chromoprotein enediyne antibiotic with anti-tumoral activity secreted by the bacteria *Streptomyces macromomyceticus*. It consists of two parts, a labile chromophore (bicyclic dienediyne structure shown) and a 113 amino acid apoprotein with the chromophores non-covalently bound with a high affinity. The *chromophore* is a very potent DNA-damaging agent because it is very labile and plays a role to protect and release the cleaved target DNA. Opening of the epoxide under reductive conditions present in cells creates favorable conditions and leads to a diradical intermediate and subsequent double-stranded DNA cleavage.

17. Which functional groups is NOT present in the molecule of neocarzinostatin?

A. thiol
B. hydroxyl
C. ester
D. epoxide

18. What is the hybridization of the two carbon atoms and the oxygen atom indicated by the arrows in Figure 1?

A. C_1 is sp^2, C_2 is sp^2 and O is sp^2 hybridized
B. C_1 is sp^2, C_2 is sp and O is sp hybridized
C. C_1 is sp, C_2 is sp^2 and O is sp^2 hybridized
D. C_1 is sp, C_2 is sp^3 and O is sp^3 hybridized

19. How many chiral carbons are in the molecule of neocarzinostatin?

A. 4
B. 8
C. 10
D. 12

20. How many π bonds are in the molecule of neocarzinostatin?

A. 7
B. 9
C. 11
D. 13

21. Which of the following is correct about the absolute configuration of the carbon atom indicated (*)?

A. it has an *S* absolute configuration
B. it has an *R* absolute configuration
C. it is not chiral
D. absolute configuration cannot be determined

Passage 4
(Questions 22–26)

The human digestive system functions by a highly coordinated chain of mechanisms consisting of ingestion, digestion and nutrient absorption. Digestion is a progressive process that begins with ingestion into the mouth and continues with digestion in the stomach and with digestion and absorption in the three sections of the small intestine.

Digestion involves macromolecules being broken down by enzymes into their component molecules before absorption through the villi of the small intestine. Nutrients from digested food such as vitamins, mineral and subunits of macromolecules (e.g. monosaccharides, amino acids, di– or tripeptides, glycerol and fatty acids) are absorbed via either diffusion or transport (facilitated or active) mechanisms. These transport mechanisms may occur with or without mineral co-transport.

Digestive enzymes at the intestinal brush border work with digestive enzymes secreted by salivary glands and the pancreas to facilitate nutrient absorption. Digestion of complex carbohydrates into simple sugars is an example of this process. Pancreatic α-amylase hydrolyzes the 1,4–glycosidic bonds in complex starches to oligosaccharides in the lumen of the small intestine. The membrane-bound intestinal α-glucosidases hydrolyze oligosaccharides, trisaccharides and disaccharides to glucose and other monosaccharides in the small intestine.

Acarbose is a starch blocker used as an anti-diabetic drug to treat type-2 diabetes mellitus. Acarbose is an inhibitor of α–1,4-glucosidase (an enteric brush-border enzyme) and pancreatic α-amylase that release glucose from complex starches. The inhibition of these enzyme systems reduces the rate of digestion of complex carbohydrates resulting in less glucose being absorbed because the carbohydrates are not broken down into glucose molecules. For diabetic patients, the short-term effect of such drug therapy is a decreased current blood glucose levels and the long-term effect is a reduction of the HbA1C levels.

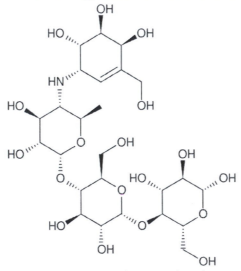

Figure 1. Acarbose molecule

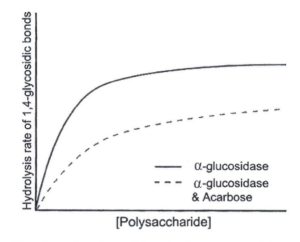

Figure 2. The kinetics of α-glucosidase in the presence/absence of acarbose.

22. According to the graph (Figure 2), how are α-1,4-glucosidase enzyme kinetics affected by acarbose?

    A. The concentration of available enzyme is reduced

    B. Enzyme specificity for the substrate is changed

    C. The K_{eq} binding of the ligand : enzyme complex is changed

    D. Covalent bonds that irreversibly inactivate the enzyme's active site are formed

23. Which type of α-1,4–glucosidase inhibition is most closely demonstrated by acarbose?

    A. irreversible covalent modification   **C.** competitive

    B. Allosteric   **D.** noncompetitive

24. Which condition most closely resembles the symptoms resulting from α-1,4-glucosidase inhibition by acarbose?

    A. infection by *V. cholera*   **C.** deficiency of lactase

    B. deficiency of intrinsic factor   **D.** deficiency of bile acid

25. Which molecule does NOT require micelle formation for intestinal absorption?

    A. vitamin A   **B.** triglycerides   **C.** cholesterol   **D.** bile acid

26. Glucosidase is best characterized as a:

    A. hydrolase   **B.** isomerase   **C.** ligase   **D.** phosphatase

Questions 27 through 30 are not based on any descriptive passage and are independent of each other

27. Which of the following is required for the proper function of the DNA-dependent DNA polymerase?

     I. DNA template strand
     II. primase (RNA primer)
     III. 4 different nucleotides
     IV. RNA polymerase

  A. I and II only
  B. I and III only
  C. I, II and III only
  D. I, II, III & IV

28. Given that the availability of the carbon source determines energy yield, catabolism of which molecule will result in the highest energy yield?

  A. short-chain unsaturated fatty acid
  B. short-chain saturated fatty acid
  C. long-chain conjugated fatty acid
  D. long-chain saturated fatty acid

29. Which molecule has the closest to 3000-3500 cm^{-1} infrared (IR) stretch?

  A. $H_2C=CH_2CH_3$
  B. CH_3CH_2COOH
  C. CH_3CH_2OH
  D. $(CH_3CH_2)_2CO$

30. Which of these compounds have a dipole moment?

     I. CCl_4
     II. CH_3CH_2OH
     III. $CH_3CHBrCH_3$

  A. II only
  B. III only
  C. I and III only
  D. II and III only

Passage 5
(Questions 31–35)

Penicillins are one of the most successful classes of antibiotics derived from *Penicillium* fungi. They include penicillin G, penicillin V, procaine penicillin and benzathine penicillin. Penicillin antibiotics were the first drugs that treated serious diseases such as syphilis, staphylococci and streptococci. Penicillins are still widely used today but many types of bacteria are now resistant to them. All penicillins are β-lactam antibiotics and are used in the treatment of bacterial infections caused by susceptible, usually Gram-positive, organisms.

The initial efforts to synthesize penicillin proved difficult with discrepancies in the structure being reported from different laboratories. In 1957, chemist John Sheehan at the Massachusetts Institute of Technology (MIT) completed the first chemical synthesis of penicillin. However, the synthesis developed by Sheehan was not appropriate for mass production of penicillins. One of the intermediate compounds was 6-aminopenicillanic acid (6-APA). Attaching different groups to the 6-APA allowed the synthesis of new forms of penicillin.

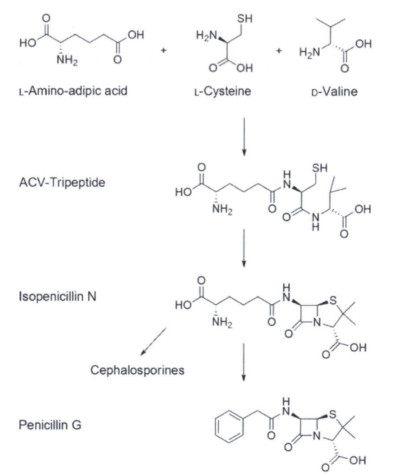

Figure 1. Penicillin biosynthesis

The structure of the penicillins includes a five-membered ring containing both sulfur and nitrogen (i.e. thioazolidine ring) joined to a four-membered ring containing a cyclic amide (i.e. β-lactam). These two rings are necessary for the biological activities of penicillin and cleavage of either ring disrupts antibacterial activity.

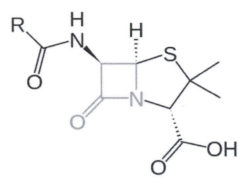

Figure 2. Core structure of penicillins (beta-lactam ring highlighted)

A medical student performed three experiments to elucidate how penicillin resulted in the death of bacterial cell.

Experiment 1

Two bacterial species were cultured and grown on agar plates. Both species had normal peptidoglycan cell walls. One population was exposed to penicillin while the other was not exposed to penicillin. About 93% of the bacteria treated with penicillin underwent cytolysis and did not survive while the bacteria which were not exposed to penicillin were unaffected.

Experiment 2

Two bacterial species were cultured and grown on agar plates. One species had an intact peptidoglycan cell wall while the other species had an incomplete cell wall. Both groups were exposed to penicillin on the agar plates and the bacteria with incomplete cell walls survived while 93% of those with intact peptidoglycan cell walls did not survive.

Experiment 3

The 7% who survived the treatment of penicillin in Experiment 2 were cultured and grown on agar plates. These colonies were repeatedly inoculated with penicillin and the colonies grew continuously with no apparent affect from the antibiotic.

31. It is reasonable to hypothesize that penicillin causes the bacterial death likely by:

   A. blocking the colonies' access to nutrients

   B. disrupting the integrity of the bacterial cell wall

   C. establishing excessive rigidity in the bacterial cell wall

   D. inducing mutations in bacteria from gram negative to gram positive strains

32. Knowing that penicillin G is rapidly hydrolyzed under acidic conditions, which limitation applies to its use?

   A. it is not active in the range of plasma pH

   B. it must be administered intravenously

   C. it must be taken 30 to 60 minutes before eating

   D. it should be avoided by young children and elderly patients

33. From the experiments, which bacterial species are most resistant to penicillin?

   A. Species unable to transcribe DNA to RNA

   B. Species with complete peptidoglycan cell walls

   C. Species with incomplete cross-linked cell walls

   D. Species with the greatest intracellular osmotic pressure

34. What causes the bacterial cells to undergo cytolysis upon weakening of their cell wall?

   A. water enters the cells due to osmotic pressure

   B. proteins are not able to exit the cell through vesicles

   C. solutes are forced out of the cells through active transport mechanisms

   D. facilitated diffusion causes lipid-insoluble substances to cross the cell membrane

35. It is a reasonable hypothesis that 7% of the cell-walled bacteria treated with penicillin in experiments 1 and 2 survived due to:

   A. bacterial cell wall's impermeability to penicillin

   B. agar on the growth plates that hydrolyzed and degraded penicillin

   C. plasmids that synthesize penicillinase

   D. limitation of diffusion which resulted in select colonies not being exposed to penicillin

Passage 6
(Questions 36–41)

Adipose tissue is loose connective tissue composed of adipocytes and stores free fatty acids as triglycerides. A fatty acid is a carboxylic acid with a long aliphatic tail (often with even numbers of carbons between 4 to 28) that is either saturated or unsaturated. Saturated refers to the aliphatic chain which lacks double bonds while unsaturated chains contain one or more double bonds.

Glycerol, a three-carbon molecule, contains three hydroxyl groups with a single OH on each of the three carbons. Glycerol is the backbone for triglycerides and each hydroxyl group is the attachment point for a free fatty acid. The hydroxyl on the glycerol attacks the carboxylic acid group of the free fatty acid to form an ester linkage bond.

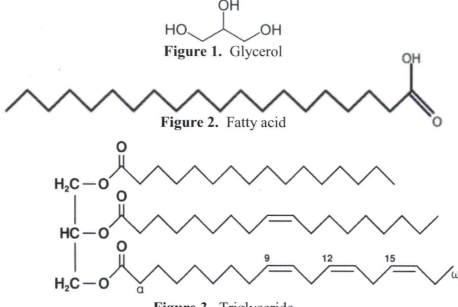

Figure 1. Glycerol

Figure 2. Fatty acid

Figure 3. Triglyceride

Triglycerides are released from adipose tissue into the circulatory system during high demands for energy by peripheral muscle tissue. The release of free fatty acids is controlled by a complex series of reactions tightly modulated by *hormone-sensitive lipase* (HSL). HSL hydrolyzes the first fatty acid from a triglyceride freeing a fatty acid and a diglyceride. HSL is activated when the body needs to mobilize energy stores and responds positively to catecholamines and adrenocorticotropic hormone (ACTH), but is inhibited by insulin. Lipase activators bind receptors that are coupled to adenylate cyclase which increases cAMP for activation of an appropriate *kinase* (PKA) that then activates HSL.

Free fatty acids targeted for breakdown are transported bound to *albumin* through the circulation. However, fatty acids targeted for adipose storage sites in adipocytes are transported in large lipid-protein micelle particles termed *lipoproteins* (i.e. LDL). During high rates of mitochondrial fatty acid oxidation, acetyl CoA is produced in large amounts. If the generation of acetyl CoA from glycolysis exceeds utilization by the Krebs cycle, an alternative pathway is ketone body synthesis. During the onset of starvation, skeletal and cardiac muscles preferentially metabolize ketone bodies which preserves endogenous glucose for the brain.

36. Albumin is the most abundant protein distributed throughout circulatory system and accounts for about 50% of plasma proteins. Which bond and for what reason binds albumin to free fatty acids?

  A. hydrogen bonding to albumin stabilizes fatty acid absolute configuration
  B. covalent bonding to albumin increases lipid solubility
  C. ionic bonding to albumin stabilizes free fatty acid structure
  D. van der Waals binding to albumin increases lipid solubility

37. A person suffering untreated diabetes can experience ketoacidosis due to a reduced supply of glucose. Which of the following correlates with diabetic ketoacidosis?

  A. high plasma insulin levels
  B. increase in fatty acid oxidation
  C. ketone bodies increase plasma alkalinity to clinically dangerous levels
  D. decreased levels of acetyl CoA lead to increased production of ketone bodies

38. Which of the following is the site of the breakdown for β-oxidation?

  A. mitochondria   **B.** lysosomes   **C.** cytoplasm of the cell   **D.** nucleolus

39. The main regulation point for fatty acid catabolism is *lipolysis*. All of the following are direct products of adipose tissue breakdown EXCEPT:

  A. acetyl CoA   **B.** glycerol   **C.** free fatty acids   **D.** ketone bodies

40. Which organ is the last to use ketone bodies as an energy source?

  A. kidneys   **B.** brain   **C.** cardiac tissue   **D.** skeletal muscle

41. Which of the following bonds between glycerol and the free fatty acids is cleaved by phosphorylated *hormone-sensitive lipase* via hydrolysis?

  A. hydrogen bond   **C.** ionic bond
  B. ester bond   **D.** disulfide bond

> Questions 42 through 46 are not based on any
> descriptive passage and are independent of each other

42. What is the correct sequence of organelles passed by the proteins targeted for the secretory pathway?

  A. ER → vesicle → Golgi → vesicle → plasma membrane
  B. ER → vesicle → Golgi → cytoplasm → plasma membrane
  C. Golgi → ER → vesicle → cytoplasm → proteosome
  D. cytoplasm → vesicle → Golgi → ER → vesicle → plasma membrane

43. During replication, which molecule do single stranded binding proteins (SSBP) attach to for maintaining the uncoiled configuration of the nucleotide strands of the double helix uncoiled by the helicase enzyme?

  A. dsDNA   **B.** ssDNA   **C.** dsRNA   **D.** ssRNA

44. A biochemist hypothesized that the glucose transport protein is located only on the outer surface of the cell membrane. Is such hypothesis correct?

  A. Yes, because transport proteins are located only on the outer surface of the lipid bilayer
  B. Yes, because transport proteins are located only on the inner surface of the lipid bilayer
  C. No, because transport proteins are transmembrane and span the entire lipid bilayer
  D. No, because the hydrophilic heads of the lipid bilayer attract polar residues of the protein

45. Beta-oxidation occurs in the same location as:

  I. Glycolysis   II. Krebs cycle   III. Pyruvate decarboxylation into acetyl-CoA

A. I only   **B.** I and II only   **C.** II and III only   **D.** I, II and III

46. Which molecule has an infrared stretch closest to 1700 cm^{-1}?

  A. $CH_3CH_2CH_2CPh_3$ **C.** $CH_3CH_2CH_2CH_2CHO$
  B. $CH_3CH_2CH_2CH_2OH$ **D.** $CH_3CHClCH_2CH_2OCH_2CH_3$

This page is intentionally left blank

Passage 7
(Questions 47–52)

Esters are compounds consisting of a carbonyl adjacent to an ether linkage. They are derived by reacting a carboxylic acid (or its derivate) with a hydroxyl of an alcohol or phenol. Esters are often formed by condensing *via* dehydration (removal of water) of an alcohol acid with an acid.

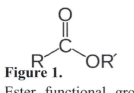

Figure 1. Ester functional group (R and R' represent alkyl chains)

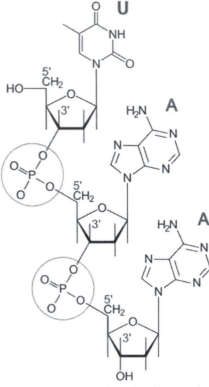

Esters are ubiquitous in biological molecules. Most naturally occurring fats and oils are the fatty acid esters of glycerol while phosphoesters form the backbone of nucleic acids (e.g. DNA and RNA molecules) as shown in Figure 2. Esters with low molecular weight are commonly used as fragrances and found in essential oils and pheromones.

Acid-catalyzed esterification is a mechanism of nucleophilic attack by the oxygen on an alcohol to the carboxylic acid as diagrammed below. The isotope of oxygen labeled in the alcohol as $R'^{18}OH$ was used to elucidate the reaction mechanism. The ester product was separated from unused reactants and side reaction contaminants in the reaction mixture. The water from the reaction mixture was collected as a separate fraction via distillation.

Figure 2. Two phosphodiester bonds are formed by connecting the phosphate group (PO_4^{3-}) between three nucleotides.

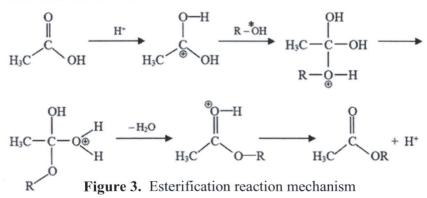

Figure 3. Esterification reaction mechanism

47. Which of these carboxylic acids has the lowest pK_a?

   A. $ClCH_2CH_2CH_2COOH$ **C.** $Cl_3CCH_2CH_2COOH$

   B. $CH_3CH_2CH_2COOH$ **D.** $CH_3CH_2CHClCOOH$

48. Given that esterification may occur between parts of the same molecule, which compound would most easily undergo intramolecular esterification to form a cyclic ester?

   A. $HOOCCH_2CH_2OH$ **C.** $HOOCCH_2CH_2CH_2CH_2OH$

   B. $HOOCCH_2CH_2CH_2OH$ **D.** $HOOCCH_2CH_2CH_2CH_2CH_2CH_2OH$

49. An alternative method for forming esters is:

$$CH_3CH_2COO^- + RX \rightarrow CH_3CH_2COOR + X^-$$

The reason that this reaction occurs is because:

   A. carboxylates are good nucleophiles   **C.** halide acts as a good electrophile

   B. carboxylates are good electrophiles   **D.** halide is a poor conjugate base

50. The rate of the reaction is negligible without the acid catalyst. The catalyst is attacked by the:

   A. carbonyl carbon and facilitates the attack of the carbonyl nucleophile

   B. carbonyl carbon and facilitates the carbonyl oxygen electrophile

   C. carbonyl oxygen and facilitates the attack of the alcohol nucleophile

   D. carbonyl oxygen and facilitates the carbonyl carbon electrophile

51. Which alkyl halide most readily forms an ester with sodium pentanoate ($CH_3CH_2CH_2CH_2COO^-Na^+$)?

   A. CH_3Br **C.** $CH_3(CH_2)_6CH_2Br$

   B. $(CH_3)_2CHBr$ **D.** $CH_3CH_2CH_2CH_2Br$

52. Which statement is correct, assuming that only the forward reaction occurs (Figure 3)?

   A. ester fraction does not contain labeled oxygen while the water fraction does

   B. water fraction does not contain labeled oxygen while the ester does

   C. neither the ester fraction nor the water fraction contains labeled oxygen

   D. both the ester fraction and the water fraction contain labeled oxygen

Questions 53 through 59 are not based on any
descriptive passage and are independent of each other

53. Which of the following amino acids is an essential amino acid in the diets of children but not adults?

    A. Asparate   **B.** Glycine   **C.** Arginine   **D.** Lysine

54. At room temperature, triglycerols containing only saturated long chain fatty acids remain:

    A. oils   **B.** solid   **C.** liquid   **D.** unsaturated

55. Which of the following is an inactive precursor of protease enzymes synthesized in the pancreas?

    A. Ribozyme   **C.** Zymogen
    B. Isozyme   **D.** Allosteric enzyme

56. The most common naturally occurring fatty acids have:

    A. 12-20 carbon atoms with an odd number of carbon atoms
    B. 12-20 carbon atoms with an even number of carbon atoms
    C. 20-50 carbon atoms with an odd number of carbon atoms
    D. 20-50 carbon atoms with an even number of carbon atoms

57. The anticodon is located on the:

    A. DNA   **B.** tRNA   **C.** mRNA   **D.** rRNA

58. Which disaccharide, when present in large excess over glucose, can be metabolized by *E. coli* by use of the operon?

    A. galactose   **B.** lactose   **C.** sucrose   **D.** cellobiose

59. Which mechanism is used to interconvert anomers?

    A. Isotopic exchange reaction
    B. Mutarotation
    C. Conformational change around carbon-carbon bonds
    D. Anomers cannot be interconverted

PART II.II

Explanatory Answers

BIOLOGICAL & BIOCHEMICAL FOUNDATIONS OF LIVING SYSTEMS
MCAT® PRACTICE TEST #1: ANSWER KEY

Passage 1
1 : B
2 : C
3 : A
4 : D
5 : D

Passage 2
6 : B
7 : D
8 : C
9 : D
10 : A

Independent questions
11 : A
12 : B
13 : D
14 : C

Passage 3
15 : A
16 : B
17 : A
18 : A
19 : C
20 : D

Passage 4
21 : D
22 : B
23 : D
24 : C
25 : B
26 : A

Independent questions
27 : C
28 : C
29 : D

Passage 5
30 : A
31 : B
32 : D
33 : C
34 : B
35 : D

Passage 6
36 : B
37 : B
38 : B
39 : B
40 : A

Independent questions
41 : A
42 : A
43 : C
44 : D
45 : D
46 : C

Passage 7
47 : C
48 : C
49 : B
50 : D
51 : A
52 : B

Independent questions
53 : B
54 : C
55 : D
56 : D
57 : B
58 : A
59 : C

Passage 1
(Questions 1–5)

An antibiotic is a soluble substance derived from a mold or a bacterium that inhibits the growth of other microorganisms. Despite the absence of the bacterial beta-lactamase gene that typically confers penicillin resistance, there is a strain of penicillin-resistant pneumococci bacteria. Additionally, some of the cells in this strain are unable to metabolize the disaccharides of sucrose and lactose. A microbiologist studying this strain discovered that all of the cells in this strain were infected with two different types of bacteriophage: phage A and phage B. Both, phage A and phage B, insert their DNA into the bacterial chromosome. The researcher infected wildtype pneumococci with the two phages to determine if the bacteriophage infection could give rise to this new bacterial strain.

Experiment 1
Two separate 25ml nutrient broth solutions containing actively growing wild-type pneumococci were mixed with 15μl of phage A and 15μl of phage B. In addition, another 25ml broth solution containing only wild-type pneumococci was used as a control. After 30 minutes of room temperature incubation, the microbiologist diluted 1μl of the broth solutions in separate 1ml aliquots of sterile water. These dilutions were plated on three different agar plates containing glucose, sucrose, and lactose, respectively. The plates were incubated at 37°C for 12 hours and the results are summarized in Table 1.

Plates	phage A infected cells	phage B infected cells	wild-type cells
glucose	+	+	+
sucrose	+	−	+
lactose	+	−	−

(+) plates show bacterial growth; (−) plates show no growth

Table 1

Experiment 2
10μl of each of the broth solutions from experiment 1 was again diluted in separate 5ml aliquots of sterile water. These dilutions were plated on three different agar plates containing tetracyne, ampicillin, and no antibiotic, respectively. The plates were incubated at 37°C for 12 hours and the results are summarized in Table 2.

Plates	phage A infected cells	phage B infected cells	wild-type cells
Tetracyne	−	−	−
Ampicillin	+	+	−
No antibiotic	+	+	+

(+) plates show bacterial growth; (−) plates show no growth

Table 2

1. Which of the following best accounts for the results of Experiment 2?

> **I.   wild-type bacteria has no natural resistance to either ampicillin or tetracyne**
> **II. phage A DNA and phage B DNA encode for beta-lactamase**
> III. phage A and phage B disrupted the wild-type bacteria's ability to resist ampicillin
> IV. phage A DNA and phage B DNA encode for enzymes that inhibit tetracyne's harmful effects

  A. II only
  B. I & II only
  C. III & IV only
  D. I, II & IV only

B is correct.

In Table 2, the control (e.g. wild type) bacteria were unable to grow in the presence of either tetracyne or ampicillin. Therefore, the wild-type bacteria do not have any natural resistance to these two antibiotics and so Roman numeral I is correct.

Eliminate all answer choices containing Roman numeral III because the wild-type bacteria have no natural resistance to ampicillin.

From Table 2, bacteria infected with either phage A or phage B are able to grow in the presence of ampicillin but not in the presence of tetracyne. Both phage A DNA and phage B DNA must contain the gene that encodes for beta-lactamase because this is the enzyme that confers ampicillin resistance.

Test technique: do not focus on very specific details of the experimental protocol because this can slow the reading and none of the questions actually required you to refer back to the protocol. Focus your attention on the rationale of the experiments. Don't focus on the minutiae because the passage is available to refer to at any time.

2. Plaques are transparent areas within the bacterial lawn caused by bacterial cell death. In which of the following cycles must phage A be able to produce plaques?

  A. S phase
  B. translocation
  C. lytic
  D. lysogenic

C is correct.

The lysis (e.g. lytic cycle) of the bacterial cell produces plaques that are transparent areas within a bacterial lawn caused by bacterial cell death. The lysis of the bacterial cells results from the eruption of infectious viral particles.

The question asks about the cycle of viral infection when bacteriophages assemble new viral particles and lyse (rupture) the host cell. This passage relates to strains of phage that began their infection in a lysogenic stage because the passage states that the phage DNA was integrated (i.e. inserted) into the bacterial genome.

When certain phages (i.e. viruses) infect bacteria, one of two events may occur. The viral DNA may enter the cell and initiate a lytic cycle infection whereby new viral particles are assembled and the bacterium lyses.

Alternatively, the viral DNA may become integrated into the bacterial chromosome. Once integrated into the bacterial chromosome, the viral DNA replicates with the host chromosome and passes (i.e. during cell division of the host cells) to daughter cells. The virus is dormant within the cell and this is the lysogenic cycle. Periodically, an integrated virus, (i.e. called a prophage) becomes activated, the virus DNA is excised from the host genome and the lytic cycle begins.

A common example of this alternation between the lytic and lysogenic cycle in human involves the herpes virus comparing the dormant (i.e. lysogenic cycle) virus phase vs. actively virus replicating cycle of the lytic cycle.

The eukaryotic cell cycle (Interphase and Mitosis) is not related to a viral infection. Mitosis (PMAT: stages of prophase, metaphase, anaphase and telophase) is the nuclear division of eukaryotic somatic (i.e. body) cells characterized by chromosome replication and formation of two identical daughter cells; each with a complete copy of the chromosomes within the nuclei.

3. Which of the following best describes the appearance of pneumococci, a streptococcal bacteria, when stained and then viewed with a compound light microscope?

  A. spherical
  B. rod
  C. helical
  D. cuboidal

A is correct.
Bacteria are categorized on the basis of their shape. Pneumococci bacteria, when stained and viewed under a light microscope, are spherical in shape.

The three basic bacterial shapes are 1) spherical, 2) rod, and 3) helical (or spiral).

Spherical bacteria are known as cocci (i.e. berries).

Rod-shaped bacteria are known as bacilli.

Helical bacteria are known as spirochetes (or spirilla) and are the least common of the three groups.

Streptococcus pneumoniae (pneumococcus), a member of the genus Streptococcus, is a significant human pathogenic bacterium. *S. pneumoniae* was identified as a major cause of pneumonia in the 19th century. Aside from this, the organism causes many other types of pneumococcal infection including acute sinusitis, otitis media, meningitis, bacteremia, sepsis, osteomyelitis, septic arthritis, endocarditis, peritonitis, pericarditis, cellulitis, and brain abscess.

Pneumococci is a part of respiratory tract natural flora, but (as many natural flora) can become pathogenic under certain conditions, for example if the immune system of the host is weakened.

Rod-shaped bacteria include the common bacteria, *Escherichia coli* (i.e. *E. coli*), named after the German pediatrician and bacteriologist (Escherich; 1857-1911). *E. coli* is a genus of aerobic, facultative anaerobic bacteria containing short, motile or nonmotile, Gram-negative rods. Motile cells are peritrichous; relating to cilia or other appendicular organs projecting from the periphery of a cell. Glucose and lactose are fermented with the production of acid and gas. These organisms are found in feces; some are pathogenic to man, causing enteritis, peritonitis, cystitis, etc.

Among the representatives of helical bacteria there is *Treponema pallidum* which cannot be seen on a Gram stained smear because this organism is very thin. This bacterium is known for causing syphilis and transmits via sexual contact and from mother to fetus across placenta.

Bacteria are not classified as cuboidal. Cuboidal refers to the shape of tissue type.

4. Based on the results of the experiments, which statement is most likely true of phage A?

   A. phage A reduced the ampicillin on the agar plates and therefore allows bacterial growth
   B. phage A inserted its DNA into the bacterial chromosome rendering ampicillin ineffective against the bacterial cell wall
   C. phage A inhibited the growth of the bacteria
   D. phage A contained the viral gene that encoded for beta-lactamase

D is correct.

The correct answer is that phage A contained the viral gene that encoded for beta-lactamase. All answers refer to ampicillin resistance and phage A. A bacteriophage is a virus that infects bacteria.

From Table 2, the bacteria infected with phage A were able to grow on agar plates containing ampicillin. From the passage (and Table 2), the uninfected wild-type bacterial cells do not contain the gene that encodes for beta-lactamase. Beta-lactamase confers ampicillin resistance because no bacterial growth was observed when the control dilution was incubated in the presence of ampicillin. Combining these two pieces of information, phage A must be responsible for the observed ampicillin resistance in Experiment 2.

Choice C should be eliminated because bacterial growth did occur in both Experiments 1 and 2 when the bacteria were infected with phage A.

The other choices are all possible ways in which the bacterial cells could have become resistant to ampicillin. So, decide between these three answers based on the experimental data.

The ampicillin resistance observed in the bacteria infected with phage A in Experiment 2 must have been conferred by the insertion of phage A DNA that contained the gene that codes for beta-lactamase.

Beta-lactam is the core structure of ampicillins. The term penicillin refers to over 50 chemically related antibiotics. All penicillins (e.g. ampicillin) have a common core structure of a beta-lactam ring.

Penicillins prevent the cross-linking of the peptidoglycan and interfere with the final stage of the cell wall formation in bacteria. Penicillins do not destroy fully formed bacteria but inhibit the formation of additional bacteria by inhibiting the synthesis of the cell wall.

The passage does not state the exact mechanism by which this gene functions and therefore you are not expected to know this information. Perhaps beta-lactamase does function via the mechanisms proposed by affecting the bacterium cell wall, or by reducing the penicillin on the agar plate. However, neither of these proposed mechanisms can be concluded from the experimental data.

The only conclusion is that ampicillin resistance is encoded for by the gene for beta-lactamase because the only difference between these bacterial cells and the wild-type cells of the control group is the phage A infection.

5. Which of the following conclusions is consistent with the data in Table 1?

A. phage A inserted its DNA into the bacterial chromosome region that encodes for the enzymes of glycolysis
B. phage A prevented larger molecules such as lactose and sucrose from passing through the bacterial cell wall
C. phage B utilized all of the sucrose and lactose and starved out the bacteria
D. phage B inserted its DNA into the bacterial chromosome region that encodes for enzymes that digest disaccharides

D is correct.

Phage B inserted its DNA into the bacterial chromosome region that encodes for enzymes that digest disaccharides. According to Table 1, the bacteria infected with phage B were only able to grow on glucose and not able to grow in the presence of either sucrose or lactose (both are disaccharides). Therefore, phage B inhibits the bacteria's metabolism of disaccharides.

Since phage A has no deleterious effects on bacterial metabolism, as indicated by the ability to grow on all three plates, choices A and B can be eliminated. Therefore, if phage A DNA was incorporated into the bacterial chromosome region that encodes for the enzymes of glycolysis, the bacteria would have been unable to grow on glucose, since glycolysis provides the ATP required for growth. If phage A had prevented lactose and sucrose entrance into the cells, the bacteria would have been unable to grow on either of these sugars because the cells would not have had access to metabolic fuel.

Since viruses are not autonomous life forms, they would be unable to utilize any sugar; viruses do not possess the metabolic machinery to metabolize nutrients.

Insertion of phage B DNA into the chromosome region that encodes for the enzymes that digest disaccharides such as sucrose and lactose would disrupt the metabolism of these nutrients. Therefore, no bacterial growth is expected when phage B-infected bacteria were incubated with either sucrose or lactose (i.e. Table 1).

Passage 2
(Questions 6–10)

Water is the most abundant compound in the human body and comprises about 60% of total body weight. The exact contribution of water to total body weight within a person varies with gender and also decreases with age. Daily water needs are about 2.7 liters for women and about 3.7 liters for men.

Total body water (TBW) in the body is distributed between two fluid compartments. These compartments comprise the intracellular fluid (ICF) and extracellular fluid (ECF). The sum of ICF and ECF volumes equals the TBW:

TBW volume = ECF volume + ICF volume

There are approximately 100 trillion cells in the human body. Intracellular fluid is the fluid contained within the membrane of each cell. ICF accounts for about 65% or about 2/3 of TBW. Extracellular fluid is the fluid surrounding the individual cells within the body. ECF, present outside of body cells, can be further divided into: interstitial fluid (IF), lymph fluid and blood plasma. Interstitial fluid and lymph fluid together comprise about 27% of the TBW. Blood plasma accounts for another 8% of the TBW.

Other extracellular fluids are found in specialized compartments such as the urinary tract, digestive tract, bone and synovial fluids lubricating the joints and organs.

Total body water (TBW) can be measured with isotope dilution. After ingesting a trace dose of a known isotopic marker, saliva samples are collected from the patient over several hours. The measurements are compared between experimental and baseline data. The calculation of body mass before and after the experiment provides a ratio of TBW to total body mass. The data is analyzed using the following formula:

Volume = Amount (g) / Concentration

6. In periods of low water intake, the rennin-angiotensin feedback mechanism is used to minimize the amount of water lost by the system. The kidney works in conjunction with which of the following organs to excrete acidic metabolites and regulate acid-base buffer stores?

A. brain   **B. lungs**   **C.** heart   **D.** liver

B is correct.

The kidneys are bean-shaped organs (about 11 cm long, 5 cm wide and 3 cm thick) lying on either side of the vertebral column, posterior to the peritoneum, about opposite the twelfth thoracic and first three lumbar vertebrae. The nephron is the functional cell of the kidney that produces urine.

The kidneys work in conjunction with the lungs to excrete acidic (H^+) metabolites and regulate acid-base buffer stores. CO_2, which contributes to the acidity of blood, is expelled via the lung. The lungs correct an abnormally high acid concentration by increasing expirations (i.e., hyperventilation) and thereby increase CO_2 expiration.

7. In isotope dilution technique, a dose of approximately 7 milligrams of O^{18} labeled water was used as a tracer. If 21.0 M/L was the estimated particle concentration, what is the estimate of TBW?

  A. 0.33　　　　　**B.** 33.3　　　　　**C.** 0.33 x 10^{-2}　　　　　**D.** 33.3 x 10^{-5}

D is correct.

According to the equation in the passage:
Volume = amount (g) / concentration
7 milligrams = 0.007 grams
Thus, 0.007 / 21.0 M/L = 3.33 x 10^{-4} or 33.3 x 10^{-5}

8. The movement of water into the cell from the interstitial space to the cytosol is an example of:

  A. facilitated transport　　　　**C. osmosis**
  B. active transport　　　　　　**D.** passive transport

C is correct.

The plasma membrane consists of a fluid mosaic model. The phospholipids consist of a polar head (hydrophilic phosphate group) and the non-polar tails (hydrophobic fatty acid chains). Water and small uncharged molecules are able to pass freely through the bilayer of the plasma membrane. Movement of molecules down their concentration gradient is a spontaneous process (i.e. no energy needed) known as diffusion. Osmosis is a subset of diffusion and refers to the movement of water down its concentration gradient.

Facilitated transport is the same process as passive transport (aka passive diffusion). This process requires a protein pore (or channel) through the membrane that provides the path for larger or charged molecules to move down their concentration gradient. Like diffusion and osmosis, movement of solutes down a concentration gradient does not require energy (e.g. ATP).

Active transport uses a protein pore or channel but solutes (molecules dissolved in the solution) move up their concentration gradient. Because movement is up a concentration gradient (movement from a lower concentration to a higher concentration), energy is needed for active transport.

9. Edema is characterized by the presence of excess fluid forced out of circulation and into the extracellular space of tissue or serous cavities. Often edema is due to circulatory or renal difficulty. Which of the following could be a direct cause of edema?

    A. decreased permeability of capillary walls

    B. increased osmotic pressure within a capillary

    C. decreased hydrostatic pressure within a capillary

    D. increased hydrostatic pressure within a capillary

D is correct.

An increase in hydrostatic pressure (e.g. force generated by blood volume) within a capillary would create a stronger force of the fluid inside. This increased hydrostatic pressure would increase the amount of fluid that leaks out of the capillary and moves into the extracellular space. By definition, this accumulation of fluid in the interstitial tissue leads to edema.

A: decreasing capillary permeability would not cause edema because the decreased permeability of the capillary would cause even less leakage of fluid into the extracellular space.

B: if osmotic pressure is increased within a capillary, this would only increase the reabsorption of fluid back into the capillary and no edema would result.

C: decreasing hydrostatic pressure within a capillary bed would have the opposite effect. A decreased force on the fluid in the capillary leads to decreased leakage of fluid into the extracellular space.

10. An experiment is conducted to estimate total body water. According to the passage, which of the following must be true?

    A. ECF comprises 35% of TBW and is estimated at 1/3 of body water

    B. ECF comprises 65% of TBW and is estimated at 2/3 of body water

    C. ICF comprises 50% of TBW and is estimated at 1/2 of body water

    D. ICF comprises 35% of TBW and is estimated at 1/3 of body water

A is correct.

According to the passage, ICF comprises 65% of TBW and about 2/3 of total body water.

Because ICF + ECF = TBW, ECF = TBW – ICF and equals 35% TBW which is about 1/3 of body water.

Total body water
Volume = 40 L
body weight - 60%

Extracellular fluid (ECF)
Volume = 15 L
body weight - 20%

Intracellular fluid (ICF)
Volume = 25 L
body weight - 40%

Interstitial fluid (IF)
Volume = 12 L
80% of ECF

Plasma Volume = 3 L, 20% of ECF

The major fluid compartments of the body.
Values are for 70 kg (154 lbs) male.

Questions 11 through 14 are not based on any
descriptive passage and are independent of each other

11. Which of the following compounds would be most likely to produce color?

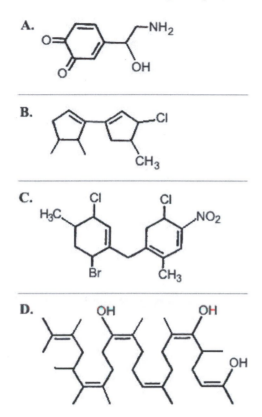

A.

B.

C.

D.

A is correct.

This molecule has four conjugated bonds and produces a brownish color. Conjugation means alternating double and single bonds and requires an sp^2 carbon (e.g. double bond, carbocation, radical or carbanion) for the delocalization of the electrons within the sp^2 carbon (double bonds).

B: has too few double bonds to produce color.

C: has three double bonds, but they are isolated and conjugated (in a set of two) and less likely to be colored.

D: has a large number of double bonds, but they are isolated (not conjugated), so its absorbance wavelength is below the visible range.

12. Which of the following molecules of digestion is NOT transported by a specific carrier in the intestinal cell wall?

   A. fructose   **B. sucrose**   **C.** alanine   **D.** tripeptides

B is correct.

Carbohydrates have a molecular formula of $C_nH_{2n}O_n$ and are composed of sugars and end in ~ose. Sucrose must first be digested, (i.e. passage) before absorption. Sucrose, unlike its component monosaccharides (glucose and fructose), is not absorbed via a carrier.

Proteins, unlike carbohydrates, do not have to be hydrolyzed to single subunits (e.g. monosaccharide for carbohydrates and amino acid for proteins) to be absorbed and transported into the small intestine. Single amino acids, dipeptides and tripeptides are all transported across intestinal cell membranes via carrier proteins. Alanine is one of twenty amino acids.

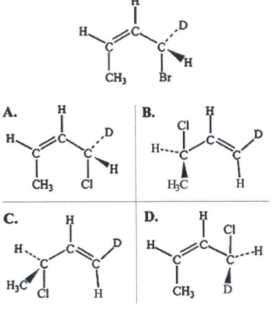

13. Which of the following answer choices would be a major product in the reaction of the molecule shown below with chloride anion in carbon tetrachloride (CCl_4)?

D is correct.

In the aprotic solvent of carbon tetrachloride (CCl_4) the preferred mechanism is S_N2. S_N2 is a concerted mechanism that produces inversion of stereochemistry. S_N2 mechanisms prefer a solvent such as CCl_4 that is nonpolar aprotic (i.e. no protons dissociate and release into the solution).

Tertiary substrates undergo the formation of a carbocation intermediate (S_N1 mechanism) and prefer a polar protic solvent (e.g. CH_3OH or H_2O). S_N1 mechanisms produce racemic mixtures with about equal probability of the two enantiomers (+) / (–) as measured with a polarimeter because the carbocation intermediate is trigonal planar (i.e. flat) and the nucleophile is likely to attack from either face of the trigonal planar intermediate.

14. The nucleus of a tadpole myocardial cell is removed and transplanted into an enucleated frog zygote. After transplant, the frog zygote develops normally. The experimental results suggest that:

A. the zygote cytoplasm contains RNA for normal adult development

B. cell differentiation is controlled by irreversible gene repression

C. cell differentiation is controlled by selective gene repression

D. the ribosomes in the zygote nucleus are the same as in an adult frog

C is correct.

The nucleus of a zygote (fertilized egg) contains all the genetic information (e.g. genome) needed by all future cells of an adult organism. As the zygote divides and segments of the growing organism differentiate, each individual cell maintains a complete complement of genetic information. However, a differentiated cell does not express all the gene-encoded protein products because some genes are selectively expressed, while others are repressed. Within individual cells, gene expression is selectively on (or off) depending on the cell type. Selective activation is very important because even though a myocardial (heart) cell contains the same genetic information as an osteoblast (bone cell), each cell in the body has a specialized function requiring selective gene expression. When certain genes that are normally turned off are aberrantly expressed, cancer (uncontrolled cell growth) may result.

This experiment involved transplantation of genetic material of a differentiated (myocardial) cell into an enucleated frog zygote and the zygote develops normally. The results suggest that a differentiated (myocardial) nucleus contains the same genetic (genome) information as the nucleus within the non-differentiated zygote. A zygote is totipotent (or omnipotent) and can differentiate and develop into a complete organism. The fact that the nucleus was originally in a differentiated cell also suggests selective repression of DNA. If the myocardial nucleus lacked genetic material essential to a developing organism, the zygote would develop into a mass of myocardial cells and, with certain essential genes absent, the zygote would not develop normally.

A: the experiment did not specifically address this question and the results do not support (or contradict) this conclusion. Another experiment, such as testing if an enucleated cell containing the RNA within the zygote would develop normally, needs to be conducted to support (or contradict) this theory.

B: the experiment proves that irreversible repression of genes is false. Inactivation of genes must be reversible, otherwise the transplanted nucleus would not direct the zygote to divide and develop into all the different cell types found in an adult frog.

D: this is not tested and the experiment does not support (or contradict) this choice. Eukaryotic ribosomes are the same in all cells and are located within the cytoplasm, not the nucleus, of the cell.

Passage 3
(Questions 15– 20)

The earth's atmosphere absorbs the energy of most wavelengths of electromagnetic energy. However, significant amounts of radiation reach the earth's surface through two regions of non-absorption. The first region transmits ultraviolet and visible light, as well as infrared light or heat. The second region transmits radio waves. Organisms living on earth have evolved a number of pigments that interact with light. Some pigments capture light energy, some provide protection from light-induced damage, some serve as camouflage and some serve signaling purposes.

Polyenes are poly-unsaturated organic compounds that contain one or more sets of conjugation. Conjugation is alternating double and single bonds which results in an overall lower energy state of the molecule. Polyenes are important photoreceptors. Without conjugation, or conjugated with only one or two other carbon-carbon double bonds, the molecule normally has enough energy to absorb within the ultraviolet region of the spectrum. The energy state of polyenes with numerous conjugated double bonds can be lowered so they enter the visible region of the spectrum and these compounds are often yellow or other colors.

Certain wavelengths of light (quanta) possess exactly the correct amount of energy to raise electrons with the molecule from their ground state to higher-energy orbitals. For most organic compounds, these wavelengths are in the UV range. However, conjugated double bond systems stabilize the electrons, so that they can be excited by lower-frequency photons with wavelengths in the visible spectrum. Such pigments are known as chromophores and transmit the complimentary color to the one absorbed. Carotene is a hydrocarbon compound with eleven conjugated double bonds that absorbs blue light and transmits orange light. The wavelength absorbed generally increases with the number of conjugated bonds. The presence of rings and side-chains within the molecule also affect the wavelengths of energy that the molecule absorbs.

Nucleic acids are biological molecules affected by light. DNA absorbs ultraviolet light and is damaged by UVC (electromagnetic energy with wavelength less that 280 nm), UVB (280-315 nm) and UVA (315-400 nm). UVA also stimulates the melanin cells during tanning and there is increasing evidence that UVA damages skin.

Wavelength	Color
390 - 460 nm	violet
460 - 490 nm	blue
490 - 580 nm	green
580 - 600 nm	yellow
620 - 790 nm	red

15. The color-producing quality of conjugated polyenes is dependent upon:

A. resonance   **B.** polarity   **C.** optical activity   **D.** antibonding orbitals

A is correct.

Resonance is responsible for reducing the energy of electromagnetic radiation (light) needed to excite an electron by promoting an electron into a higher-energy (i.e. antibonding) orbital.

B: polarity of molecules depends on electronegativity and the shape of the molecule and is a principle independent of color.

C: optical activity is the property of being able to rotate the plane-polarized light. The ability to rotate plane-polarized light (chiral molecules such as enantiomers, diastereomers & meso compounds) is not related to color.

D: antibonding orbital is incorrect because almost any molecule can absorb light and have an electron raised to an antibonding orbital. This process of absorbing light raising electrons into antibonding orbital does not normally produce color because the frequency of light involved is usually outside the visible range. Resonance reduces the amount of energy needed, bringing the frequency into the visible spectrum.

16. The four compounds represented by the electronic spectra below were evaluated as potential sunscreens. From strongest to weakest, what is the correct sequence of sunscreen effectiveness among these four absorption profiles?

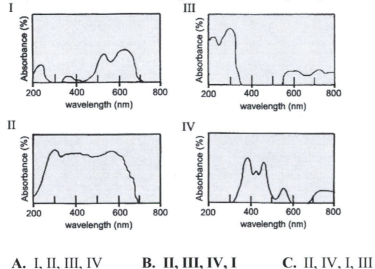

A. I, II, III, IV   **B. II, III, IV, I**   **C.** II, IV, I, III   **D.** IV, I, II, III

B is correct.

Substance II is the best sunscreen because it absorbs over a broad spectrum of wavelengths, including all three types of ultraviolet light (e.g. UVA 315-400nm; UVB

280-315nm; UVC <280nm). The absorption spectrum of the pigment which protects human skin from sunlight (i.e. melanin) has a similar absorption profile.

Spectrum III, which absorbs UVB and UVC (the most dangerous wavelengths of ultraviolet light) would be the next best choice as an effective sunscreen.

Spectrum IV absorbs UVA, so it would reduce tanning but would let through the dangerous UVB and UVC, and therefore burning symptoms would develop.

Spectrum I would be of little value as a sunscreen because it absorbs almost exclusively in the visible range (greater than 400 nm) and therefore is the weakest sunscreen among presented compounds.

17. A chromophore is the moiety of a molecule responsible for its color. Two pigments differ in the lengths of the conjugated polyene chains. The first pigment transmits yellow light and the second transmits red light. What can be said about the sizes of the chromophores?

  A. first chromophore is shorter
  B. second chromophore is shorter
  C. one of the chromophores must be a dimer
  D. comparative lengths of chromophores cannot be determined

A is correct.

When a molecule absorbs certain wavelengths of visible light and transmits or reflects others, the molecule has color. For each compound, transmitted light is complimentary in color to the light absorbed by the molecule. Thus, the first chromophore absorbs violet light (transmits yellow – intermediate wavelength) and the second absorbs green light (transmits red – longer wavelength). Violet light has a shorter wavelength than green and thus has a higher energy.

From the passage, longer chromophores generally absorb longer-wavelength light than shorter ones. Therefore, the pigment that absorbs the green light (i.e. has a red color) must be longer. Even for longer pigments, there's no basis for concluding that it is a dimer (i.e. compound made of two identical subunits).

Chemical structure of retinol (vitamin A) as an example of a conjugated molecule containing six double bonds:

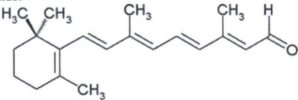

18. Many exoskeleton organisms produce a blue or green carotene-protein complex. What is the most likely cause of the color change from green to red when a lobster is boiled?

    A. the protein is separated from the carotenoid pigment
    B. increase in temperature permits the prosthetic group to become partially hydrated
    C. heat causes the prosthetic group to become oxidized
    D. the prosthetic group spontaneously disassociates

A is correct.

The color of the cooked crustacean changes because the protein is separated from the carotenoid pigment. From the passage, the carotene by itself is orange. The green color comes from absorption of light by the entire carotene-protein complex. Boiled lobsters are red because of the presence of other pigments.

Upon cooking, the heat disrupts the intermolecular attractions that attach the carotene molecule, the protein's prosthetic group, to the protein itself. This change in the molecule (i.e. dissociation of the prosthetic group) causes a change in the wavelength of light absorbed. The red color of the cooked lobster is the transmission color of the isolated carotenoid, with the conjugated bonds from the protein removed.

Cofactors can be divided into two broad groups: organic cofactors, such as flavin or heme (i.e. red blood cells use heme for binding the oxygen); and inorganic cofactors such as the metal ions Mg^{2+}, Cu^+, Mn^{2+}.

B: organic cofactors are sometimes further divided into coenzymes and prosthetic groups. Coenzymes refer specifically to enzymes and as such to the functional properties of a protein. A prosthetic group emphasizes the nature of the binding of a cofactor to a protein (tight or covalent) and thus refers to a structural property. An increase in temperature is only a physical change and therefore would not change the absorption wavelength.

C: if carotene were hydrated or oxidized, it would break the chain of conjugation completely and produce a colorless compound.

19. Why is a solution of benzene colorless?

    A. benzene does not absorb light
    B. benzene is not conjugated
    C. absorption energy is too high for a frequency to be visible
    D. absorption energy is too low for a frequency to be visible

C is correct.

The greater the number of conjugated bonds in a molecule, the more strongly electrons in excited states will be stabilized. Thus the more conjugated a molecule, the lower the frequency and the longer the wavelength that will excite it.

Benzene, with only three double bonds, requires absorption of relatively high energy light. This energy, as discussed in the passage, is higher than for the colored compounds. The light required to excite benzene electrons is in the ultraviolet range, so no color is produced when benzene absorbs light, and a solution of benzene is colorless.

20. The electrons that give color to a carotene molecule are found in:

    A. *d* orbitals   **B.** *f* orbitals   **C.** *s* orbitals   **D.** *p* **orbitals**

D is correct.

Double bonds, like in carotene, are formed by the overlap of the *p* orbitals (of the sp^2 hybridized molecule). The double bond is formed by the overlap of perpendicular *p* orbitals. The pi bond of the double bond is stabilized by the conjugated polyene system. Conjugation refers to the alternating double, single and double bond and conjugation permits the pi electrons to be excited by lower frequencies of light.

The pi (i.e. π) electrons which give conjugated bonds their stability are in the p and not in the *s* orbitals. Carbon and hydrogen bonds, which are the major component of organic molecules like carotene, lack *d* or *f* orbitals.

Chemical structure of Beta-carotene (precursor of vitamin A) as an example of a conjugated molecule containing eleven double bonds:

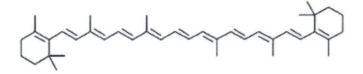

Passage 4
(Questions 21–26)

Adenosine triphosphate (ATP) is the energy source for many biochemical reactions within the cell including many membrane transport processes. However, several membrane transport processes do not use the energy liberated from the hydrolysis of ATP. Instead, these transport processes are coupled to the flow of cations and/or anions down their electrochemical gradient. For example, glucose is transported into some animal cells by the simultaneous entry of Na^+. Sodium ions and glucose bind to a specific transport protein and, together, both molecules enter the cell. A symport is a protein responsible for the concerted movement (in the same direction) of two such molecules. An antiport protein carries two species in opposite directions. The rate and extent of the glucose transport depends on the Na^+ gradient across the plasma membrane. Na^+ entering the cell along with glucose, via symport transport, is pumped out again by the Na^+/K^+ ATPase pump.

A medical student investigated a type of bacteria that transports glucose across its cell membrane by use of a sodium-glucose cotransport mechanism. She performed two experiments in which bacterial cells were placed in glucose-containing media that differed with respect to relative ion concentration and ATP content. Glycolysis was inhibited in the cells during these experiments.

Experiment 1:

Bacterial cells with relatively low intracellular Na^+ concentration were placed in a glucose-rich medium. The medium had a relatively high Na^+ concentration but lacked ATP. At regular time intervals, the glucose and sodium concentrations were analyzed from the medium (Figure 1).

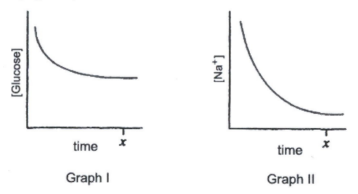

Graph I   Graph II

Figure 1. Glucose and Na+ concentrations in ATP-deficient medium

Experiment 2:

Bacterial cells with relatively low intracellular Na^+ concentration were placed in a glucose-rich medium. The medium had relatively high concentrations of both, Na^+ and ATP. At regular time intervals, the medium was analyzed for the concentration of glucose, Na^+ and ATP (Figure 2). Overtime, if radiolabeled ATP is used for the experiment, the majority of the radiolabel will be inside the cells in the form of ADP.

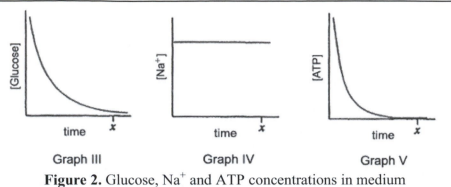

Figure 2. Glucose, Na$^+$ and ATP concentrations in medium

21. Experiments 1 & 2 provide evidence that the cells take up glucose:

  A. in exchange for Na$^+$, if the ATP concentration is zero
  B. in exchange for ATP, if the extracellular Na$^+$ concentration remains constant
  C. together with Na$^+$, if the extracellular ATP concentration gradient is increasing
  D. together with Na$^+$, if a favorable sodium concentration gradient is maintained

D is correct.

In experiment 1, both [glucose] and [Na$^+$] decrease in the medium and therefore are increased inside the cells. This suggests that a [Na$^+$] gradient was driving the transport of glucose into the cells.

In experiment 2, [Na$^+$] remains the same as glucose is transported, but ATP in the medium is decreasing. This observation suggests that the cells are importing ATP and using ATP hydrolysis to maintain the Na$^+$ gradient to drive glucose transport.

There is no evidence for exchange of ATP for glucose or for exchange of Na$^+$ for glucose. Both, ATP (Graph V, Figure 2) and Na$^+$ (Graph II, Figure 1), decrease in the medium at the same time that glucose is decreasing. This graphical data suggests that Na$^+$ is being transported in the same direction as glucose. Extracellular ATP does not increase in these experiments.

22. From experiments 1 & 2, the student hypothesized that the cells being investigated ultimately depend on energy to operate the sodium-glucose cotransport mechanism. Is this hypothesis supported by the data?

  A. yes, because Figures 1 & 2 show that glucose crosses the cell membrane in exchange for phosphate
  B. yes, because Figure 1 shows that a Na$^+$ gradient drives glucose transport and Figure 2 shows that ATP maintains the Na$^+$ gradient
  C. no, because Figure 2 shows extracellular glucose and ATP concentrations are independent
  D. no, because Figure 1 shows glucose crosses the cell membrane indefinitely in the absence of exogenous energy

B is correct.

As shown in Figures 1 & 2, both the Na^+ (Graph II) concentration gradient and ATP hydrolysis (Graph V) maintain their gradient and energy drives glucose transport. All other statements are false so they can be eliminated.

23. Based on the passage, the initial event in the transport of glucose and sodium into a cell is:

- **A.** direct hydrolysis of ATP in the cytoplasm by the sodium-glucose cotransporter
- **B.** direct hydrolysis of ATP on the extracellular surface by the sodium-glucose cotransporter
- **C.** binding of Na^+ to specific secreted proteins in the surrounding medium
- **D. binding of Na^+ and glucose in the surrounding medium to specific membrane proteins**

D is correct.

Binding of specific proteins in the membrane to Na^+ and glucose in the surrounding medium is the only possible answer. A membrane protein must bind Na^+ and glucose in the extracellular side of the membrane prior to transport.

A and B: ATP hydrolysis is not catalyzed by the Na^+/glucose cotransporter. ATPase pump produces the initial Na^+.

C: there are no secreted proteins involved in the transport process.

24. The result of experiments 1 & 2 indicate that ATP promotes the cellular uptake of glucose by serving as a source of:

- **A.** monosaccharide
- **C. metabolic energy**
- **B.** enzymes
- **D.** inorganic phosphate

C is correct.

The driving force is the energy provided in breaking (i.e. hydrolysis) of ATP into ADP + P_i. The hydrolysis of the "high energy bond" in ATP supplies energy to drive transport.

A and B: ATP (i.e. a nucleotide) is neither an enzyme (i.e. proteins are enzymes) or monosaccharide (i.e. sugar subunits of carbohydrate), nor does ATP serve as a source of inorganic phosphate.

D: inorganic phosphate is not the correct choice because, although ATP can be a source of P_i, inorganic phosphate does not drive transport.

25. Within animal cells, the transport of Na^+/K^+ ATPase pump involves:

    A. facilitated diffusion   **C.** osmosis

    B. active transport   **D.** passive transport

B is correct.

Symport transport, antiport transport and facilitated diffusion (i.e. passive transport) involve the movement of ions down the concentration gradient.

Because the transport / diffusion is from a high concentration region to a low concentration region, none of these mechanisms involve a concentration gradient or an electrochemical gradient.

Diffusion requires no hydrolysis of ATP because the process does not require energy. The Na^+/K^+ ATPase pump transports Na^+ out of the cell against an electrochemical gradient. Because the concentration is increasing, hydrolysis of ATP supplies the needed energy to drive transport.

26. According to Figure 1, as Na^+ concentration in the medium approaches the same concentration found in the cells, glucose concentration in the medium would:

    A. level off because a sodium gradient is not available to drive cotransport

    B. remain at its original level because sodium concentration does not affect glucose concentration

    C. approach zero because glucose and sodium are transported together

    D. increase because less glucose is transported into the bacterial cells

A is correct.

The Na^+ concentration gradient provides the energy to drive glucose transport. When the Na^+ concentration is the same inside and outside of the cell, there is no gradient, and thus no energy to drive glucose transport. Therefore, when Na^+ concentration levels are equal on both sides of the membrane, transport stops and the extracellular glucose concentration become equal.

In Figure 1, the Na^+ in the medium decreases but levels off before reaching zero.

> Questions 27 through 29 are not based on any
> descriptive passage and are independent of each other

27. Which one of the following structures is found in bacterial cells?

A. nucleolus   **C. ribosome**
B. mitochondria   **D.** smooth endoplasmic reticulum

C is correct.

Ribosomes are assemblies of protein and rRNA and are not organelles. The ribosomes in prokaryotes and eukaryotes are different, but both cell types have ribosomes. The ribosomes of prokaryotes are 30S (small subunit) and 50S (large subunit) making a 70S complete ribosome with both subunits assembled. The ribosomes of the eukaryote are 40S (small subunit) and 60S (large subunit) making a 80S complete ribosome with both subunits assembled.

Bacteria are prokaryotes and therefore lack all membrane-bound organelles, including mitochondria, the ER (both smooth and rough), the nucleus and nucleolus. The nucleolus is located within the nucleus in eukaryotes and is the site of rRNA synthesis.

28. Exocrine secretions of the pancreas:

A. lower blood serum glucose levels   **C. aid in protein and fat digestion**
B. raise blood serum glucose levels   **D.** regulate metabolic rate of anabolism and catabolism

C is correct.

The pancreas functions both as an exocrine gland and endocrine gland. The pancreas is an elongated lobular gland extending from the duodenum (first of three regions of the small intestine). From its exocrine part, the gland secretes pancreatic juice that is discharged into the intestine, and from its endocrine part – insulin and glucagon.

An exocrine gland excretes its products into ducts (i.e. tubes) that often empty into epithelial tissue. Endocrine glands release hormones directly into the bloodstream. Hormones are chemical substances formed in a tissue or organ and carried in the blood to stimulate or inhibit the growth or function of one or more other tissues or organs.
As an endocrine gland, the pancreas produces and secretes two hormones: insulin and glucagon. Insulin is secreted by the beta cells of the pancreas and lowers blood glucose levels by stimulating the uptake of glucose by the cells. Glucagon is secreted by the alpha cells of the pancreas and elevates blood glucose levels by stimulating the release of hepatic (e.g. liver) glycogen. One of the diseases of glycogen storage is von Gierke's.

As an exocrine gland, the pancreas secretes many enzymes that are involved in protein, fat, and carbohydrate digestion. All of the exocrine products of the pancreas are secreted into the small intestine. Pancreatic amylase hydrolyzes starch to maltose. Trypsin hydrolyzes peptide bonds and catalyzes the conversion of chymotrypsinogen to chymotrypsin. Chymotrypsin and carboxypeptidase also hydrolyze peptide bonds. Pancreatic lipase is an enzyme that hydrolyzes lipids.

The thyroid gland secretes thyroid hormone and calcitonin. Thyroxine (T_4: thyroid hormone) promotes growth and development and increases the metabolic rate in cells. Calcitonin, a peptide hormone, is produced by the parathyroid, thyroid and thymus. Calcitonin works in opposition to parathyroid hormone. Calcitonin increases deposition of calcium and phosphate in bone and lowers the level of calcium in the blood. Parathyroid hormone is a peptide hormone formed by the parathyroid glands and maintains serum calcium levels by promoting intestinal absorption and renal tubular reabsorption of calcium, and release of calcium from bone to extracellular fluid.

29. What type of protein structure describes two alpha and two beta peptide chains within hemoglobin?

    A. primary   **B.** secondary   **C.** tertiary   **D. quaternary**

D is correct.

Important MCAT fact: There are four levels of protein structure.

The primary (1°) protein structure refers to the linear sequence of amino acids.

The secondary (2°) protein structure refers to the local folding along amino acids that are within 12 amino acids. Common motifs of secondary structure are alpha helix and beta-pleated sheets within the protein.

The tertiary (3°) protein structure refers to the three dimensional shape of the properly folded polypeptide of the functional protein.

The quaternary (4°) protein structure is defined as two (or more) polypeptide chains linked together via a number of weak H-bonds and/or strong disulfide bonds (between cysteine). Cystine is formed by two –SH groups between single cysteine that become one –S–S– group.

According to the question stem, adult hemoglobin consists of four polypeptide chains and therefore is an example of 4° protein structure. The definition of quaternary structure requires that the protein contain more than two ends (more than one chain) and often separated during denaturation of the protein during experimentation.

Passage 5
(Questions 30– 35)

Thrombosis is the formation or presence of a blood clot which may cause infarction of tissue supplied by the vessel. Although the coagulation factors necessary to initiate blood clotting are present in the blood, clot formation in the intact vascular system is prevented by three properties of the vascular walls. First, the endothelial lining, which is sensitive to vascular damage, is smooth enough to prevent activation of the clotting system. Second, the inner surface of the endothelium is covered by a mucopolysaccharide (glycocalyx) that repels the clotting factors and platelets in the blood. Third, an endothelial surface protein known as thrombomodulin binds thrombin, the enzyme that converts fibrinogen into fibrin in the final stage of clotting. The binding of thrombin to thrombomodulin reduces the amount of thrombin that can participate in clotting. Also, the thrombin-thrombomodulin complex activates protein C, a plasma protein that hinders clot formation by acting as an anticoagulant.

If the endothelial surface of a vessel has been roughened by arteriosclerosis or infection, and the glycocalyx-thrombomodulin layer has been lost, the first step of the intrinsic blood clotting pathway (Figure 1) will be triggered. The Factor XII protein changes shape to become "activated" Factor XII. This conformational change within the protein initiates a cascade of reactions that result in the formation of thrombin and the subsequent conversion of fibrinogen to fibrin. Simultaneously, platelets release platelet factor 3, a lipoprotein that helps to activate the coagulation factors. A thrombus is an abnormal blood clot that develops in blood vessels and may impede or obstruct vascular flow.

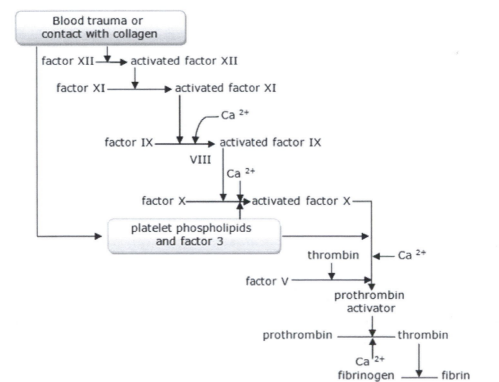

An embolus is a thrombus that dislodges and travels in the bloodstream. Typically, an embolus will travel through the circulatory system until it becomes trapped at a narrow point, resulting in vessel blockage.

30. All of the following would cause prolonged clotting time in a human blood sample EXCEPT:

A. addition of activated Factor X   C. addition of a calcium chelating agent

B. removal of platelets or fibrinogen   D. removal of Factor VIII

A is correct.

Prolonged clotting time results from a interference in the intrinsic pathway (Figure 1). A deficiency of any clotting factor (e.g. Factor VIII) or a deficiency of platelets (or platelet phospholipids) makes it more difficult for the blood to coagulate and for clot formation.

Calcium ions are required for the promotion of all but the first two reactions in the pathway. Clotting would be slowed (or prevented) by reducing the calcium ion concentration in the blood (e.g. addition of a calcium chelating agent).

However, addition of activated Factor X would not increase clotting time because activated Factor X is one of the key components in the intrinsic pathway.

31. A physician injects small quantities of heparin in patients with pulmonary emboli histories to inhibit further thrombus formation. Heparin increases the activity of antithrombin III, the blood's primary inhibitor of thrombin. One possible adverse side effect of heparin administration is:

A. dizziness   C. degradation of existing emboli

B. minor bleeding   D. blood pressure increase

B is correct.

Heparin, a highly-sulfated glycosaminoglycan, is widely used as an injectable anticoagulant and has the highest negative charge density among all known biological molecules. It prevents the formation of abnormal blood clots by enhancing the activity of antithrombin III (the anticoagulant). Antithrombin III interferes with the intrinsic pathway and blood clotting ability is significantly reduced by heparin injection. Minor damage to the patient's blood vessels will not be automatically repaired (as normal) and the patient may experience minor vascular bleeding as a result of heparin administration.

A: there is indication that the oxygen-carrying capability of the blood or that the integrity of the blood vessels would be compromised. Therefore, dizziness would be an unlikely result.

C: existing blood clots, (e.g. emboli) are degraded by fibrinolytic enzymes. Interfering with the blood clotting pathway has no effect on existing clots.

D: a patient should not experience an increased blood pressure from interfering with the blood clotting function.

32. From the picture of the passage, the function of Factor VIII in the activation of Factor X is that of:

    A. zymogen   **B.** substrate   **C.** enzyme   **D. cofactor**

D is correct.

The intrinsic clotting pathway consists of a series of reactions in which proteins, such as Factor X, are converted from their inactive proenzyme form (e.g. zymogens; ending in -ogen) to the active form of the enzyme. Proenzymes (zymogens) are enzyme precursors requiring some change (usually the hydrolysis of an inhibiting fragment that makes an active group) to render the enzyme active.

Examples of inactive enzymes include the zymogens such as pepsinogen (i.e. in the stomach for digestion of proteins) and trypsinogen. Trypsinogen, like pepsin, trypsin and chymotrypsin are proteolytic enzymes of the pancreas that cleave only the peptide linkage of certain amino acids. Trypsin splits the peptide bond adjacent to lysine and arginine; chymotrypsin splits peptide bonds adjacent to tyrosine, phenylalanine, tryptophan and, to a lesser degree, methionine and leucine.

Factor X is the proenzyme that undergoes a transformation to the active form. Factor X serves as the substrate for activated Factor IX (enzyme) that catalyzes the conversion of Factor X to its active form.
Factor VIII, Ca^{2+} and platelet phospholipids all serve as cofactors for the reaction because they accelerate the conversion of Factor X to its active form.

33. The initial formation of thrombin in the intrinsic clotting pathway:

    A. deactivates the blood factors
    B. increases conversion of Factor XII to activated Factor XII
    C. has a positive feedback effect on thrombin formation
    D. causes a platelet reduction within plasma

C is correct.

When the cascade begins, Factor V and Factor VIII are initially inactive because no thrombin is present. Once clotting begins, thrombin is formed and thrombin then activates

Factors V and VIII. Factors V and VIII serve as cofactors in the reactions that activate Factor X and prothrombin activator. Thus, thrombin accelerates its own synthesis and the initial formation of thrombin has a positive feedback effect and that supports accelerated thrombin formation.

A: thrombin is responsible for activation of several factors involved in the clotting cascade.

B: blood trauma (or contact with collagen) enhances the activation of Factor XII.

D: thrombin has no effect on the number of circulating platelets.

34. Based on information in the passage, which of the following is the most likely mechanism of action of protein C?

    A. activation of Factors XII and X
    B. deactivation of activated Factors V and VIII
    C. accelerates formation of prothrombin
    D. negative feedback effect of thrombomodulin

B is correct.

According to the passage, protein C is an anticoagulant that prevents clotting.

All other choices are mechanisms of coagulation and are incorrect because protein C is an anticoagulant.

A and C: the promotion of the formation of prothrombin and activation of Factors X and XII would increase clotting (see Figure 1). Deactivation of activated Factors V and VIII, however, would prevent thrombin from having a positive feedback effect on its own formation, which is essential for clot formation. Deactivation of these factors (the actual mechanism of protein C function), renders protein C an effective anticoagulant.

D: a negative feedback regulation of thrombomodulin facilitates clotting because thrombomodulin acts to slow the process.

35. Which of the following is most likely the origin of a pulmonary embolus that blocks the pulmonary artery?

    A. left side of the heart   **C.** pulmonary veins
    B. aorta   **D. veins within the lower extremities**

D is correct.

A pulmonary embolus is an abnormal blood clot that has been dislodged from its point of origin and carried through the circulatory system to the lungs. Within the lungs, the embolus blocks the pulmonary artery (or its branch). The movement of an embolus is impeded when it reaches a narrow point in the circulatory system. Therefore, there is a limited number of possible locations from which a pulmonary embolism could originate.

A: the embolus could not originate from the left side of the heart because the passage through the systemic circulation to the right side of the heart and then to the pulmonary arteries would be a virtually impossible one for the embolus to make. The embolism would most likely lodge in some systemic vessel.

B and C: an embolus coming from the aorta, or the pulmonary veins, would also likely become lodged somewhere in a systemic vessel such as the upper limbs, the lower extremities, or the brain.

Most pulmonary emboli originate in the veins of the lower legs. From the veins in the lower extremities, the embolism flows freely with venous blood up into the right side of the heart (right atrium and then right ventricle) and then into the pulmonary arteries (toward the lungs), where the embolism typically lodges.

Passage 6
(Questions 36–40)

Fermentation is an anaerobic process that results in the conversion of high-energy substrates to various waste products. Fermentation harvests only a small amount of the energy stored in glucose. There are two common types: alcoholic fermentation and lactic acid fermentation.

Alcoholic fermentation (also called ethanol fermentation) is a biological process whereby sugars (e.g. glucose, fructose and sucrose) are converted into cellular energy and produce ethanol and carbon dioxide as metabolic waste products. Because yeasts perform this conversion in the absence of oxygen, alcoholic fermentation is considered an anaerobic process. Anaerobic respiration is a form of respiration that uses electron acceptors other than oxygen.

Lactic acid fermentation is a biological metabolic process where glucose, fructose, and sucrose are converted into cellular energy and the metabolite lactate. It is also an anaerobic fermentation that occurs in some bacteria and animal cells (e.g. muscle cells). In homolactic fermentation, one molecule of glucose is converted to two molecules of lactic acid. By contrast, heterolactic fermentation yields carbon dioxide and ethanol in addition to lactic acid via a process called the phosphoketolase pathway.

In alcoholic fermentation, the conversion of pyruvic acid to ethanol is a two-step process. In heterolactic acid fermentation, the conversion of pyruvic acid to lactic acid is a one-step process.

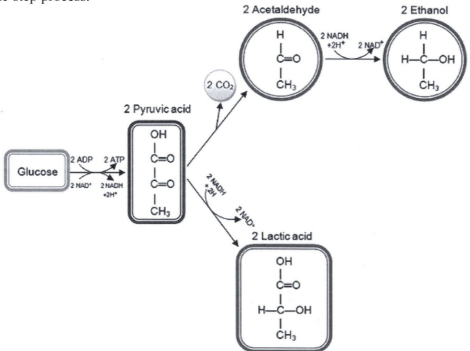

Figure 1. Alcoholic fermentation and lactic acid fermentation pathways.

36. Lactic acid accumulates in muscles and is carried by the blood and transported to the liver. What is the effect of lactic acid on the respiratory rate?

    A. decreases respiratory rate

    B. increases respiratory rate

    C. no effect on respiratory rate

    D. respiratory rate initially decreases and then quickly level off

B is correct.

Lactic acid decreases the pH of blood plasma. Carbon dioxide dissolved in blood plasma also decreases the pH through conversion to carbonic acid.

The respiratory rate increases when the blood plasma becomes acidic because the person needs to exhale more CO_2. An increased respiratory rate achieves homeostasis by making the blood plasma slightly alkaline. Normally, blood plasma is slightly alkaline at about pH 7.35.

37. In lactic acid fermentation, pyruvate functions as an:

    A. electron acceptor for the reduction of NAD^+

    B. electron acceptor for the oxidation of NADH

    C. electron donor for the reduction of NAD^+

    D. electron donor for the oxidation of NADH

B is correct.

Pyruvate is reduced by gaining electrons. NADH is oxidized by loss of electrons.

Other choices are incorrect because in fermentation, NADH is oxidized to NAD^+. Fermentation occurs under anaerobic conditions where the organism has a deficiency of O_2 and therefore pyruvate cannot enter the Krebs cycle due to the deficiency of O_2. Pyruvate is shunted to the lactic acid cycle for the purpose of regenerating NAD^+ because glycolysis (aerobic and anaerobic) requires NAD^+ for reduction to NADH that is needed for glycolysis to yield a total of 4ATP (net of 2ATP) from glycolysis.

"LEO the Lion says GER" is a common mnemonic. LEO: Loss of Electrons is Oxidation. GER: Gain of Electrons is Reduction.

In organic chemistry, oxidation is an increase of the number of bonds to oxygen (or electronegative atoms) or conversely, the loss of bonds to hydrogen (and the accompanying gain of electrons to electronegative atoms / oxygen).

38. Fermentation differs from glycolysis because in fermentation:

    A. glucose is oxidized   **C.** high-energy electrons transferred to NAD^+

    B. NAD^+ is regenerated   **D.** ATP is produced

B is correct.

Fermentation occurs during anaerobic cellular respiration due to an oxygen debt because the demand for ATP exceeds the capacity of the lungs / blood to transport O_2 to the tissue where O_2 is needed for the electron transport chain.

In fermentation, NAD^+ is regenerated. Glycolysis requires the availability of NAD^+. Glycolysis converts NAD^+ by reduction (gain of electrons) to NADH. Under anaerobic conditions, NADH is oxidized to regenerate NAD^+/ concurrently reducing pyruvate to lactic. This is similar to metabolism in facultative anaerobes, which are able to use either fermentation or oxidative phosphorylation, depending on the availability of oxygen.

Muscle cells can use lactic-acid fermentation (without oxygen) during periods of strenuous physical activity.

Muscle cell preferentially use aerobic respiration except during strenuous exercise. Strenuous exercise uses oxygen faster than it can be supplied.

ATP, CTP, GTP, TTP and UTP are nucleotides. GTP is produced in the Krebs cycle of cellular respiration. During cellular respiration, ATP is produced during glycolysis (gross production is 4 ATP less 2 invested = net of 2 ATP) by substrate level phosphorylation (not requiring O_2).

During the ETC (electron transport chain), 32 ATP are produced via oxidation of NADH → NAD^+ and $FADH_2$ → FADH.

NADH produces three H^+ and $FADH_2$ produces two H^+. H^+ is pumped into the intermembrane space of the mitochondrion and each H^+ produces 1 ATP by oxidative phosphorylation as the H^+ passes through the ATP synthase (i.e. ATPase), a protein embedded in the inner membrane of the mitochondria.

39. During alcoholic fermentation, pyruvic acid and acetaldehyde are, respectively:

   A. decarboxylated and oxidized   **C.** reduced and decarboxylated

   B. decarboxylated and reduced   **D.** decarboxylated and phosphorylated

B is correct.

Pyruvate is decarboxylated (loses a CO_2) to become lactic acid while acetaldehyde is reduced by NADH that becomes oxidized to NAD^+.

40. During fermentation, the final electron acceptor from NADH is:

   A. organic molecule   **B.** alcohol   **C.** NAD^+ **D.** ½ O_2

A is correct.

During oxidative phosphorylation, the final electron acceptor from NADH (high energy intermediate similar to $FADH_2$) during the electron transport chain (ETC) in aerobic cellular respiration is O_2. Molecular oxygen ($\frac{1}{2}$ O_2) is often referred to as the ultimate electron acceptor because of its role (accepting electrons and two H^+ to form H_2O) during the last stage of cellular respiration, the electron transport chain.

Fermentation is anaerobic cellular respiration. During fermentation, the final electron acceptor (from NADH to regenerate NAD^+) is the organic molecule of lactate (lactic acid).

Questions 41 through 46 are not based on any descriptive passage and are independent of each other

---

41. Which two atomic orbitals interact to form the D—D bond in D_2?

  A. *s* and *s*   **B.** *p* and *p*   **C.** *sp* and *sp*   **D.** sp^3 and sp^3

A is correct.

Deuterium is an isotope of hydrogen. Like hydrogen, deuterium has a single valence electron and therefore has a one *s* orbital. The single *s* orbital is not hybridized.

The D–D bond is formed by the internuclear σ (sigma) bond overlap of an *s* orbital from each deuterium and σ bond refers to a single bond.

Carbon is the atom that undergoes hybridization of the 4 orbitals of: $s + p + p + p$ (*s* is lower in energy than the p orbitals) to form 4 equal energy sp^3 orbitals pointing to the corners of a tetrahedron (shape) with a bond angle of 109.5°.

42. During skeletal muscle contraction, which bands of the sarcomere shorten?

  A. I and H bands   **C.** I bands and Z discs
  B. A and H bands   **D.** Z discs

A is correct.

It is the overlap between thick and thin filaments which increases during contraction. The nonoverlapping regions decrease in length. During contraction, I bands (actin thin filaments only) and H bands (myosin thick filament only) shorten.

B: the A bands are the length of myosin (thick filaments) and includes the overlapping portion of the actin (thin filaments). The lengths of the A (actin and myosin overlap) bands do not change during contraction.

C and D: the Z discs are the connection points for the I band (actin) connection and demarcate the ends of the sarcomeres.

---

43. Human muscle cells behave in a manner similar to:

A. anaerobes   **C. facultative anaerobes**
B. obligate aerobes   D. strict aerobes

C is correct.

Muscle cells generate ATP through aerobic respiration. Aerobic respiration links glycolysis to the Krebs cycle and then to the ETC for oxidative phosphorylation.

Under anaerobic conditions, muscle cells can produce ATP through fermentation, using NADH to reduce pyruvate to lactic acid and regenerate NAD^+. Anaerobic respiration is similar to metabolism in facultative anaerobes, which are able to use either fermentation or oxidative phosphorylation, depending on availability of oxygen.

A: muscle cells will preferentially use aerobic respiration except during strenuous exercise which depletes oxygen faster than it can be supplied to the tissue.

B and D: muscle cells can use lactic acid fermentation (anaerobic respiration) to survive without using oxygen during periods of strenuous physical activity.

44. During the production of urine, the nephron controls the composition of urine by all of the following physiological processes EXCEPT:

A. reabsorption of H_2O C. secretion of solutes into urine
B. counter current exchange with blood   **D. filtration for Na^+ to remain in blood**

D is correct.

The answer choice of filtration for Na^+ to remain in the blood is a false statement and therefore the correct answer.

Only large solutes like proteins are filtered at the glomerulus and do not pass into the nephron. Ions such as Na^+ pass freely into the filtrate and must be reabsorbed in the proximal tubule (active transport), ascending loop of Henle (passive transport) and distal tubule (active transport) during the processing of filtrate to make urine.

45. Which of the following molecules is NOT transported via Na^+ dependent transport?

A. bile acids   B. galactose   C. proteins   **D. fatty acids**

D is correct.

The MCAT requires understanding of the absorption mechanisms for dietary nutrients such as carbohydrates, proteins and lipids.

Lipids are enclosed, absorbed and transported in the circulatory system as micelles (membrane enclosed vesicles). Lipids (dietary fat) are composed of glycerol and fatty acids.

A: bile is stored in the gall bladder. Bile acts as emulsifier of dietary lipids to increase their surface area because bile is amphiteric (hydrophobic and hydrophilic portion). The hydrophobic portion of the bile becomes embedded within the hydrophobic core of the lipid while the hydrophilic portion of the lipid remains in contact with the hydrophilic chyme (dietary contents of the stomach and small intestine). Bile acids are reabsorbed via Na^+ dependent transport.

B and C: galactose (i.e. not fructose) and proteins (single amino acids, dipeptides and tripeptides) are transported across the small intestine membrane via Na^+ dependent cotransport.

46. Which of the following characteristics of water make it the most important solvent on earth?

    I.   water is non-polar   **III. water is a Bronsted-Lowry Acid**

    II.   water is a Bronsted-Lowry Base   **IV. water forms hydrogen bonds**

  A. I & II only   **C. II, III & IV only**

  B. II & III only   **D.** I, II, III & IV

C is correct.

Important MCAT topic: Water can act as both an acid (H_2O dissociates into → H^+ + OH^-) and a base (H_2O abstracts H^+ → H_3O^+).
Water is a polar compound, therefore statement I is false. Additionally, water makes hydrogen bonds to other water molecules. Hydrogen bonds occur when H is bonded directly to an electronegative atom such as F, O, N or Cl. Note, many textbooks exclude Cl from the examples of hydrogen bond when hydrogen is directly bonded to either F (electronegativity: 3.98), O (3.44) or N (3.04). Due to its electronegativity of 3.16, Cl does form hydrogen bonds. However, these hydrogen bonds are weaker than predicted by electronegativity alone. Because of the larger orbital size of chlorine, the electron density is lower than necessary for strong hydrogen bonding (i.e. strong dipole-dipole attractions).

Hydrogen bonding between water molecules contributes to water having surface tension, capillary tension, and high specific heat *et al* therefore statement IV is correct.

A Bronsted-Lowry acid is any molecule that donates protons (H^+). A Bronsted-Lowry base is any molecule or ion that combines with a proton; ^-OH, ^-CN, NH_3. This definition replaces the older and more limited definition of bases. The Bronsted-Lowry acid is a substance (i.e. charged ions or uncharged molecules) liberating hydrogen ions in solution. A Bronsted-Lowry base is a substance that removes H^+ from solution. This Bronsted-Lowry concept is useful for weak electrolytes (i.e. substances that dissociate into ions within the solution) and for buffers (i.e. solutions that resist changes in pH). Therefore statement II & III apply to water and are correct.

Passage 7
(Questions 47–52)

The reaction between alkyl bromide and chloride anion may proceed via any one of four possible reaction mechanisms. The observed pathway is a function of the solvent polarity. Although all four reactions involve substitution, each mechanism produces a distinct product.

Researchers calculated the free energies of activation (ΔG) in kcal mol^{-1} for the different mechanisms in two different solvents.

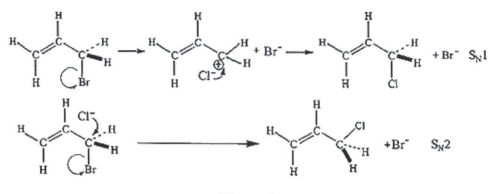

Figure 1.

Experiments demonstrated that the preferred pathway for the molecules in non-polar organic solvents is S_N2. However, as the solvent polarity increases, the difference in energy between the pathways narrows. In water, the preferred pathway, with a lower energy of activation, is S_N1.

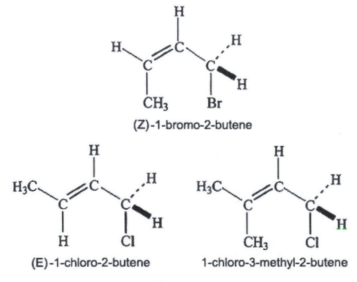

(Z)-1-bromo-2-butene

(E)-1-chloro-2-butene   1-chloro-3-methyl-2-butene

Figure 2.

47. Which of the following is true regarding the reaction of (Z)-1-bromo-2-butene with the chloride anion in carbon tetrachloride?

    A. reaction is unimolecular   **C. reaction is a concerted mechanism**

    B. reaction produces a racemic mixture of products   **D.** reaction rate is increased by increasing [Cl$^-$]

C is correct.

In CCl$_4$, the reaction undergoes the profile of an S$_N$2 mechanism. S$_N$2 reaction rates dependent on concentration of substrates and nucleophile (i.e. second order kinetics). S$_N$2 occurs in a concerted mechanism within one step whereby the nucleophile attacks the carbon and the nucleophile displaces the leaving group. The concerted (single step) mechanism accounts for inversion of stereochemistry and the fact that a stereospecific (e.g. R vs. S) single product is produced (i.e. not a racemic mixture). Racemic mixtures result from the S$_N$1 reaction involving a planar intermediate (carbocation) and the nucleophile attacks the trigonal planar (flat) intermediate to produce a mixture (racemate) of the stereospecific (R and S) products.

48. Which of the following molecules forms the most stable carbocation following the dissociation of the halide ion?

    A. (E)-1-chloro-2-butene   **C. 1-chloro-3-methyl-2-butene**

    B. (Z)-1-bromo-2-butene   **D.** no difference is expected

C is correct.

1-chloro-3-methyl-2-butene has an additional electron donating group (methyl) to help stabilize the positive charged carbocation. After the halide dissociates, the 1-chloro-3-methyl-2-butene resonances to form a tertiary cation.

(Z)-1-bromo-2-butene and (E)-1-chloro-2-butene can resonate but form a less stable secondary carbocation.

49. Regarding the reaction of 1-chloro-3-methyl-2-butene with Cl$^-$ in water, which of the following statements is supported by the passage?

    A. strong nucleophile is required for the reaction to proceed

    B. carbocation is formed

    C. reaction occurs with the inversion of stereochemistry

    D. reaction occurs with a single ΔG in the reaction profile

B is correct.

The mechanism is an S$_N$1 pathway with the formation of a carbocation.

All other answers are accurate for the concerted mechanism of an S$_N$2 pathway.

50. What hypothesis explains the difference in the mechanism pathway (Figure 1) when the solvent is changed from CCl_4 to H_2O?

    A. hydrogen bonding of the H_2O solvent stabilizes the transition state of the S_N2 pathway

    B. hydrogen bonding of the H_2O solvent stabilizes the intermediate of the S_N2 pathway

    C. hydrogen bonding of the H_2O solvent stabilizes the nucleophile of the S_N2 pathway

    D. hydrogen bonding of the H_2O solvent stabilizes the carbocation intermediate of the S_N1 pathway

D is correct.

Hydrogen bonding in water stabilizes the carbocation formed in the S_N1 pathway because the charged intermediate is stabilized to decrease the activation energy.

S_N2 mechanisms are favored in non-polar aprotic solvents such as CCl_4 because the aprotic solvent does not liberate H^+ that would solvate (shield) the strong nucleophile (often charged species) that favors the concerted reaction mechanisms of the S_N2. Strong (charged) nucleophiles initiate the reaction prior to the formation of a carbocation. The substrate is important for determining if the reaction proceeds by S_N1 or S_N2. S_N1 favors tertiary (3°) substrates that can support a stable carbocation while S_N2 favor the less sterically hindered primary (1°) substrate that do not form stable carbocation.

51. Which of the following reagents must be reacted with (E)-1-chloro-2-butene for a saturated alkyl halide to be formed?

    A. H_2, Pd   **C.** $Hg(OAc)_2$, H_2O / $NaBH_4$

    B. BH_3, THF / H_2O_2, ^-OH **D.** concentrated H_2SO_4

A is correct.

The conversion of an alkene (double bond) to an alkane (single bond) is a reduction. Hydrogenation (adding H_2 with metal catalyst) is the only reducing reagent among the choices listed.

B: BH_3, THF / H_2O_2, ^-OH (Hydroboration to alkenes) adds an –OH group at the non-Markovnikov (less substituted carbon) along the double bond.

C: $Hg(OAc)_2$, H_2O / $NaBH_4$ (Oxymercuration to alkenes) adds an –OH group at the Markovnikov (more substituted carbon) along the double bond.

D: Concentrated H_2SO_4 is used for reduction of an alcohol to form an alkene.

52. Which of the following reagents, when reacted with 1-chloro-3-methyl-2-butene will produce an alcohol with the hydroxyl group on C2?

    A. Lindlar   **C.** $Hg(OAc)_2$, H_2O / $NaBH_4$

    B. BH_3, THF / H_2O_2, ^-OH   **D.** Grignard

B is correct.

Hydroboration (BH_3, THF followed by H_2O_2, ^-OH) yields a non-Markovnikov orientation with hydroxyl group at the less substituted carbon (carbon 2) on 1-chloro-3-methyl-2-butene.

A: Lindlar is the reagent that converts an alkyne (triple bond) to a cis alkene. Another reaction, Li / NH_3 is the reagent that converts an alkyne (triple bond) to a trans alkene.

C: $Hg(OAc)_2$, H_2O / $NaBH_4$ (Oxymercuration to alkenes) adds an –OH group at the Markovnikov (more substituted carbon) along the double bond.   This is the opposite regiospecificity desired from the question.

D: Grignard (Mg^{2+} inserted between the carbon-halide bond) is a common method for generation a carbanion (C with a pair of electrons – negative charged species). Grignard is used for extending the carbon-carbon chain length by attacking (often) an alkyl halide and displacing the leaving group during the new carbon-carbon bond formation. Note: the solution cannot contain a source of H^+ (protons such as from a protic solvent of water or alcohols) because the highly reactive (basic) Grignard will abstract the H^+ and the reaction will be quenched with the resulting alkane (undesired product) formation.

Questions 53 through 59 are not based on any descriptive passage and are independent of each other

53. How many amino acids are essential in the human diet?

A. 4   **B. 9**   **C.** 11   **D.** 12

B is correct.

Essential amino acids cannot be synthesized *de novo* (i.e. made new) within the human body and therefore must be supplied in the diet. The nine amino acids humans cannot synthesize endogenously are histidine, isoleucine, leucine, lysine, methionine, phenylalanine, threonine, tryptophan and valine. Mnemonic for essential amino acids: *PVT TIM HaLL*

Six amino acids are conditionally essential for humans, meaning their endogenous synthesis can be limited under special pathophysiological conditions (e.g. for infants or persons under severe catabolic distress). These six amino acids are arginine, cysteine, glutamine, glycine, proline and tyrosine. Five amino acids are neither essential nor conditionally essential in humans because they can be synthesized in the body: alanine, asparagine, aspartic acid, glutamic acid and serine.

54. In eukaryotic cells, most of the ribosomal RNA are transcribed by RNA polymerase [   ], major structural genes are transcribed by RNA polymerase [   ], and tRNAs are transcribed by RNA polymerase [   ].

A. II; I; III   **B.** II; III; I   **C. I, II, III**   **D.** I; III; II

C is correct.

55. Cellulose is not highly branched because it does not have:

A. β (1→4) glycosidic bonds   **C.** a polysaccharide backbone
B. α (1→4) glycosidic bonds   **D. α (1→6) glycosidic bonds**

D is correct.

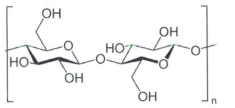

Cellulose linked by β(1→4) glycosidic bonds

56. Which formula represents palmitic acid?

   A. $CH_3(CH_2)_8COOH$ **C.** $CH_3(CH_2)_{16}COOH$
   B. $CH_3(CH_2)_{18}COOH$ **D.** $CH_3(CH_2)_{14}COOH$

D is correct.

Palmitic acid is the most common saturated fatty acid (IUPAC: hexadecanoic acid) found in animals, plants and microorganisms with the molecular formula $CH_3(CH_2)_{14}COOH$. Per its name, it is a major component of the oil from palm trees (e.g. palm oil) but can also be found in meats, cheeses, butter, and dairy products. Palmitate refers to the salts and esters of palmitic acid.

57. Lipids can be either:

   A. hydrophobic or hydrophilic   **C.** amphipathic or hydrophilic
   B. hydrophobic or amphipathic   **D.** amphipathic or amphoteric

B is correct.

An amphipathic substance contains both a hydrophilic and hydrophobic region.
An amphoteric substance can act as an acid or as a base, depending on pH (e.g. water).

58. Given that K_M measures the affinity of enzyme and substrate, then:

   A. k_{cat} is much smaller than k_{-1}   **C.** k_{cat} must be smaller than K_M
   B. k_{cat} is about equal to k_1 **D.** k_{cat} must be larger than K_M

A is correct.

59. Which amino acid-derived molecule transports amino acids across the cell membrane?

   A. S-adenosylmethionine   **C. Glutathione**
   B. Insulin   **D.** γ-aminobutyric acid

C is correct.

In addition to transporting amino acids across the cell membrane, glutathione has multiple functions such as being a major antioxidant produced by the cells, regulation of the nitric oxide cycle, participating in metabolic and biochemical reactions of DNA synthesis and repair, protein synthesis, prostaglandin synthesis and enzyme activation, as well as playing a vital role in iron metabolism.

BIOLOGICAL & BIOCHEMICAL FOUNDATIONS OF LIVING SYSTEMS
MCAT® PRACTICE TEST #2: ANSWER KEY

Passage 1
1 : A
2 : D
3 : B
4 : B
5 : C
6 : B
7 : C

Passage 2
8 : B
9 : A
10 : C
11 : C
12 : C
13 : B

Independent questions
14 : A
15 : B
16 : C
17 : A

Passage 3
18 : A
19 : C
20 : B
21 : C
22 : C
23 : A

Passage 4
24 : D
25 : B
26 : C
27 : C
28 : A

Independent questions
29 : B
30 : D
31 : A
32 : A
33 : C

Passage 5
34 : C
35 : B
36 : B
37 : B
38 : D

Passage 6
39 : B
40 : C
41 : D
42 : D
43 : B

Independent questions
44 : C
45 : D
46 : A
47 : D

Passage 7
48 : D
49 : B
50 : C
51 : A
52 : D

Independent questions
53 : A
54 : D
55 : D
56 : A
57 : D
58 : A
59 : C

Passage 1
(Questions 1–7)

Researchers are studying a eukaryotic organism that has a highly active mechanism for DNA replication, transcription and translation. The organism has both a haploid and a diploid state. In the haploid state, only one copy of each chromosome complement is present. In the diploid state, two copies of each chromosome complement, usually homozygous for most traits, are present. To investigate this organism, two mutations were induced and the resulting cell lines were labeled as mutants #1 and #2, and these mutants demonstrated unique phenotypes.

To elucidate the events of transcription and translation, a wild-type variant of the organism was exposed to standard mutagens, including intercalating agents such as Ethidium bromide, which resulted in the creation of the two mutants. The researchers analyzed the exact sequence of events leading from DNA to RNA, and from RNA to protein products. Figure 1 illustrates this sequence of the wild-type and the sequences of the two mutant organisms.

Wild Type

GAC	TCA	CGA	ATG	GTA		←	DNA - sense strand
CTG	AGT	GCT	TAC	CAT		←	DNA - template strand
1 2 3	4 5 6	7 8 9	10 11 12	13 14 15		←	Nucleotide position number

transcription ↓

GAC	UCA	CGA	AUG	GUA		←	RNA strand
Asp	— Ser	— Arg	— Met	— Val		←	Amino acids

Mutant #1

GAC	TCA	CGA	GTG	GTA		←	DNA - sense strand
CTG	AGT	GCT	CAC	CAT		←	DNA - template strand

GAC	UCA	CGA	GUG	GUA		←	RNA strand
Asp	— Ser	— Arg	— Val	— Val		←	Amino acids

Mutant #2

GAC	TCA	TGA	ATG	GTA		←	DNA - sense strand
CTG	AGT	ACT	TAC	CAT		←	Template DNA strand

GAC	UCA	UGA	AUG	GUA		←	RNA strand
Asp	— Ser	— stop codon				←	Amino acids

Asp = asparagines, Ser = Serine, Arg = Arginine, Met = Methionine, Val = Valine

Experiment A:

Mutant #1 was plated onto a Petri dish and grown with a nutrient broth. The mutant #1 organism showed growth and reproduction patterns similar to the wild type, including the generation of a haploid stage. Mutant #2 was similarly treated and this organism also displayed stable growth and reproductive patterns.

Experiment B:

Mutants #1 and #2 were exposed to a virus to which the wild type is resistant. Mutant #1 was also found to be resistant, while the virus infected and destroyed mutant #2. The haploid form of mutant #2 was then fused with the haploid form of the wild type. The diploid fused organisms were protected against virus infection. The diploid forms of mutant #2 were not protected against virus infection.

1. Mutant #2 codon aberrations eventually results in a nonfunctioning and nonproductive polypeptide due to:

A. **termination of translation**   **C.** initiation of DNA replication
B. aberration of centriole reproduction   **D.** repression of RNA replication

A is correct.

Translation is the conversion of the mRNA into proteins (i.e. from language of nucleotides to amino acids). During translation of mRNA, stop codons cause translation to cease and the nascent polypeptide to be released from the ribosome. Mutant #2 caused translation to terminate earlier compared to the normal polypeptide. This termination event creates a shorter and potentially nonfunctional protein.

Mistakes can occur during translation (RNA into protein). A nonsense mutation involves a premature stop codon. A missense mutation results from a change in a nucleotide (within the codon) and causes a different amino acid to be incorporated into the growing polypeptide.

Central dogma of molecular biology is the flow of genetic information from DNA to RNA to protein. For RNA viruses (obligate parasites), the general premise is the same, but the retrovirus (RNA virus) uses its enzyme of reverse transcriptase on the host cell's machinery to convert genetic material of the virus (RNA) into the DNA genetic material of the infected host.

2. If mutants #1 and #2 are separated within individual Petri dishes and subsequent mutations arise where the two mutant strains are no longer able to reproduce sexually with each other, the process can be described as:

A. population control resulting from genetic variation
B. population control resulting from random mating
C. niche variability resulting in phenotypic variation
D. **speciation arising from geographic isolation**

D is correct.

Speciation refers to a barrier to reproduction between organisms. When populations (e.g. groups of organisms) are in contact with other populations and interbreeding (mating) occurs, barriers to reproduction are less likely to arise and speciation will most likely not occur. However, geographic isolation allows a population to change its allelic (gene) frequency from other population. Additionally, reproductive isolation can arise and the two populations will no longer be able to mate and produce fertile offspring – speciation has occurred.

3. Consistent with Darwin's views about evolution, mutant #2 represents a less "fit" organism than mutant #1 because:

    A. mutant #1 and #2 produce protein products of variable length
    B. mutant #1 is immune against a naturally-occurring virus while mutant #2 is susceptible
    C. mutant #1 is endogenous in humans while mutant #2 is found in amphibians
    D. mutant #1 replicates at a different rate than mutant #2

B is correct.

Fitness is measured by the number of future offspring that inherits the alleles (i.e. alternative forms of the gene) of the organisms.

If the mutants reproduce at different rates, it would indicate different fitness, but the passage states that the growth rate is the same.

Since mutant #1 is immune to the virus and mutant #2 is susceptible to the viral infection, mutant #2 would be expected to produce fewer offspring (in the population) and, therefore, has a lower fitness.

Fitness cannot be compared between two different species because of factors such as gestation periods, inherent survival rates, life cycle etc. The protein length is not related to the fitness of an organism as a whole.

4. In Experiment B, how many copies of mutant #2 were present in the surviving diploid?

    A. 0   **B. 1**   **C.** 2   **D.** 4

B is correct.

The diploid cell in Experiment B which survived was formed by the fusion of two haploid cells (fusion of wild-type & mutant #2). Haploid (gametes: egg and sperm) cell contain a single copy (1n) while diploid (somatic) cells contain 2 copies (2n) of the genetic material. Ploidy number refers to n (1n or 2n in humans). Thus, the surviving diploid (2n) cell contained a single copy of the wild-type and a single copy of the genome from mutant #2.

5. From Figure 1, a biomedical researcher concluded that a single point mutation in DNA altered the size of the translated product. What observations supported this conclusion?

   A. valine is encoded by two different codons
   B. mutant #2 translated a longer polypeptide than mutant #1
   C. DNA point mutations created a stop codon which terminated the growing polypeptide
   D. point mutations within the DNA increased the length of the RNA molecule

C is correct.

A nonsense mutation terminates protein translation by prematurely introducing a stop codon into the mRNA.

The genetic code converts the language of nucleotides – DNA & RNA – into the language of amino acids – proteins. The genetic code is redundant which means that a single amino acid can be encoded for by more than a single codon (sequence of three nucleotides). The third base is more permissive and this interchange of nucleotides for the same amino acid is referred to as wobble. Often, changing the third nucleotide does not change the amino acid. The genetic code has information (triplet code) that would include the possibility for 64 codes. There are 20 naturally occurring amino acids, 1 start codon (AUG for the amino acid methionine) and three stop (termination) codons.

6. In labeling the RNA in mutants #1 and #2, which of the following labeled radioactive molecules would be most useful to label the RNA?

   A. thymine   **B. uracil**   **C.** D-glucose   **D.** phosphate

B is correct.

Both DNA and RNA are nucleotides that contain a sugar-phosphate backbone of deoxyribose (DNA) and ribose (RNA) sugars.

Only DNA contains the thymine base and only RNA contains the uracil base.

Ribose sugar is unique to RNA while deoxyribose sugar is unique to DNA.

Deoxyribonucleotides (DNA) are synthesized from deoxyribose sugars and consist of the deoxyribose sugar, bases (A, C, G, T) and phosphate.
Labeled ribose becomes incorporated into the RNA as ribonucleotides. The nucleotide of RNA consists of ribose sugar, bases (A, C, G, U) and phosphate.

7. In Figure 1, the mutation in mutant #2 is caused by a defect in:

    A. RNA transcription
    B. protein translation
    C. DNA replication
    D. post-translational modification

C is correct.

Replication occurs in the S (synthesis) phase of interphase within the cell cycle. Replication is the duplication of DNA into two newly synthesized DNA daughter strands. DNA replication occurs via semiconservative replication with one new DNA strand and one original DNA (template) strand in the daughter DNA helix. For the mutation in Figure 1, changes (mutations) within the DNA nucleotides (genome) must occur during DNA replication.

A: RNA transcription is the synthesis of an mRNA molecule with bases complimentary to the DNA nucleotides.

B: protein translation is the assembly of amino acids from the information (sequence) of the mRNA molecule.

Passage 2
(Questions 8–13)

Phenols are compounds containing a hydroxyl group attached to a benzene ring. Derivatives of phenols, such as naphthols (II) and phenanthrols (III), have chemical properties similar to many substituted phenols. Like other alcohols, phenols have higher boiling points than hydrocarbons of similar molecular weight. Like carboxylic acids, phenols are more acidic than their alcohol counterparts. Phenols are highly reactive and undergo several reactions because of the hydroxyl groups and the presence of the benzene ring. Several chemical tests distinguish phenols from alcohols and from carboxylic acids.

Thymol (IUPAC name: 2-isopropyl-5-methylphenol) is a phenol naturally occurring from thyme oil and can also be synthesized from *m*-cresol in Reaction A. Reaction B illustrates how thymol can be converted into menthol, another naturally-occurring organic compound.

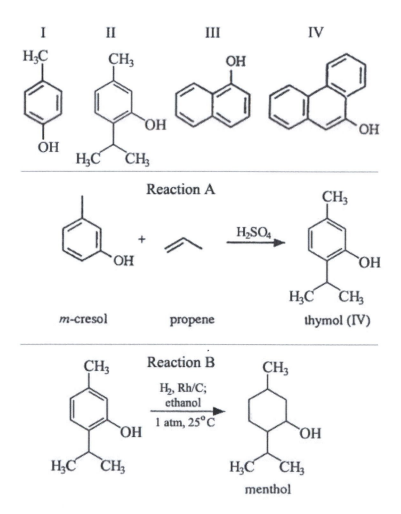

8. Which of the following is the sequence of decreasing acidity among the four compounds below?

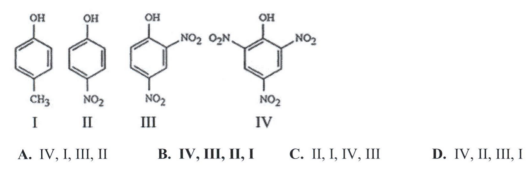

I II III IV

A. IV, I, III, II   **B. IV, III, II, I**   C. II, I, IV, III   D. IV, II, III, I

B is correct.

Consider the characteristics of a substituted phenol towards increasing acidity of the hydroxyl group on the molecule. The more electron-withdrawing groups attached to the phenol, the greater the negative charge (phenoxide) resulting from deprotonation of the H^+ on the alcohol can be dispersed and stabilized.

Since resonance (delocalization of electron density) stabilizes the phenoxide (~O$^-$) ion, increased number of valid resonance structures stabilizes the phenol and makes the molecule more acidic.

Comparing the four phenols, three molecules have nitro (strong electron-withdrawing) groups and the fourth molecule has a methyl group (electron-donating via hyperconjugation). The trinitrophenol (IV) has the most nitro groups and is the most acidic. This resonance stability is followed by dinitrophenol (III), then *para*-nitrophenol (II) and then *para*-cresol (I) where methyl group replaces the nitro group.

9. Which of the following structures corresponds to Compound Y ($C_{10}H_{14}O$) that dissolves in aqueous sodium hydroxide but is insoluble in aqueous sodium bicarbonate. The proton nuclear magnetic resonance (NMR) spectrum of Compound Y is as follows:

chemical shift	integration #	spin-spin splitting
δ 1.4	(9H)	singlet
δ 4.9	(IH)	singlet
δ 7.3	(4H)	multiplet

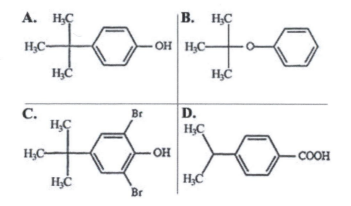

A is correct.

All four answer choices are aromatic compounds, so Compound Y must be aromatic. The chemical formula for this compound consists of carbons, hydrogens and oxygen. Eliminate choice C because the molecule contains bromine atoms absent from the molecular formula of the question.

From the question, Compound Y is soluble in aqueous sodium hydroxide but not in aqueous sodium bicarbonate. Eliminate a substituted benzoic acid (D) which would dissolve in sodium bicarbonate (weak base). The ability to dissolve in aqueous sodium hydroxide (strong base), but not in aqueous sodium bicarbonate, is characteristic of highly acidic phenols. This suggests that Compound Y is a phenol and not a phenyl ether (B) because phenyl ethers are not acidic.

The NMR spectrum has three separate peaks. The multiplet with an integration number (i.e. hydrogens producing the area under the peak) of four has a chemical shift of δ 7.3 (higher numbers: downfield from deshielding) and represents the aromatic ring. Additionally, the spin-spin splitting (coupling) is consistent with four aromatic hydrogens. The singlet at a chemical shift of δ 1.4, with an integration number of 9, indicates a chemical shift of carbon-hydrogen single bonds. The second singlet peak at a chemical shift of δ 4.9 has an integration number of one.

The fact that the single hydrogen is shifted further downfield (δ 4.9) indicates that the proton is deshielded, suggesting that the hydrogen is attached to a more electronegative element than carbon. This magnitude of shift (δ 4–5) is characteristic of the hydrogen of a phenol and data agrees with the conclusion that Compound Y is choice A.

10. Which of the following compounds is the product of the reaction of phenol with dilute nitric acid?

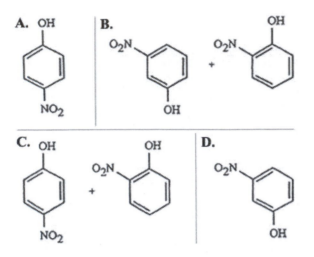

C is correct.

The hydroxyl (~OH) groups have two lone pairs of electrons on the oxygen and therefore the hydroxyl is electron-donating. Electron-donating groups activate aromatic rings towards electrophilic aromatic substitution (EAS). Like all electron-donating groups (via the resonance of the lone pair electrons), hydroxyl groups are *ortho*-directors and *para*-directors. The nitro group adds to phenol to form two products of *ortho*-nitrophenol (minor product due to steric hindrance) and *para*-nitrophenol (major product due to less steric hindrance).

Compound A is incomplete because only the *para*-nitrophenol is shown. The *meta*-nitrophenol (D) is not formed because the *meta*-substituted product involves intermediates with an anion on less stable atoms (compared to the stable intermediates) resulting from *ortho*- and *para*-substituents.

11. Comparing the pK$_a$ values for cyclohexanol (pK$_a$ = 16) to phenol (pK$_a$ = 9.95), phenol is more acidic than cyclohexanol. Which of the following explains the greater acidity of phenol compared to cyclohexanol?

I. phenoxide delocalizes the negative charge on the oxygen atom over the benzene ring
II. phenol is capable of strong hydrogen bonding which increases the ability of
phenol to disassociate a proton, making it more acidic than cyclohexanol
**III. phenoxide, the conjugate base of phenol, is stabilized by resonance more than for
cyclohexanol**

  A. I only   **B.** I and II only   **C. I and III only**   **D.** I, II and III

C is correct.

Resonance stabilization is important to support the observation that phenols are more acidic than aliphatic alcohols (e.g. cyclohexanol). In the phenoxide ion (i.e. deprotonated phenol), the negative charge on the oxygen is dispersed, via resonance, throughout the benzene ring. These resonance structures stabilize the anion by distributing electron density. This delocalizing charge effect stabilizes the phenoxide ion (Statement III), which is included in the correct answer. Therefore, eliminate answer choices that do not include Statement III.

Similarly, the phenoxide ion (from phenol) has more possible resonance structures than the alkoxide (from hydroxyl) and supported by Statement I. Statements I & III draw the same conclusion and both imply that resonance (delocalization of electrons through a pi system of bonds) contributes to the stability of the anion.

Statement II is a true fact because phenols can hydrogen-bond more strongly than aliphatic alcohols as supported by the higher boiling points mentioned in the passage. Hydrogen bonding is a consequence (not the reason) for the greater anion stability of phenol (compared to cyclohexanol) but hydrogen bonding does not account for the acidity of phenol. Therefore, statement II cannot be included in the correct answer choice.

12. Reaction A is an example of:

> **A.** free radical substitution   **C. electrophilic aromatic substitution**
> **B.** electrophilic addition   **D.** nucleophilic aromatic substitution

C is correct.

Like benzene, Reaction A is an electrophilic aromatic substitution (EAS) reaction where *meta*-cresol is converted to thymol. In *meta*-cresol, both the hydroxyl and methyl substituents are *ortho-para* directing (i.e. relative position) and activators (i.e. rate of reaction compared to benzene). Consider the direction of the substitution. The hydroxyl substituent is a more powerful activator (compared to a methyl substituent) and the electrophilic aromatic substitution occurs in the *ortho* position (one carbon away) relative to the hydroxyl group.

Analyze the reaction mechanism. Initially, the pi electrons of the propene abstract an H^+ (proton) from the sulfuric acid (i.e. Lewis acid), creating a secondary carbocation on the propene. This carbocation then acts as an electrophile and adds to the electron rich benzene ring at the *ortho* position (relative to hydroxyl). Addition of the propene carbocation forms an arenium (i.e. benzene) ion. The aromaticity of the benzene is restored by the loss of a proton to produce thymol. Therefore, this mechanism is an electrophilic aromatic substitution.

Although the carbocation adds to the ring, a proton is lost in order to restore aromaticity of the ring. The derivatives of benzene do not undergo addition (would result in the loss of aromaticity). The derivatives of benzene undergo EAS to restore the aromatic ring in the final product. Therefore, Reaction A is an example of substitution (not addition). The carbocation, which adds to the ring, is an electrophile (not a nucleophile) because benzene is electron rich and the substituents on *meta*-cresol enhance this electron density of the ring.

The sulfuric acid (Lewis acid) will not induce radical formation. In general, radical formation (e.g. unpaired electron) involves starting material of either a dihalide (Br_2 or Cl_2; and light/heat or alkyl halides) or other molecules such as BH_3 or HBr (in presence of peroxides: RO-OR, H_2O_2 or R_2O_2).

13. Which chemical test could distinguish between the two following compounds?

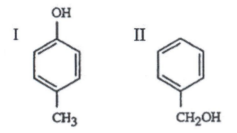

I   II

    A. compound I is soluble in $NaHCO_3$ **C.** compound II decolorizes a solution of Br_2
    B. compound I is soluble in NaOH   **D.** compound II is soluble in $NaHCO_3$

B is correct.

Compound I is *para*-cresol (or *para*-methylphenol) and Compound II is benzyl alcohol. Benzyl alcohol (with the OH not attached directly to benzene) behaves more like an aliphatic alcohol than phenol and this difference can be used to distinguish the two compounds. The main distinction of these molecules is their solubility and this can be used to separate them from a mixture.

Phenols are acidic and are quite soluble in aqueous NaOH (sodium hydroxide is a strong base). Aliphatic alcohols (including benzyl alcohol here) are not acidic and therefore not soluble in aqueous sodium hydroxide. An exception to solubility is observed for very short chain alcohols (with fewer than five carbons) that are water-soluble because short chain alcohols can dissolve in aqueous solution.

However, benzyl alcohol is not a short chain molecule and therefore is not water-soluble. Benzyl alcohol is not soluble in sodium hydroxide solution. The solubility of *para*-cresol (I) in aqueous sodium hydroxide would provide an effective test to distinguish between the two compounds.

A mixture of these two compounds could be separated by dissolving them in an organic solvent, and then extracting the solution in a separatory funnel with aqueous sodium hydroxide. The benzyl alcohol would remain in the organic layer (not soluble in an aqueous solution) and the *para*-cresol (soluble in aqueous solution) would move into the aqueous layer.

Compound I would not react with a bromine solution and decolorize it. Both compounds will react under stronger conditions (presence of a Lewis acid) but bromine in solution is too mild of a reagent to react with the stable aromatic ring. Therefore, both compounds I and II would not decolorize a bromine solution.

Neither of the two compounds is soluble in $NaHCO_3$ (sodium bicarbonate is a weak base). Since phenols are fairly weak acids, it requires a fairly strong base (NaOH) to cause deprotonation (abstraction of the acidic proton) of the phenol. Thus, *para*-cresol is not soluble in sodium bicarbonate. The benzyl alcohol is a weaker acid (than *para*-cresol) and would not dissolve in sodium bicarbonate.

Since neither compound I nor II will be soluble in sodium bicarbonate, sodium bicarbonate cannot be used to distinguish between them.

Questions 14 through 17 are not based on any
descriptive passage and are independent of each other

---

14. In thin layer chromatography (TLC), a sheet of absorbent paper is partially immersed in a non-polar solvent. The solvent rises through the absorbent paper through capillary action. Which of the following compounds demonstrates the greatest migration when placed on the absorbent paper near the bottom and the solvent is allowed to pass?

A. $CH_3CH_2CH_3$ **B.** CH_3Cl **C.** NH_3 **D.** R-COOH

A is correct.

In thin layer paper chromatography, the non-polar compounds dissolve into the migrating non-polar solvent and non-polar compounds are carried with the solvent front.

Propane ($CH_3CH_2CH_3$) is the only non-polar compound listed. Propane will interact less strongly with the polar cellulose of the TLC paper and the propane dissolves into and moves with the mobile non-polar solvent. Thus, non-polar compounds move farther than more polar compounds because polar molecules bond more strongly to the polar chromatography paper.

All other compounds are polar and thus will interact via bonds to the TLC paper and therefore these polar compounds migrate less than the non-polar propane.

15. During meiosis, in which phase of oogenesis development does anaphase I occur?

A. 1
B. 2
C. 3
D. 4

B is correct.

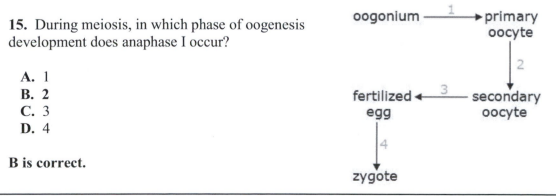

Stage 2, the progression from primary to secondary oocytes includes anaphase I.

Meiosis refers to the cell cycle that occurs for gamete formation. Gametes are sperm (males) and eggs (females). For meiosis, there are two sequential rounds of cell division referred to as meiosis I and meiosis II. During embryonic development of females, oogenesis (formation of eggs) proceeds up to the formation of primary oocytes (diploid female gamete).

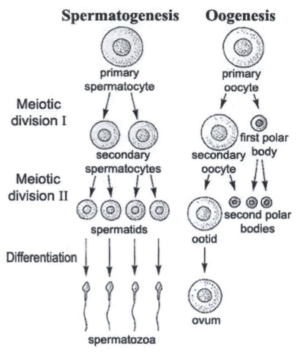

The primary oocytes (within the ovaries) are arrested in meiotic prophase I. The primary oocytes remain suspended at this stage until ovulation and then the primary oocytes complete meiosis I. Meiosis I continues through anaphase I to form secondary oocytes which are ovulated.

16. Why do acetoacetate and other ketone bodies form during low carbohydrate availability?

    A. Because acetyl-CoA is converted into glucose
    B. Because acetoacetate spontaneously decarboxylates into acetone
    C. Because citrate cannot be formed due to low level of oxaloacetate that binds to acetyl-CoA
    D. Because acetyl-CoA cannot combine with citrate because of a low level of citrate

C is correct.
Oxaloacetate combines with acetyl-CoA to form citrate at the initiation of the Krebs cycle. During low carbohydrate availability (e.g. fasting), oxaloacetate is used for gluconeogenesis (synthesis of glucose from non-carbohydrate sources) and its availability to the Krebs cycle is reduced. Lack of oxaloacetate inhibits acetyl-CoA from forming citrate.

Excess acetyl-CoA is converted to acetoacetate and other ketone bodies which can be used by heart and skeletal muscle to produce energy. Brain, which usually depends on glucose as sole energy source, can also use ketone bodies during a long fasting period.

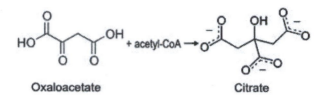

Oxaloacetate   Citrate

A: a small amount of glucose is necessary to provide oxaloacetate needed for the Krebs cycle, but acetyl-CoA cannot be converted into glucose.

B: is true, but doesn't answer the question.

D: citrate is formed when oxaloacetate combines with acetyl-CoA in the Krebs cycle.

17. In DiGeorge syndrome, caused by a deletion of a large portion of chromosome 22, there is defective embryonic development of the parathyroid glands. A patient with this syndrome would be expected to have:

 A. low serum calcium
 B. high serum calcium
 C. low serum thyroid hormone
 D. high serum PTH

A is correct.

The parathyroid glands must develop normally to be able to secrete PTH. A deficiency in the ability to synthesize PTH permits the serum calcium levels in the patient to remain low. In the absence of PTH, calcium is not reabsorbed by the kidney (i.e. ascending loop and distal tubule) or released (i.e. osteoclast activity) by bone.

B: high serum calcium level is the negative feedback stimulus to inhibit PTH secretion. The negative feedback mechanism involves the antagonistic hormone calcitonin. Calcitonin is synthesized in the thyroids and released into the blood from high serum Ca^{2+}.

Passage 3
(Questions 18–23)

The parathyroid glands are part of the endocrine system. The parathyroid glands are two small endocrine glands that detect low plasma calcium levels and respond by releasing parathyroid hormone (i.e. PTH). The parathyroid hormone affects bone, kidneys and intestine to regulate serum calcium levels.

PTH acts on the bone to release stored calcium into the bloodstream. Osteoclasts dissolve bone matrix by secreting acid and collagenase onto the bone surface to release calcium. In the presence of PTH and 1,25-$(OH)_2$ D, the maturation of osteoclasts is accelerated, resulting in increased resorption and release of calcium from the bone mineral compartment.

In the kidneys, PTH acts within the nephron to increase calcium reabsorption in the thick ascending loop of Henle and in the distal tubule. These modifications to mechanisms within the kidneys recapture some calcium that was filtered by the kidney and reduce the amount of calcium excreted in the urine. PTH also upregulates the conversion of 25-hydroxyvitamin D (25-OH D) to 1,25-dihydroxyvitamin D (1,25-OH_2 D) in renal cells.

Additionally, Vitamin D stimulates calcium absorption within the intestine. 1,25-dihydroxyvitamin D is the active form of vitamin D, which promotes the active transport of calcium through the mircovilli of intestinal epithelium. Thus, PTH works indirectly in the intestines, via 1,25-$(OH)_2$ D to maximize dietary calcium absorption.

18. Although converted from 25-hydroxyvitamin D to 1,25-$(OH)_2$ D in the kidneys, the sites of action of 1,25-$(OH)_2$ D include cells within the intestine and within peripheral bone. Based on its mode of action, 1,25-$(OH)_2$ D may be classified as:

A. hormone   **B.** neuropeptide   **C.** coenzyme   **D.** enzyme

A is correct.

Hormones are substances released into the bloodstream, enabling them to exert effects on distant tissues. Hormones can be classified into two broad categories: steroid hormones and peptide hormones.

B: the activity of a neuropeptide (e.g. neurotransmitter) is confined to the synapse. The synapse is the space between adjacent neurons (nerve cells) or between neurons and muscle cells (e.g. neuromuscular junction).

A and D: enzymes and coenzymes affect the rate of the reaction by binding to the substrate (molecule being acted upon) and lowering the energy of activation (barrier from reactant to product formation). Note, enzymes have no effect on the relative stability of the reactants or products (ΔG of the reaction). Equilibrium is the rate of the forward reaction equal to the rate of the reverse reaction; enzymes have no effect on equilibrium. The passage does not mention vitamin D affecting a reaction rate, therefore, it cannot be classified as enzyme or coenzyme.

19. Hormone secretion is often regulated by negative feedback inhibition. Which of the following signals is used to decrease PTH secretion for homeostasis?

A. high serum PTH   **C. high serum calcium**

B. low bone density   D. high serum phosphate

C is correct.

Parathyroid hormone (PTH) increases concentration of calcium level in the blood. A hormone is a molecule that is released into the blood and acts on a distant target organ or tissue. The antagonistic actions of calcitonin (from thyroid glands) and parathyroid hormone (from parathyroid glands) maintain the blood calcium levels within normal limits (i.e. homeostasis).

A and B: increased serum calcium levels exert a negative feedback inhibition on PTH secretion. Parathyroid glands are only sensitive to serum calcium levels, not bone density. PTH does not inhibit itself because it does not function as an autocrine. An autocrine is a cell that releases a molecule and the molecule acts upon the cell that released it. Autocrines are common during embryogenesis. A paracrine is a cell that releases a molecule that acts on a cell nearby to the cell that released that molecule.

D: the choice high serum phosphate (HPO_4^{2-}) is an electrolyte imbalance and high level of serum phosphate (indirectly) stimulates PTH secretion. Phosphate was not mentioned in the passage but parathyroid hormone causes the blood phosphate level to decrease (and increase the level of calcium in the blood).

20. The precursor to $1,25\text{-}(OH)_2$ D is 7-dehydrocholesterol. Cholesterol derivatives are also precursors of:

A. epinephrine and norepinephrine   C. adenine and guanine

B. cortisol and aldosterone   D. prolactin and oxytocin

B is correct.

Cortisol (i.e. glucocorticoids) and aldosterone (i.e. mineralcorticoids) are steroid hormones synthesized by the adrenal cortex. Glucocorticoid denotes the type of biological activity. Glucocorticoids are steroid-like compounds capable of promoting hepatic glycogen deposition and of exerting a clinically useful anti-inflammatory effect. Cortisol is the most potent of the naturally occurring glucocorticoids. Mineralcorticoids are one of the steroids of the adrenal cortex that influence salt (e.g. sodium and potassium) metabolism.

A: epinephrine and norepinephrine are derived from the tyrosine amino acid. These modified amino acid proteins are synthesized by the adrenal medulla.

C: adenine and guanine are purine bases of nucleic acids (i.e. DNA and RNA).

D: prolactin (from anterior pituitary) and oxytocin (from posterior pituitary) are peptide (short amino acid chain) hormones that participate in lactogenesis.

21. Homeostasis regulation of serum calcium is necessary for the proper function of nervous system. Low blood Ca^{2+} levels may result in numbness and tingling in the hands and feet. Insufficient serum calcium would have the greatest effect on which of the following neuronal structures?

   A. axon   **B.** dendrites   **C. axon terminal**   **D.** axon hillock

C is correct.

When the action potential reaches the axon terminal, voltage-gated Ca^{2+} channels open and Ca^{2+} enters the cell. The Ca^{2+} influx causes vesicles containing neurotransmitters to fuse to the presynaptic membrane, releasing their contents into the synapse. Thus, a decrease in Ca^{2+} levels would decrease neurotransmitter release.

A: the axon is the elongated portion of a neuron that conducts nerve impulses (e.g. action potential), typically from the cell body to the synapse.

B: the dendrite is the process extending from the relatively short cell body of a neuron and is typically branched to receive signals from axons of other neurons.

D: the axon hillock is located within the cell body of the neuron. The axon hillock aggregates depolarization stimuli and transmits the summation of depolarization to the neuron process for the action potential propagation if threshold stimulation is achieved.

22. PTH most likely acts on target cells by:

   A. increasing Na^+ influx into the cell
   B. decreasing Na^+ influx into the cell
   C. increasing synthesis of secondary messenger cAMP
   D. increasing 1,25-$(OH)_2D$ transcription

C is correct.

Hormones can be classified as steroid hormones, peptide hormones or amine hormones. PTH is a peptide hormone (i.e. consisting of a small chain of amino acids) and therefore utilizes secondary messengers (secondary messenger for PTH is cAMP).

A and B: PTH does not affect Na^+ transport across the cell membrane.

In review, only steroid hormones are able to pass through the plasma membrane, bind with a receptor in the cytoplasm and then, bound together pass into the nucleus to act at the transcription level.

D: $1,25\text{-}(OH)_2 D$ is a vitamin, not a gene product, and thus cannot be transcribed. Additionally, the passage states that PTH catalyzes the conversion of vitamin D, not transcription.

23. McCune-Albright syndrome is a hereditary disease of precocious puberty and results in low serum calcium levels, despite elevated serum PTH levels. Which of the following is the most likely basis of the disorder?

    A. G_s-protein deficiency which couples cAMP to the PTH receptor
    B. defective secretion of digestive enzymes by osteoclast
    C. absence of nuclear receptor which couples PTH to the parathyroid transcription factor
    D. osteoblast autostimulation

A is correct.

The chronic low serum calcium in the presence of elevated PTH suggests the target organ resistance to PTH. As PTH is a peptide hormone, G protein dysfunction is a reasonable hypothesis. The correct choice is deficiency of the G_s-protein which couples the PTH receptor to adenylate cyclase. The syndrome is affected by a mutation in the guanine nucleotide-binding protein gene (GNAS1) on 20q. This mutation prevents downregulation of cAMP signaling.

B: for nonfunctional osteoclast cells, PTH and $1,25\text{-}(OH)_2D$ would still be able to elevate serum calcium levels through their actions on the kidney and on the intestine.

C: peptide hormones, that PTH belongs to, do not enter the cell or bind to receptors within the cell. Steroid hormones migrate as a hormone/receptor complex and move into the nucleus.

D: the passage does not mention autostimulation of osteoblast bone cells.

Passage 4
(Questions 24–28)

The kidneys regulate hydrogen ion (H^+) concentration in extracellular fluid primarily by controlling the concentration of bicarbonate ion (HCO_3^-). The process begins inside the epithelial cells of the proximal tubule, where the enzyme carbonic anhydrase catalyzes the formation of carbonic acid (H_2CO_3) from CO_2 and H_2O. The H_2CO_3 then dissociates into HCO_3^- and H^+. The HCO_3^- enters the extracellular fluid, while the H^+ is secreted into the tubule lumen via a Na^+/H^+ counter-transport mechanism that uses the Na^+ gradient established by the Na^+/K^+ pump.

Since the renal tubule is not very permeable to the HCO_3^- filtered into the glomerular filtrate, the reabsorption of HCO_3^- from the lumen into the tubular cells occurs indirectly. Carbonic anhydrase promotes the combination of HCO_3^- with the secreted H^+ to form H_2CO_3. The H_2CO_3 then dissociates into CO_2 and H_2O. The H_2O remains in the lumen while the CO_2 enters the tubular cells.

From Figure 1, inside the cells, every H^+ secreted into the lumen is countered by an HCO_3^- entering the extracellular fluid. Thus, the mechanism by which the kidneys regulate body fluid pH is by the titration of H^+ with HCO_3^-.

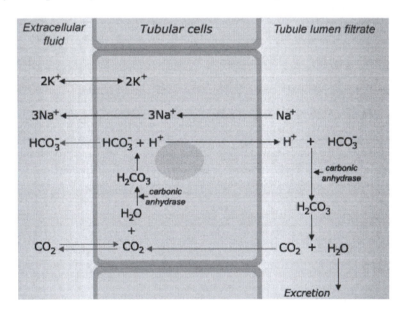

Figure 1

The drug Diamox (i.e. acetazolamide) is a potent carbonic anhydrase inhibitor. Acetazolamide is available as a generic drug and used as a diuretic because it increases the rate of urine formation and thereby increases the excretion of water and other solutes from the body. Diuretics can be used to maintain adequate urine output or excrete excess fluid.

24. Spironolactone (an adrenocorticosteroid) is a competitive aldosterone antagonist and functions as a diuretic. Administering this drug to a patient would most likely result in:

A. Na^+ plasma concentration increase and blood volume increase

B. Na^+ plasma concentration increase and blood volume decrease

C. Na^+ plasma concentration decrease and blood volume increase

D. Na^+ plasma concentration decrease and blood volume decrease

D is correct.

According to the question, spironolactone is a diuretic that inhibits aldosterone. Aldosterone is the hormone that increases in the re-absorption of sodium ions from the nephron lumen and increases the potassium ions secretion into the nephron lumen.

Aldosterone increases the Na^+ plasma concentration. A medication that inhibits aldosterone will inhibit the re-absorption of Na^+ and decreases the Na^+ plasma concentration. Therefore, eliminate choices A and B.

Comparing choices C and D, aldosterone affects blood volume. Osmolarity is the number of solute particles per volume of liquid. In two compartments divided by a water permeable membrane, water diffuses from the area of lower concentration (lower osmolarity) to the area of higher concentration (higher osmolarity). Sodium is re-absorbed from the tubular filtrate into the tubular cells and eventually enters the bloodstream. Movement of sodium from the tubular lumen to the cells (and to the blood) increases the osmolarity of these regions, resulting in a corresponding movement of water from the filtrate because water follows the movement of Na^+ and blood volume increases.

Inhibiting aldosterone reduces both, the re-absorption of Na^+ and the movement of water, which results in decreased blood volume.

The question states that spironolactone is a diuretic and the passage states that diuretics increase the excretion of water and other solutes. Therefore, administration of a diuretic results in a decrease concentration of solutes in plasma followed by a decrease of blood volume due to high urine excretion.

25. Excretion of acidic urine by a patient results from:

A. more H^+ transported into the glomerular filtrate than HCO_3^- secreted into the tubular lumen

B. more H^+ secreted into the tubular lumen than HCO_3^- transported into the glomerular filtrate

C. more HCO_3^- secreted into the tubular lumen than H^+ transported into the glomerular filtrate

D. more HCO_3^- transported into the glomerular filtrate than H^+ secreted into the tubular lumen

B is correct.

From the passage, the H^+ secretion into the lumen is balanced by HCO_3^- transport from the glomerular filtrate into the extracellular fluid. This mechanism results in the regulation of body fluid pH by the kidneys. Acidity depends on H^+ concentration. Therefore, acidic urine has a higher concentration of H^+ compared to the concentration of HCO_3^-.

Acidic urine is produced when the lumen fluid (filtrate) has a high H^+ concentration relative to the HCO_3^- because more H^+ is secreted into the tubular lumen than HCO_3^- is transported into the glomerular filtrate.

26. What mechanism described in the passage is used to transport Na^+ into the tubular cells?

   A. endocytosis   **B.** exocytosis   **C. facilitated diffusion**   **D.** active transport

C is correct.

From Figure 1 and the passage, H^+ is secreted into the lumen using the mechanism of Na^+/H^+ countertransport. Carbonic anhydrase catalyzes the formation of carbonic acid inside the tubular cell which spontaneously degrades into bicarbonate ion and H^+, resulting in an H^+ increase within the cell. The H^+ is secreted into the lumen in exchange for Na^+. The Na^+ binds to a carrier protein on the luminal side of the cell membrane, while concurrently an H^+ binds to the opposite side of the same carrier protein. Because of the greater concentration of Na^+ outside the cell (compared to inside), the Na^+/K^+ pump moves Na^+ down its concentration gradient into the cell. This movement supplies the energy for transporting H^+ into the tubular lumen. As Na^+ moves into the cell via facilitated diffusion no energy is required because movement is down its concentration gradient.

A: endocytosis is the uptake of extracellular material via invagination of the plasma membrane. In this question, one ion is being transported in exchange for another ion.

B: exocytosis is the release of intracellular material via budding of the plasma membrane.

D: active transport requires both a protein carrier and energy (e.g. ATP).

27. Acetazolamide administration increases a patient's excretion of:

   I. H_2O **II.** H^+ **III.** HCO_3^- **IV.** Na^+

   A. III only   **B.** III & IV only   **C. I, III & IV only**   **D.** I, II, III & IV

C is correct.

Figure 1 shows that carbonic anhydrase is both within the lumen and in the kidney tubular cells. H^+ and HCO_3^- (bicarbonate ions) are converted into H_2CO_3 (carbonic acid) in the lumen. Carbonic anhydrase catalyzes the further disassociation of H_2CO_3 into CO_2

(carbon dioxide) and H_2O. CO_2 is transported into the cells while H_2O remains in the lumen.

Inside cells, carbonic anhydrase catalyzes the production of H_2CO_3 from H_2O and CO_2.

Carbon dioxide dissolved in water is in equilibrium with carbonic acid:

$$CO_2 + H_2O \overset{\text{carbonic anhydrase}}{\rightleftharpoons} H_2CO_3$$

Carbonic acid

H_2CO_3 dissociates into HCO_3^- and H^+ ions. The HCO_3^- exits the cell and enters the extracellular fluid while the H^+ is secreted into the lumen in exchange for Na^+. Since acetazolamide is a carbonic anhydrase inhibitor, administering this drug to a patient would inhibit reactions catalyzed by the carbonic anhydrase enzyme. The Na^+ / H^+ countertransport and the reabsorption of HCO_3^- from the lumen into the tubular cells would be inhibited. Since the lumen filtrate is excreted as urine, acetazolamide lowers the H^+ concentration while increasing HCO_3^- and Na^+ concentrations in urine. The increase in urinary osmolarity draws water into the lumen to counter the increase of lumen osmolarity. Thus, Na^+, HCO_3^- and H_2O increase in the urine while H^+ decreases.

28. Which of the following hormones would affect the patient's blood volume to oppose the effect of administering acetazolamide?

   A. ADH   **B.** somatostatin   **C. LH**   **D.** calcitonin

A is correct.

Acetazolamide is a carbonic anhydrase inhibitor that reduces excretion of H^+ into the lumen and re-absorption of HCO_3^-. The excretion of H^+ into the lumen is necessary to provide means for Na^+ transport into tubular cells. If carbonic anhydrase is inhibited and no H^+ is produced in the tubular cell, Na^+ will remain in the lumen and increase the filtrate osmolarity. With increased filtrate osmolarity, water diffuses into the lumen causing the urine volume to increase. Diuretics use this mechanism to excrete excess body fluids.

The hormone with the effect opposite to diuretics would decrease water excretion by increasing water reabsorption. ADH (antidiuretic hormone) is such a hormone that increases water reabsorption in the kidneys.

B: somatostatin is a hormone secreted by the hypothalamus which acts as a potent inhibitor of many other hormones such as: growth hormone, TRH (thyroid-releasing hormone), ACTH, insulin, glucagon, gastrin, rennin and some others.

C: LH (luteinizing hormone) is a hormone produced by the anterior pituitary gland and it stimulates the release of an egg to mature.

D: calcitonin is a 32-amino acid peptide hormone that reduces blood calcium. Calcitonin is secreted by the thyroid gland in response to high plasma calcium ion concentration. Calcitonin is an antagonist of parathyroid hormone (PTH) function. PTH increases blood calcium levels by stimulating osteoclasts to degrade mineralized bone.

> Questions 29 through 33 are not based on any
> descriptive passage and are independent of each other

29. Which of the following functions describes the purpose of the lysosome membrane?

    A. creating a basic environment for hydrolytic enzymes of the lysosome within the cytoplasm

    B. creating an acidic environment for hydrolytic enzymes of the lysosome within the cytoplasm

    C. serving as an alternative site for peptide bond formation during protein synthesis

    D. the lysosome membrane is a continuation of the nuclear envelope

B is correct.

Lysosomes are membrane-bound sacs containing hydrolytic enzymes involved in intracellular digestion. Lysosomes fuse with intracellular vesicles and digest the macromolecules of proteins, polysaccharides, fats and nucleic acids. These macromolecules are degraded into their monomers and the subunits are reused by cells. Lysosomes also play a role in the recycling of cell organelles by engulfing and digesting depleted organelles and releasing their component molecules into the cytosol for reuse. These hydrolytic enzymes are contained within the lysosome and are optimally functional at acidic pH 5. Similar to the stomach (pH of 2 for pepsin), the lysosome pumps H^+ from the cytosol for an internal pH of 5. The lysosomal enzymes would not function properly in the neutral pH of the cytosol. The lysosome membrane enables the lysosome to maintain its acidic environment.

C: the lysosomes are not an alternate site for protein synthesis because ribosomes are the site of protein synthesis. The ribosomes are free in the cytosol (proteins remaining in the cell) or attached to endoplasmic reticulum (rough ER) for production of proteins exported from the cell, or for the plasma membrane proteins, or for lysosome proteins. Lysosomes are involved in protein degradation, not the synthesis of proteins.

D: lysosome membranes are not in physical contact with the nuclear envelope (membrane). Lysosomes, like other membrane-bound organelles, are part of the cell's endomembrane system (a system of membranes linked through direct contact or communication via vesicles). The endoplasmic reticulum is continuous with the nuclear membrane at certain points.

30. How many σ bonds and π bonds are there in ethene?

    A. 1 σ and 2 π   **B.** 1 σ and 5 π   **C.** 6 σ and 2 π   **D. 5 σ and 1 π**

D is correct.

Ethene ($CH_2 = CH_2$) is a two carbon alkene.

Each C–H bond is a σ (sigma) single bond and there are four C–H bonds. Ethene also has one C–C σ bond and a C-C π (pi) double bond. Therefore, there are five σ (single) bonds and one π (double) bond in ethene.

31. Why is PCC a better oxidant for the conversion of an alcohol into an aldehyde compared to other oxidizing agents?

A. PCC is a less powerful oxidant which does not oxidize the alcohol to a carboxylic acid

B. PCC is a less powerful oxidant which does not oxidize the aldehyde to an alcohol

C. PCC is a more powerful oxidant which oxidizes the alcohol to a carboxylic acid

D. PCC is a more powerful oxidant which oxidizes the carboxylic acid to an alcohol

A is correct.

A primary alcohol is oxidized to an aldehyde by PCC (pyridinium chlorochromate) or a carboxylic acid with a stronger oxidizing agent (e.g. $KMnO_4$ or CrO_3). To stop oxidation at the aldehyde, a weaker oxidant (e.g. PCC) is needed. PCC oxidizes the primary alcohol to the aldehyde because it is a weaker oxidizing agent and will not fully oxidize the primary alcohol to the carboxylic acid as $KMnO_4$ (potassium permanganate) or Jones reagent (CrO_3).

32. Which of the following describes the reaction of acyl-CoA to enoyl-CoA conversion?

A. oxidation **B.** reduction **C.** hydrogenation **D.** hydrolysis

A is correct.

The conversion of acyl-CoA into enoyl-CoA involves the removal of two C-H bonds to generate a C=C double bond. Creating a double bond from a single bond is an oxidation. Oxidation-reduction is coupled; FAD is reduced as acyl-CoA is oxidized.

An enoyl consists of a carbonyl group plus a double bond between α (adjacent) carbon and β (two carbons away) carbon.

FAD is reduced (gains electrons) to $FADH_2$, consistent with the oxidation of acyl-CoA into enoyl-CoA. Oxidations are always accompanied by reductions (and vice versa).

33. *Biology > Generalized Eukaryotic cells*

For breeding, salmon travel from saltwater to freshwater. The salmon maintain solute balance by reversing their osmoregulatory mechanism when entering a different solute environment. Failure to reverse this mechanism results in:

A. no change because movement between saltwater and freshwater does not affect osmotic pressure in salmon

B. metabolic activity increase due to an increase in enzyme concentration

C. death because water influx causes cell lysis

D. death because cells become too concentrated for normal metabolism

C is correct.

Freshwater is hypotonic relative to saltwater. In freshwater, the cells of the salmon have higher osmotic pressure than the surrounding environment. If salmon were unable to reverse their osmoregulatory mechanism, water would flow into the cells, causing them to swell and eventually lyse (burst).

Tonicity: A hypertonic solution contains a greater concentration of the impermeable solutes than cytosol. The resulting osmotic pressure causes a net movement of water out of the cell.

A hypotonic solution contains a lower concentration of impermeable solutes than cytosol. The resulting osmotic pressure causes a net movement of water into the cell.

Passage 5
(Questions 34–38)

Simple acyclic alcohols are an important class of alcohols. Their general formula is $C_nH_{2n+1}OH$. An example of simple acyclic alcohols is ethanol (C_2H_5OH) – the type of alcohol found in alcoholic beverages.

The terpenoids (aka isoprenoids) are a large and diverse class of naturally occurring organic chemicals derived from five-carbon isoprene units. Plant terpenoids are commonly used for their aromatic qualities and play a role in traditional herbal remedies. They are also being studied for antibacterial, antineoplastic (i.e. a chemotherapeutic property that stops abnormal proliferation of cells) and other pharmaceutical applications. Terpenoids contribute to the scent of eucalyptus; menthol and camphor are well-known terpenoids.

Citronellol is an acyclic alcohol and natural acyclic monoterpenoid that is found in many plant oils, including (-)-citronellol in geraniums and rose. It is used in synthesis of perfumes, insect repellants and moth repellants for fabrics. Pulegone, a clear colorless oily liquid, is a related molecule found in plant oils and has a camphor and peppermint aroma.

Below is the synthesis of pulegone from citronellol.

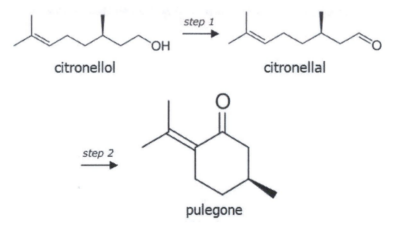

Figure 1. Synthesis of pulegone from citronellol

34. Pulegone has the presence of the following functional groups:

A. aldehydes and an isopropyl alkene

B. ketone and isobutyl alkene

C. ketone and isopropyl alkene

D. hydroxyl and tert-butyl alkene

C is correct.

Ketones end in ~one, alcohols (hydroxyl) ends in ~ol and aldehydes end in ~al. The carbon double bond oxygen within the carbon chain (as opposed to the terminal aldehyde) describes the ketone. The presence of a double bond within the hydrocarbon describes an alkene. Isopropyl refers to a three carbon chain with attachment to the C2 (middle) carbon.

35. What is the absolute configuration of pulegone?

A. *R* **B.** *S* **C.** *cis* **D.** *trans*

B is correct.

There is a single stereogenic center at the methyl substituent within the ring. The hydrogen (not shown) points into the page. The Cahn-Inglold-Prelog (CIP) priorities around the stereogenic center are the carbonyl (#1), cyclic portion of the ring towards the alkene (#2) and the methyl (#3). The priorities are arranged counterclockwise and thus are (S).

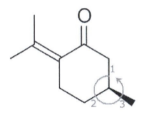

Carbon 1, according to IUPAC, is the carbon with the most oxidized atom (e.g. ketone). The groups are then prioritized according to Cahn-Ingold-Prelog rules (i.e. atomic number of the atom at the point of attachment – and not the aggregation of atoms - to determine priorities). Note the counterclockwise arrangement (lowest priority points into page).

Clockwise rotation denotes an R while counterclockwise rotation denotes an S configuration.

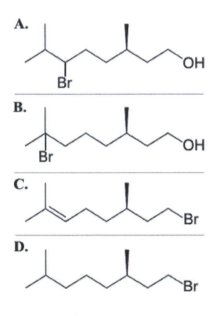

36. Which of the following structures is the most likely product when HBr is added to citronellol?

B is correct.

HBr results in the addition of H and Br across the double bond. The intermediate is a carbocation upon addition of H^+ with the most stable carbocation formation. Br then adds to the carbocation with the Markovnikov regiospecificity.

In general, ⁻OH does not dissociate as a leaving group because hydroxyl is a strong base (i.e. unstable) and therefore a poor leaving group, and Br will not replace the OH on the molecule. Hydroxyl groups can be converted to alkyl halides with special reagents such as $SOCl_2$ (substitution of Cl) or PBr_3 and PBr_5 (substitution of Br).

37. PCC promotes conversion of citrinellol to which molecule?

    A. citrinellone   **B. citrinellal**   **C.** citric acid   **D.** no reaction

B is correct.

PCC, discovered in 1975, is formed by the reaction of pyridine with chromium trioxide.

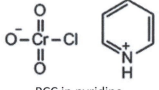

PCC in pyridine

Pyridinium chlorochromate (PCC) is a reddish orange solid reagent used to oxide primary alcohols (citrinellol) into aldehydes (~al ending) such as citrinellal, and secondary alcohols into ketones (~one ending).

PCC is a weaker oxidizing agent and will not fully oxidize the primary alcohol to the carboxylic acid as the Jones reagent (CrO_3) does. Jones reagent (CrO_3) oxidizes a primary alcohol – past aldehydes – to a carboxylic acid; a secondary alcohol is oxidized to a ketone. Therefore, PCC is the choice for an oxidizing agent that converts the primary alcohol to the aldehydes (and not to the completed oxidation of carboxylic acid).

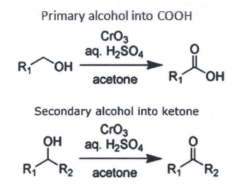

38. What is the relationship between citronellol and citronellal?

    A. enantiomers   **C.** geometric isomers
    B. diastereomers   **D. constitutional isomers**

D is correct.

Bonds must be broken for the conversion between citronellol and citronellal and therefore the molecules are constitutional (i.e. structural) isomers.

A: enantiomers are chiral molecules with a non-superimposable mirror image. If the mirror images are superimposable, the molecules are nonchiral – a carbon that is not attached to 4 different substituents. A chiral molecule and its mirror image are enantiomers (stereoisomers).

B: diastereomers result from chiral molecules with 2 or more chiral carbons (stereogenic centers). The diastereomers are not the mirror image – the mirror image is the enantiomer.

C: geometric isomers are a special class of diastereomers where a double bond is present in the molecule. Geometric isomers are designated *cis* or *trans* if the same substituents are attached to each side of the double bond. If the atoms are different on each side of the double bond, E and Z are used to designate the geometric isomer. E is analogous to *trans* and Z (zame side) to *cis*. Determination of E or Z requires prioritizing the substituents according to atomic number (Cahn-Ingold-Prelog priorities).

Passage 6
(Questions 39–43)

Beta-oxidation is the process when fatty acids are broken down in the mitochondria. Before fatty acids are oxidized, they are covalently bound to coenzyme A (CoA) on the mitochondrion's outer membrane. The sulfur atom of CoA attacks the carbonyl carbon of the fatty acid and H_2O dissociates. The hydrolysis of two high-energy phosphate bonds drives this reaction producing acyl-CoA.

Special transport molecules shuttle the acyl-CoA across the inner membrane and into the mitochondria matrix. Further fatty acids beta-oxidation involves four recurring steps whereby acyl-CoA is broken down by sequential removal of two-carbon units in each cycle to form acetyl-CoA. Acetyl-CoA is the initial molecule that enters the Krebs cycle.

The beta-carbon of the fatty acyl-CoA is oxidized to a carbonyl that is attacked by the lone pair of electrons on the sulfur atom of another CoA. The CoA substrate molecule and the bound acetyl group dissociate. The acetyl-CoA, produced from fatty acid oxidation, enters the Krebs cycle and is further oxidized into CO_2. The Krebs cycle yields 3 NADH + 1 FADH$_2$ + 1 GTP, which are converted into ATP.

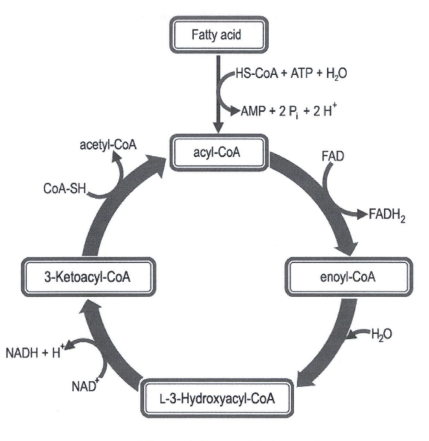

Figure 1. Beta-oxidation cycle

39. For an 18-carbon fatty acid to be completely oxidized, how many turns of the beta-oxidation cycle must be completed?

A. 1 **B. 8** **C.** 9 **D.** 18

B is correct.

To complete the oxidation of 18-carbon fatty acid, 8 rounds of beta-oxidation need to be completed because each round removes 2 carbon units.

40. How many ATP would be produced if a 12-carbon fatty acid was completely oxidized to CO_2 and H_2O?

A. 5ATP **B.** 51 ATP **C. 78 ATP** **D.** 80 ATP

C is correct.

To complete the oxidation of 12-carbon fatty acid, 5 rounds of beta-oxidation need to be completed. Each cycle produces 5 NADH, 5 $FADH_2$, and 6 acetyl-CoA. Every acetyl-CoA enters the Krebs cycle and yields 3 NADH, 1 $FADH_2$, and 1 GTP per turn. The 6 acetyl-CoA produce the total of 18 NADH, 6 $FADH_2$ and 6 GTP. Adding the products of β-oxidation and Krebs cycles yields: NADH = 18 + 5 = 23, $FADH_2$ = 5 + 6 = 11 and GTP = 6.

During oxidative phosphorylation (e.g. electron transport chain), one NADH produces 2.5 ATP and one $FADH_2$ produces 1.5 ATP. Total ATP production is (23 NADH x 2.5 ATP) + (11 $FADH_2$ x 1.5 ATP) + (6 GTP x 1 ATP) = 80 ATP. Deduct 2 ATP that are required to activate the fatty acid, which results in a total of 78 ATP.

41. Which of the following enzymes is involved in the conversion of acyl-CoA to enoyl-CoA?

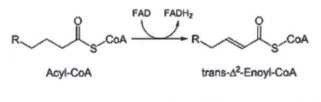

A. reductase **B. ketothiolase** **C. isomerase** **D. dehydrogenase**

D is correct.

Dehydrogenase catalyzes the formation of a trans alkene (double bond) from the alkane of the acyl-CoA thioester substrate.

A: reductase catalyzes the reduction (addition of Hs) across a double bond.

C: isomerase converts the molecule into a related structural isomer (same molecular formula but different connectivity among the atoms) by catalyzing breakage / formation of bonds during this conversion and acyl-CoA is not an isomer of acetyl-CoA.

42. The equation for one turn of the fatty acid degradation cycle is:

A. C_n-acyl-CoA + $H_2O \rightarrow$ acetyl-CoA

B. C_n-acyl-CoA $\rightarrow C_{n-2}$-acyl-CoA + acetyl-CoA

C. C_n-acyl-CoA + NAD^+ + FAD + $H_2O \rightarrow C_{n-2}$-acyl-CoA + NADH + $FADH_2$ + acetyl-CoA

D. C_n-acyl-CoA + NAD^+ + FAD + H_2O + CoA $\rightarrow C_{n-2}$-acyl-CoA + NADH + $FADH_2$ + acetyl-CoA + H^+

D is correct.

The balanced equation includes H_2O as a reactant and includes changes in NAD^+ (reduced to NADH) and FAD (reduced to $FADH_2$) redox states. The resulting acyl-CoA formed after one turn of the cycle is two carbons shorter than the original acyl-CoA.

A: the equation does not include NAD^+ and FAD as redox reactants.

B: the equation is not a balanced equation and does not include changes in the redox state of NAD^+ and FAD.

C: the equation is not balanced because reactants on the left side lack CoA and the products on the right side lack H^+.

43. Which of the following traits are shared by the reactions of beta-oxidation and fatty acid biosynthesis?

A. both biochemical pathways use or produce NADH

B. both biochemical pathways use or produce acetyl alcohol

C. both biochemical pathways occur in the mitochondrial matrix

D. both biochemical pathways use the same enzymes

B is correct.

Fatty acid biosynthesis builds fatty acids from two-carbon units of acetyl-CoA. Beta-oxidation produces acetyl-CoA by the cleavage of two-carbon units during degradation of fatty acids.

A: fatty acid biosynthesis requires NADPH as a reducing agent, while beta-oxidation produces NADH.

C: fatty acid biosynthesis takes place in the cytosol, while beta-oxidation takes place within the matrix of the mitochondria.

D: since fatty acid biosynthesis and beta-oxidation are opposing biochemical pathways, they require different enzymes to catalyze the reactions.

Questions 44 through 47 are not based on any
descriptive passage and are independent of each other

44. The deletion of nucleotides occurs during DNA replication. For mutations involving the addition or deletion of three base pairs, the protein encoded for by the mutated gene is relatively normal. A reasonable explanation for this observation is that:

    A. cellular function is not affected by most DNA mutations
    B. the size of amino acid codons often varies
    C. the original reading frame is retained after removal of three nucleotide multiples
    D. non-mutated mRNA are translated successfully by ribosome one-third of the time

C is correct.

Codons consist of three nucleotides (base pairs: A, C, G, U) located on the mRNA. The deletion of one or two nucleotides (bases) changes the reading frame along the entire mRNA and (often) results in a completely nonfunctional protein past the point of the base pair deletion. This mutation (i.e. change in nucleotides) is referred to as a frame-shift mutation because the reading frame (and corresponding amino acids incorporated into the growing polypeptide) has changed.

An addition or deletion of three base pairs, however, deletes one entire codon which codes for one amino acid of the protein. Such mutation retains the original reading frame, but results in one less amino acid in the protein. The loss of one amino acid is a subtle change compared to changing the entire reading frame of a protein. Therefore, with an alteration of 3 nucleotides (1 amino acid) the protein may fold and function normally.

45. Which sequence is the correct cycle of spermatogenesis?

    A. spermatids → spermatogonia → spermatocytes → spermatozoa
    B. spermatids → spermatogonia → spermatozoa → spermatocytes
    C. spermatogonia → spermatids → spermatozoa → spermatocytes
    D. spermatogonia → spermatocytes → spermatids → spermatozoa

D is correct.

Spermatogenesis is the process that produces gametes in males and proceeds from spermatogonia → spermatocytes → spermatids → spermatozoa.
In the testis of males, primary spermatocytes (i.e. diploid as 2n) with 46 chromosomes divide to form two secondary spermatocytes (i.e. haploid as 1n), each with 23 duplicated chromosomes.

Secondary spermatocytes divide to produce four spermatids (i.e. 1n), also with 23 daughter chromosomes.

The spermatid is a round, unflagellated cell that looks nothing like a mature vertebrae sperm. Spermatids then differentiate into spomataozoa (i.e. sperm). The process of meiosis in males produces 4 haploid cells that become sperm.

Each day, some 100 million sperm are made in each testicle, and each ejaculation releases 200 million sperm. Unused sperm are either reabsorbed or passed out of the body in urine.

46. What is the IUPAC name for the molecule shown below?

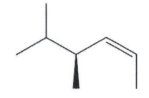

A. (S)-4,5 dimethyl-(Z)-2-hexene
B. (S)-4,5 dimethyl-(E)-2-hexene
C. (R)-4,5 dimethyl-(Z)-2-hexene
D. (R)-4,5 dimethyl-(E)-2-hexene

A is correct.

The longest possible carbon backbone contains 6 carbons and corresponds to hexene. In naming organic molecules containing double bonds, the E (i.e. *trans*) and Z (i.e. *cis*) notation is required for alkenes. R and S refer to stereospecificity according to Cahn-Inglold-Prelog priorities.

For R and S: refer to the chiral (stereogenic) center with 4 different substituents, assign priorities according to atomic number (from first point of difference). The alkene branch is labeled as (1), the isopropyl is labeled as (2), the methyl as (3) and the hydrogen (not shown and pointing into the page) as (4). Orientation is counterclockwise and thus, (S).

The molecule is (Z) because the highest priorities across the double bond (isopropyl and alkene) are on the same (*cis*) side of the double bond in the alkene.

47. Which of the following is the site for collagen polypeptide synthesis?

A. lysosome   **C.** smooth endoplasmic reticulum
B. mitochondrion   **D. rough endoplasmic reticulum**

D is correct.

Rough endoplasmic reticulum (rough ER) contains ribosomes, which serve as the site for protein synthesis.

A: lysosomes are cytoplasmic organelles involved in cellular digestion (recycle macromolecule building blocks).

B: the mitochondrion is the "powerhouse" of the cell and produces ATP during cellular respiration. The three stages of cellular respiration are: 1) glycolysis (occurs in cytoplasm), 2) Krebs (TCA) cycle (occurs in mitochondrion), and 3) electron transport chain (ETC) (occurs in intermembrane space between the inner and outer membrane of mitochondrion).

C: smooth endoplasmic reticulum (smooth ER) is responsible for cell detoxification (i.e. liver cells) and lipid synthesis.

Passage 7
(Questions 48–52)

With the advent of recombinant biology, *gene therapy* is a technique used to insert foreign genes into cells. Researchers are now able to introduce DNA into cells to treat genetic defects. One technique for gene therapy uses a small bore pipette to microinject a gene into a target cell. This technique worked in many cases but is very time consuming and requires high technical skills. Another method is electroporation whereby cells undergo electric shock to increase the permeability of the plasma membrane and DNA can enter cells. However, this procedure can destroy the cell. Alternative and highly effective gene therapy technique is when foreign genes are introduced into cells via a viral vector where foreign genes enter the cell through the mechanism of normal viral infection.

Viral genomes consist of DNA or RNA and the nucleic acid can be either single- or double-stranded. Simple RNA viruses use a mechanism where their genome is directly translated into mRNA (by the RNA *replicase* enzyme) without integration into hosts's DNA. On the other hand, when a DNA virus enters a cell, its DNA may be inserted into the host's genome via the lysogenic cycle. After integration into the host's genome, viral genes can be transcribed into mRNA and, subsequently, into proteins.

Retroviruses contain an RNA (either single- or double-stranded) genome and viral genome is transcribed into DNA by the enzyme *reverse transcriptase*. The newly synthesized DNA is then inserted into the host's genome, and viral genes can then be expressed to synthesize viral RNA and proteins. Retroviruses consist of a protein core that contains viral RNA and reverse transcriptase and are surrounded by an outer protein envelope. The RNA of a retrovirus is made up of three coding regions – *gag, pol* and *env* – which encode for core proteins, reverse transcriptase and the coat protein, respectively.

Retroviruses present a more promising gene therapy technology than simple RNA viruses or DNA viruses. A retrovirus, carrying a specific gene, enters a target cell by receptor-mediated endocytosis. Its RNA gets transcribed into DNA which then randomly integrates into the host's DNA, forming a provirus. The provirus would be copied along with the chromosomal DNA during the S phase of cell division. Retroviral vectors are constructed in a way that the therapeutic gene replaces *gag* or *env* coding region.

However, there are some practical problems associated with retroviral vector gene therapy because of the risk of random integration leading to activation of *oncogenes*. Oncogenes arise when newly integrated fragments of nucleic acids stimulate the cell to divide and increase protein production beyond desirable levels. A major limitation is that due to the randomness of the virus vector integration into the host's genome, gene expression of desired genes can't be controlled. Future research is underway to target integration of the virus vector into specific regions of the host's genome; similar to transposons in maze described by Nobel laureate Barbara McClintock. Additionally, integration can take place only in the cells that can divide.

48. To successfully integrate a retrovirus into the cell's genome, which of the following events must take place?

    A. New virions must be produced

    B. The retroviral proteins encoded by *gag*, *pol* and *env* must be translated after integration

    C. Reverse transcriptase must translate the retroviral genome

    D. The retroviral protein envelope must bind to the cell's surface receptors

D is correct.

Several events must take place for a retrovirus to successfully infect a cell and integrate into the host's genome. Foremost, the retrovirus must enter the cell which occurs when viral protein tail fibers bind to the cell's surface receptors. Then, the retroviral RNA is reverse transcribed into DNA by reverse transcriptase.

A: to produce virions the virus needs to enter a lytic cycle in which case the host cell would be destroyed. This is not the desired outcome and does not occur in successful gene therapy.

B: would not take place during gene therapy because the proteins encoded by *gag*, *pol* and *env* genes are not synthesized after integration. Since *gag* encodes for the retroviral core proteins and *env* encodes for the protein envelope, these proteins are synthesized only if the retrovirus enters a lytic cycle. *Pol* encodes for reverse transcriptase and because it is necessary for integration, it must be synthesized before integration into host's DNA.

C: translation (mRNA → protein) is different from transcription (DNA → mRNA). Transcription is the process of synthesizing genetic information from nucleic acids – DNA or RNA are converted to another form of nucleic acids (e.g. DNA to RNA per the central dogma of molecular biology, or retrovirus RNA to DNA via reverse transcriptase as reverse transcription)

49. All of these cells would be good targets for retroviral gene therapy EXCEPT?

    A. hepatocytes

    B. neuronal cells

    C. bone marrow cells

    D. epidermal cells

B is correct.

Neuronal cells are not good targets for retroviral gene therapy because they do not divide and the therapeutic gene cannot integrate. A retrovirus integrates its DNA reverse-transcribed from RNA into host's DNA during host cell replication. Therefore, cells that do not undergo division are not able to integrate reverse-transcribed viral DNA into their chromosomes. Of the four cell types in the answer choices, only nerve cells remain in G_O and cannot divide.

A: hepatocyte is a liver cell. Liver cells are productive targets for retroviral gene therapy because they continuously divide and the therapeutic gene would be replicated along with the host's DNA during division. After cell replication, each daughter cell inherits the integrated therapeutic gene in its DNA for expression of the therapeutic protein.

C: bone marrow cells are good targets for retroviral vector gene therapy. While the procedure would require the removal of bone marrow cells from the body to infect them, they can be placed back into the body. Furthermore, these cells divide and give rise to important blood cells (red blood cells, white blood cells and platelets) and therefore are a good cell type for gene replacement therapy. Clinically, bone marrow replacement procedures are used to treat lymphomas.

D: while the top layer of the skin consists of the epithelial skin cells which are are dead and are continually sloughed from the surface of the epidermis, they are replaced through cell division by living precursor skin cells. Only these precursor cells could be successfully infected by a retrovirus because they undergo cell division. Once the retrovirus infects this cell, the therapeutic gene would be inherited by daughter cells.

50. From in vitro gene therapy experiments, retroviral delivery system is preferred over physical techniques (i.e. microinjection or electroporation) of introducing therapeutic genes into cells. Which of the following statements is the most likely explanation for this?

    A. Retroviral gene delivery allows more control over the site of integration
    B. Retroviral gene delivery results in more cells that integrate the new gene successfully
    C. Retroviral gene delivery is less damaging to the cells and less labor-intensive
    D. Retroviral gene delivery permits the insertion of therapeutic genes into all cell types

C is correct.

Microinjection is very time consuming and requires a high level of technical skills while electroporation is traumatic to the cells. These drawbacks do not apply to retroviral gene delivery because it occurs through a regular viral infection mechanism (receptor-mediated endocytosis). Inducing a retroviral infection simply involves mixing the virus with the cells to be infected. This technique does not harm the cells' integrity during the infection and the virus integrates in the host's genome and enters a lysogenic (not lytic where virions are produced) cycle.

A: the site of gene integration cannot be predetermined in retroviral vector delivery because, from the passage, the retroviral DNA integrates into the host's DNA randomly.

B: the passage contains no evidence that a retroviral gene delivery results in a greater number of cells to integrate the therapeutic gene as compared to electroporation or microinjection. In fact, as far as integration ratio numbers, microinjection is the most efficient method of gene therapy.

D: not all cell types are suitable for retroviral gene therapy because provirus integration takes place during DNA replication. Therefore, cells that do not divide cannot be treated by retroviral gene therapy.

51. Simple RNA viruses are not suitable for gene therapy vectors because:

A. therapeutic gene introduced within a viral RNA cannot be replicated
B. RNA genome becomes unstable due to an insertion of a therapeutic gene
C. their genome size is not sufficient to carry a therapeutic gene
D. only specific cell types can be infected by simple RNA viruses

A is correct.

Simple RNA viruses are not optimal for gene therapy vectors while retroviruses make good vectors. The reason for this is related to the cellular mechanism of retroviruses.

If simple RNA viruses were used as the viral vector for a therapeutic gene, the cell's DNA genome would not express the genes contained in the virus. DNA integration is a necessary step of successful gene therapy and can take place only if the foreign gene is reverse transcribed into DNA. Since DNA integration cannot occur for simple RNA viruses, the viral RNA (containing the therapeutic gene) gets degraded by the cell. By contrast, the retrovirus has an RNA genome that is not directly transcribed into messenger RNA, but instead is reverse transcribed into a DNA.

B: the passage contains no evidence that incorporation of a therapeutic gene into an RNA genome makes it unstable for being used as a vector. Opposite to that, the passage states that all viruses can contain therapeutic genes but retroviruses, due to other reasons, are the best vectors.

C: the passage contains no evidence that simple RNA viruses have smaller genomes than DNA viruses or retroviruses and cannot carry a therapeutic gene.

D: certain viruses are able to infect only specific cell types – this is known as host specificity. Host specificity applies to all viruses, not only simple RNA viruses; therefore this cannot be the reason why simple RNA viruses are a poor choice for gene therapy.

52. Following an integration of a therapeutic gene into a cell's DNA, the retroviral DNA:

    A. causes nondisjunction to correct the genetic defect
    B. is deemed "foreign" by the host's immune system and degraded
    C. replicates and produces infectious virions
    D. remains in the cell in a noninfectious form

D is correct.

The purpose of successful viral gene therapy is to introduce a therapeutic gene into a genetically defective cell and have the cell produce desired protein without causing an infection. Therefore, the retroviral DNA must remain in the host's DNA in a noninfectious form.

A: nondisjunction is a failure of either sister chromatids (during mitosis) or homologous chromosomes (during meiosis) to properly separate during anaphase. Nondisjunction during mitosis or meiosis results in some daughter cells inheriting multiple copies of one chromosome while others lack the chromosome completely. In either case, it is not desirable and often is lethal. Therefore, it is unlikely for a therapeutic gene to cause nondisjunction. Additionally, nondisjunction would not correct a genetic defect.

B: the host's immune system is not able to recognize the retroviral DNA as foreign because it integrates into the host cell's genome along with the therapeutic gene.

C: to produce infectious virions, the virus must enter a lytic cycle and destroy the host cell. This is not the desired outcome and does not occur in successful gene therapy.

> Questions 53 through 59 are not based on any
> descriptive passage and are independent of each other

53. Incomplete proteins lack one or more:

A. essential amino acids

C. sulfur-containing amino acids

B. nonpolar amino acids

D. polar amino acids

A is correct.

A complete protein is a protein that contains all nine essential amino acids. Complete proteins come from animal products (meat, poultry, dairy, eggs, fish etc.), soy and quinoa (a grain). Incomplete proteins contain fewer than all nine essential amino acids and come from plant-based foods (beans, rice, grains, vegetables and legumes other than soy). In diet, incomplete proteins can be combined in meals to make a complete protein. Incomplete proteins don't need to be consumed at the same time in order to be used by the body to build protein but may be consumed within 24 hour period.

54. Which statement regarding the number of initiation and STOP codons is correct?

A. There are multiple initiation codons, but a single STOP codon

B. There are two STOP codons and four initiation codons

C. There is a single STOP codon and single initiation codon

D. There are multiple STOP codons, but a single initiation codon

D is correct.

55. How many carbon atoms are in a molecule of stearic acid?

A. 12   **B.** 14   **C.** 16   **D. 18**

D is correct.

Stearic acid is a waxy solid 18-carbon chain saturated fatty acid (IUPAC: octadecanoic acid) with the molecular formula $CH_3(CH_2)_{16}CO_2H$. The salts and esters of stearic acid are called stearates. Stearic acid is one of the most common saturated fatty acids found in nature following palmitic acid.

56. Fatty acids that mammals must obtain from nutrition are:

A. essential

C. dietary

B. saturated

D. esters

A is correct.

Essential fatty acids (EFAs) are fatty acids required for biological processes but do not include the fats that only act as fuel. Humans and other animals cannot synthesize them and therefore these fatty acids must be ingested with food because they are required by the body. Only two fatty acids are known to be essential for humans: alpha-linolenic acid (omega-3) and linoleic acid (omega-6). Some other fatty acids are sometimes considered *conditionally essential*, meaning that they may become essential under some physiological conditions.

57. What type of amino acid is phenylalanine?

   A. Basic   **B.** Acidic   **C.** Polar   **D. Hydrophobic aromatic**

D is correct.

Phenylalanine is a precursor for tyrosine. It also is a precursor for the monoamine signaling molecules epinephrine (adrenaline), norepinephrine (noradrenaline) and dopamine along with melanin (skin pigment).

58. The simplest lipids that can also be either a part of or a source of many complex lipids are:

   A. Fatty acids   **B.** Terpenes   **C.** Waxes   **D.** Triglycerols

A is correct.

59. What type of macromolecule is a saccharide?

   A. protein   **B.** nucleic acid   **C. carbohydrate**   **D.** lipid

C is correct.

The carbohydrates (i.e. saccharides) are divided into four groups: monosaccharides, disaccharides, oligosaccharides and polysaccharides. Monosaccharides and disaccharides are smaller (i.e. lower molecular weight) and are generally referred to as sugars.

BIOLOGICAL & BIOCHEMICAL FOUNDATIONS OF LIVING SYSTEMS
MCAT® PRACTICE TEST #3: ANSWER KEY

Passage 1
1 : A
2 : D
3 : C
4 : D
5 : C
6 : B

Passage 2
7 : D
8 : A
9 : A
10 : C
11 : B

Independent questions
12 : C
13 : A
14 : A
15 : C

Passage 3
16 : D
17 : A
18 : C
19 : B
20 : D
21 : A
22 : C

Passage 4
23 : D
24 : C
25 : B
26 : D
27 : A
28 : D

Independent questions
29 : B
30 : C
31 : B
32 : B
33 : A

Passage 5
34 : A
35 : B
36 : C
37 : C
38 : B
39 : B

Passage 6
40 : D
41 : C
42 : B
43 : D

Independent questions
44 : A
45 : A
46 : A
47 : D

Passage 7
48 : A
49 : C
50 : A
51 : B
52 : D

Independent questions
53 : C
54 : A
55 : B
56 : C
57 : C
58 : A
59 : C

Passage 1
(Questions 1–6)

Aerobic respiration is the major process that provides cellular energy for oxygen requiring organisms. During cellular respiration, glucose is metabolized to generate chemical energy in the form of ATP:

$$C_6H_{12}O_6 + 6O_2 \rightarrow 6CO_2 + 6H_2O + 36 \text{ ATP}$$

Mitochondrion is the biochemical machinery within the cell utilized for cellular respiration. Mitochondria are present in the cytoplasm of most eukaryotic cells. The number of mitochondria per cell varies depending on tissue type and individual cell function.

Mitochondria have their own genome independent from the cell's genetic material. However, mitochondrial replication depends upon nuclear DNA to encode essential proteins required for replication of mitochondria. Mitochondria replicate randomly and independently of cell cycle.

The mitochondrial separate genome and the ribosomes of the protein synthesizing machinery became the foundation for the endosymbiotic theory. Endosymbiotic theory proposes that mitochondria originated as a separate prokaryotic organism that was engulfed by a larger anaerobic eukaryotic cell millions of years ago. The two cells formed a symbiotic relationship and eventually became dependent on each other. The eukaryotic cell sustained the bacterium, while the bacterium provided additional energy for the cell. Gradually the two cells evolved into the present-day eukaryotic cell, with the mitochondrion retaining some of its own DNA. Mitochondrial DNA is inherited in a non-Mendelian fashion because mitochondria, like other organelles, are inherited from the maternal gamete that supplies the cytoplasm to the fertilized egg. The study of individual mitochondria is used to investigate evolutionary relationships among different organisms.

1. Which of the following statements distinguishes the mitochondrial genome from the nuclear genome?

  A. most mitochondrial DNA nucleotides encode for protein
  B. specific mitochondrial DNA mutations are lethal
  C. mitochondrial DNA is a double helix structure
  D. some mitochondrial genes encode for tRNA

A is correct.

The nuclear genome is comprised of double helix DNA that encodes for mRNA, tRNA and rRNA. The mitochondrial genome is small compared to the size of the nuclear genome. Almost every nitrogen base of mitochondrial genome encodes for a protein and, like bacterial genomes, does not contain noncoding regions. Bacteria, mitochondria and chloroplasts do not have noncoding sequences because they lack introns within the transcribed mRNA molecule. Coding / noncoding refer to bases on the DNA nucleotide strand while exon / intron refer to bases on the RNA nucleotide strand. Three nucleotides on the mRNA strand are referred to as a codon. Anticodons correspond to the codons and are located on the tRNA.

B: nuclear genome mutations can render a necessary characteristic of the nuclear genome ineffective. Although nuclear genome encodes for many products, most of the bases of DNA are noncoding because these nucleotides regulate gene expression and do not directly encode for protein. Mitochondria are vital to cell function and their replication is highly accurate. Mutations that change the mitochondrial DNA affect dramatically a cell's ability to produce proteins needed for ATP production and would be lethal to the cell. Therefore, statement B is true, but it doesn't distinguishes mitochondrial genome from the nuclear genome.

C: mitochondrial DNA is a double helix, but this does not answer the question.

D: is false and describes the nuclear, not mitochondrial, genome.

2. In which phases of the eukaryotic cell cycle does mitochondrial DNA replicate?

I. G_1 II. S   III. G_2 IV. M

A. I only   **B.** II only   **C.** II & IV only   **D. I, II, III & IV**

D is correct.

From the passage, mitochondria replicate randomly and independently of the phase of the cell cycle and from other mitochondria. Mitochondrial DNA must replicate prior to the mitochondria dividing into daughter mitochondria. It is inferred that mitochondrial DNA replicates throughout the cell cycles: G_1, S, G_2, and M.

During G_1, the cell undergoes intense biochemical activity associated with cell growth. During S (synthesis), the nuclear DNA replicates. During G_2, other organelles replicate, nuclear DNA condenses and structures used during mitosis (e.g. spindle fibers) begin to assemble.

During M (mitotic), mitosis occurs where nuclear envelope disintegrates, spindle fibers assemble, condensed DNA segregates to opposite poles of the cell, replicated organelles (e.g. mitochondria and others) also are partitioned within the cell, and the cell divides (cytokinesis) forming two identical daughter cells.

3. A wild-type strain of cyanobacteria (algae) is crossed with the opposite mating type of a mutant strain of cyanobacteria. All mitochondrial functions of the mutant strain are lost because of deletions within mitochondrial genome and all progeny also lack mitochondrial functions. From the passage, which of the following best explains this observation?

  A. presence of genetic material in mitochondria distinct from nuclear DNA
  B. recombination of mitochondrial DNA during organelle replication
  C. non-Mendelian inheritance of mitochondrial DNA
  D. endosymbiotic hypothesis

C is correct.

Mating type is analogous to male and female for species that do not have opposite genders (e.g. algae and yeast). The progeny lack functional mitochondria because offspring have the deleted mitochondrial genome like the parental mutant strain. Precisely, the mutant strain must have been the organelle-donating parent (e.g. female). Therefore, the non-Mendelian inheritance pattern of mitochondrial DNA best explains the result of the experiment. If the wild-type strain had been the organelle-donating parent, all progeny would have wild-type mitochondrial function.

The endosymbiotic theory explains the origin of mitochondria in eukaryotic cells but not the pattern of mitochondrial inheritance.

A: is a correct statement, but does not explain the inheritance patterns observed in this cross.

B: the term recombination indicates the formation of new gene combinations from crossing over during reproduction (e.g. prophase I of meiosis in eukaryotes). If recombination occurred, some of offspring would regain mitochondrial functions because wild-type mitochondrial DNA would replace the deleted segments of DNA.

4. Four human cell cultures (colon cells, epidermal cells, erythrocytes and skeletal muscle cells) were grown in a radioactive adenine medium. After several days of growth, centrifugation was used to isolate the mitochondria. The radioactivity level of the mitochondria was measured by a liquid scintillation counter. Which of the following cell types would have the highest level of radioactivity?

  A. colon cells   **C.** erythrocytes
  B. epidermal cells   **D. skeletal muscle cells**

D is correct.

During DNA replication, cells incorporate radioactive adenine. Since all autosomal human cells have the same amount of nuclear DNA, the difference in radioactivity is related to mitochondrial DNA. Cells with the largest number of mitochondria have the highest radioactive count. The cell type with the greatest number of mitochondria depends on the energy needs of the tissue. Skeletal muscle cell is the correct choice because muscle cells have high energy demands needed for contraction.

A and B: the epidermal (deep skin) and colon (large intestine) cells do not have any special energy requirements.

C: the erythrocytes (red blood cells) are enucleated (without nucleus) and do not contain any mitochondria. If red blood cells were metabolically active, it would consume a portion of the O_2 it carries to tissue.

5. Which of the following facts does NOT support the endosymbiotic theory?

    A. mitochondrial DNA is circular and not enclosed by a nuclear membrane

    B. mitochondrial DNA encodes for its own ribosomal RNA

    C. mitochondrial ribosomes resemble eukaryotic ribosomes more than prokaryotic ribosomes

    D. many present day bacteria live within eukaryotic cells and digest nutrients within the hosts

C is correct.

The endosymbiotic theory originated from the hypothesis that mitochondrion was once an independent unicellular organism, prokaryotic in origin, which formed a symbiotic relationship within a eukaryotic cell that was mutually beneficial. If mitochondria were prokaryotic in origin, then similarities between mitochondria and bacteria support the hypothesis.

The statement that mitochondrial ribosomes resemble eukaryotic ribosomes more than prokaryotic ribosomes is false. If true, this fact would not support the endosymbiotic theory. Mitochondrial ribosomes do resemble prokaryotic ribosomes, thereby providing further support for the endosymbiotic hypothesis.

A: mitochondrial DNA is circular and not enclosed by a nuclear membrane. Bacteria have a single circular (like mitochondria) chromosome located in a cytoplasmic region of the prokaryotic cell known as the nucleoid. The nucleoid region is not enclosed by a membrane. These observations are correct and support the endosymbiotic hypothesis.

B: the fact that mitochondrial DNA encodes for its own ribosomal RNA, provides evidence that mitochondria may have existed as independent cells, capable of directing their own protein synthesis and cell division. These processes of protein synthesis and replication are cellular activities associated with independently living organisms.

D: the fact that many present day bacteria live within eukaryotic cells, digesting nutrients within their hosts, supports the endosymbiotic theory. If many present day bacteria have symbiotic relationships within eukaryotic cells, this supports the hypothesis that the mitochondrial ancestor may have lived within an ancestral eukaryotic cell in a mutualistic relationship.

6. Experimental data shows that mitochondrial DNA of humans mutates at a relatively low frequency. Due to mitochondria having an important role in the cell, these mutations are most likely:

    A. nondisjunctions
    B. point mutations
    C. frameshift mutations
    D. lethal mutations

B is correct.

Mitochondria supply the cell with energy in the form of ATP. Mitochondrial DNA produces mitochondrial proteins essential for cell survival. Mitochondria are vital to eukaryotic cell and replication of mitochondrial DNA is very accurate. Mutations that cause a dramatic change in the mitochondrial DNA and its ability to produce proteins needed for ATP production would be lethal to the cell.

Since some mutations do occur, the most likely type of mutation would be the type that causes the least damage. A point mutation is a single change of a nitrogenous base. For example, a cytosine is substituted for an adenine during replication. Point mutations are not usually lethal because of the redundancy of the genetic code. Redundancy means that most amino acids are coded for by more than one codon. For example, glycine is coded for by codons: GGU, GGC, GGA, and GGG. If the codon GGU undergoes a point mutation at the third base then any of the three remaining bases (C, A, G) is substituted for U (uracil), the amino acid product is still glycine. Therefore, point mutations are least likely to affect the cell function.

A: nondisjunction is the failure of homologous chromosomes, during meiosis, to separate. Only specialized eukaryotic cells (e.g. gametes) in sexually reproducing organisms undergo meiosis to produce egg or sperm. Mitochondria are not gametes and therefore do not undergo meiosis.

C: a frameshift mutation causes bases to be either inserted or deleted during DNA replication (or during transcription). Frameshift mutations shift the reading frame of the mRNA strand being translated, usually forming non functional polypeptides. Changes in protein synthesis would most likely be dangerous for the mitochondria and the cell itself.

D: lethal mutations cause the mitochondria to become nonfunctional.

Passage 2
(Questions 7–11)

Protons adjacent to a carbonyl functional group are referred to as α and are significantly more acidic than protons adjacent to carbon atoms within the hydrocarbon chain. The increased acidity characteristic for α hydrogens results from the electron withdrawing effect of the neighboring carbon-oxygen double bond. In addition, the resulting anion is stabilized by resonance shown below:

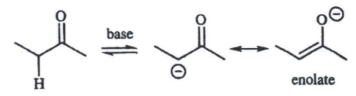

A reaction of the enolate anion with an alkyl halide or carbonyl compound forms a carbon-carbon bond at the α position. Condensation of an enolate with an aldehyde or ketone forms an unstable alcohol which is a reaction intermediate and not an isolated product. The intermediate spontaneously reacts, via dehydration, to form an α,β-unsaturated compound.

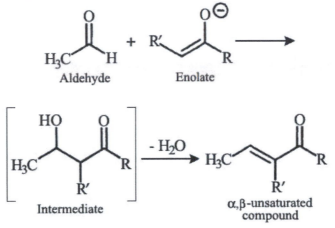

7. Which of the following ketones would NOT react with the strong base LDA?

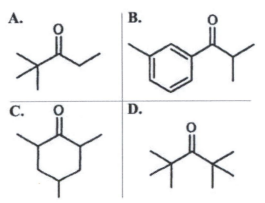

D is correct. Ketone D has no α protons to react with LDA.

8. Which one of the following compounds would be the intermediate alcohol from the condensation reactions shown below?

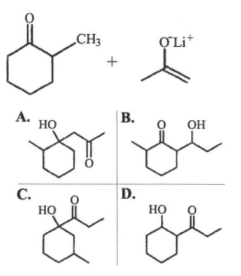

A.   B.

C.   D.

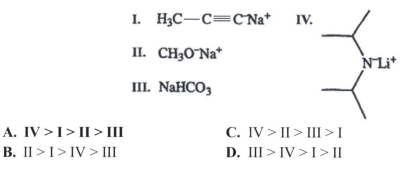

A is correct.

Attack of the enolate of 2-propanone occurs at the carbonyl carbon of 2-methylcyclohexanone and yields a tertiary alcohol adjacent to the methyl group on the ring.

9. What is the order of decreasing basicity for the following reagents?

I. $H_3C-C\equiv C^-Na^+$ IV.

II. $CH_3O^-Na^+$

III. $NaHCO_3$

A. IV > I > II > III   C. IV > II > III > I
B. II > I > IV > III   D. III > IV > I > II

A is correct.

The more stable the negatively-charged anion, the less basic is the molecule.

Resonance stabilization or powerful electron withdrawing groups decrease basicity. The only anion fitting such criteria is HCO_3^-, which has resonance structures.

10. Which carbonyl compounds has the most acidic proton?

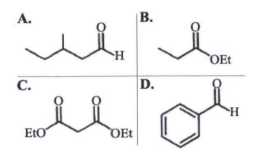

C is correct.

The α protons between two carbonyl groups would be most acidic.

B: does not have any α protons.

C and D: have about the same acidity, but far less acidity than the correct choice.

11. Which set of the following reactants would result in the formation of ethyl-2-hexanoate?

A. step 1: propanol, ethyl acetate & LDA; step 2: H^+
B. step 1: butanal, ethyl acetate & LDA; step 2: H^+
C. step 1: pentanal, ethyl acetate & LDA; step 2: H^+
D. step 1: hexanal, ethyl acetate & LDA; step 2: H^+

B is correct.

Ethyl-2-hexanoate contains eight carbons. All answer choices have the same functional groups but differ in chain length of the parent molecule. Ethyl acetate contains four carbons, so butanal (aldehyde with a four carbon chain) must be the correct answer. LDA is a strong base that abstracts α protons in this reaction.

Ethyl acetate   Butanal

Ethyl-2-hexanoate

> Questions 12 through 15 are not based on any
> descriptive passage and are independent of each other

12. In the graph below, the solid line represents the reaction profile $A + B \rightarrow C + D$ in the absence of a catalyst. Which dotted lines best represents the reaction profile in the presence of a catalyst?

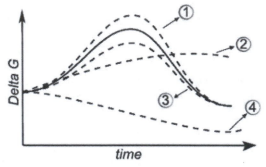

A. 1   C. 3
B. 2   D. 4

C is correct.

Catalysts are typically enzymes (i.e. proteins) that increase the rate of reaction by lowering the energy of activation. The activation energy is the energy required by the reactants to form product. Catalysts are neither altered nor consumed during the reaction. Furthermore, catalysts have no effect on the reactant's initial potential energy or the product's potential energy. Catalysts do not change the delta G of a reaction.

In the graph, the solid curve represents the reaction rate without a catalyst. In the presence of a catalyst, the dotted line must begin (reactant) and end (products) at the same points as the solid line. Since the activation energy of the uncatalyzed reaction (solid line) corresponds to the potential energy of reactant and the potential energy is highest at the peak, the activation energy of the catalyzed reaction would be lower. In the catalyzed reaction, the difference between the highest potential energy and the initial potential energy is smaller.

13. How would the beta-oxidation cycle be effected by depleting oxygen of the cell?

A. NADH and FADH$_2$ accumulate and the cycle slows
B. Krebs cycle replaces beta-oxidation
C. CoA availability decreases
D. beta-oxidation accelerates to satisfy energy needs

A is correct.

Acetyl-CoA is the initial molecule entering the Krebs cycle. With O_2 depletion, the electron transport chain is inhibited and acetyl-CoA accumulates as each turn of the cycle produces additional NADH and FADH$_2$. NADH and FADH$_2$ are high-energy intermediates used by the electron transport chain for oxidative phosphorylation of ATP. Without entry into the electron transport chain, NADH and FADH$_2$ products accumulate and slow the beta-oxidation cycle.

14. Rank the C–O bond length from shortest to longest for the following compounds:

A. $CO < CO_2 < CO_3^{2-}$ **C.** $CO_3^{2-} < CO < CO_2$

B. $CO < CO_3^{2-} < CO_2$ **D.** $CO_3^{2-} < CO_2 < CO$

A is correct.

Bond length depends on the hybrid orbitals forming the bond. The sp hybridized orbitals form shorter bonds than sp^2 orbitals because sp hybridization contains more s character. The sp^2 hybridized orbitals form shorter bonds than sp^3 orbitals because sp^2 hybridization contains more s character.

Therefore, CO and CO_2 have shorter bond lengths than CO_3^{2-}, since their carbon atom is sp hybridized, while the carbon in CO_3^{2-} is sp^2 hybridized. CO has a shorter bond length than CO_2, since oxygen orbitals are sp hybridized with one σ and two π bonds towards the single O. The hybridized orbital in CO_2 is sp with one σ and one π bond towards each O.

15. Which of the following properties distinguish fungal and animal cells from bacterial cells?

    I.   presence of cell walls   III. asexual reproduction

    II. presence of ribosomes   **IV. presence of membrane bound organelles**

  A. I & II only   **B.** III & IV only   **C. IV only**   **D.** I, II & IV only

C is correct.

All animal and plant cells are eukaryotic. Bacterial cells are prokaryotic. Although fungi have their own kingdom, they were originally classified in the plant kingdom. Fungal cells are eukaryotic and heterotrophic (uses organic substances to derive chemical energy) organisms of a variety of shapes and sizes. Fungi can be either multicellular (e.g. mushrooms) or unicellular (e.g. yeast). Like plant cells, fungi have cell walls and other membrane bound organelles present within eukaryotic cells.

I: bacteria have cell walls (i.e. peptidoglycan) different in structure from plant (cellulose) and fungal (glucosamine polymer such as chitin) cell walls. However, the plasma membrane of animal cells is not enclosed by a cell wall.

II: both animal cells and fungal cells are eukaryotic and have ribosomes. Ribosomes are organelles responsible for translation: conversion of mRNA (nucleotides) into protein (amino acids). Bacteria also use ribosomes to synthesize proteins. Note, prokaryotic ribosomes (30S small subunit; 50S large subunit and 70S complete unit) are structurally different from eukaryotic ribosomes (40S small subunit; 60S large subunit and 80S complete unit). However, ribosomes are common to both cell types.

III: animals reproduce sexually while the primary method of reproduction in fungi is asexual (via spores). Bacteria reproduce asexually (via binary fission). Therefore, asexual reproduction is not a common characteristic of animal and fungal cells and can be eliminated as an answer choice. The only property characteristic to animal and fungal cells that is not found in bacterial cells is the presence of membrane bound organelles.

Passage 3
(Questions 16–22)

Viruses are classified into two major groups: DNA viruses and RNA viruses. Herpes simplex virus type 1 (HSV-1) infection, also known as Human Herpes Virus 1 (HHV-1) is almost universal among humans.

HSV-1 infects humans and hides in the nervous system via retrograde movement through afferent sensory nerve fibers. During latency period, the nervous system functions as a viral reservoir from which infection can recur and this accounts for virus's durability in a human body. Reactivation of the virus is usually expressed by watery blisters commonly known as cold sores or fever blisters. During this phase, viral replication and shedding occur as the most common way of herpes simplex transmission.

Following initial contact, production of the herpes virus growth mediators takes place. Viral growth factors bind axon terminal receptors and are related to tumor necrosis factors.

The structure of herpes viruses consists of a relatively large double-stranded, linear DNA genome encased within an icosahedral protein cage called the capsid, which is wrapped in a lipid bilayer called the envelope. The envelope is joined to the capsid by means of a tegument. This complete particle is known as the virion. Replication and assembly of the virus takes place via nuclear machinery.

HSV-1 infection is productive if the cell is permissive to the virus and allows viral replication and virion release. HSV-1 cell infection is often not productive due to a viral genome integration block that occurs upstream. However, stimulation of an infected cell will eliminate this block and allow for virion production. Abortive infection results when cells are non-permissive. In this case restrictive attacks occur when a few virion particles are produced. Viral production then ceases, but the genome integration persists.

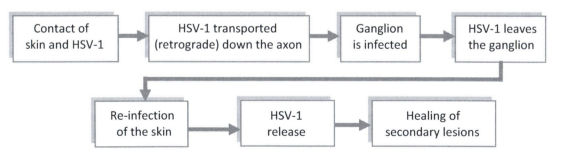

Figure 1. Steps of HSV-1 infection

16. Where in the nervous system will the latent virus of herpes simplex be localized?

A. neurotransmitter

C. lower motor neuron dendrites

B. axon hillock

D. afferent nervous system ganglion

D is correct.

Figure 1 of the passage describes the steps of HSV infection. It indicates that, immediately before re-infecting the skin, the virus leaves a ganglion (collection of neuron cells bodies) to return to the surface of the skin. Therefore, latent HSV virus must be localized there.

17. The spreading of HSV-1 virus occurs during shedding by direct contact with the lesion. Which of the following locations is the source for the virus to acquire its glycoprotein-covered envelope?

A. nuclear membrane after transcription

C. outer cell wall during lysis

B. storage vacuoles during lysis

D. rough ER during protein synthesis

A is correct.

Most viruses acquire their envelopes from the plasma membrane, which isn't an answer choice.

The second logical answer would be a nuclear membrane since the passage states that the viral assembly takes place in the nucleus.

C: can be eliminated because human cells lack a cell wall.

18. Which infection type results in the integration of the viral genome into the host cell chromosome?

I. restrictive　　　　**II. productive**　　　　III. abortive

A. I only　　　**B.** II only　　　**C. I & II only**　　　**D.** I, II & III

C is correct.

From the passage, productive infection is the type of infection when the cell is permissive to the virus and allows for viral integration, replication and virion release. During restrictive attacks viral production ceases, but the genome integration still persists.

Abortive infection occurs when cells are non-permissive and don't allow the viral genome to integrate into the host cell's chromosome.

19. If the infectivity/particle ratio of picornaviruses is about 0.1%, what is the number of infectious particles present in a culture of 25,000 virions?

A. 5　　　**B. 25**　　　**C.** 250　　　　**D.** 2500

B is correct.

0.1% of 25,000 is 25.

Picornavirus is non-enveloped, positive-stranded RNA virus with an icosahedral capsid. The genome RNA is unusual because it has a protein on the 5' end that is used as a primer for transcription by RNA polymerase. The name is derived from "pico" meaning "small", so "picornavirus" literally means "small RNA virus."

20. Which of the following statements is NOT the cause of the abortive viral cycle?

A. infected esophagus cells lack DNA replication machinery
B. hepatitis C patients lack the majority of viral liver cell receptors
C. host autoimmune antibodies bind to the viral antigen and prevent infection
D. **random mutations of influenza virus plasma membrane antigens causes genetic drift**

D is correct.

From the passage, abortive viral infection results from non-permissive cells where no virion particles are produced. The host does not present symptoms of infection. Viruses, bacteria and fungi are infecting organisms that possess antigens (e.g. surface markers) that are detected by the host's immune system. When the influenza virus undergoes rapid random mutation, its ability to cause an infection (i.e. virulence) increases because the immune system has difficulty detecting rapidly changing surface markers and therefore the infection is productive and not abortive.

All other statements are characteristic of abortive infection.

A: esophagus cells that lack DNA replication machinery cannot replicate and therefore are unable to produce new virions.

B: viral particles of hepatitis C are not able to bind to liver tissue cells which lack cell surface receptors.

C: viral surface markers (antigens) that match the host's antibodies will be detected and suppressed by the immune system.

21. Where will radioactive tegument dye be localized?

A. **protein-filled area between capsid and envelope**
B. protein-filled area between envelope and extracellular glycoprotein
C. protein-filled area between DNA core and nucleosome
D. protein-filled area between capsid and DNA core

A is correct.

From the passage, the envelope is joined to the capsid by means of a tegument (viral matrix) which is a protein-filled area. Therefore, radioactive tegument dye would adhere to that area between the capsid and the envelope.

22. From the information provided in the passage, which statement must be true for tumor necrosis factors (TNF)?

    A. TNF are taken up by dendrites and transported toward the neuron cell body

    B. TNF are produced following a malignant cancerous spread through the basement membrane

    C. TNF uptake and transport are inhibited following an injury to the axon terminal

    D. TNF function with nerve growth factors to stimulate voltage gated Na^+ channels

C is correct.

According to passage, tumor necrosis factors (TNF) are similar to viral growth factors, which bind the axon terminal receptors, so it can be assumed that tumor necrosis factors also bind axon terminal receptors. Therefore, axon terminal injury will prevent TNF transport.

Tumor necrosis factors refers to a group of cytokines family that can cause cell death. In 1975 a protein responsible for this process was identified and called tumor necrosis factor alpha – TNF-alpha (TNF-α is the most well-known member of this class, and sometimes referred to when the term "tumor necrosis factor" is used; TNF-β is a cytokine that is induced by interleukin 10).

TNF acts via the TNF Receptor (TNF-R) and is part of the extrinsic pathway for triggering apoptosis. TNF-R is associated with procaspases through adapter proteins that can cleave other inactive procaspases and trigger the caspase cascade, irreversibly leading the cell to apoptosis (programmed cell death).

TNF interact with tumor cells to trigger cytolysis or cell death. TNF also interact with receptors on endothelial cells, which leads to increased vascular permeability allowing for leukocytes to access the site of infection – localized inflammatory response.

Passage 4
(Questions 23–28)

Translation is the mechanism of protein synthesis. Proteins are synthesized on ribosomes that are either free in the cytoplasm or bound to the rough endoplasmic reticulum (rough ER). The *signal hypothesis* states that about 8 initial amino acids (known as a leader sequence) are joined initially to the growing polypeptide. In the absence of a leader sequence, the ribosomes remain free in the cytosol. If the leader sequence is present, translation of the nascent polypeptide pauses and the ribosomes, along with the attached mRNA, migrate and attach to the ER.

Proteins used for transport to organelles, the plasma membrane, or to be secreted from the cell have *N-terminus signal peptide* of about 8 amino acids which are responsible for the insertion of the nascent polypeptide through the membrane of the ER. After the leading end of the polypeptide is inserted into the lumen of the ER, the leader sequence (i.e. signal peptide) is cleaved by an enzyme within the ER lumen.

With the aid of chaperone proteins in the endoplasmic reticulum, proteins produced for the secretory pathway are folded into tertiary and quaternary structures. Those that are folded properly are packaged into transport vesicles that bud from the membrane of the ER via endocytosis. This packaging into a vesicle requires a region on the polypeptide that is recognized by a receptor of the Golgi membrane. The receptor-protein complex binds to the vesicle and then brings it to its destination where it fuses to the cis face (closest to the ER) of the Golgi apparatus.

A pathway of vesicular transport from the Golgi involves lysosomal enzymes that carry a unique mannose-6-phosphate (M6P) marker that was added in the Golgi. The marker is recognized by specific M6P-receptor proteins that concentrate the polypeptide within a region of the Golgi membrane. This isolations of the M6P-receptor proteins facilitates their packaging into secretory vesicle and after vesicle buds from the Golgi membrane, it moves to the lysosome and fuses with the lysosomal membrane. Because of the low pH of the lysosome, the M6P-receptor releases its bound protein. The lysosomal high H^+ concentration also produces the conformation change of the lysosomal enzymes.

23. The lumen of the endoplasmic reticulum most closely corresponds to:

A. cytoplasm   C. intermembrane space of the mitochondria
B. ribosome   **D. extracellular environment**

D is correct.

The interior of endoplasmic reticulum (the ER lumen) is similar to the interior of the Golgi. The interior of secretory vesicles is similar to the interior of the transport vesicles (proteins from ER to Golgi). The Golgi and the extracellular environment are similar because the contents of the ER are transported via secretory vesicles to the Golgi, an organelle or to the extracellular space (e.g. peptide hormones).

A: cytoplasm is the gel-like substance (70-90% water) within the cell membrane that holds all the cell's organelles outside the nucleus. All the contents of prokaryotic cells are contained within the cytoplasm, while in eukaryotes the nucleus is separated from the cytoplasm. Most cellular activities (including glycolysis and processes of cell division) occur within the cytoplasm. The inner granular mass is called the *endoplasm* and the outer clear layer is the cell cortex or the *ectoplasm*.

B: ribosome is a large complex molecular machinery, found in all living cells, that serves as the primary site of protein synthesis – translation. It is made from complexes of RNAs and proteins (making it a *ribonucleoprotein*) and is divided into two subunits: the smaller subunit binds to the mRNA pattern, the larger subunit binds to the tRNA and the amino acids.

C: the intermembrane space of the mitochondria is used for the electron transport chain in cellular respiration; it has a low pH due to the high concentration of H^+ which create the proton motive force as the protons pass through the ATPase to synthesize ATP via oxidative phosphorylation during the last stage of cellular respiration.

24. If a protein destined to become a lysosomal enzyme was synthesized lacking a signal peptide, where in the cell is the enzyme targeted?

A. Golgi apparatus   **B.** lysosome   **C. cytosol**   **D.** plasma membrane

C is correct.

The signal peptide is located at the N-terminus of the growing polypeptide (protein). The N-terminus is the initial amino acid residue portion within a polypeptide. The C-terminus is the final amino acid incorporated into the polypeptide chain. The N-terminus is written on the left ($-NH_2$) and the C-terminus is written on the right ($-COOH$).

A signal peptide is used by the ribosome, including the small and the large subunits (40S and 60S respectively), to adhere to the membrane of the ER for the translation completion. The ER is a continuous membrane structure with the nuclear envelope membrane and functions to fold proteins into their proper three-dimensional shape. The correct three-dimensional shape is the necessary condition for the protein to be functional and for being transported in vesicles out of the ER. Proteins not folded properly are destined for the proteosome to be degraded.

Without a signal peptide, the protein is translated on the free ribosomes and remains in the cytoplasm. It will not enter the secretory pathway (the ER to *cis* Golgi, *medial* Golgi and *trans* Golgi).

25. In a cell that failed to label proteins with the M6P marker, which of the following processes would be disrupted?

A. oxidative phosphorylation

C. Lysosomal formation

B. intracellular digestion of macromolecules

D. protein synthesis

B is correct.

In the Golgi apparatus, lysosomal proteins are targeted with the M6P marker. Without this marker, the proteins are not targeted to the lysosome. If specific proteins do not get transported to the lysosome, lysosome cannot properly hydrolyze macromolecules.

A: oxidative phosphorylation (i.e. requires oxygen) produces ATP by the electron transport chain (ETC) of cellular respiration. Both glycolysis and the Krebs cycle are substrate-level phosphorylation because oxygen is not required for the production of ATP. Note, the nucleotide analog of ATP (GTP) is produced in the Krebs cycle and then converted into ATP for use as energy.

Aerobic respiration during ETC (via oxidative phosphorylation) is different than ATP production during glycolysis and the Krebs cycle (i.e. the citric acid cycle – TCA) because glycolysis and the Krebs cycle do not use oxygen (substrate level phosphorylation). A common misconception is that the Krebs cycle is aerobic because it does cease to function in the absence of oxygen. The reason that the Krebs cycle cannot continue in the absence of oxygen is that its products (i.e. NADH and $FADH_2$) are utilized by the ETC. The ETC does require oxygen and its inhibition (due to the lack of oxygen) causes the Krebs cycle products to accumulate and the overall reaction is halted (i.e. Le Chatelier's principle).

D: the M6P marker does not target polypeptides meant for other organelles, the plasma membrane or the secretory pathway (e.g. peptide hormones) out of the cell.

26. Within the cell, where is the M6P receptor transcribed?

A. nucleolus   **B.** smooth ER   **C.** ribosome   **D. nucleus**

D is correct.

Transcription is the conversion of DNA nucleotide sequences into messenger RNA. The enzyme that completes RNA synthesis from the sense strand of DNA is RNA polymerase. In eukaryotes, transcription (like replication, copying of the DNA during S phase of interphase in the cell cycle) occurs in the nucleus.

A: nucleolus is inside the nucleus and involved in rRNA synthesis. The nucleolus is often visualized via staining that is denser than the positive stain that highlights the nucleus because the rRNA nucleotides in the nucleolus are more concentrated than the DNA in the larger nucleus. rRNA is transported into the cytoplasm and anneals with proteins to form the ribosomes.

C: translation is the conversion of mRNA into proteins (using ribosomes) which occurs in the cytoplasm of the cell.

27. Which of these enzymes functions in an acidic environment?

A. pepsin   **B.** lingual lipase   **C.** signal peptidase   **D.** salivary amylase

---

A is correct.

Pepsin is a digestive enzyme that breaks down proteins in the stomach. Therefore its catalytic activity is optimal at a very low pH (e.g. 2 to 3) as the stomach has a very acidic environment due to the presence of hydrochloric acid.

B: lingual lipase is an enzyme that functions in the pre-digestion of long chain triglycerides (lipids composed of glycerol and fatty acids) and is also secreted in the mouth with the saliva.

C: signal peptidase targets growing polypeptides into the endoplasmic reticulum (ER). The interior lumen of ER is not acidic; therefore this enzyme would not function in acidic environment.

D: salivary amylase is an enzyme released in the mouth with saliva for the pre-digestion of starch – conversion of long polymers of glucose into maltose.

Saliva is a clear, tasteless, odorless, slightly acidic (pH 6.8) fluid consisting of the secretions from the parotid, sublingual and submandibular salivary glands and mucous glands of the oral cavity. Food ingested into the mouth undergoes mastication by chewing to increase surface area of the bolus (food).

28. Which of the following is required for the transport of proteins to the lysosome?

   A. endocytosis   **C.** acidic pH of the Golgi

   B. absence of leader sequence   **D. vesicular transport from the rough ER to the Golgi**

D is correct.

Before being transported to the lysosome, proteins are synthesized and inserted into the lumen of the ER via the signal peptide. After being properly folded (via the assistance of chaperone molecules), they are transported by vesicles from the rough ER (protein synthesis site) to the Golgi for protein modification and sorting. Then to the target organelle, lysosome.

A: endocytosis is invagination of the plasma membrane that forms transport vesicles that take extracellular material into the cell's interior. Transporting proteins via endocytosis from the extracellular space into the cell for their degradation is a different process from targeting proteins via a signal peptide sequence for integration into the plasma membrane of the lysosome.

B: a leader sequence (also known as a signal peptide sequence) is a 6-10 amino acid sequence which targets the nascent polypeptide from the synthesis on a free (cytosolic) ribosome to the endoplasmic reticulum. Signal peptidase (targeting the leader sequence) is an enzyme that converts secretory and some membrane proteins to their mature forms by cleaving their signal peptides from their N-terminals (the start of a protein or polypeptide terminated by an amino acid with a free amine group). Absence of the leader sequence is not a condition for protein targeting to the lysosome. Proteins destined for organelles (e.g. lysosomes), the plasma membrane or for excretion from the cell contain a leader sequence.

C: the pH of the Golgi is not acidic, the lysosome is the organelle with an acidic pH (about 5).

> Questions 29 through 33 are not based on any
> descriptive passage and are independent of each other

29. Which of the following properties within a polypeptide chain determines the globular conformation of a protein?

A. number of individual amino acids   **C.** relative concentration of amino acids
B. linear sequence of amino acids   **D.** peptide optical activity measured in the polarimeter

B is correct.

The primary ($1°$) structure is the linear sequence of amino acids in the polypeptide.

$1°$ determines subsequent local folding for the secondary ($2°$) structure - alpha helix & beta pleated sheets. The alpha helix and beta-pleated sheets of $2°$ structure give rise to the tertiary ($3°$) structure for the overall 3-D shape of a functional protein. The overall 3-D shape determines the function of the protein. A functional enzyme (protein) has proper folding for the formation of the active site for substrate binding.

The joining of two separate polypeptide chains defines the quaternary ($4°$) structure. A classic example of $4°$ structure is hemoglobin with 2 alpha and 2 beta chains forming a functional hemoglobin protein.

30. In the Newman projection shown below, what does the circle represent?

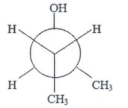

A. first carbon along the C_1–C_2 axis of the bond
B. first carbon along the C_2–C_3 axis of the bond
C. second carbon along the C_2–C_3 axis of the bond
D. second carbon along the C_3–C_4 axis of the bond

C is correct.

Newman projections represent carbon-carbon bonds for the C_2–C_3 atoms. The molecule is rotated (conformational change) to looking down the C_2–C_3 bond axis. The carbon in front is C_2 and represents the intersection of the three front lines. The back carbon (obscured) is C_3 and drawn as a larger circle in the Newman projection.

31. What is the degree of unsaturation for a molecule with the molecular formula $C_{18}H_{20}$?

A. 2   **B. 9**   **C.** 18   **D.** 36

B is correct.

The degree of unsaturation is given by the formula C_2H_{2n+2} or $(2C + 2 - H)/2$, where C is the number of carbon atoms and H is the number of hydrogen atoms. Therefore, $C_{18}H_{20}$ contains $(36 + 2 - 20)/2 = 9$ degrees of unsaturation.

A single degree of unsaturation corresponds to 2 Hs and the molecule has a structure of either a double bond or a ring.

Two degrees of unsaturation corresponds to 4 Hs and the molecule has a structure of a triple bond, two double bonds, a double bond and a ring, or two rings.

Three degrees of unsaturation corresponds to 6 Hs and the structure is either a triple bond and a double bond, three double bonds, two double bonds and a ring, a double bond and two rings, or a three ring structure.

32. If distillation was used to separate hexanol from butanol, which product would distill first?

A. hexanol   **B. butanol**   **C.** they distill simultaneously   **D.** cannot be determined

B is correct.

Hexanol and butanol contain hydroxyl groups. Hydroxyl groups form hydrogen bonds because hydrogen is attached directly to an electronegative atom (e.g. F, O, N or Cl). The partial delta charge (i.e. due to electronegativity differences in the atoms compared to hydrogen) permits the formation of the strongest of the dipole-dipole bonds (i.e. hydrogen bonding).

With the H attached directly to O, hydrogen bonding is possible in both molecules. However, butanol (i.e. 4-carbon chain) is a smaller alcohol (i.e. less molecular weight) than hexanol (i.e. 6-carbon chain) and has a lower boiling point, making it the first compound to be distilled.

Always consider molecular weight as the greater factor in boiling point and then dipole interactions (e.g. hydrogen bonding) between molecules.

33. All of the following are involved in energy production within the mitochondrion EXCEPT:

A. glycolysis   **C.** electron transport chain
B. Krebs cycle   **D.** oxidative phosphorylation

A is correct.

Glycolysis is involved in the net production of 2 ATP during cellular respiration. Glycolysis is important in energy production, but it occurs in the cytoplasm, not the mitochondria. All other choices name processes that occur in the mitochondria.

Passage 5
(Questions 34–39)

Acetylsalicylic acid (known by the brand name Aspirin) is one of the most commonly used drugs. It has analgesic (pain relieving), antipyretic (fever-reducing) and anti-inflammatory properties. The drug works by blocking the synthesis of *prostaglandins*. A prostaglandin is any member of a lipid compound group enzymatically derived from fatty acids. Every prostaglandin is a 20-carbon (including a 5-carbon ring) unsaturated carboxylic acid.

Prostaglandins are involved in a variety of physiological processes and have important functions in the body. They are mediators and have strong physiological effects (e.g. regulating the contraction and relaxation of smooth muscle). These *autocrine* or *paracrine* hormones (i.e. messenger molecules acting locally) are produced throughout the human body with target cells present in the immediate vicinity of the site of their secretion.

Acetylsalicylic acid is a white crystalline substance that is an acetyl derivative and is a weak acid with a melting point of 136 °C (277 °F) and a boiling point of 140 °C (284 °F). Acetylsalicylic acid can be produced through acetylation of salicylic acid by acetic anhydride in the presence of an acid catalyst and is shown in the following reaction:

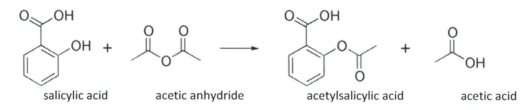

salicylic acid   acetic anhydride   acetylsalicylic acid   acetic acid

Reaction 1. Synthesis of acetylsalicylic acid

The acetylsalicylic acid synthesis is classified as an *esterification* reaction. Salicylic acid is treated with acetic anhydride, an acid derivative, which causes a chemical reaction that turns salicylic acid's hydroxyl group into an ester group (R-OH → R-OCOCH$_3$). This process yields acetylsalicylic acid and acetic acid, which for this reaction is considered a byproduct. Small amounts of sulfuric acid (and sometimes phosphoric acid) are almost always used as a catalyst.

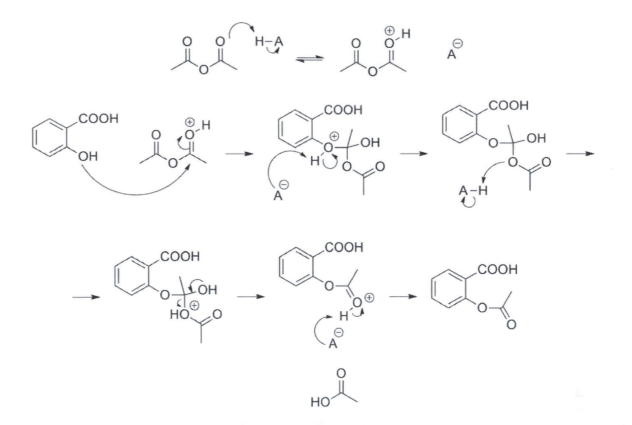

Reaction 2. Mechanism of acetylsalicylic acid synthesis

In a college lab, this synthesis was carried out via the following procedure:

10 mL of acetic anhydride, 4 g of salicylic acid and 2 mL of concentrated sulfuric acid were mixed and the resulting solution was heated for 10 minutes. Upon cooling the mix in an ice bath, a crude white product X precipitated. 100 mL of cold distilled water was added to complete the crystallization. By suction filtration the product X was isolated and then washed with several aliquots of cold water.

Product X was dissolved in 50 mL of saturated sodium bicarbonate and the solution was filtered to remove an insoluble material. Then, 3 M of hydrochloric acid was added to the filtrate and product Y precipitated. It was collected by suction filtration and recrystallized in a mixture of petroleum ether (benzine) and common ether.

After analyzing product X, it showed the presence of acetylsalicylic acid, trace levels of salicylic acid and a contaminate of a high molecular weight.

34. In the experiment described in the passage, salicylic acid primarily acts as an alcohol. What is the likely product when salicylic acid is reacted with an excess of methanol in the presence of sulfuric acid?

A. methyl salicylate   **B.** benzoic acid   **C.** phenol   **D.** benzaldehyde

A is correct.

Salicylic acid has two different functional groups – an alcohol and a carboxylic acid – both of which can undergo esterification reactions. From the passage, in the synthesis of acetylsalicylic acid, the alcohol functional group of salicylic acid reacts with acetic anhydride to form an ester.

Under acidic conditions, the carboxylic acid group forms an ester linkage when it is reacted with an excess of alcohol. The oxygen in methanol (i.e. nucleophile) attacks the carboxyl carbon in salicylic acid and salicylic acid acts as a carboxylic acid.

The reaction mechanism in the problem stem is similar to salicylic acid and acetic anhydride whereby a series of protonation / deprotonation steps lead to the formation of the ester (e.g. methyl salicylate). This is nucleophilic acyl substitution with the OH group on the carboxylic acid being substituted (i.e. not the hydroxyl group).

B: the hydroxyl group would be removed from the aromatic ring but this is unlikely because the aromatic ring is stable and the hydroxyl group remains attached.

C: if phenol were formed, salicylic acid would have to undergo decarboxylation but, under these conditions, decarboxylation is highly unlikely. For decarboxylation, high temperatures and either 1,3-dicarboxylic acids or β-keto acids spontaneously release carbon dioxide.

D: the hydroxyl group would need to be removed from benzene and the carboxyl group would have to be reduced to an aldehyde. Reduction of the carboxylic acid would occur with a strong reducing agent such as lithium aluminum hydride ($LiAlH_4$).

35. When acetylsalicylic acid is exposed to humid air, it acquires a vinegar-like smell because:

    A. moist air reacts with residual salicylic acid to form citric acid
    B. it undergoes hydrolysis into salicylic and acetic acids
    C. it undergoes hydrolysis into salicylic acid and acetic anhydride
    D. it undergoes hydrolysis into acetic acid and citric acid

B is correct.

Since acetylsalicylic acid is an ester it reacts with water whereby the ester linkage is cleaved and forms an alcohol and a carboxylic acid. From moisture (i.e. humidity), acetylsalicylic acid is cleaved to produce salicylic acid and acetic acid. Acid is present as H_3O^+ and through a series of intermediates, the ester linkage is cleaved in acetylsalicylic acid yielding salicylic acid (alcohol) and acetic acid (carboxylic acid). Acetic acid generates the aroma of vinegar.

A: there should not be any residual salicylic acid in acetylsalicylic acid. Even if small levels of salicylic acid were present, salicylic acid does not react with water-saturated air to form citric acid.

C: acetic anhydride will not be formed. Acetic anhydride is often a reactant in the synthesis of molecules of acetic acid with the side product of water. However, the question states that acetylsalicylic acid undergoes hydrolysis and the hydrated product (not the dehydrated product) is formed. Acetic acid (not acetic anhydride) is formed with salicylic acid.

D: acetylsalicylic acid does cleave to produce citric acid (smell of lemon juice) and acetic acid. For citric acid to form, the ester would have to be aliphatic (e.g. hydrocarbon chain) and not aromatic (e.g. benzene). Acetylsalicylic acid contains an aromatic ring, so upon hydrolysis (i.e. cleavage by the addition of water), a phenyl (i.e. aromatic) group would be one of the products. Neither citric nor acetic acid contain a phenyl group.

36. What is the purpose of dissolving product X in saturated $NaHCO_3$ in the experiment conducted in a college lab?

    A. precipitate any side product contaminants as sodium salts

    B. remove water from the reaction

    C. form the water-soluble sodium salt of aspirin

    D. neutralize any remaining salicylic acid

C is correct.

Bicarbonate ($NaHCO_3$) is commonly used for syntheses and extractions. In the experiment, acetylsalicylic acid was formed when the solution of acetic anhydride, salicylic acid and sulfuric acid was heated. The formation of the crude white precipitate containing acetylsalicylic acid following the cooling indicates that acetylsalicylic acid is relatively insoluble in water.

Acetylsalicylic acid has two functional groups: a carboxylic acid and an ester. Therefore, when dissolving product X in sodium bicarbonate, acetylsalicylic acid dissolves in this solution because the proton of the carboxylic acid dissociates (i.e. –COOH into –COO⁻ Na⁺). The hydrogen on the carboxyl group is slightly acidic with a pK_a of about 3.5 and acetylsalicylic acid is converted into its corresponding sodium salt.

Salicylic acid is present in product X as an impurity and is converted to its corresponding sodium salt which is removed in the recrystallization step. By filtration, the acetylsalicylic acid salt is then isolated in the filtrate and can be converted back to its solid form by acidification with hydrochloric acid (HCl).

A: the contaminant cannot form a water soluble sodium salt because acetylsalicylic acid forms a water soluble sodium salt. If the contaminant could be dissolved in water as its corresponding salt, it would mix with acetylsalicylic acid preventing its isolation.
B: sodium bicarbonate is not a desiccant that would dry the solution.

D: sodium bicarbonate converts acetylsalicylic acid into its corresponding sodium salt. Bicarbonate (NaHCO$_3$) is often used to deprotonate a weak acid which (as an ion) becomes soluble. The choice of sodium hydroxide would not be proper because –OH is a strong base.

37.

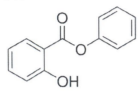 Phenyl salicylate is a molecule different from acetylsalicylic acid that also possesses analgesic properties. Which of the following could be reacted with salicylic acid in the presence of sulfuric acid to produce phenyl salicylate?

   A. PhCH$_2$OH   **B.** PhCO$_2$H   **C. PhOH**   **D.** Benzene

C is correct.

This question tests the basic concepts of carboxylic acid and alcohol reactions similar to the mechanism in the synthesis of acetylsalicylic acid (Reaction 1). Under acidic conditions, the oxygen of phenol is a nucleophile that attacks and adds to the carboxyl carbon of salicylic acid. Through a series of intermediates, water dissociates (i. dehydration) and the product is the substitution of the carboxyl hydroxyl by the aromatic ring to form an ester linkage between the carboxyl group (salicylic acid) and the alcohol (phenol) to form phenyl salicylate.

A: note the extra CH$_2$ group. Even though this molecule contains a nucleophilic alcohol, the product would not be phenyl salicylate.

B: salicylic acid would function as an alcohol undergoing nucleophilic attack of its hydroxyl oxygen on the carboxyl carbon of benzoic acid resulting in *o*-benzoylbenzoic acid.

D: benzene is very stable and would not react directly with salicylic acid. Even under extreme conditions (e.g. high temperature), a reaction between the two molecules is not likely.

38. For the synthesis of acetylsalicylic acid, what is the reaction mechanism?

   A. Nucleophilic addition   **C.** Nucleophilic aromatic substitution
   B. Nucleophilic acyl substitution   **D.** Electrophilic aromatic substitution

B is correct.

Acetylsalicylic acid is synthesized when a molecule of salicylic acid reacts with a molecule of acetic anhydride. Anhydrides are formed during dehydration of either two carboxylic acids or a carboxylic acid and an alcohol. The oxygen on the alcohol is the nucleophile and attacks and adds to one of the carbonyl carbons in acetic anhydride. The carbonyl oxygen of acetic anhydride is protonated by sulfuric acid (i.e. acid catalyzed reaction) which makes it more susceptible to a nucleophilic attack because the O is deficient in electron density (i.e. yielding a greater partial plus on the O). A series of intermediates are formed which leads to the formation of acetylsalicylic acid and the dissociation of acetic acid.

A: no addition reaction occurs for benzene because this would interrupt aromaticity and the overall molecule would be less stable. From the product, the hydrogen on the phenol group has been replaced (i.e. substituted) by an acyl group.

C and D: in the synthesis of acetylsalicylic acid, the stable benzene ring does not undergo a reaction but the reaction occurs with the functional groups attached to stable (i.e. aromatic) benzene. Under relatively mild reaction conditions, the benzene ring is unlikely to be attacked by either electrophilic (EAS) or nucleophilic aromatic substitution (NAS). Electrophilic aromatic substitution is restricted to a few reactions (e.g. halogenations, nitration, sulfonation, Friedel-Crafts alkylation and Friedel-Crafts acylation) and each requires a Lewis acid as a catalyst to generate a "carbocation" that the electrons of benzene attack.

39. Which of the following is the likely structure of the high-molecular weight contaminant in product X?

B is correct.

Because the contaminant must be a derivative of salicylic acid, analyze the structure of salicylic acid and consider other possible reactions it can undergo in acidic environment. Salicylic acid has an alcohol and carboxylic acid functional groups.

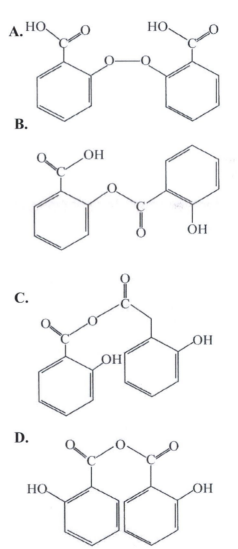

These two functional groups both react with other molecules (i.e. intermolecular attack) and also react with each other (i.e. intramolecular attack). The contaminant is the product of the hydroxyl group of one of the salicylic acid molecules forming an ester linkage with the carboxyl group of another salicylic acid. The oxygen (i.e. hydroxyl group) in salicylic acid acts as a nucleophile and attacks the carboxyl carbon of another salicylic acid molecule to form a protonated intermediate.

Water can then dissociate from this intermediate with an ester linkage between the two molecules. The hydroxyl and carboxyl groups remaining at each end can react further. A large number of molecules can react via polymerization of these repeating units (i.e. benzene ring attached to an ester moiety). However, the length of the polymer is limited by entropy and by depletion of the substrate. The polymer has repeating units and is formed via dehydration whereby the oxygen of the hydroxyl group attacks the carbon of the carbonyl and water is released when the ester linkage is formed.

Passage 6
(Questions 40–43)

The ovaries of a female at birth contain on average 300,000 follicles (with a range from 35,000 to 2.5 million). These follicles are immature (*primordial*) and each contains an immature primary oocyte. By the time of puberty the number decreases to an average of 180,000 (the range is 25,000-1.5 million). Only about 400 follicles ever mature and produce an oocyte. During the process of *folliculogenesis* (i.e. maturation), a follicle develops from a *primary follicle* to a *secondary follicle*, to a *vesicular* (Graafian) follicle. The whole process of folliculogenesis, from primordial to a preovulatory follicle, belongs to the stage of *ootidogenesis* of *oogenesis*. A secondary follicle contains a secondary oocyte with a reduced number of chromosomes. The release of a secondary oocyte from the ovary is called *ovulation*.

Unlike male *spermatogenesis*, which can last indefinitely, folliculogenesis ends when the remaining follicles in the ovaries are incapable of responding to the hormonal signals that previously prompted some follicles to mature. The depletion in follicle supply sets the beginning of menopause in women.

The ovarian cycle is controlled by the *gonadotropic hormones* released by the pituitary: follicle-stimulating hormone (FSH) and luteinizing-hormone (LH). Imbalances of these hormones may often cause infertility in females. For treatment of many female reproductive disorders, therapies that act similar to FSH and LH are often used successfully.

In a pharmaceutical laboratory, scientists test two of such drugs. Drug X binds to LH receptors, while drug Y binds to FSH receptors. The scientists separated 15 mice with fertility disorders into three experimental groups. Mice in group I were administered drug Y, while mice in group II were administered drug X, and mice in group III received a placebo. After 1 month, the scientists performed an *ovariectomy* (i.e. surgical removal of ovaries in laboratory animals) and counted the number of developing follicles in the mice ovaries.

Note: a normal female mouse has on average 10-12 developing follicles at any point in the menstrual cycle.

Mice	Group I	Group II	Group III
#1	5	6	6
#2	11	4	5
#3	8	16	6
#4	11	11	4
#5	8	5	9

Table 1. Number of developing follicles per mouse

40. From the data, which of the following conditions is most likely the cause of infertility observed in mice #3 in all three groups given that they all are affected by the same reproductive disorder?

A. inability of FSH to bind FSH receptors   **C.** elevated levels of LH

B. benign tumor of the pituitary   **D. gene mutation LH hormone**

D is correct.

The LH receptors are likely functional in all mice # 3 because the LH agonist induced follicular development. An agonist is a molecule that combines with receptors to initiate (e.g. drug) actions because the agonist possesses affinity and intrinsic activity.

The cause for infertility is either insufficient LH synthesis or the synthesis of nonfunctional LH. A mutation of the LH gene can result in nonfunctional LH.

41. Which of the following conditions is LEAST likely to result in female infertility?

A. downregulation of LH receptors   **C. release of multiple follicles**

B. inflammation of oviducts   D. FSH gene mutation

C is correct.

The release of multiple follicles may lead to the occurrence of multiple conceptions. This effect is the opposite of infertility and is often used in *in vitro* fertilization where hyperovulation is induced in a woman and multiple fertilized eggs are transferred into the uterus for implantation.

A and D: from the passage, the imbalances of FSH and LH hormones often result in fertility problems.

B: a released egg must travel down the oviduct (i.e. fallopian tube) to be fertilized; therefore an inflammation of the oviducts may interfere with successful zygote implantation.

42. Overstimulation of follicular development during reproductive therapies increases the probability of multiple ovulations often resulting in multiple pregnancies. Which of the test subjects is the best example for this case?

A. mouse #2 of group I   C. mouse #4 of group II

B. mouse #3 of group II   D. mouse #5 of group III

B is correct.

According to the passage, the average female mouse has a 10-12 mature follicles. Mouse #3 in group II had 16 mature follicles and was the only mouse with a greater (than average) number of mature follicles. Therefore, this mouse exhibits therapeutic follicular overstimulation. To demonstrate a therapeutic effect, the mouse must be in an experimental group (groups I & II) and not in the placebo group (group III).

43. Which treatment is most likely responsible for the number of maturing follicles observed in the mouse #5 in group III?

A. stimulation of the pituitary

B. FSH receptor inhibition

C. LH receptor stimulation

D. no relationship to treatment

D is correct.

The passage states that group III is the control group that received a placebo. A placebo is a medicinally inactive compound that is administered in drug testing for its suggestive effect. Therefore, the number of follicles observed in all the mice of group III is unrelated to the treatment.

Questions 44 through 47 are not based on any descriptive passage and are independent of each other

---

44. During DNA replication, individual dNTP nucleotides are joined by bond formation that releases phosphate. Which of the following describes the bond type between two dNTP nucleotides?

A. covalent bond   **B.** peptide bond   **C.** van der Waals bond   **D.** ionic bond

A is correct.

Covalent bonds involve equal (or about equal) sharing of electrons between two atoms when the two atoms have the same electronegativity (attraction for electron density). Covalent bonds are the most common intramolecular bond (i.e. covalent or ionic) because carbon (which comprises the backbone of organic molecules) has an intermediate electronegativity and shares electrons almost equally with most other atoms.

B: peptide bonds refer to a bond between adjacent amino acids formed during the dehydration whereby the lone pair of electrons on the nitrogen (amino group) attacks the carbonyl carbon (carboxylic acid) of the adjacent amino acid and is not applicable to this question. A peptide bond is rigid (no rotation around a single bond) because of the double bond character (due to resonance) between the amino end (NH) of one amino acid and the carboxyl end (COO) of the adjacent amino acid. The resonance of the lone pair of electrons of the NH being shared to form a double bond with the carboxyl group provides the rigidity of the peptide bond and is important for protein shape (protein shape determines function).

C: van der Waals (also known as London dispersion forces) results from an attraction between molecules based on the momentary flux of electron density within / among molecules that results in a weak (and short ranged) attraction between the oppositely charge polarity within the molecules. Van der Waals forces are the weakest of the intermolecular forces (between molecules). The strongest intermolecular force results from hydrogen bonding where H is attached directly to a strongly electronegative atom such as F, O, N or Cl (see explanation on pg. 409 to question 46 in *Biological and Biochemical Foundations Practice Test 1* regarding

Cl). Weaker than hydrogen bonding is dipole-dipole interactions which does not have as strong an electronegativity difference as in H-bonding. Dipole–induced dipole is the third in the series of intermolecular forces, followed by van der Waals (London dispersion forces.

D: ionic bonds involve unequal sharing of electrons and occur between two atoms with great differences in electronegativity (e.g. salts such as KCl: K^+ cations and Cl^- anions). Ionic bonds dissociate in water because the ions each interact with the polar water molecule. For example, the cation associates with the partial negative charge on the O in water, while the anion associates with the partial plus charge on the H of water.

45. Which of the following is true about polar amino acids?

A. side chains project towards the exterior of the protein chain
B. side chains contain only hydrogen and carbon atoms
C. side chains are hydrophobic
D. side chains have neutral moieties

A is correct.

The R groups of the polar side chains project towards the exterior of the protein chain because the polar side chains (hydrophilic moieties) hydrogen bond with the H_2O solution in biological systems.

Hydrocarbons include only hydrogens and carbons without any heteroatom (i.e. atoms other than H & C) such as electronegative O or N that create polarity due to the unequal sharing of bonded electrons (polar covalent bonds). This unequal sharing generates hydrophilic regions that interact with H_2O either by hydrogen bonds or electrostatic interactions (e.g. dipole or ionic bonds).

46. What is the net number of ATP produced per glucose in an obligate anaerobe?

A. 2 ATP   **B.** 4 ATP   **C.** 36 ATP   **D.** 38 ATP

A is correct.

Obligate anaerobes require the absence of oxygen. Obligate anaerobes produce ATP only via fermentation which includes both glycolysis and the reactions necessary to regenerate NAD^+ needed for subsequent glycolysis. Obligate anaerobes produce a net of 2 ATP produced during glycolysis with no additional ATP produced during fermentation where pyruvate is converted to lactic acids (i.e. mammals) or to ethanol (i.e. yeast).

B: Glycolysis produces a total (gross) of 4 ATP, but the initial process of glycolysis requires the hydrolysis (investment) of 2 ATP to add phosphates to each end of the glucose molecule at the onset of the process.

C and D: aerobic eukaryote organisms produce a net of 36 ATP per glucose, while prokaryotes (e.g. bacteria) produce a net of 38 ATP per glucose because in prokaryotes, the NADH produced during glycolysis does loose energy by needing to be shuttled into the double membrane-layered mitochondria. In prokaryotes: glycolysis, Krebs cycle and the electron transport chain all occur in the cytoplasm of the prokaryote. The reported ATP values (e.g. 36 vs. 38) are theoretical and the actual yield is often less due to "leaky" membranes of mitochondria.

47. All of the following hormones are released by the anterior pituitary gland EXCEPT:

A. luteinizing hormone	**C.** thyroid stimulating hormone
B. prolactin	**D. Vasopressin**

D is correct.

Vasopressin (aka ADH - antidiuretic hormone) and oxytocin are synthesized in the posterior pituitary. ADH targets the kidneys for water retention and arterioles for vasoconstriction to raise blood pressure. Oxytocin targets the uterus for contractions during child birthing and the mammary glands for lactation.
The anterior pituitary synthesizes seven hormones:

- Adrenocorticotropic hormone (ACTH) targets the adrenal glands for the secretion of glucocorticoid & mineralcorticoid;
- Beta-endorphin targets the opioid receptor for inhibition of pain perception;
- Thyroid-stimulating hormone (TSH) targets the thyroid gland for the secretion of thyroid hormones;
- Follicle-stimulating hormone (FSH) targets the gonads for growth of the reproductive system;
- Luteinizing hormone (LH) targets the gonads for sex hormone production (including testosterone, estrogens and progesterone);
- Growth hormone (aka somatotropin) targets the liver and adipose tissue to promote growth, lipid and carbohydrate metabolism;
- Prolactin (PRL) targets the ovaries for secretion of estrogen / progesterone and the mammary glands for milk production.

Passage 7
(Questions 48–52)

The genome of all cells of the human body except germ line cells (i.e. gametes of either sperm or egg) and mature red blood cells (i.e. erythrocytes) contain identical DNA on chromosomes. Even with the same genetic material, cells of different tissue are diverse and specialized. This diversity of cellular function is due primarily to cell-specific variations in protein expression which is regulated mostly at the transcriptional level. Different genes are expressed by transcriptional controls that determine cellular function and growth.

Specifically, gene transcription is controlled by upstream regulatory sequences which include regulatory genes and promoters. Regulators and promoters are controlled by extracellular signals (e.g. hormones) and intracellular signals (e.g. calcium or glucose). Regulators stimulate or inhibit gene transcription of a gene while activated promoters only increase transcription.

A major cause of cancer is the cell's inability to regulate the cell cycle. Genetic mutations may occur at any level of the cell growth regulation system. There are two gene categories that, if mutated, often result in cancer: *oncogenes* and *tumor suppressor genes*. Oncogenes regulate cell growth and division and a mutation of the oncogene itself or its promoters can result in uncontrolled cell growth and division. Tumor suppressor genes regulate the cell cycle and may induce cell death when a cell has abnormal function. Mutations of tumor suppressor genes impair this regulatory ability and, without this control mechanism, the malfunctioning cells are able to proliferate.

When regulators or promoter sequences for genes involved in oncogenesis (also called carcinogenesis or tumorigenesis) are identified, it is possible to use drug treatments to regulate transcription of these genes. Certain drugs are effective at controlling the growth of cancerous cells, but have significant side effects that include diarrhea, significant hair loss, decreased immunity and kidney damage.

48. Given that oncogenes and tumor suppressor genes mutations usually arise during DNA replication, which phase of the cell cycle is most likely the phase for cancerous mutations?

A. S   **B.** metaphase   **C.** cytokinesis   **D.** G_0

A is correct.

DNA is replicated in the S phase of the cell cycle whereby the result is still a diploid cell (i.e. 2 copies of the chromosomes) but each strand is duplicated to form sister chromatids. The number of chromosomes is counted by the number of centromeres. Centromeres are a tightly coiled (i.e. heterochromatin) region that joins the chromatin arms forming sister chromatids of the newly replicated DNA.

B and C: interphase includes the sequence of cellular growth (i.e. G_1), DNA replication (i.e. S) and organelle replication (i.e. G_2). The cell cycle is divided into interphase (i.e. G_1, S, G_2 phases) and mitosis (i.e. PMAT: prophase, metaphase, anaphase, telophase / cytokinesis). The cell spends most of its life cycle in G_1 and once it proceeds into S phase, the cell cycle checkpoints ensure that properly dividing cells undergo cytokinesis at the end of the cycle and form 2 diploid cells that are identical to the parental cell.

D: G_0 is the phase for nondividing cells (e.g. brain and spinal cord cells). Other cells can enter G_0 at the end of mitosis and then, via cell cycle signals, the cell proceeds into G_1 where the cell remains until the onset of S phase. In interphase, the DNA is accessible for transcription and is uncoiled (i.e. euchromatin).

49. What is the likely action mechanism of the cancer drugs mentioned in the passage?

    A. changes at the nucleotide level of an oncogene
    B. upregulation of the activator for an oncogene
    C. increased expression of a tumor suppressor gene
    D. blocking the promoter of a tumor suppressor gene from binding transcription factors

C is correct.

According to the passage, the drug curtails the growth of cancerous cell whereby anticancer drugs target rapidly proliferating cells. Like cancer cells, rapidly dividing cells include hair follicles, cells of the gastrointestinal system and antibodies. Therefore, anticancer therapies result in hair loss, poor absorption of nutrients and a suppression of immune activity as side effects.

The drug must be increasing the expression of tumor suppressor genes (i.e. p53 being the most common tumor suppression gene). If the drug decreased oncogenic activity, it would suppress the expression of proteins and slow the growth of cancerous cells. Tumor suppressor genes and oncogenes work in contrast. Oncogenes increase the expression of cancer by producing protein products which yield more cell growth (i.e. uncontrolled cell growth is the hallmark of cancer cells) while tumor suppressor genes inhibit cancer by blocking the over-expression of proteins that would move the cell at an accelerated rate through the cell cycle.

50. A new cancer drug with the brand name Colcrys acts to prevent cell division by inhibiting microtubule formation. In what stage of mitosis this drug would be most effective?

    A. prophase   **B.** metaphase   **C.** anaphase   **D.** telophase

A is correct.

Microtubules assemble from the polymerization of tubulin subunits. Microtubules (i.e. spindle fibers) are essential for cell division because they connect centromeres (on the chromosomes) to the centriole (at the pole of the cell). Microtubule formation is essential for chromosomes to align along the midline of the cell (i.e. metaphase plate).

The microtubules pull the chromosomes apart by splitting the centromeres during anaphase and separating the chromatids. Without the polymerization of tubulin to form microtubules, chromosomes fail to align at the metaphase plate, separate during anaphase or become segregated into respective nuclei during telophase.

51. Along with its corresponding gene, a promoter sequence may be transcribed in one mRNA transcript. The mRNA sequence containing the transcribed promoter must be cleaved to make translation possible. Which cell region is most likely the site of this cleavage?

A. Golgi apparatus   **B. nucleus**   **C.** cytoplasm   **D.** nucleolus

B is correct.

The primary transcript (i.e. heteronuclear RNA or hnRNA) undergoes processing in the nucleus to produce mRNA. The hnRNA processing includes the addition of a 5'-G cap and a poly-A tail, excision and removal of introns, and ligation of exons. All three post-transcriptional activities (i.e. processing) must take place for the formation of mRNA. Only after hnRNA has been processed (i.e. capping, adding a tail and splicing), mRNA will migrate through the nuclear pores of the nuclear membrane and enter the cytoplasm. Once in the cytoplasm, the mRNA is the template for protein synthesis (known as translation).

A: the Golgi apparatus structure resembles a stack of flattened sacs located close to the endoplasmic reticulum. The Golgi functions in protein processing and sorting of proteins for the secretory pathways (proteins destined for exocytosis from the cell, placement into the plasma membrane or targeted for an organelle within the cell). Secretory proteins arrive at the Golgi in vesicles that bud off from the rough endoplasmic reticulum.

C: the cytoplasm (also called cytosol) is the gel-like area outside of the nucleus. Cytosol is where organelles are located. It contains biomolecules used by the cell and is the site of translation for protein synthesis – the conversion of the nucleic acids language into amino acids.

D: the nucleolus is a membrane-bound structure within the nucleus. rRNA is synthesized in the nucleolus and then transported to the cytosol to anneal with proteins and assemble into the two subunits of the ribosomes (e.g. 30S & 50S subunits for prokaryotes and 40S & 60S subunits for eukaryotes). The complete ribosome for prokaryotes is 70S and 80S for eukaryotes.

52. A novel approach to cancer treatment employs modified tRNA molecules that carry inappropriate combinations of amino acids and anticodons. The tRNA molecule with the nucleotide triplets on one end is *charged* with mismatched amino acids on the other end. What is the likely mechanism of the anticancer action of these modified tRNA molecules?

    A. inhibition of cancer cells to translate protein
    B. inhibition of cancer cells to transcribe protein
    C. inhibition of ribosomes to bind to the mRNA
    D. change in the tertiary structure of the translated protein

D is correct.

Translation occurs in the cytoplasm and is the synthesis of proteins from mRNA. tRNAs (contain the anticodon) are used to bring the corresponding amino acid to the growing polypeptide based on the nucleotide sequence of the mRNA (contain the codon).

Translation occurs but the synthesized proteins have incorrect amino acids (mismatch between the codon-anticodon). A change in the primary structure (linear sequence of amino acids) gives rise to a change in the overall shape of the folded protein making it likely dysfunctional.

Without translation of the mRNA template into the correct linear sequence of amino acids, the cancerous cells cannot synthesize proteins necessary for cellular function and subsequent reproduction. Such abnormal and dysfunctional cells would likely undergo apoptosis (i.e. programmed cell death).

Questions 53 through 59 are not based on any
descriptive passage and are independent of each other

---

53. How many carbon atoms are in a molecule of oleic acid?

    A. 14   **B.** 16   **C. 18**   **D.** 20

C is correct.

Oleic acid is an odorless, colorless fatty acid oil that occurs naturally in many animal and vegetable fats and oils. The term "oleic" refers to oil or olive; olive oil is predominantly composed of oleic acid which is a monounsaturated omega-9 fatty acid, abbreviated as 18:1 cis-9.

Oleic acid has the molecular formula of $CH_3(CH_2)_7CH=CH(CH_2)_7COOH$.

54. Amylose is different from amylopectin because amylose:

A. forms a helix with no branch points
B. is highly branched while amylopectin is linear
C. has more glucose residues than amylopectin
D. is composed of a different monomer than is amylopectin

A is correct.

55. What value is expressed by the slope in a Lineweaver-Burke plot?

A. V_{max} / K_m **B. K_m / V_{max}**   C. K_m D. $1 / [S]$

B is correct.

The Lineweaver-Burke plot is a graphical representation of enzyme kinetics.

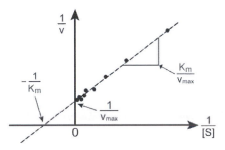

The Lineweaver-Burke plot is a graphical method for analysis of the Michaelis–Menten equation:

$V = V_{max}[S] / K_m + [S]$

Taking the reciprocal:

$1/V = K_m + [S] / V_{max}[S] = K_m / V_{max}[S] + 1 / V_{max}$

where V is the reaction velocity (i.e. reaction rate)

K_m is the Michaelis–Menten constant

V_{max} is the maximum reaction velocity

[S] is the substrate concentration.

56. Which statement about the initiation codon is correct?

A. It is part of the TATA box   **C. It specifies methionine**
B. It binds a protein complex that begins replication   D. It specifies uracil

C is correct.

57. Which tyrosine-derived molecule has the correct relationship?

- **A.** Norepinephrine – thyroid hormone
- **B.** Thyroxine – catecholamine
- **C. Dopaquinone – precursor of melanin**
- **D.** Dopamine – thyroid hormone

C is correct.

A: Norepinephrine (also called noradrenaline) is the hormone and neurotransmitter most responsible for vigilant concentration in contrast to its most chemically similar hormone, dopamine, which is primarily responsible for cognitive alertness. One of its most important functions is as the neurotransmitter released by the sympathetic neurons to affect the heart.

B: Thyroxine (T_4) is an intra-glandular precursor of a hormone triiodothyronine (T_3) produced by the thyroid gland and primarily responsible for regulation of metabolism. Iodine is necessary for the production of T_3 and T_4.

D: dopamine is a hormone that functions as a neurotransmitter in the brain.

58. Which statement is correct about essential amino acids?

- **A. They are not synthesized *de novo* by the body and must be part of the diet**
- **B.** They are not synthesized by the body in sufficient amounts
- **C.** There are twelve essential amino acids
- **D.** They are plentiful in all animal protein

A is correct.

59. A term used for a carbohydrate polymer is:

- **A.** Multimer
- **B.** Oligosaccharide
- **C. Glycan**
- **D.** Polycarb

C is correct.

The IUPAC defines terms glycan and polysaccharide as synonyms that refer to "compounds consisting of a large number of monosaccharides linked glycosidically." In practice, *glycan* can also refer to the carbohydrate portion of a glycoconjugate (e.g. glycoprotein, glycolipid or proteoglycan) even if the carbohydrate is only an oligosaccharide.

BIOLOGICAL & BIOCHEMICAL FOUNDATIONS OF LIVING SYSTEMS
MCAT® PRACTICE TEST #4: ANSWER KEY

Passage 1
1 : B
2 : D
3 : B
4 : A
5 : A
6 : D
7 : B

Passage 2
8 : A
9 : D
10 : B
11 : C
12 : D

Independent questions
13 : D
14 : C
15 : A
16 : D

Passage 3
17 : A
18 : D
19 : C
20 : D
21 : B

Passage 4
22 : A
23 : C
24 : C
25 : D
26 : A

Independent questions
27 : C
28 : D
29 : C
30 : D

Passage 5
31 : B
32 : B
33 : C
34 : A
35 : C

Passage 6
36 : D
37 : B
38 : A
39 : D
40 : B
41 : B

Independent questions
42 : A
43 : B
44 : C
45 : C
46 : C

Passage 7
47 : D
48 : C
49 : A
50 : C
51 : A
52 : B

Independent questions
53 : C
54 : B
55 : C
56 : B
57 : B
58 : B
59 : B

Passage 1
(Questions 1–7)

There are two proteins that are involved in transporting O_2 in vertebrates. Hemoglobin (Hb) is found in red blood cells and myoglobin (Mb) is found in muscle cells. The hemoglobin protein accounts for about 97% of the dry weight of red blood cells. In erythrocytes, the hemoglobin carries O_2 from the lungs to the tissue undergoing cellular respiration. Hemoglobin has an oxygen binding capacity of 1.3 ml O_2 per gram of hemoglobin which increases the total blood oxygen capacity over seventy-fold compared to dissolved oxygen in blood.

When a tissue's metabolic rate increases, carbon dioxide production also increases. In addition to O_2, Hb also transports CO_2. Of all CO_2 transported in blood, 7-10% is dissolved in blood plasma, 70% is bicarbonate ions (HCO_3^-) and 20% is bound to the globin to Hb as carbaminohemoglobin.

CO_2 combines with water to form carbonic acid (H_2CO_3), which quickly dissociates. This reaction occurs primarily in red blood cells, where *carbonic anhydrase* reversibly and rapidly catalyzes the reaction:

$$CO_2 + H_2O \leftrightarrow H_2CO_3 \leftrightarrow H^+ + HCO_3^-$$

Hb of vertebrates has a quaternary structure comprised of four individual polypeptide chains: two α and two β protein polypeptides each with a heme group bound as a prosthetic group. The four polypeptide chains are held together by hydrogen bonding.

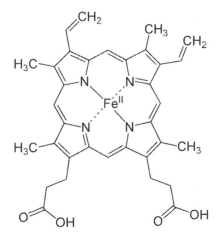

Figure 1. Hemoglobin

The binding of O_2 to Hb depends on the cooperativity of the Hb subunits. Cooperativity means that the binding of O_2 at one heme group increases the binding of O_2 at another heme within the Hb molecule through conformational changes of the entire hemoglobin molecule. This shape (conformational) change means it is energetically favorable for subsequent binding of O_2. Conversely, the unloading of O_2 at one heme increases the unloading of O_2 at other heme groups by a similar conformational change of the molecule.

Oxygen's affinity for Hb varies between different species and within species depending on multiple factors like blood pH, developmental stage (i.e. fetal versus adult), and body size. For example, small animals dissociate O_2 at a given partial pressure more readily than large animals because they have a higher metabolic rate and require more O_2 per gram of body mass.

Figure 2 represents the O_2-dissociation of Hb shown as sigmoidal curves B, C and D and myoglobin as hyperbolic curve A where saturation is the percent of O_2-binding sites occupied at specific partial pressures of O_2.

The *utilization coefficient* is the fraction of O_2 diffusing from Hb to the tissue as blood passes through the capillary beds. A normal value for the *utilization coefficient* is about 0.25.

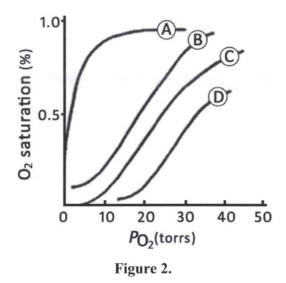

Figure 2.

In 1959, Max Perutz determined the molecular structure of myoglobin by x-ray crystallography which led to his sharing of the 1962 Nobel prize with John Kendrew. Myoglobin is a single-chain globular protein made up from 154 amino acids that transports and stores O_2 in muscle. Mb contains a heme (i.e. iron-containing porphyrin) prosthetic group with a molecular weight of 17.7 kd (kilodalton where 1 dalton is defined as 1/12 the mass of a neutral unbound carbon atom). As seen in Figure 2, Mb (curve A) has a greater affinity for O_2 than Hb. Unlike the blood-borne hemoglobin, myoglobin does not exhibit cooperative binding because cooperativity is present only in quaternary proteins that undergo allosteric changes. A high concentration of myoglobin in muscle cells allows organisms to hold their breath for extended periods of time. Diving mammals such as whales and seals have muscles with abundant myoglobin levels.

1. The mountain goat has developed a type of hemoglobin adapted to the unusually high altitudes. If curve C represents the O_2 dissociation curve for a cow's Hb, which curve most closely resembles the the O_2 dissociation curve for the mountain goat's Hb?

A. curve A   **B. curve B**   **C.** curve C   **D.** curve D

B is correct.

At high altitudes, atmospheric pressure is low and there is less oxygen in the air than at sea level. The mountain goat has adapted to life at high altitudes by evolving a different type of hemoglobin. Since the partial pressure of O_2 is less at high altitudes, mountain goat's hemoglobin must be able to bind oxygen with increased affinity at these lower O_2 partial pressures.

For a given value of O_2 pressure on the X-axis of Figure 2, the mountain goat's hemoglobin becomes more saturated with O_2 than the cow's hemoglobin, since cows have not adapted to live in regions of unusually high altitude. From Figure 2, the mountain goat oxygen-dissociation curve is to the left compared to the cow.

If curve C is for a cow, then the curve for a mountain goat would most closely resemble curve B.

From the passage, curves B, C and D represent O_2-dissociation for Hb (i.e. sigmoid shape curve displays cooprerativity) while curve A is for the myoglobin.

2. If curve C represents the O_2-dissociation curve for a hippopotamus's Hb, which curve would most closely correspond with the Hb of a squirrel?

A. curve A   **B.** curve B   **C.** curve C   **D. curve D**

D is correct.

From the passage, small animals have higher metabolic rates (i.e. cellular respiration rate) and require more O_2 per gram of tissue than larger animals. Therefore, small animals have Hb that dissociates O_2 more rapidly than the Hb of large animals.
A high metabolic rate indicates increased aerobic respiration where metabolically active tissues need O_2. Hb that easily dissociates O_2 is capable of delivering more oxygen to metabolically active tissue.

At a given value of O_2 partial pressure, a squirrel's Hb is less saturated with O_2 than that of a hippopotamus because the hippopotamus is much larger than a squirrel and has a much lower metabolic rate. From Figure 2, a squirrel's Hb curve will be to the right of the hippopotamus Hb curve.

3. If curve C represents the O_2-dissociation curve for Hb of an adult human, which of the following best explains why curve B most closely corresponds with the curve for fetal Hb?

    A. O_2 affinity of fetal Hb is lower than adult Hb

    B. O_2 affinity of fetal Hb is higher than adult Hb

    C. metabolic rate of fetal tissue is lower than adult tissue

    D. metabolic rate of fetal tissue is higher than adult tissue

B is correct.

Fetal Hb has a higher affinity for O_2 than adult Hb because oxygen is delivered to the fetus by diffusion across the placenta.

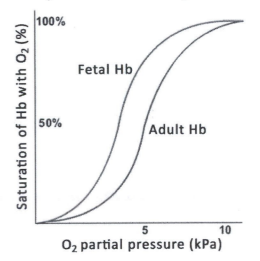

Curve B most closely resembles the oxygen-dissociation curve for fetal Hb assuming that curve C is the curve for adult Hb. At a given oxygen pressure (P_{O_2}), fetal Hb is more saturated with O_2 than adult Hb, which implies that fetal Hb has a greater affinity for O_2 than adult Hb. Due to differences in the Hb subunits, at low P_{O_2}, fetal Hb has a 20 to 30% greater affinity for O_2 than adult Hb. Oxygen binds preferentially to fetal Hb in the capillaries of the placenta.

In addition, fetal blood has a 50% higher concentration of Hb than maternal blood and this, combined with greater O_2 affinity, also increases the amount of O_2 in fetal circulation.

4. Which of the following best explains the sigmoidal shape of the Hb O_2-dissociation curve?

    A. conformational changes in the polypeptide subunits of the Hb molecule

    B. heme groups within the Hb are being reduced and oxidized

    C. changing $[H^+]$ in the blood

    D. changing $[CO_2]$ transported by Hb in the blood

A is correct.

Cooperative binding of O_2 to the two α and two β polypeptide chains of Hb yields the sigmoidal shape dissociation curve. Co-operative binding of Hb is due to conformational changes in the heme group when O_2 binds to one subunit. The conformational change results in greater affinity of Hb to bind O_2 after a subunit has bound O_2. Therefore, Hb has greatest affinity for O_2 (highest cooperativity) when three of the four heme polypeptide chains are bound to O_2.

Each heme unit is capable of binding one molecule of O_2 so Hb is capable of binding four O_2. O_2 binding to the first heme group induces a conformational (shape) change in the Hb which causes an increase in the second heme's affinity for O_2. The binding of O_2 at the second heme group increases the affinity of the third heme for O_2. The binding of O_2 at the third heme groups increases the fourth's affinity for O_2. Because of cooperativity, the graph of percent oxygen-saturation *vs* PO_2 is not linear but sigmoidal.

Fe is a necessary component of Hb. A cofactor is a non-protein (inorganic or organic) component bound to a protein (often an enzyme) that is required for the biological activity of the protein.

Loosely bound cofactors are termed *coenzymes* (often organic molecules such as vitamins) while tightly bound (iron in hemoglobin) cofactors are termed *prosthetic groups*.

Organic cofactors are often vitamins and many contain the nucleotide adenosine monophosphate (AMP).

An inactive enzyme (without its cofactor) is known as an *apoenzyme* while the complete enzyme (with cofactor) is referred to as the *holoenzyme*.

While myoglobin does have a higher affinity for oxygen than hemoglobin (Figure 2), this difference in affinity does not explain the sigmoidal shape of the curve.

B: oxidation and reduction on the Hb heme groups is a true statement. O_2 is reduced when it binds to the Fe atom of the heme group. Fe is oxidized when it releases O_2. However, this does not result in the sigmoidal shape of the curve.

C: The Bohr effect is a physiological observation where Hb's O_2 binding affinity is inversely related both to the $[CO_2]$ and acidity of the blood. An increase in blood $[CO_2]$ or decrease in blood pH (increase in H^+) results in Hb releasing its O_2 at the tissue.

Conversely, a decrease in CO_2 or an increase in pH results in hemoglobin binding O_2 and loading more O_2. CO_2 reacts with water to form carbonic acid which causes a decrease in blood pH. Carbonic anhydrase (present in erythrocytes) accelerates the formation of bicarbonate and protons, which decreases pH at the tissue and promotes the dissociation of O_2 to the tissue. In the lungs where PO_2 is high, binding of O_2 causes Hb to release H^+ which combines with bicarbonate to release CO_2 via exhalation. Since these two reactions are closely matched, homeostasis of the blood pH is maintained at about 7.35.

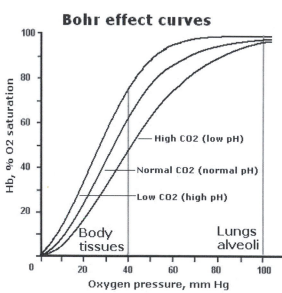

Bohr effect curves

High CO2 (low pH)

Normal CO2 (normal pH)

Low CO2 (high pH)

Body tissues

Lungs alveoli

Hb, % O2 saturation

Oxygen pressure, mm Hg

D: $[CO_2]$ in the blood affects Hb's affinity for O_2 and therefore affects the location of the curve on the O_2-dissociation graph, but $[CO_2]$ is not the reason for the sigmoidal shape. A high $[CO_2]$ in the blood decreases Hb's affinity for O_2 and shifts the curve to the right (known as the *Bohr effect*).

5. A sample of adult human Hb was placed in an $6M$ urea solution which resulted in the disruption of nonconvalent bonds. After that, the Hb α chains were isolated. If curve C represents the O_2-dissociation curve for adult human Hb *in vivo,* which curve most closely corresponds with the curve of the isolated α chains?

A. curve A   **B.** curve B   **C.** curve C   **D.** curve D

A is correct.

From the passage, the four polypeptide subunits in Hb are held together by noncovalent interactions. A $6M$ urea solution disrupts noncovalent interactions (hydrogen bonds, dipole–dipole, van der Waals and hydrophobic) and causes the subunits to dissociate. The alpha chains of this sample of hemoglobin were isolated, therefore the oxygen dissociation curve for one polypeptide chain of Hb should look similar to the dissociation curve for myoglobin (single polypeptide chain).

The isolated, single chain of the dissociated Hb polypeptide does not resemble a sigmoid curve because the unique shape of the sigmoid curve results from cooperativity of the four hemoglobin subunits. Therefore, for a single α chain dissociated by the $6M$ urea solution, cooperativity is absent.

6. In response to physiological changes, the utilization coefficient of an organism is constantly being adjusted. What value most closely represents the utilization coefficient for human adult Hb during strenuous exercise?

A. 0.0675   **B.** 0.15   **C.** 0.25   **D. 0.60**

D is correct.

Utilization coefficient is the fraction of the Hb that release its O_2 to tissues under normal conditions and is approximately 0.25. During strenuous exercise there is a greater demand for O_2 in cells undergoing an accelerated level of cellular respiration (e.g. skeletal muscle) therefore, a greater fraction of erythrocytes unload O_2 at the tissue and the utilization coefficient would be greater than 0.25.

During strenuous exercise, the utilization coefficient can reach 0.70 to 0.85 where 70-85% of the Hb dissociates O_2 in the capillaries of the tissue.

7. The Mb content in muscle of a humpback whale is about 0.005 moles/kg. Approximately how much O_2 is bound to Mb of a humpback that has 10,000 kg of muscle (assuming the Mb is saturated with O_2)?

    A. 12.5 moles   **B. 50 moles**   **C.** 200 moles   **D.** 2×10^7 moles

B is correct.

Calculate how many moles of myoglobin are present in the humpback whale's muscles.

Calculate the moles of O_2 by determining how many molecules of O_2 bind to a single molecule of myoglobin. Myoglobin binds 1 O_2 (compared to 4 O_2 for Hb) because myoglobin has a single heme group on a single polypeptide chain.

There are 0.005 moles of myoglobin per kg of muscle and the whale has 10,000 kg of muscle. Multiply 0.005 moles x 10,000 kg which equals 50 moles of myoglobin. The whale has 50 moles of myoglobin in its muscles.

One molecule of myoglobin binds to one molecule of O_2. Since the whale has 50 moles of myoglobin in its muscle (i.e. each binding 1 molecule of O_2), then 50 moles of O_2 bind to myoglobin when myoglobin is completely saturated with O_2.

Passage 2
(Questions 8–12)

Corpus luteum (from the Latin "yellow body") is a temporary endocrine structure (yellow mass of cells) in female mammals involved in the production of relatively high levels of progesterone and moderate levels of estradiol (predominant potent estrogen) and inhibin A. The estrogen it secretes inhibits the secretion of LH and FSH by the pituitary which prevent future ovulation.

The corpus luteum is essential for establishing and maintaining pregnancy in females. It is typically very large relative to the size of the ovary (in humans, the size ranges from under 2 cm to 5 cm in diameter) and its color results from concentrating carotenoids from the diet.

The corpus luteum develops from an ovarian follicle during the luteal phase of the menstrual cycle or estrous cycle, following the release of a secondary oocyte from the follicle during ovulation. While the *oocyte* (subsequently the *zygote* if fertilization occurs) traverses the *oviduct* (Fallopian tube) into the uterus, the corpus luteum remains in the ovary.

Progesterone secreted by the corpus luteum is a steroid hormone responsible for the development and maintenance of the endometrium – thick lining of the uterus that provides area rich in blood vessels in which the zygote(s) can develop. If the egg is fertilized and implantation occurs, by day 9 post-fertilization the cells of the blastocyst secrete the hormone called *human chorionic gonadotropin* (hCG) which signals the corpus luteum to continue progesterone secretion. From this point on, the corpus luteum is called the *corpus luteum graviditatis*. The presence of hCG in the urine is the indicator used by home pregnancy test kits.

If the egg is not fertilized, the corpus luteum stops secreting progesterone and decays after approximately 14 days in humans. If fertilization occurred, throughout the first trimester, the corpus luteum secretes hormones at steadily increasing levels. In the second trimester of pregnancy, the placenta (in placental animals, including humans) eventually takes over progesterone production and the corpus luteum degrades without embryo/fetus loss.

8. Could high estrogen levels be used in home pregnancy tests to indicate possible pregnancy?

   A. No, because estrogen levels also rise prior to ovulation
   B. Yes, because estrogen is secreted at high levels during pregnancy
   C. No, because antibodies in the pregnancy test kit only recognize epitopes of proteins
   D. No, because estrogen is a steroid hormone and is not excreted into the urine by kidneys

A is correct.

High levels of estrogen would not be a good indicator of pregnancy because estrogen levels fluctuate during the menstrual cycle and reach high levels just before the ovulation (release of the egg) because the ovarian follicle cells secrete estrogen in high amounts during that time. In the absence of progesterone, elevated levels of circulating estrogen actually cause active secretion of FSH and LH via a positive feedback mechanism.

Before ovulation, progesterone is at low levels and the body uses a different mechanism for LH and FSH regulation. After ovulation (and also during pregnancy), the combination of high estrogen and moderate levels of progesterone trigger a negative feedback inhibition of FSH and LH production.

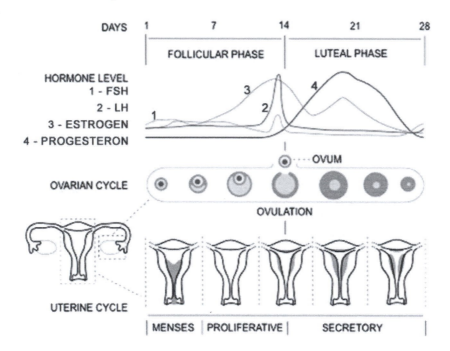

C: antibodies are composed of protein but the epitope (i.e. what the antibodies recognize as foreign and bind to) may not be a protein.

D: steroids, including estrogen, are excreted in the urine which is why urine is used for testing professional athletes for the use of anabolic steroids. Nevertheless, when testing estrogen levels, blood or saliva samples are more preferable since the test is done not to simply indicate the presence of estrogen (as most women would have it present to some extent), but to measure the specific level of the hormone for a diagnostic or therapeutic purpose.

9. All of these methods, if administered prior to ovulation, could theoretically be used as a method of female birth control, EXCEPT injecting:

    A. monoclonal antibodies for progesterone and estrogen

    B. antagonists of LH and FSH

    C. agonists that mimic the actions of estrogen and progesterone

    D. agonists that mimic the actions of LH and FSH

D is correct.

If agonist compounds were injected that mimicked the activity of FSH and LH, ovulation would occur and pregnancy would not be prevented. The FSH and LH hormones do not have inhibitory (e.g. negative feedback) effects on estrogen or progesterone and these hormones are required for pregnancy. If FSH and LH agonists (i.e. analogs) were injected they would not prevent pregnancy.

A: antibodies bind to a ligand (i.e. moiety or epitope that the antibody recognizes and binds), the ligand is either removed (from the circulatory or interstitial fluid) or inactivated. In this example, the ligand is estrogen and is bound to large antibody molecules. Estrogen and progesterone can be inactivated with monoclonal antibodies and ovulation and (subsequent) pregnancy would be blocked because the activity of these hormones is required for female reproductive function (see passage). This blocking of progesterone and estrogen could (theoretically) be used as a method for female birth control.

B: if FSH and LH activities are inhibited (i.e. by antagonists), ovulation is blocked and fertilization is not possible.

C: estrogen and progesterone are common in birth control pills. These hormones can be used to prevent pregnancy because these hormones have a negative feedback effect on LH and FSH and thereby prevent ovulation (see passage). The birth control pill inhibits ovulation because high plasma levels of progesterone and estrogen are characteristic of pregnancy.

10. How would pregnancy be affected by the removal of the ovaries in the fifth month of gestation?

  A. Not affected because LH secreted by ovaries is not necessary in the 5th month of gestation
  B. Not affected because progesterone secreted by ovaries is not necessary in the 5th month of gestation
  C. Terminated because LH secreted by ovaries is necessary in the 5th month of gestation
  D. Terminated because progesterone secreted by ovaries is necessary in the 5th month of gestation

B is correct.

The ovaries produce the female gametes (e.g. egg or ova) and are female endocrine organs that secrete estrogen and progesterone. Other endocrine organs secrete hormones that regulate the activities of the female reproductive system:

The hypothalamus secretes gonadotropin releasing hormone (GnRH) that stimulates follicle-releasing hormone (FSH) and luteinizing hormone (LH) release from the anterior pituitary. FSH and LH regulate gametogenesis and the menstrual cycle. Tropic hormones have other glands as their target and most tropic hormones are produced and secreted by the anterior pituitary.

A mnemonic for secretions from the anterior pituitary is FLAT PEG - **F**ollicle stimulating hormone (FSH), **L**uteinizing hormone (LH), **A**drenocorticotropic hormone (ACTH), **T**hyrotropic hormone (TSH), **P**rolactin (PRL), **E**nkephalins (endorphins) & **G**rowth hormone (GH or STH for somatotropin).

The posterior pituitary stores hypothalamic hormones. The posterior pituitary secretes oxytocin and vasopressin (ADH). Oxytocin stimulates uterine contractions and stimulates release of milk from mammary glands for lactation. Vasopressin stimulates increased water reabsorption by kidneys (ADH is antidiuretic hormone) and vasoconstriction of arterioles and other smooth muscle.

LH is secreted by the anterior pituitary (not the ovaries). The normal period of human gestation is nine months; the second trimester of pregnancy begins after the third month of pregnancy, and the third trimester of pregnancy begins after six months. From the passage, the corpus luteum secretes progesterone until the second trimester. At the second trimester, the placenta then continues to secrete the progesterone through the third trimester.

11. Very low levels of circulating progesterone and estrogen:

    A. inhibit the release of LH and FSH, thereby not inhibiting ovulation
    B. inhibit the release of LH and FSH and thereby inhibiting ovulation
    C. do not inhibit the release of LH and FSH, thereby not inhibiting ovulation
    D. do not inhibit the release of LH and FSH and thereby inhibiting ovulation

C is correct.

From the passage, high levels of circulating estrogen and progesterone present during pregnancy prevent ovulation (similar to the actions of birth control pills) by inhibiting the secretion of FSH and LH by the anterior pituitary. However, very low levels of estrogen and progesterone do not inhibit the secretion of FSH and LH and ovulation occurs. After menstruation, estrogen and progesterone levels are very low. Because of these low levels, the negative feedback inhibition of FSH and LH secretion is removed. The subsequent rise in FSH and LH levels indicates the onset of a new menstrual cycle.

12. Which of these hormones must be present at high levels in a blood sample of a female patient who suspects to be 10 week pregnant to confirm the pregnancy?

    I. Estrogen and progesterone
    II. FSH and LH
    III. hCG

    A. I only   **B.** I and II only   **C.** II and III only   **D. I and III only**

D is correct.

From the passage, hCG (human chorionic gonadotropin) levels rise after fertilization and the presence of hCG in urine is the basis of some pregnancy tests. hCG is secreted until the 2nd trimester of pregnancy (through the 3rd month of pregnancy). Therefore, hCG could be used as an indicator for pregnancy between the 1st and 3rd months of gestation.

High levels of estrogen and progesterone are present throughout pregnancy. Estrogen and progesterone levels also rise during the menstrual cycle. Therefore, high levels of these two hormones alone do not indicate pregnancy. However, in conjunction with the presence of hCG, high levels of estrogen and progesterone are consistent with pregnancy.

II: FSH and LH secretion are inhibited (by high levels of estrogen and progesterone) during pregnancy to prevent ovulation.

> Questions 13 through 16 are not based on any descriptive passage and are independent of each other

13. Which of the following molecules is the site of NMR spin-spin coupling?

A. CH_4 **B.** FCH_2CH_2F **C.** $(CH_3)_3CCl$ **D.** CH_3CH_2Br

D is correct.

Splitting pattern is determined by the formula $n + 1$ where n is the number of (non-equivalent) adjacent hydrogens.

CH_3CH_2Br has two peaks (two sets of non-equivalent hydrogens) with one peak (-CH_3) split into a triplet with an integration number of 3 and the other peak (-CH_2) split into a quartet with an integration number of 2.

A: CH_4 has a single peak with an integration number of 4.

B: FCH_2CH_2F has a single peak with an integration number of 4.

C: $(CH_3)_3CBr$ has a single peak with an integration number of 9.

14. Which of the following is correct about the hybridization of the three carbon atoms in the following molecule indicated by arrows?

A. C_1 is *sp* hybridized, C_2 is *sp²* hybridized and C_3 is *sp³* hybridized
B. C_1 is *sp²* hybridized, C_2 is *sp²* hybridized and C_3 is *sp* hybridized
C. C_1 is *sp* hybridized, C_2 is *sp²* hybridized and C_3 is *sp²* hybridized
D. C_1 is *sp²* hybridized, C_2 is *sp²* hybridized and C_3 is *sp²* hybridized

C is correct.

C_1 is in a triple bond of an alkyne. The carbon of alkynes has two σ (single) bonds and two π (the double and the triple) bonds. The carbon of an alkyne is *sp* hybridized.

C_2 is in a double bond of an alkene. The carbon of alkenes has three σ (single) bonds and one π (double) bond. The carbon of an alkene is *sp²* hybridized.

C_3 is a carbocation and *sp²* hybridized. The carbocation has a vacant unhybridized p orbital that corresponds to the carbocation.

The *sp³* hybridized carbon is part of a single bond in the alkane. All hybridized *sp³* hybridized orbitals create 4 σ (single) bonds.

The *sp²* hybridized carbon uses three orbitals for 3 σ (single) bonds and also contains an unhybridized p orbital. An unhybridized p orbital can be one of 4 species: a π of the alkene with a double bond to the adjacent carbon; a vacant unhybridized p orbital of the carbocation; a single electron of the radical; or two electrons of the carbanion. Carbanions are reactive species with the carbon having a negative formal charge due to the additional valence electron.

The *sp* hybridized carbon uses two orbitals for 2 σ (single) bonds and also contains two unhybridized p orbitals ($sp + p + p$). The unhybridized p orbitals can be one of 5 species: two π of the triple bond (i.e. most common variant); two π of the alkene with two double bonds on both adjacent carbons (cumulated double bonds); double bond with a vacant unhybridized *p* of the carbocation; double bond with a single electron of the radical; or double bond with two electrons of the carbanion.
Note: carbocations exist with vacant unhybridized p orbitals.

Radicals exist as a single (unpaired) electron in unhybridized p orbitals.

Carbanions (i.e. carbons with negative charges) exist with a pair of electrons in the unhybridized p orbital.

15. The extracellular fluid volume depends on the total sodium content in the body. The balance between Na^+ intake and Na^+ loss regulates Na^+ level. Which of the following will occur following the administration of digoxin, a poison that blocks the Na^+/K^+ ATPase?

A. **increased intracellular $[H_2O]$**   **C.** increased extracellular $[Na^+]$
B. increased intracellular $[Cl^-]$ **D.** increased intracellular $[K^+]$

A is correct.

The Na^+/K^+ ATPase transports 3 Na^+ ions out and 2 K^+ ions into the cell.

Digoxin (also known as digitalis) is similar to ouabain since both disrupt the ATPase pump and therefore degrade the ion concentration gradient normally maintained (Na^+ ions outside of the cell and K^+ ions inside of the cell) by the ATPase pump. With the ATPase pump absent, 3 Na^+ and 2 K^+ ions move down their concentration gradient and in the direction of their natural equilibrium where Na^+ enters the cell and K^+ flows out of the cell and into in the extracellular space.

Then water follows the Na^+ into the cell, causing massive swelling and, eventually, lysis (i.e. plasmolysis – rupturing of the plasma membrane) of the cell.

16. To selectively function on ingested proteins and avoid digestion of a body's proteins in the digestive system, pancreatic peptidases must be tightly regulated. Which mechanism activates pancreatic peptidases?

    A. osmolarity   **C.** carbohydrate moieties
    B. coenzyme binding   **D.** **proteolytic cleavage**

D is correct.

Zymogens are inactive enzymes that are synthesized in an inactive form at one location within the body and then are transported to their target location where they undergo *proteolytic cleavage* (i.e. cutting of the peptide bond that connects the inactive portion from the active portion of the functional protein) and convert into an active form. pH is often a controlling factor of proteolytic cleavage.
Pancreatic peptidases (enzymes end in ~ase) must be tightly controlled to prevent degradation of endogenous human proteins. The enzymes, once in the intestinal lumen, are activated by brush border enzymes. Pepsin (within the stomach) is the classic example of pH-dependent activation.

The pancreas secretes HCO_3 (sodium bicarbonate) to neutralize gastric (stomach) acidity. Once the chyme (food) enters the small intestine, HCO_3 adjusts the pH of chyme exiting the stomach with the pH of 2 to pH to 7.2 of the small intestine. The stomach has a low pH because HCl (hydrochloric acid) is secreted into the stomach for pre-digestion of dietary proteins. Once chyme leaves the stomach and enters the small intestine, there is a significant change in pH via HCO_3.

Temperature, ion concentration and osmolarity are all tightly regulated – homeostasis – within the body and, because they do not fluctuate widely, could not function as the triggers for proteolytic cleavage as zymogens move from the origin of synthesis to the site of activation.

Peptidases are enzymes that do not require coenzymes or cofactors. A cofactor is an inorganic substance bound to an enzyme and is classified depending on how tightly it binds to an enzyme. Loosely-bound cofactors are termed coenzymes and tightly-bound cofactors are termed prosthetic groups.

Organic cofactors are often vitamins (or made from vitamins). Many cofactors contain nucleotide monophosphate (AMP) as part of their structure: including ATP, coenzyme A, FAD and NAD^+. Other examples of cofactors are magnesium in chlorophyll and heme in hemoglobin.

A prosthetic group is a non-amino acid component of a protein. Prosthetic groups are often bound tightly in a reversible manner to the enzyme and confer new properties upon the conjugated enzyme.

An apoenzyme is an inactive enzyme (without the cofactor bound). The complete (active) enzyme with the cofactor attached is a holoenzyme.

A coenzyme is a non-protein organic molecule that plays an accessory (but not a necessary) role in the catalytic action of an enzyme.

Passage 3
(Questions 17–21)

In pharmacology, a natural product is a chemical compound or substance produced by a living organism found in nature that usually has a pharmacological or biological activity for pharmaceutical drug discovery and drug design. However, a natural product can be classified as such even if it can be prepared by laboratory synthesis. Not all natural products can be fully synthesized because many have very complex structures making it too difficult or expensive to synthesize on an industrial scale. These compounds can only be harvested from their natural source - a process which can be tedious, time consuming, expensive, and wasteful on the natural resource.

Enediynes are a class of natural bacterial products characterized by either nine- or ten-membered rings containing two triple bonds separated by a double bond. Many enediyne compounds are extremely toxic to DNA. They are known to cleave DNA molecules and appear to be quite effective as selective agents for anticancer activity. Therefore, enediynes are being investigated as antitumor therapeutic agents.

Classes of enediynes target DNA by binding with DNA in the minor groove. Enediynes then abstract hydrogen atoms from the deoxyribose (sugar) backbone of DNA which results in strand scission. These small molecules are active ingredient of the majority of FDA-approved agents and continue to be one of the major biomolecules for drug discovery. This enediyne molecule is proven to be a potent antitumor agent:

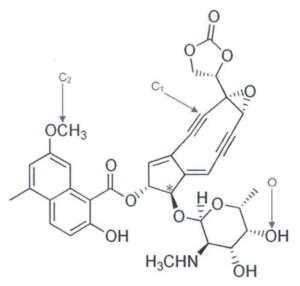

Figure 1. Neocarzinostatin

Neocarzinostatin is a chromoprotein enediyne antibiotic with anti-tumoral activity secreted by the bacteria *Streptomyces macromomyceticus*. It consists of two parts, a labile chromophore (bicyclic dienediyne structure shown) and a 113 amino acid apoprotein with the chromophores non-covalently bound with a high affinity. The *chromophore* is a very potent DNA-damaging agent because it is very labile and plays a role to protect and release the cleaved target DNA. Opening of the epoxide under reductive conditions present in cells creates favorable conditions and leads to a diradical intermediate and subsequent double-stranded DNA cleavage.

17. Which functional groups is NOT present in the molecule of neocarzinostatin?

A. thiol   **B.** hydroxyl   **C.** ester   **D.** epoxide

A is correct.

The functional group not present on the molecule is a thiol (-SH).

The functional groups present in the molecule include: three hydroxyl (–OH of an alcohol) groups; one epoxide (a three-membered ring that has oxygen bridging the two carbons); a secondary amine group (–NHR); one ether (–COC–); two esters and a diester are present.

18. What is the hybridization of the two carbon atoms and the oxygen atom indicated by the arrows in Figure 1?

    A. C_1 is sp^2, C_2 is sp^2 and O is sp^2 hybridized
    B. C_1 is sp^2, C_2 is sp and O is sp hybridized
    C. C_1 is sp, C_2 is sp^2 and O is sp^2 hybridized
    D. C_1 is sp, C_2 is sp^3 and O is sp^3 hybridized

D is correct.

Carbon has 4 hybridized orbitals of $s + p + p + p$ for the sp^3 hybridization for single bonds. The C_1 atom has two σ (sigma) bonds and two π (pi) bonds with two electrons shared for each the double and triple bond. Therefore the C_1 atom is sp hybridized, which refers to hybridized orbitals of s and p. Hence the other two unhybridized orbitals (p and p) are used for the double (two electrons in the p orbital) and triple bond (two electrons in the p orbital) for each of the π bonds.

The C_2 atom has 4 σ (single) bonds and is neutral because it has 4 bonds. Variations from the neutral C atom could include a positive charged carbocation (vacant p orbital) or radical (single unpaired electron in the p orbital) or a negative charged carbanion (with two nonbonding electrons in the p orbital).

The neutral oxygen atom has two σ bonds and two lone electron pairs and is therefore sp^3 hybridized.

19. How many chiral carbons are in the molecule of neocarzinostatin?

    A. 4   **B.** 8   **C. 10**   **D.** 12

C is correct.

The neocarzinostatin molecule has 10 chiral centers (as indicated by the asterisks in the diagram below).

The total number of possible stereoisomers is 2^n. The value of $2^{10} = 1,024$ possible stereoisomers. Among these 1,024 stereoisomers, one is the original molecule and one is the mirror image (i.e. enantiomer) and the others are non-mirror images (i.e. diasteriomers).

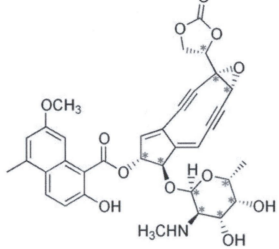

20. How many π bonds are in the molecule of neocarzinostatin?

   A. 7   **B.** 9   **C.** 11   **D.** 13

D is correct.

Single bonds contain only σ bonds.

Every bond other than single (σ) contains a π bond. Double bonds have one σ bond and one π bond (with two electrons in each π bond). Triple bonds have one σ bond and two π bonds (with two electrons in each π bond).

21. Which of the following is correct about the absolute configuration of the carbon atom indicated (*)?

   A. it has an *S* absolute configuration
   B. it has an *R* absolute configuration
   C. it is not chiral
   D. absolute configuration cannot be determined

B is correct.

Since the order of the prioritized groups is clockwise, the absolute configuration is *R* (versus *S* for counterclockwise).

Note, there is no connection between the absolute configuration (*R vs S*) and the rotation of plane polarized light (+ *vs* –) when measured by the polarimeter. (+) is designated for clockwise rotation of plane-polarized light versus (–) for counterclockwise rotation of plane-polarized light.

For absolute configuration (R vs S stereospecific) notation about a tetrahedral carbon atom, two bonds (i.e. lines) are in the plane of the paper while one bond is pointing out (i.e. wedge) and one bond is pointing back (i.e. dashed line).

First assign priorities to each moiety (i.e. group attached). When assigning priority (according to Cahn-Ingold-Prelog), use the first point of difference in atomic number of the attached atoms and not the aggregate atomic number for all substituents attached to an atom.

Priority group #1 (a single oxygen) is higher in priority than group #2 (carbon attached to an oxygen, a carbon and a hydrogen) and is higher in priority than group #3 (carbon attached to three carbons). Group #4 is a H (not shown) pointing back into the plane as a dash line (not shown).

Passage 4
(Questions 22–26)

The human digestive system functions by a highly coordinated chain of mechanisms consisting of ingestion, digestion and nutrient absorption. Digestion is a progressive process that begins with ingestion into the mouth and continues with digestion in the stomach and with digestion and absorption in the three sections of the small intestine.

Digestion involves macromolecules being broken down by enzymes into their component molecules before absorption through the villi of the small intestine. Nutrients from digested food such as vitamins, mineral and subunits of macromolecules (e.g. monosaccharides, amino acids, di– or tripeptides, glycerol and fatty acids) are absorbed via either diffusion or transport (facilitated or active) mechanisms. These transport mechanisms may occur with or without mineral co-transport.

Digestive enzymes at the intestinal brush border work with digestive enzymes secreted by salivary glands and the pancreas to facilitate nutrient absorption. Digestion of complex carbohydrates into simple sugars is an example of this process. Pancreatic α-amylase hydrolyzes the 1,4–glycosidic bonds in complex starches to oligosaccharides in the lumen of the small intestine. The membrane-bound intestinal α-glucosidases hydrolyze oligosaccharides, trisaccharides and disaccharides to glucose and other monosaccharides in the small intestine.

Acarbose is a starch blocker used as an anti-diabetic drug to treat type-2 diabetes mellitus. Acarbose is an inhibitor of α–1,4-glucosidase (an enteric brush-border enzyme) and pancreatic α-amylase that release glucose from complex starches. The inhibition of these enzyme systems reduces the rate of digestion of complex carbohydrates resulting in less glucose being absorbed because the carbohydrates are not broken down into glucose molecules. For diabetic patients, the short-term effect of such drug therapy is a decreased current blood glucose levels and the long-term effect is a reduction of the HbA1C levels.

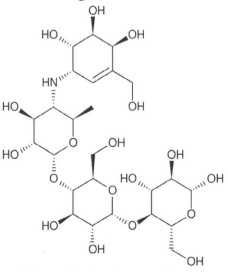

Figure 1. Acarbose molecule

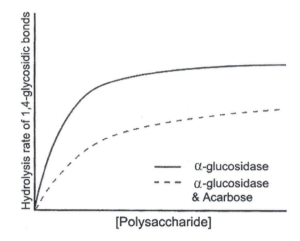

Figure 2. The kinetics of α-glucosidase in the presence/absence of acarbose.

22. According to the graph (Figure 2), how are α-1,4-glucosidase enzyme kinetics affected by acarbose?

    A. The concentration of available enzyme is reduced
    B. Enzyme specificity for the substrate is changed
    C. The K_{eq} binding of the ligand : enzyme complex is changed
    D. Covalent bonds that irreversibly inactivate the enzyme's active site are formed

A is correct.

The enzyme kinetics graph shows the reaction rate as a function of [substrate] and not acarbose (inhibitor) concentration. Note: [ ] signifies a reference to concentration.

Acarbose directly blocks the glucosidase enzyme's binding site and reduces the amount of free enzyme available to bind the ligand. A ligand is a molecule that binds to the active site of an enzyme (or to a receptor within a membrane). The substrate is the molecule that the enzyme acts upon after the substrate binds to the active site of the enzyme. Acarbose directly blocks binding of the substrate and decreases the observed rate because there are fewer unbound enzymes available to bind to the substrate.

From the graph, acarbose is acting as a competitive inhibitor because the V_{max} (on y axis) is reduced. Therefore, increasing the concentration of the acarbose decreases the relative rate (V_{max}) of the reaction.

Reversible inhibition involves weak bonds such as hydrogen bonds (i.e. normally observed for enzymes). Competitive inhibitors are reversible (not permanently bond via strong covalent bonds) and competitive inhibitors do not inactivate the amino acid residues within the active site of the enzyme.

Irreversible inhibition involves strong bonds such as covalent bonds. Poisons are a classic example of a molecule that binds irreversibly to enzymes.

Allosteric regulation means that the enzymes' shape changes due to conformational change. Conformational changes (e.g. chair conformers of cyclohexane or Newman projections) are examples of shape changes due to free rotation around single bonds.

23. Which type of α-1,4–glucosidase inhibition is most closely demonstrated by acarbose?

    A. irreversible covalent modification   **C. competitive**
    B. allosteric   **D.** noncompetitive

C is correct.

Competitive inhibition "directly inhibits" binding of the enzyme to the substrate. Figure 2 illustrates that in the absence of the competitor (e.g. acarbose), as [substrate] increases, the reaction rate approaches the V_{max}. Therefore, when [ligand] increases, it outcompetes acarbose for the same binding site on the enzyme.

V_{max} and K_m are concepts of enzyme kinetics and how they are affected by inhibition is important.

Competitive inhibition is when the competitor binds directly to the active site of the enzyme. Competitive inhibition can be altered by increasing or decreasing the relative ratio of [ligand] and [inhibitor].

Noncompetitive inhibition is when the competitor binds to a site other than the active site (i.e. allosteric site) of the enzyme which induces a conformational change (i.e. shape change) of the enzyme. With allosteric inhibition (noncompetitive inhibition), the competitor is either prevented (i.e. steric interference) or has less affinity (after the conformational change) for binding to the active site. Some conformational changes result in increased affinity of the ligand to the active site and this modulation is referred to as positive cooperativity.

Noncompetitive inhibition is not altered by increasing or decreasing the relative ratio of [ligand] and [inhibitor] because the competitor is not competing with the ligand for the same active site on the enzyme.

24. Which condition most closely resembles the symptoms resulting from α-1,4-glucosidase inhibition by acarbose?

    A. infection by *V. cholera*   **C. deficiency of lactase**
    B. deficiency of intrinsic factor   **D.** deficiency of bile acid

C is correct.

If the glucosidase (i.e. enzymes end in –ase) is blocked, polysaccharides are not digested and therefore not absorbed because only monosaccharides can be absorbed across the lining of the small intestine. If polysaccharides are not digested, they pass as indigestible material and, like indigestible dietary fiber from cellulose, are excreted in feces.

Lactase (ending in –ase) is an enzyme that digests the lactose (milk sugar) disaccharide. Normally, the intestinal villi secrete the enzyme lactase (β-D-galactosidase) to digest lactose into glucose and galactose monosaccharides that are absorbed across the wall of the small intestine. Without lactase, the disaccharide lactose cannot be cleaved into monosaccharides (glucose and galactose) to be absorbed within the small intestine, and is excreted in the feces.

Deficiency of lactase (commonly called lactose intolerance) is characterized by abdominal bloating, cramps, flatulence, diarrhea. Acarbose treatment of type 2 diabetes often produces similar side effects because undigested carbohydrates remain in the intestine and pass through the colon where bacteria digest complex carbohydrates causing these gastrointestinal side-effects.

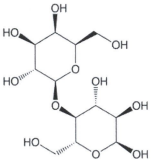

Lactose: β-D-galactopyranosyl-(1-4)-D-glucose

A: cholera is an infection of the small intestine caused by the bacterium *Vibrio cholerae*. Cholera affects ion channels in the intestinal mucosa resulting in profuse, watery diarrhea and vomiting.

B: an intrinsic factor deficiency results in vitamin B_{12} malabsorption (i.e. pernicious anemia). Intrinsic factor (IF) also known as gastric intrinsic factor (GIF) is a glycoprotein synthesized in the stomach by parietal cells (i.e. stomach epithelium cells that secrete gastric acid – HCl). Intrinsic factor is necessary for the absorption of vitamin B_{12} later in the small intestine.

D: bile acid deficiency results in fat malabsorption (i.e. steatorrhea). The main function of bile acid is to facilitate the formation of micelles which promote processing of dietary fat. Bile acids are steroid acids found predominantly in the bile of mammals. Bile is dark green to yellowish brown fluid, produced by the liver that aids the process of digestion of lipids in the small intestine. In many species, bile is stored in the gallbladder and upon eating is discharged into the duodenum.

25. Which molecule does NOT require micelle formation for intestinal absorption?

   A. vitamin A   **B.** triglycerides   **C.** cholesterol   **D. bile acid**

D is correct.

Bile acids are made in the liver by oxidation of cholesterol.

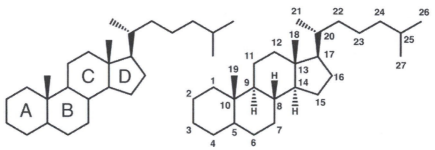

Cholesterol-steroid ring nomenclature

Only lipid components (e.g. cholesterol, triglycerides and fat-soluble vitamins such as A, D and E) are absorbed within micelles through the brush border of the intestine and enter the circulatory system. Bile acids function to stabilize micelle formation. Bile acids are stored in the gallbladder and may be excreted or reabsorbed via Na^+-dependent transport. The human body produces about 800 mg of cholesterol per day and about half of that is used for bile acid synthesis. About 20-30 grams of bile acids are secreted into the intestine daily and about 90% are reabsorbed by active transport in the ileum and recycled in the enterohepatic circulation, which moves the bile salts from the intestinal system back to the liver and the gallbladder.

26. Glucosidase is best characterized as a:

   A. hydrolase   **B.** isomerase   **C.** ligase   **D.** phosphatase

A is correct.

The *y*-axis (vertical axis) of the graph is labeled hydrolysis whereby a water molecule acts as a nucleophile with the lone pair of electrons on the oxygen breaking a bond: hydrolysis is the breaking (i.e. lysis) by the addition of H_2O.

There are six categories of enzymes:

- *Hydrolases* break bonds via hydrolysis (i.e. adding water).

- *Oxidoreductases* catalyze oxidation/reduction reactions.

- *Lyases* (commonly known as synthetases or synthases) catalyze the breaking of chemical bonds via hydrolysis and oxidation and often form new double bonds or a new ring structure (e.g. ATP → cAMP and PP_i). Lyases are unusual for enzymes because they require only one substrate in one direction but two substrates for the reverse reaction.

- *Isomerases* catalyze the structural rearrangement of isomers.

- *Ligases* catalyze the joining of two large molecules (e.g. nucleotides in synthesis of nucleic acid) by forming a new chemical bond usually via dehydration (i.e. condensation).

- *Transferases* catalyze the transfer of a functional group (e.g. methyl, phosphate, and hydroxyl) from one molecule to another.

  Two common examples include kinases and phosphatase. Kinases transfer phosphate groups from high–energy donor molecules (e.g. ATP) to specific substrates known as phosphorylation. Kinases function as the reverse of a phosphatase. Phosphatases remove phosphate groups (e.g. alkaline phosphatase) from its substrate. Phosphatases function as the reverse of a kinase.

Questions 27 through 30 are not based on any descriptive passage and are independent of each other

---

27. Which of the following is required for the proper function of the DNA-dependent DNA polymerase?

> **I. DNA template strand**   **III. 4 different nucleotides**
> **II. primase (RNA primer)**   IV. RNA polymerase

  A. I and II only   **B.** I and III only   **C. I, II and III only**   **D.** I, II, III & IV

C is correct.

DNA polymerase requires four different nucleotides (dNTPs) with A, C, G, T bases, a DNA template and a short strand RNA primer for the DNA polymerase to bind for initiation of replication.

DNA polymerase binds to a short segment of RNA (primer) and begins replication by complimentary binding to the DNA template strand. Without an RNA primer, the DNA polymerase cannot bind to the sense strand of DNA and replication cannot occur. RNA primase (an enzyme that joins about 8 RNA nucleotides) synthesizes the RNA strand for DNA polymerase to bind. The DNA polymerase (after the short RNA primer) then adds individual nucleotides complementary to the DNA strand. In DNA, base A is a compliment to base T, while C is a compliment to G. The DNA polymerase catalyzes

---

nucleotides to join along the sugar-phosphate backbone with hydrogen bonds between the bases of the nucleotide.

IV: RNA polymerase synthesizes mRNA from the DNA template during transcription.

28. Given that the availability of the carbon source determines energy yield, catabolism of which molecule will result in the highest energy yield?

    A. short-chain unsaturated fatty acid   **C.** long-chain conjugated fatty acid
    B. short-chain saturated fatty acid   **D. long-chain saturated fatty acid**

D is correct.

Acetyl CoA is an important 2-carbon metabolic intermediate entering the Krebs cycle in cellular respiration and free fatty acids serve as a carbon source for acetyl CoA production. The longer the carbon backbone of the fatty acid, the greater is the energy yield from the catabolism of the molecule because of the cleaving of a greater number of bonds.

Conjugation refers to a molecule with alternating single and double bonds. Both the presence of unsaturation and the added stability of conjugation result in less energy yield from conjugated fatty acids as the original molecule undergoing catabolism.

Double bonds refer to unsaturated (not saturated with Hs) molecules and result in a decrease in the potential (chemical) energy storage in the bonds. Therefore, unsaturated fatty acid catabolism yields less energy compared to saturated fatty acids of the same carbon chain length.

29. Which molecule has the closest to 3000-3500 cm^{-1} infrared (IR) stretch?

    A. $H_2C=CH_2CH_3$ **C. CH_3CH_2OH**
    B. CH_3CH_2COOH **D.** $(CH_3CH_2)_2CO$

C is correct.

CH_3CH_2OH is an alcohol which shows a broad, deep absorption in the region from 3000-3500 cm^{-1} of the infrared spectrum.

A: $H_2C=CH_2CH_3$ is an alkene which shows the absorption in the 2100-2300 cm^{-1} region of the infrared spectrum and this is characteristic of C≡C and C≡N triple bonds.

B: CH_3CH_2COOH is a carboxylic acid where the hydroxyl absorption shows a broad, deep absorption shifted to 2800-3200 cm^{-1} (compared to 3000-3500 cm^{-1} for alcohols) and it is also characteristic of strong, sharp absorption of the carbonyl in the region 1630-1740 cm^{-1}

D: $(CH_3CH_2)_2CO$ is a ketone which shows a strong, sharp absorption in the 1630-1740 cm^{-1} region of the infrared spectrum which is characteristic of carbonyls. Carbonyls are present in seven molecules: aldehyde, ketone, acyl halide, anhydrides, carboxylic acid, ester and amide.

30. Which of these compounds have a dipole moment?

     I. CCl_4
   II. **CH_3CH_2OH**
   III. **$CH_3CHBrCH_3$**

  A. II only   **B.** III only   **C.** I and III only   **D.** **II and III only**

D is correct.

A dipole moment is the vector sum of the individual bond dipoles in a molecule.

I: is carbon tetrachloride and the individual C-Cl dipoles of the symmetric molecule cancel so CCl_4 has no net dipole moment.

II and III: are asymmetric because they each have one highly polar bond (C-Br and C-O) and both have dipole moments originating from these polar covalent bonds.

Passage 5
(Questions 31–35)

Penicillins are one of the most successful classes of antibiotics derived from *Penicillium* fungi. They include penicillin G, penicillin V, procaine penicillin and benzathine penicillin. Penicillin antibiotics were the first drugs that treated serious diseases such as syphilis, staphylococci and streptococci. Penicillins are still widely used today but many types of bacteria are now resistant to them. All penicillins are β-lactam antibiotics and are used in the treatment of bacterial infections caused by susceptible, usually Gram-positive, organisms.

The initial efforts to synthesize penicillin proved difficult with discrepancies in the structure being reported from different laboratories. In 1957, chemist John Sheehan at the Massachusetts Institute of Technology (MIT) completed the first chemical synthesis of penicillin. However, the synthesis developed by Sheehan was not appropriate for mass production of penicillins. One of the intermediate compounds was 6-aminopenicillanic acid (6-APA). Attaching different groups to the 6-APA allowed the synthesis of new forms of penicillin.

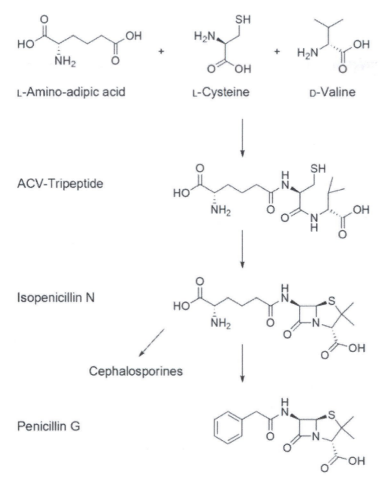

Figure 1. Penicillin biosynthesis

The structure of the penicillins includes a five-membered ring containing both sulfur and nitrogen (i.e. thioazolidine ring) joined to a four-membered ring containing a cyclic amide (i.e. β-lactam). These two rings are necessary for the biological activities of penicillin and cleavage of either ring disrupts antibacterial activity.

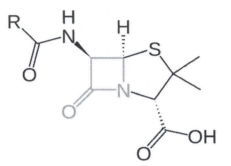

Figure 2. Core structure of penicillins (beta-lactam ring highlighted)

A medical student performed three experiments to elucidate how penicillin resulted in the death of bacterial cell.

Experiment 1

Two bacterial species were cultured and grown on agar plates. Both species had normal peptidoglycan cell walls. One population was exposed to penicillin while the other was not exposed to penicillin. About 93% of the bacteria treated with penicillin underwent cytolysis and did not survive while the bacteria which were not exposed to penicillin were unaffected.

Experiment 2

Two bacterial species were cultured and grown on agar plates. One species had an intact peptidoglycan cell wall while the other species had an incomplete cell wall. Both groups were exposed to penicillin on the agar plates and the bacteria with incomplete cell walls survived while 93% of those with intact peptidoglycan cell walls did not survive.

Experiment 3

The 7% who survived the treatment of penicillin in Experiment 2 were cultured and grown on agar plates. These colonies were repeatedly inoculated with penicillin and the colonies grew continuously with no apparent affect from the antibiotic.

31. It is reasonable to hypothesize that penicillin causes the bacterial death likely by:

    A. blocking the colonies' access to nutrients
    B. disrupting the integrity of the bacterial cell wall
    C. establishing excessive rigidity in the bacterial cell wall
    D. inducing mutations in bacteria from gram negative to gram positive strains

B is correct.

Peptidoglycan cross-linking of the bacterial cell wall is needed for the cell to resist osmotic pressure and the subsequent cytolysis of the bacteria. Penicillin inhibits the last step of cross-linking of peptidoglycan during the synthesis of the bacterial cell wall.

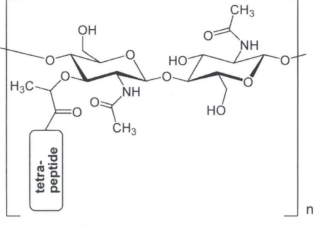

Peptidoglycan monomer

The peptidoglycan layer in the bacterial cell wall is a crystal lattice structure formed from linear chains of two alternating amino sugars. The alternating sugars are connected by a β-(1,4)-glycosidic bond (i.e. between the hemiacetal of one sugar with the hydroxyl on the adjacent sugar). One sugar is attached to a short (4- to 5-residue) amino acid chain which helps protect the bacteria against attacks by most peptidases.

Bacteria constantly remodel their peptidoglycan cell walls, simultaneously building and breaking down portions of the cell wall as they grow and divide. β-lactam antibiotics inhibit the formation of peptidoglycan cross-links in the bacterial cell wall. The enzymes that normally hydrolyze the peptidoglycan cross-links continue to function which weakens the bacteria's cell wall and osmotic pressure increases – eventually causing cell death via cytolysis.

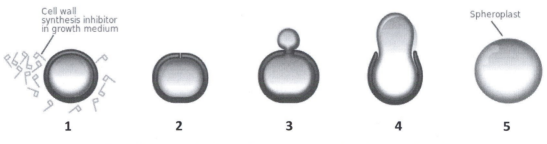

Penicillin's mechanism of action on peptidoglycan cell wall.

32. Knowing that penicillin G is rapidly hydrolyzed under acidic conditions, which limitation applies to its use?

    A. it is not active in the range of plasma pH
    B. it must be administered intravenously
    C. it must be taken 30 to 60 minutes before eating
    D. it should be avoided by young children and elderly patients

B is correct.

Benzylpenicillin, also known as penicillin G, is the "gold standard" type of penicillin (G in its name refers to "gold standard"). Penicillin G is typically given intravenously (injected directly into the venous circulation) or by other parenteral (not oral) route of administration because it is unstable in the hydrochloric acid of the stomach.

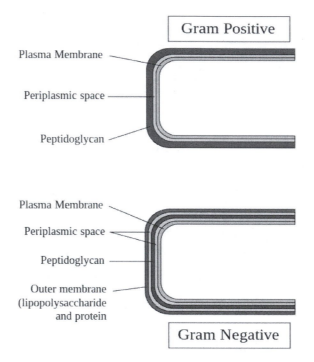

Phenoxymethylpenicillin (also called penicillin V) is an orally active penicillin type as it is more acid-stable than penicillin G, which allows it to be given orally. However, it is less active than penicillin G against Gram-negative bacteria.

33. From the experiments, which bacterial species are most resistant to penicillin?

    A. Species unable to transcribe DNA to RNA
    B. Species with complete peptidoglycan cell walls
    C. Species with incomplete cross-linked cell walls
    D. Species with the greatest intracellular osmotic pressure

C is correct.

From experiment 2, bacteria with incomplete cell walls survived while 93% of bacteria with a normal peptidoglycan cell wall underwent cytolysis.

Bacterial cell walls are composed of peptidoglycan while plants have cell walls made of cellulose (i.e. dietary fiber) consisting of glucose monomers.

34. What causes the bacterial cells to undergo cytolysis upon weakening of their cell wall?

> **A. water enters the cells due to osmotic pressure**
> **B.** proteins are not able to exit the cell through vesicles
> **C.** solutes are forced out of the cells through active transport mechanisms
> **D.** facilitated diffusion causes lipid-insoluble substances to cross the cell membrane

A is correct.

Osmotic pressure is a force that allows water to enter bacterial cells through the plasma membrane because bacterial cells have a high solute concentration compared to the medium in which the bacterium is located. The cell wall with cross-linked peptidoglycan is a rigid structure that opposes this pressure and prevents the bacterial cell from swelling and undergoing cytolysis. In the absence of an intact peptidoglycan cross-linked cell wall, the osmotic pressure causes swelling as water enters the bacteria and lyses the bacteria (i.e. cytolysis or plasmolysis).

35. It is a reasonable hypothesis that 7% of the cell-walled bacteria treated with penicillin in experiments 1 and 2 survived due to:

> **A.** bacterial cell wall's impermeability to penicillin
> **B.** agar on the growth plates that hydrolyzed and degraded penicillin
> **C. plasmids that synthesize penicillinase**
> **D.** limitation of diffusion which resulted in select colonies not being exposed to penicillin

C is correct.

The variation of survival rate is not simply a matter of penicillin concentration. The 7% of the bacteria that survived required the cells to be genetically different and not dependant on the penicillin. Plasmids are extrachromosomal pieces of DNA that confer antibiotic resistance to bacteria by synthesizing enzymes that cleave the antibiotic. Penicillinase is an enzyme that inactivates penicillin.

The resistant bacteria cells pass the plasmids and the corresponding antibiotic resistance to future generations during cell replication (experiment 3). Plasmids can also be transferred to other (non daughter cell) bacteria by transformation (uptake of genetic information from the solution), transduction (viral vector) or conjugation (via a sex pili). A plasmid within the bacteria that increases the expression of the penicillinase enzyme likely confers penicillin resistance in bacterial cells that survived.

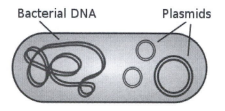

Bacterium with chromosomal DNA and plasmids

Passage 6
(Questions 36–41)

Adipose tissue is loose connective tissue composed of adipocytes and stores free fatty acids as triglycerides. A fatty acid is a carboxylic acid with a long aliphatic tail (often with even numbers of carbons between 4 to 28) that is either saturated or unsaturated. Saturated refers to the aliphatic chain which lacks double bonds while unsaturated chains contain one or more double bonds.

Glycerol, a three-carbon molecule, contains three hydroxyl groups with a single OH on each of the three carbons. Glycerol is the backbone for triglycerides and each hydroxyl group is the attachment point for a free fatty acid. The hydroxyl on the glycerol attacks the carboxylic acid group of the free fatty acid to form an ester linkage bond.

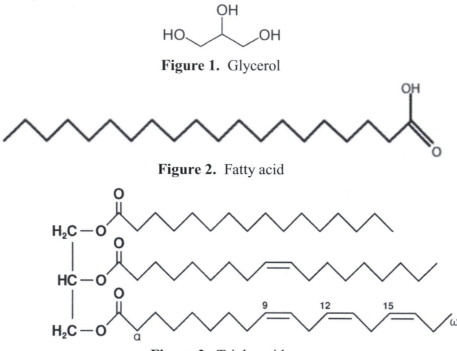

Figure 1. Glycerol

Figure 2. Fatty acid

Figure 3. Triglyceride

Triglycerides are released from adipose tissue into the circulatory system during high demands for energy by peripheral muscle tissue. The release of free fatty acids is controlled by a complex series of reactions tightly modulated by *hormone-sensitive lipase* (HSL). HSL hydrolyzes the first fatty acid from a triglyceride freeing a fatty acid and a diglyceride. HSL is activated when the body needs to mobilize energy stores and responds positively to catecholamines and adrenocorticotropic hormone (ACTH), but is inhibited by insulin. Lipase activators bind receptors that are coupled to adenylate cyclase which increases cAMP for activation of an appropriate *kinase* (PKA) that then activates HSL.

Free fatty acids targeted for breakdown are transported bound to *albumin* through the circulation. However, fatty acids targeted for adipose storage sites in adipocytes are transported in large lipid-protein micelle particles termed *lipoproteins* (i.e. LDL). During high rates of mitochondrial fatty acid oxidation, acetyl CoA is produced in large amounts. If the generation of acetyl CoA from glycolysis exceeds utilization by the Krebs cycle, an alternative pathway is ketone body synthesis. During the onset of starvation, skeletal and cardiac muscles preferentially metabolize ketone bodies which preserves endogenous glucose for the brain.

36. Albumin is the most abundant protein distributed throughout circulatory system and accounts for about 50% of plasma proteins. Which bond and for what reason binds albumin to free fatty acids?

  A. hydrogen bonding to albumin stabilizes fatty acid absolute configuration
  B. covalent bonding to albumin increases lipid solubility
  C. ionic bonding to albumin stabilizes free fatty acid structure
  D. van der Waals binding to albumin increases lipid solubility

D is correct.

Albumin is synthesized in the liver and is the most abundant plasma protein. It is a very important because it provides substantial oncotic pressure (i.e. osmotic pressure in the circulatory system) in blood vessels which maintains proper vascular pressure (due to osmolarity of the blood). Oncotic pressure from proteins (e.g. albumin) in the blood plasma attracts plasma (e.g. water) back into the circulatory system. Oncotic pressure counteracts the hydrostatic pressure (i.e. blood pressure) that forces blood into the interstitial space.

Without vascular osmolarity (from albumin and other proteins), fluid would leak out of the circulatory system (and cells) and flow into the interstitial space causing swelling known as edema.

Some lipid-soluble (i.e. hydrophobic) molecules also bind to albumin and thereby increase their solubility in the blood plasma (i.e. hydrophilic). Molecules transported by albumin are bonded *via* weak, non-covalent intermolecular bonds (e.g. hydrogen bonding, dipole-dipole and van der Waals attractions). In general, hydrogen bonding is used for attraction/dissociation for reversible reactions.

37. A person suffering untreated diabetes can experience ketoacidosis due to a reduced supply of glucose. Which of the following correlates with diabetic ketoacidosis?

  A. high plasma insulin levels
  B. increase in fatty acid oxidation
  C. ketone bodies increase plasma alkalinity to clinically dangerous levels
  D. decreased levels of acetyl CoA lead to increased production of ketone bodies

B is correct.

Ketoacidosis is a metabolic state associated with high concentrations of ketone bodies. In ketoacidosis, the body fails to adequately regulate ketone production causing such a severe accumulation of keto acids that the pH of the blood is decreased substantially which, in extreme cases, can be fatal.

Ketone bodies are three water-soluble compounds that are produced as by-products when fatty acids are broken down by the liver for energy. Although termed *bodies*, they are substances dissolved in the plasma. Ketone bodies are produced from acetyl-CoA (i.e. ketogenesis) mainly in the mitochondrial matrix of hepatocytes (e.g. liver cells) when carbohydrates (i.e. glucose) are so scarce that energy must be obtained from catabolism of fatty acids (and also deamination of amino acids).

A: diabetes is characterized by the inability of the beta cells of the pancreas to synthesize insulin.

Insulin stimulates cell's uptake of glucose from the blood plasma within the circulation. Insulin-dependent diabetes results from either deficient or absent insulin synthesis by the β-cells of the pancreas. In diabetes type I patients, insulin production and the associated glucose uptake does not occur. Although the plasma glucose levels of a diabetic are very high, only a small amount of glucose is transported into the cells because insulin is needed for the primary transport of glucose into cells.

As a result of the inability of the pancreas to synthesize insulin, the cell functions as though there were no plasma glucose and is similar to starvation mode. Therefore, ketone bodies are made which causes ketoacidosis observed in type I diabetes.

C: ketone bodies are acidic and lower the pH, if untreated, to dangerous levels.

D: the passage states that increased acetyl CoA levels lead to ketone body production.

38. Which of the following is the site of the breakdown for β-oxidation?

A. mitochondria   **B.** lysosomes   **C.** cytoplasm of the cell   **D.** nucleolus

A is correct.

According to the passage, beta-oxidation occurs in the mitochondrial matrix which is the location for the Krebs (i.e. TCA) cycle.

B: lysosomes are cellular organelles that contain hydrolase enzymes (i.e. catalysis via hydrolysis) for the degradation of waste material and cellular debris. They are used for the digestion of macromolecules from phagocytosis (i.e. ingestion of other dying cells or larger extracellular material such as foreign invading microbes), endocytosis (i.e. whereby receptor proteins are recycled from the cell surface), and autophagy (i.e. damaged or unneeded organelles / proteins, or invading microbes are delivered to the lysosome).

C: glycolysis occurs in the cytoplasm and begins with the catabolism (i.e. breakdown) of glucose and produces two 3-carbon pyruvates (i.e. pyruvic acid) per glucose. The pyruvate is shuttled through the double membrane of the mitochondria into the matrix that, via decarboxylation, produces acetyl CoA (2-carbon chain) that enters the Krebs cycle.

D: nucleolus is a membrane-bound organelle located within the nucleus. The nucleolus is the site of rRNA synthesis which are the main component (along with proteins) of the ribosome.

39. The main regulation point for fatty acid catabolism is *lipolysis*. All of the following are direct products of adipose tissue breakdown EXCEPT:

   A. acetyl CoA   **B.** glycerol   **C.** free fatty acids   **D. ketone bodies**

D is correct.

Lipolysis is the breakdown of lipids and is hormonally induced by epinephrine, norepinephrine, ghrelin, growth hormone, testosterone, and cortisol (yet unknown role in the mechanism). Adipocytes comprise the adipose tissue as lipid storages (i.e. fat cells) within the body and functions as the main storage site for triglycerides (e.g. glycerol plus three fatty acid tails).

Ketone bodies are produced from acetyl-CoA mainly in the mitochondrial matrix of liver cells (i.e. hepatocytes) when carbohydrates (e.g. glucose) are so scarce that energy must be obtained from breaking down fatty acids. The production of ketone bodies is not considered a direct product of lipolysis. Ketone bodies are produced only when levels of acetyl CoA exceed the utilization capacity by the Krebs cycle.

Pyruvate (3-carbon chain) is oxidized into lactate (3-carbon chain) during anaerobic fermentation for the concurrent reduction of NAD^+ to NADH. In both cellular respiration (proceeding to the Krebs cycle) and lipolysis, acetyl CoA (2-carbon chain) is formed by the decarboxylation (loss of CO_2) of pyruvate (precursor for Krebs cycle) or lactate (precursor for ketone bodies).

From the passage, the ester bonds within triglycerides are broken *via* hydrolysis by the hormone-sensitive lipase (HSL) to produce glycerol and free fatty acids. Free fatty acids are converted to acetyl CoA that is either oxidized within the Krebs (TCA) cycle into ATP or used to produce ketone bodies.

40. Which organ is the last to use ketone bodies as an energy source?

   A. kidneys   **B. brain**   **C.** cardiac tissue   **D.** skeletal muscle

B is correct.

Ketone bodies are formed by ketogenesis when liver glycogen stores are depleted and fat (triacylglycerol) is cleaved to yield 1 glycerol and 3 fatty acid chains in a process known as lipolysis. Ketone bodies are a group of ketones (carbonyl carbon linked between two carbon chains) including acetone, acetoacetic acid and β-hydroxybutyric produced in high levels during ketosis as in diabetes mellitus and during starvation. The ketone body acetoacetate slowly decarboxylates into acetone which is a volatile compound that is both metabolized as an energy source and lost in both the breath and urine.

Most of the cells in the body are able to use fatty acids as an alternative source of energy in a process known as beta-oxidation. One of the products of beta-oxidation is acetyl-CoA which can be used in the Krebs cycle (citric acid cycle).

During prolonged fasting or starvation, acetyl-CoA in the liver is used to produce ketone bodies instead, leading to a state of ketosis whereby the body starts using fatty acids instead of glucose. The brain cannot use long-chain fatty acids for energy because they are albumin-bound and cannot cross the blood–brain barrier. However, not all medium-length fatty acids are bound to albumin. The unbound medium-chain fatty acids are soluble in the blood and can cross the blood–brain barrier. The ketone bodies produced in the liver can also cross the blood–brain barrier. In the brain, these ketone bodies are then converted to acetyl-CoA and used in the citric acid cycle.

According to the passage, cardiac and other muscle tissues metabolize ketone bodies to preserve any available glucose for the brain. The brain uses glucose preferentially as the molecule for oxidation into ATP. The brain, as starvation proceeds and after the depletion of residual glucose (i.e. initially from food and then from glycogen stores in liver and muscle cells), utilizes ketone bodies to sustain metabolic function. Therefore, under extreme conditions of prolonged starvation, the brain ultimately uses ketone bodies.

41. Which of the following bonds between glycerol and the free fatty acids is cleaved by phosphorylated *hormone-sensitive lipase* via hydrolysis?

   A. hydrogen bond   **B. ester bond**   **C.** ionic bond   **D.** disulfide bond

B is correct.

From the passage, *hormone-sensitive lipase* hydrolyzes the bond *via* the addition of water (hydrolysis). The free fatty acids bond to a glycerol molecule *via* an *esterification* reaction (i.e. the hydroxyl groups on glycerol attacks the carbonyl carbon of the carboxylic acid of a fatty acid) to form an ester bond. These ester bonds are cleaved by *hormone-sensitive lipase* during hydrolysis of the triglyceride.

A common theme in biology is the breaking of bonds *via hydrolysis* (i.e. addition of water). The making of covalent bonds occurs *via dehydration* (i.e. loss of water) during bond formation involving condensation (joining of two subunits) reactions.

> Questions 42 through 46 are not based on any
> descriptive passage and are independent of each other

42. What is the correct sequence of organelles passed by the proteins targeted for the secretory pathway?

   A. ER → vesicle → Golgi → vesicle → plasma membrane
   B. ER → vesicle → Golgi → cytoplasm → plasma membrane
   C. Golgi → ER → vesicle → cytoplasm → proteosome
   D. cytoplasm → vesicle → Golgi → ER → vesicle → plasma membrane

A is correct.

The secretory pathway for a secreted protein is rough ER → vesicle → Golgi → vesicle → extracellular fluid (or to the plasma membrane or to the organelle within the cell).

Vesicular transport is used for the properly folded protein to migrate from the rough ER (site of protein folding using chaperones) to the Golgi. The Golgi is involved in protein modification (i.e. trimming of the properly folded polypeptide and/or adding of sugar moieties) and sorting of proteins destined for 1) the extracellular space (secreted from cell), 2) the plasma membrane (as a membrane receptor or channel), or 3) targeted for a cellular organelle (e.g. lysosome or nucleus).

Transport to the proteosome is not in the pathway for properly folded proteins. The proteosome is used for (misfolded) proteins that are destined to be degraded because the protein failed to fold properly within the lumen (interior) of the endoplasmic reticulum.

43. During replication, which molecule do single stranded binding proteins (SSBP) attach to for maintaining the uncoiled configuration of the nucleotide strands of the double helix uncoiled by the helicase enzyme?

   A. dsDNA   **B. ssDNA**   **C.** dsRNA   **D.** ssRNA

B is correct.

Nucleotides comprise the double helix of DNA. Helicase is an enzyme (along with topoisomerase) that uncoils the double stranded DNA molecule during replication (copying) of the nucleotides along the DNA. Once uncoiled and awaiting replication, the single stranded DNA strands are protected (coated with the SSBP) to avoid degradation by nucleases (enzymes that cleave nucleotides).

Replication occurs during the S phase of interphase. Transcription is the synthesis of an RNA molecule from the DNA template and transcription occurs for the generation of proteins (translation).

44. A biochemist hypothesized that the glucose transport protein is located only on the outer surface of the cell membrane. Is such hypothesis correct?

    A. Yes, because transport proteins are located only on the outer surface of the lipid bilayer

    B. Yes, because transport proteins are located only on the inner surface of the lipid bilayer

    C. No, because transport proteins are transmembrane and span the entire lipid bilayer

    D. No, because the hydrophilic heads of the lipid bilayer attract polar residues of the protein

C is correct.

Transport proteins are integral membrane proteins that span the entire phospholipid bilayer of membranes and allow molecules to pass through the membrane. By contrast, peripheral membrane proteins adhere only temporarily to the phospholipid bilayer with which they are associated and attach to integral membrane proteins, or penetrate the peripheral regions of the phospholipid bilayer.

Molecules are shuttled to the other side of the phospholipid bilayer by passage within the protein-lined channel of the transmembrane protein. Integral membrane proteins have membrane-spanning domains with hydrophobic amino acids projecting into the hydrophobic tail regions of the phospholipid bilayer. The presence of these hydrophobic amino acids allows the integral membrane protein to span the hydrophobic interior of the membrane.

45. Beta-oxidation occurs in the same location as:

    I. Glycolysis

    II. Krebs cycle

    III. Pyruvate decarboxylation into acetyl-CoA

A. I only   **B.** I and II only   **C. II and III only**   **D.** I, II and III

C is correct.

Beta-oxidation occurs in the same location as the Krebs cycle and pyruvate decarboxylation. The Krebs cycle, like beta-oxidation, occurs in the matrix of the mitochondria. Pyruvate (from glycolysis) decarboxylation into acetyl-CoA (Krebs cycle) also occurs in the mitochondrial matrix.
II: glycolysis occurs in the cytoplasm.

46. Which molecule has an infrared stretch closest to 1700 cm^{-1}?

    A. $CH_3CH_2CH_2CPh_3$ **C. $CH_3CH_2CH_2CH_2CHO$**

    B. $CH_3CH_2CH_2CH_2OH$ **D.** $CH_3CHClCH_2CH_2OCH_2CH_3$

C is correct.

An infrared (IR) absorption in the $1640 - 1750$ cm^{-1} region is an absorption characteristic of the carbonyl (C=O) bond. Carbonyls are present in seven molecules: aldehydes, ketones, acyl halides, anhydrides, carboxylic acids (with a second spectra of hydroxyl absorption between $2500 - 3000$ cm^{-1}), esters and amides.

Aldehydes (represented as ~CHO) contain a carbonyl.

Compare the ~CHO of the aldehyde

~CH$_2$OH of an alcohol

~COC of a ketone

~COX of an acyl halide (where X = F, Cl, Br or I)

~COOOC of an anhydride

~COOH of a carboxylic acid

~COOC of an ester

~CONH$_2$ of an amide

Passage 7
(Questions 47–52)

Esters are compounds consisting of a carbonyl adjacent to an ether linkage. They are derived by reacting a carboxylic acid (or its derivate) with a hydroxyl of an alcohol or phenol. Esters are often formed by condensing *via* dehydration (removal of water) of an alcohol acid with an acid.

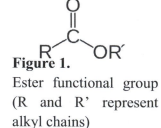

Figure 1.
Ester functional group (R and R' represent alkyl chains)

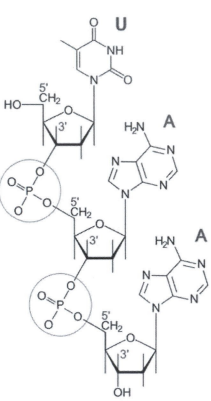

Esters are ubiquitous in biological molecules. Most naturally occurring fats and oils are the fatty acid esters of glycerol while phosphoesters form the backbone of nucleic acids (e.g. DNA and RNA molecules) as shown in Figure 2. Esters with low molecular weight are commonly used as fragrances and found in essential oils and pheromones.

Acid-catalyzed esterification is a mechanism of nucleophilic attack by the oxygen on an alcohol to the carboxylic acid as diagrammed below. The isotope of oxygen labeled in the alcohol as $R'^{18}OH$ was used to elucidate the reaction mechanism. The ester product was separated from unused reactants and side reaction contaminants in the reaction mixture. The water from the reaction mixture was collected as a separate fraction via distillation.

Figure 2. Two phosphodiester bonds are formed by connecting the phosphate group (PO_4^{3-}) between three nucleotides.

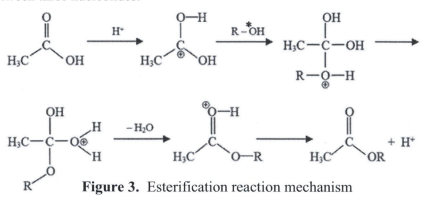

Figure 3. Esterification reaction mechanism

47. Which of these carboxylic acids has the lowest pK$_a$?

A. ClCH$_2$CH$_2$CH$_2$COOH

C. Cl$_3$CCH$_2$CH$_2$COOH

B. CH$_3$CH$_2$CH$_2$COOH

D. CH$_3$CH$_2$CHClCOOH

D is correct.

Carboxylic acids are strong organic acids (with pK$_a$ ranges between 2.5 and 5) but are weak acids compared to the inorganic acids (with pK$_a$ ranges between –10 and 3). The acidity of a carboxylic acid can be increased by the presence of electronegative substituents (e.g. F, O, N, Cl) because electronegative substituents' bonds pull electron density along σ (sigma – single) bonds. This inductive effect (along σ bonds) increases the stability of the resulting anion (conjugate base) of the deprotonated acid.

This electron withdrawal along the σ bond (i.e. induction) stabilizes the conjugate base compared to anions without electronegative moieties. Since the anion (i.e. conjugate base) is more stable (i.e. weaker base), the acid is stronger because it has an increase tendency to dissociate the proton. Overall, the more electron withdrawing groups present and the closer they are to the carboxyl group, the stronger the acid (i.e. lower pK$_a$). Note, resonance structures (delocalization of π electron) are a much larger contributor than induction (electronegative atoms pull along the σ bond) to anion stability.

Comparing resonance (i.e. π / pi electron delocalization) to induction (i.e. σ / sigma bonds), resonance has the greater effect on stabilizing the anion.

48. Given that esterification may occur between parts of the same molecule, which compound would most easily undergo intramolecular esterification to form a cyclic ester?

A. HOOCCH$_2$CH$_2$OH

C. HOOCCH$_2$CH$_2$CH$_2$CH$_2$OH

B. HOOCCH$_2$CH$_2$CH$_2$OH

D. HOOCCH$_2$CH$_2$ CH$_2$CH$_2$CH$_2$CH$_2$OH

C is correct.

For an intramolecular attack, the stability of a ring structure is important. The least amount of ring strain (i.e. angle or Baeyer strain) occurs in structures that can form six-membered rings as in cyclohexane (i.e. six-membered rings) chair conformational isomers. Angle strains occur when cyclic molecules are forced to deviate from the ideal sp^3 hybridized (i.e. tetrahedral) bond angle of 109.5°.

A: a four-membered ring produces substantial bond angle (i.e. 90°) and eclipsing steric strain.

B: a five-membered ring is not as stable as a six-membered ring.

D: an eight-membered ring is less stable than a six-membered ring because of angle strain resulting from a larger bond angle which deviates from the 109.5° bond angle of an sp^3 carbon.

49. An alternative method for forming esters is:

$$CH_3CH_2COO^- + RX \rightarrow CH_3CH_2COOR + X^-$$

The reason that this reaction occurs is because:

A. carboxylates are good nucleophiles   **C.** halide acts ss a good electrophile
B. carboxylates are good electrophiles   **D.** halide is a poor conjugate base

A is correct.

This reaction occurs between a carboxylate (i.e. anion of the deprotonated carboxylic acids) and alkyl halides. This reaction is a nucleophilic substitution reaction with the carboxylate ion (i.e. nucleophile) and the halide (i.e. leaving group).

Leaving groups always dissociate with their electrons and become an anion if neutral before dissociation, or become neutral if protonated before dissociation. A better leaving group dissociates more readily because the conjugate base (e.g. leaving group) is more stable. Halides are very good leaving groups because the anion is stable. The series of leaving group stability for the halides is I > Br > Cl > F. The same series is observed for nucleophilic strength of the halides.

50. The rate of the reaction is negligible without the acid catalyst. The catalyst is attacked by the:

A. carbonyl carbon and facilitates the attack of the carbonyl nucleophile
B. carbonyl carbon and facilitates the carbonyl oxygen electrophile
C. carbonyl oxygen and facilitates the attack of the alcohol nucleophile
D. carbonyl oxygen and facilitates the carbonyl carbon electrophile

C is correct.

Esterification of a carboxylic acid with an alcohol should be carried out under acid (H^+) catalysis whereby (according to the mechanism presented in figure 3) the H^+ of the acid catalyst is attacked by the lone pair of electrons on the oxygen of the carboxylic acid. The protonated oxygen (with a positive charge), through resonance, produces a carbocation (positively charged carbon) of the carbonyl carbon.

The positively charged carbocation is susceptible to a nucleophilic attack by the lone pair of electrons on the alcohol. Thus, the reaction is between the lone pair of electrons on the alcohol oxygen (i.e. nucleophile) and the positive charged carbonyl carbon (i.e. electrophile).

51. Which alkyl halide most readily forms an ester with sodium pentanoate ($CH_3CH_2CH_2CH_2COO^-Na^+$)?

A. CH_3Br
B. $(CH_3)_2CHBr$
C. $CH_3(CH_2)_6CH_2Br$
D. $CH_3CH_2CH_2CH_2Br$

A is correct.

Pentanoate results from the deprotonation of pentanoic acid. The reaction between a carboxylate anion and an alkyl halide is an S_N2 mechanism. The sodium pentanoate reacts with alkyl halides to form an ester according to the relative trend for alkyl halides: methyl > 1° > 2° > 3°.

As an S_N2 reaction (i.e. concerted mechanism) the reaction involves partial bonding between the attacking nucleophile (i.e. carboxylate) and the substrate containing the leaving group (i.e. alkyl halide). The reaction is favored with less bulky (e.g. methyl) substrates. Bulky substrates (i.e. 2° or 3°) sterically hinder the reaction by blocking (i.e. physically obstructing) the attacking nucleophile from approaching the carbon atom where the leaving group is attached.

The methyl bromide (CH_3Br) molecule has only hydrogens and the bromine substituent while the other choices have bulkier alkyl substituents. The methyl bromide is the least sterically hindered and reacts most readily with sodium pentanoate.

52. Which statement is correct, assuming that only the forward reaction occurs (Figure 3)?

A. ester fraction does not contain labeled oxygen while the water fraction does
B. water fraction does not contain labeled oxygen while the ester does
C. neither the ester fraction nor the water fraction contains labeled oxygen
D. both the ester fraction and the water fraction contain labeled oxygen

B is correct.

The acid-catalyzed esterification of a carboxylic acid involves the carbonyl carbon (of the carboxylic acid) reacting with the alcohol oxygen to form an ester (R-COO-R') linkage. Therefore, the labeled oxygen of the alcohol is incorporated into the ester product.

The water fraction does not contain labeled oxygen because the oxygen of the water comes from the unlabelled hydroxyl group (on the carboxylic acid) and not the labeled oxygen from the alcohol. The dehydration ($-OH + H^+$) is a common mechanism for condensation when two molecules are joined during biosynthetic processes.

Questions 53 through 59 are not based on any
descriptive passage and are independent of each other

53. Which of the following amino acids is an essential amino acid in the diets of children but not adults?

A. Asparate   **B.** Glycine   **C. Arginine**   **D.** Lysine

C is correct.

Arginine, a *semiessential* or *conditionally essential* amino acid in humans, is one of the most metabolically versatile amino acids and serves as a precursor for the synthesis of urea, nitric oxide, polyamines, proline, glutamate, creatine and agmatine. The sources of free arginine within the body are dietary protein, endogenous synthesis, and turnover of body proteins. At the whole-body level, most de novo arginine synthesis occurs in a metabolic collaboration between the small intestine and kidney in the intestinal-renal axis of arginine synthesis. The magnitude of endogenous synthesis is sufficient for healthy adults making, therefore it is not an essential dietary amino acid. However, endogenous arginine synthesis cannot fully meet the needs of infants and growing children or of adults with certain metabolic or physiological conditions. This is why arginine is classified as a *semiessential* or *conditionally essential* amino acid.

54. At room temperature, triglycerols containing only saturated long chain fatty acids remain:

A. oils   **B. solid**   **C.** liquid   **D.** unsaturated

B is correct.

55. Which of the following is an inactive precursor of protease enzymes synthesized in the pancreas?

A. Ribozyme   **C. Zymogen**
B. Isozyme   **D.** Allosteric enzyme

C is correct.

A zymogen (also called proenzyme) is an inactive enzyme precursor which requires a biochemical change (e.g. hydrolysis or configuration change to reveal the active site) to become an active enzyme. The pancreas secretes zymogens like pepsin in the form of pepsinogen (an inactive zymogen). When chief cells release pepsinogen into HCl, it becomes partially activated. Another partially activated pepsinogen completes the activation by removing the peptide and turning the pepsinogen into pepsin.

56. The most common naturally occurring fatty acids have:

    A. 12-20 carbon atoms with an odd number of carbon atoms
    B. **12-20 carbon atoms** with **an even number of carbon atoms**
    C. 20-50 carbon atoms with an odd number of carbon atoms
    D. 20-50 carbon atoms with an even number of carbon atoms

B is correct.

57. The anticodon is located on the:

    A. DNA   **B. tRNA**   **C.** mRNA   **D.** rRNA

B is correct.

An anticodon is made up of three nucleotides that correspond to the three bases of the codon on the mRNA. Each tRNA has a specific anticodon triplet sequence that can base-pair to one or more codons for an amino acid. Some anticodons can pair with more than one codon due to a phenomenon known as wobble base pairing.

58. Which disaccharide, when present in large excess over glucose, can be metabolized by *E. coli* by use of the operon?

    A. galactose   **B. lactose**   **C.** sucrose   **D.** cellobiose

B is correct.

59. Which mechanism is used to interconvert anomers?

    A. Isotopic exchange reaction
    B. **Mutarotation**
    C. Conformational change around carbon-carbon bonds
    D. Anomers cannot be interconverted

B is correct.

Mutarotation was first described in 1846 by French chemist Augustin-Pierre Dubrunfaut. Dubrunfaut observed that the specific rotation of aqueous sugar solution changes with time.

Mutarotation is the change in the optical rotation due to the change in the equilibrium between two anomers when the corresponding stereocenters interconvert (e.g. cyclic sugars experience mutarotation as α and β anomeric forms interconvert). The optical rotation of the solution depends on the optical rotation of each anomer and their concentration ratio in the solution.